FUNDAMENTALS OF PROGRAMMING
AN INTRODUCTION TO
COMPUTER PROGRAMMING USING C++

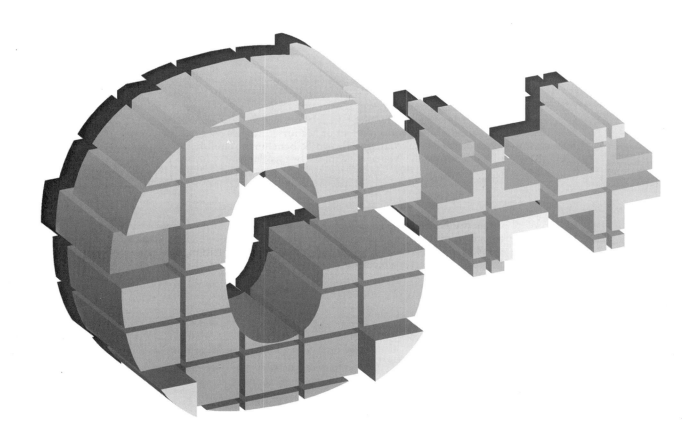

RICHARD HALTERMAN

B&E TECH

**Business and
Educational Technologies**

A Division of Wm. C. Brown Communications, Inc.

Business and Educational Technologies

A Division of Wm. C. Brown Communications, Inc.

Vice President and Publisher *Susan A. Simon*
Acquisitions Editor *Linda Meehan Avenarius*
Sales Manager *Paul Ducham*
Advertising/Marketing Coordinator *Jennifer Wherry Finders*
Product Development Assistant *Carrie Langas*

 Wm. C. Brown Communications, Inc.

Chief Executive Officer *G. Franklin Lewis*
Corporate Senior Vice President and Chief Financial Officer *Robert Chesterman*
Corporate Senior Vice President and President of Manufacturing *Roger Meyer*
Executive Vice President/General Manager, Brown & Benchmark Publishers *Tom Doran*
Executive Vice President/General Manager, Wm. C. Brown Publishers *Beverly Kolz*

Copyright ©1995 by Wm. C. Brown Communications, Inc.
All rights reserved

A Times Mirror Company

Library of Congress Catalog Card Number: 94-78011

ISBN 0-697-25110-1

Printed in the United States of America by Wm. C. Brown Communications, Inc.,
2460 Kerper Boulevard, Dubuque, IA 52001

10 9 8 7 6 5 4 3 2 1

CONTENTS

PREFACE

C++ is becoming a dominant programming language for developing today's computer software systems. It offers the runtime efficiency and economy of expression of C and adds advanced features for data abstraction and object-oriented programming. Knowledge of C++ is a valuable asset for any individual seeking employment in computer programming or systems development. Application software for modern operating environments and graphical user interfaces is best developed in an object-oriented fashion; indeed, most of these environments and graphical user interfaces work best when developed in an object-oriented fashion. Many of these environments have C++ based "application frameworks" that insulate the programmer from many of the complicated details that must be managed by programs designed to run on these systems.

Knowledge of the structure and syntax of the C++ language is useless without well-honed fundamental programming skills. The features that have been a part of higher-level procedural programming languages for nearly forty years—conditional execution (if statements), loops, array manipulation, function calls, etc.—must still be mastered to do competent object-oriented programming in C++. The principles presented in the first seven chapters of this book are not that much different from the principles presented in an introductory Pascal programming textbook from ten years ago. The language is different and admittedly offers some additional flexibility, but the underlying principles are the same. Pascal does provide a distinct pedagogical advantage over C++; namely, it was designed to teach the principles of solid structured programming. It imposes certain restrictions that C++ does not. It has a more limited way of doing almost everything that C++ can do. These limitations give a novice programmer fewer opportunities for misusing language features that lead to errors in programs that are difficult to resolve without knowledgeable assistance. While used quite successfully in some niches, Pascal is not a popular programming language for commercial software development, largely due to its label as an educational language. C++, the *programmer-friendly* language, can be intimidating for beginning programmers. It offers fewer safety nets than Pascal. It was designed to get the job done efficiently and not get in the way of a competent programmer.

Is it possible to teach students with no programming experience how to program using C++? Why not introduce the students to programming with Pascal (or another similar language) and then use C++ when advanced concepts are to be addressed? This approach has its merits, but consider the advantages of using C++ from start to finish:

- Students generally feel most comfortable using the language that they first learned. This applies to programming languages as well as conversational natural languages. This is not to say that the second programming language cannot be readily embraced and displace the original language as "most favored." (Indeed, it is almost assured that the strongest advocates for C++ did not learn how to program using C++, and most likely did not even get started with its predecessor, C.) Students who must eventually develop more advanced programs appreciate not having to take the time to learn a language that will be quickly discarded when the "real work" begins.
- The process of "unlearning" a programming language when confronted with a new language is nontrivial, especially when the structure of the two languages is similar. Students learning C++ trained in Pascal or Modula-2 (or BASIC for that matter) can become frustrated with minor differences that consume a lot of time to get right (assignment vs. equality operator, zero-based array subscripting, use of semicolons). Even though the student may totally understand the programming principle involved, these minor syntactical differences can sometimes require hours in front of the computer to correct.

- C++ can be introduced in a way that promotes good programming style and sound design principles as promoted in Pascal or Modula-2. It takes a bit of work with attention to pointing out possible pitfalls that the compiler will not detect, but the process is not as difficult as it might appear. For example, multiple initializations might be possible within a C++ for statement, but the single counter variable/single initialization approach (required by Pascal) can be presented as the best way to go.

- When advanced principles such as data abstraction, elementary data structures, and object-oriented programming are introduced, students are not burdened with simultaneously learning a new language and, possibly, a new development environment. These concepts are difficult enough without subjecting students to the first point mentioned above.

Nearly every other C++ book assumes that the reader has some prior programming experience. Most assume a knowledge of C. This book starts at the beginning. The basics of computer hardware are briefly introduced so that some basic terms, when used in subsequent chapters, will be understood well enough to support the discussion of programming concepts in which they are involved. After a brief history of C++ and a discussion of some general software development issues, the actual task of computer programming begins.

The main objectives of this text are outlined below:

- To develop the ability to correctly analyze a variety of problems and generate appropriate algorithmic solutions

- To instill the principles of top-down, structured design when using the procedural programming paradigm

- To introduce the concepts of object-oriented programming

- To explore the syntax and usage of the C++ programming language as a means of accomplishing all of the above objectives.

History shows that it is unrealistic to master a particular programming language with the intention of using it alone for the rest of one's programming career (assuming that one's career exceeds ten years). It was mentioned that few of today's C++ programmers learned to program using C++. (C++ is still a relatively young language, after all.) These programmers had to adapt their existing skills to a new language. These *generic* programming skills are much more valuable in the long run than is complete knowledge of the syntax of C++ with no idea of how to use it productively. Programming languages come and go; in ten years, C++ will likely be eclipsed by some super post-object-oriented visual code generator. Despite the differences in the programming paradigms that evolve over time, all software development requires well-developed logical and sequential reasoning skills. The problem to be solved must be understood completely, and a plan of attack must be correctly formulated given the tools at hand. Forty years ago, the tools consisted of computer machine language, teletypewriter terminals, and little else. Today, graphical user interfaces, higher-level languages like C++, source code debuggers, visual interface builders, comprehensive class libraries, and code generators are available to expedite the development process. All of the fancy tools available to the modern programmer are useless without the underlying problem analysis, organizational, and logical reasoning skills. As the tools get better, the problems get harder. Relevant software development today is just as difficult, or more so, than it was forty years ago.

While a large portion of the book is devoted to explaining C++ syntax and usage, the examples provide exposure to a variety of problem types that are typically encountered by programmers. Their programming solutions provide an insight into the problem-solving process. The best way to learn how to solve problems is to solve problems that are similar to problems whose solutions are known. Many of the programming assignments found at the end of each chapter are modifications of problems solved in the chapter or extensions of less demanding assignments from previous chapters.

This text can be used in several ways. It can be used in a two course sequence in which chapters 1–15 are covered in sequence. The instructor may spend at least part of the first class period introducing the students to the C++ development environment available. The text assumes no particular system; the procedure for editing, compiling, copying files, and so forth may be different on different systems (PC, Macintosh, Windows, Unix, etc.). On a semester schedule, chapters 1–8 could be covered in the first semester; chapters 9–15 would naturally follow in the second semester. This leaves the discussion of pointers and dynamic memory to the second course. Chapter 15 (Lower-level Programming) is optional, depending on the nature of the course. The table below contains a course outline based on 16 week semesters.

This book can be used for a second programming course that emphasizes elementary data structures and introduces abstract data types and object-oriented programming. If the students have had exposure to C++ or C, the first seven chapters may be reviewed in the first class period or two. Chapters 8–14 should be covered in detail. Chapter 15 (Lower-level Programming) is optional, depending on the nature of the class. If the students have no prior knowledge of C++ or C but have experience with another structured language (like Pascal or Modula-2), then the first seven chapters should be covered quickly but completely, emphasizing the syntactical deviations that might confuse experienced programmers unfamiliar with C++ or C. (The students should already know, for example, what loops are, how they are entered and exited, and how conditions for termination are checked; the task is translating that knowledge into the C++ form.)

Semester 1

Week	Chapter	Topic
1	1	Introduction
2	2	Variables, I/O
3	2,3	Expressions, data types
4	3	Binary representations
5	4	Relational ops, `if`
6	4	More `if`s, `switch`
7	5	`while`, `do. . .while`
8	5	`for`, loop termination
9	6	Functions
10	6	Storage classes
11	7	Arrays
12	7	Strings
13	7	Multidim. arrays
14	8	Structs
15	8	Classes, OOP
16	8	OOP
17	—	Final Examination

Semester 2

Week	Chapter	Topic
1	8	Review, OOP
2	9	Pointers
3	9	Dynamic memory
4	10	Self-referential structs
5	10	Linked lists
6	10	Recursion
7	11	Class operators
8	11	Copy semantics
9	11	Templates
10	12	Stacks, queues
11	13	Trees, BSTs
12	13	N-ary trees
13	14	Inheritance
14	14	Polymorphism
15	14,15	Class design
16	15	Lower-level prog.
17	—	Final Examination

The C++ code presented conforms to the American National Standards Institute (ANSI) base document as described in *The Annotated C++ Reference Manual* (commonly referred to as the *ARM*) by Margaret Ellis and Bjarne Stroustrup. Presently, a joint ANSI and International Standards Organization (ISO) committee is working on a C++ language standard. The *ARM* is the document that is currently identified as the "standard." The code herein conforms to AT&T release 3.0 of C++. (This corresponds to a level of C++ functionality, not to any particular compiler vendor's C++ version number). Templates are used heavily, beginning in chapter 11. Exception handling (AT&T release 4.0) is not presented since this feature was not widely available on many popular compilers at the time of this writing. If a site's development system supports exception handling, this topic could be introduced at any time after chapter 6, but it would naturally fit into the topics discussed in chapters 9 or 11.

Even though a great deal of time is spent examining the syntax and usage of C++, this book is not meant to be a comprehensive reference for the language. Its primary objective is teaching programming, and C++ is merely the medium. There are other books (the *ARM*, among others listed in the bibliography) that should be consulted when the limits of the language are to be explored. Unlike its predecessor C, C++ is a complex language. Indeed, C's simplicity was a virtue that even its critics had to concede. The syntactical and semantic structures of C++ are much more elaborate. This added complexity is mostly due to the advanced object-oriented programming features that were added, but some of it results from the additional baggage that C++ compilers must bear to insure compatibility with older C code. The result is that it is much more difficult for an individual to comprehend the full scope of the language. In this book, the most practical aspects of, for example, inheritance are covered in chapter 14. Public inheritance is the most popular and is presented with several examples. One example of private inheritance is also provided, but there are many other options available through combinations of public, protected, or private inheritance in conjunction with the public, protected, and private visibility specifications of members of the base class(es). Similarly, pointers to members, overloading `new` and `delete`, function pointers, and other tidbits that can be quite useful in certain situations are omitted to keep the text to a reasonable size.

This book would not exist in its present form without the assistance and understanding of many individuals. All of the students in my *Fundamentals of Programming I and II* classes at Southern College from the Fall of 1987 to present provided inspiration and ideas for this text through all of their questions, compiler errors, program design woes, innovative and insightful observations, and brilliant programming achievements. The reviewers of the manuscript provided welcome comments and criticisms that allowed me to make some sections clearer and fix some technical errors. They also provided guidance that prompted me to rearrange some of the chapters to produce a better organized text. Paul Ducham, Linda Meehan Avenarius, and Carrie Langas, editors at B&E Tech, provided much needed direction. Paul had enough faith in the original manuscript to start the publishing process. Linda oversaw the review process and helped me shore up its weaknesses to produce a viable book.

I wish to thank the following reviewers: Barbara Boucher Owens, St. Edward's University; Suzanne Sever, Wayne State College; Edward S. Miller, Lewis-Clark State College; Robert A. McDonald, East Stroudsburg University; William J. Moon, Palm Beach Community College; and Dr. Wm. C. Muellner, Elmhurst College.

Linden deCarmo, of IBM Corporation, contributed the PowerPC assembly code in chapter 1.

Janet, my lovely wife, served as my immediate proofreader, saving me from countless opportunities for grammatical embarrassment. She, as well as my daughters Jessica and Rachel, endured the whole process and provided much needed intangible support.

RLH

CHAPTER 1

INTRODUCTION TO COMPUTER SYSTEMS AND THE ROLE OF C++ IN SOFTWARE DEVELOPMENT

1.1 INTRODUCTION

A computer is a complex system. Like other complex systems, such as the human body or the U.S. government, it is composed of smaller systems and components. Computer systems are made up of two major systems—*hardware* and *software*. Each component is useless without the other. This book is concerned primarily with a particular kind of software development—*applications programming*. It is, however, impractical to discuss software development without knowledge of the hardware involved. In fact, since we will be writing programs and running these programs on actual machines, some knowledge of the hardware system is essential. The next section is an overview of computer hardware. It is far from comprehensive; in fact, it is merely enough to get us started. More information on the hardware will be provided later as the need arises.

1.2 COMPUTER HARDWARE

Hardware comprises the parts of the computer that can actually be seen and touched. The integrated circuits (chips), circuit boards, cables, keyboards, monitors, disk drives, etc. are all part of the hardware system. At the heart of the hardware is the *processor* or *central processing unit* (CPU). (See figure 1.1.)

The processor, or *microprocessor* in a microcomputer, is a chip (integrated circuit) that is the "brain" of the computer. The processor controls most of the other hardware. When a microcomputer is described as a 486 or Pentium machine, the name comes from the particular Intel

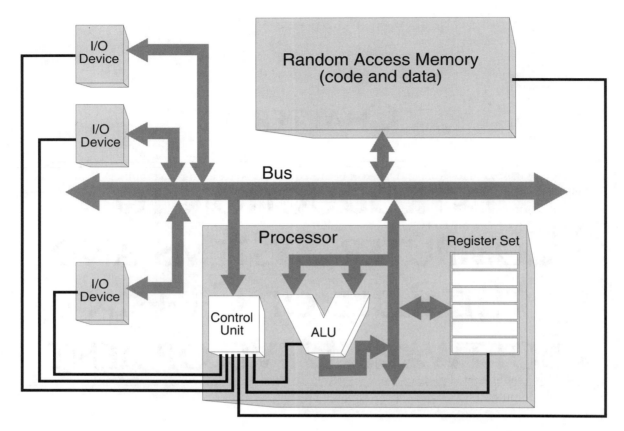

A Simplified View of Hardware
Figure 1.1

microprocessor around which the system was built. The Motorola 680x0 and the PowerPC chip are other examples of microprocessors used within today's microcomputers. The processor is responsible for moving data around from one part of the system to another, performing calculations on the data, and otherwise comparing and modifying the data. (Consider data here to mean some "chunks" of information.) The processor contains the *arithmetic-logic unit* (ALU) that performs calculations and comparisons and the *control unit* (CU) that sends signals to other parts of the hardware system controlling their function. The processor also contains a small number of *registers* that are used to store data temporarily for calculations. The software that we create will be translated into instructions for the processor. The programs we write control the computer by controlling the processor.

The processor is connected to the other primary hardware components through a link known as the *bus*. At the simplest level, the bus is merely a bunch of parallel wires running between the processor, memory, input devices, and output devices. Data is passed from an input device to the processor through the bus. You can think of the bus as an interstate highway system. Devices are connected to the highway by on and off ramps or "exits." Data can get from one component to another by getting on and off at the correct exits.

Memory, sometimes called *main memory* or *RAM (Random Access Memory)*, is where data are stored. The programs that we write (translated into processor instructions) are also stored in memory. Memory is simply a large storage area for data and machine instructions. A computer does all of its magic by performing some ridiculously simple steps over and over. The processor fetches an instruction from memory. Based on the particular instruction, it is likely to grab a piece of data from memory, do something to that datum element, and place it back somewhere (possibly the same place) in memory. This is called the "fetch-execute cycle" because the processor fetches an instruction from memory and then executes that instruction. The instructions that the processor fetches constitute the computer's *software*.

Input and output (I/O) devices are responsible for putting data into memory or retrieving data from memory. The keyboard is one example of an input device. When you use a wordprocessor or text editor, the letters you type not only appear on the screen, but also are stored in a particular place in the computer's memory. The screen is a type of output device. What is visible on the screen corresponds in some way to data stored in memory. Disk drives allow information to be both stored and retrieved from memory. The *diskette* and *fixed disk* (hard disk) are also known as secondary memory or secondary storage. Data can be stored on a diskette as in the computer's main memory; however, the data in main memory are lost when the power is removed to the computer. Data stored on diskette remain until erased or overwritten. Other I/O devices include mice, printers, trackballs, joysticks, and so forth.

1.3 COMPUTER SOFTWARE

As mentioned, software controls the processor, which in turn controls the rest of the computer system. Without hardware, obviously, you could not have a computer; however, without software, you would have a computer that could do nothing. The processor would be unable to communicate with memory or I/O devices.

Software can be categorized as *systems software* and *applications software*. An *operating system* (OS) is a sophisticated piece of systems software that oversees the whole computer system. On a personal computer, DOS (Disk Operating System) is an OS that is often used. Other choices include IBM's OS/2 and Microsoft's Windows NT. Unix and the Macintosh System 7 are other popular OSs. The OS directs the processor's communication with the other hardware components. It is the platform upon which the other type of software, applications software (programs), may be executed.

To better understand how systems software and the OS work, consider what happens when the computer is turned on. Recall that the hardware can do nothing without software; all the processor can do is "fetch and execute." Upon power-up, the processor is in a reset condition; it immediately looks to a particular place in memory for an instruction to execute. It is built to look in a part of memory known as *ROM (Read-Only Memory)*. ROM is a small part of memory with two special characteristics—it cannot be modified (unlike the memory mentioned above, RAM, where data and programs are stored), and it is not erased when the power is off (otherwise the computer could not start itself up the next time). The ROM contains the instructions for the processor to check the other hardware (memory, I/O devices, etc.) and load the OS into memory from disk. Once the OS is in memory, the processor follows the instructions dictated by the OS. On a PC under DOS, this same start-up sequence occurs but may look different on the screens of computers from different manufacturers since different ROMs may be used (Phoenix, Award, AMI, and others all make ROM-BIOS memories for PC compatibles). A DOS program called `command.com` (among others) is loaded into memory. The job of `command.com` is to interpret commands typed in from the keyboard.

Applications software consists of the programs that take advantage of the hardware and OS facilities. Applications software include wordprocessors, spreadsheets, databases, games, drawing programs, and just about every program you can think of. The C++ programs that are examined in this text are examples of applications software. Applications programs are typically easier to write than systems programs. Usually, the programmer does not have to worry about the details of how to access the I/O devices or memory. Programs are written that correspond to some real world problem, such as balancing a checkbook or simulating a game of tennis. The computer is simply a medium for solving these problems.

An *algorithm* is a finite sequence of well-understood steps that are followed to solve a particular problem or produce a particular result. For example, in a crude sense, a cake recipe is an algorithm for the production of a cake. There is a starting point—step 1 in the recipe. Following the recipe consists of performing a series of individual, simple, sequential (do this, then that—order is important) instructions that culminate at the stopping point—the finished cake. The technical definition of an algorithm is a bit more refined, but the essential principles are illustrated in the recipe example. An algorithm is a finite set of operations that must be performed in a particular sequence. Each operation must be well defined (that is, unambiguous), and each operation also must be able to be performed in a finite length of time. An algorithm must have a definite stopping place.

An algorithm is used in algebra to find the equation of the line (in the useful slope-intercept form) that passes between two points (x_1, y_1) and (x_2, y_2).

1. Find the slope, *m,* of the line passing through the points

$$m = \frac{y_2 - y_1}{x_2 - x_1}$$

2. Use the slope and one of the points in the point-slope form for the equation of a line

$$y - y_1 = m(x - x_1)$$

3. Solve for *y* (add y_1 to both sides)

$$y = m(x - x_1) + y_1$$

4. Distribute *m* to find *b* (the slope intercept)

$$y = mx - mx_1 + y_1, \; b = y_1 - mx_1$$

A program is an algorithm that has been implemented in a particular programming language. Programs can be written using many different computer languages. *Assembly language* offers absolute control over the processor because its instructions are converted directly into *machine language*— the instructions that the processor executes. It is difficult to develop programs in assembly language; the programmer must take care of all the details; namely, where values are to be placed in memory, how those values are to be manipulated with only very rudimentary operations possible, and so forth. Initially, assembly language was the only language available. It is called a *low-level* language. To solve problems in assembly language, not only must the programmer completely understand the problem at hand, but he or she must also have a good understanding of the inner workings of the microprocessor.

In the late 1950s, *higher-level* languages began to appear. These languages (FORTRAN is the oldest still in wide use) allowed the programmer to write programs in a form closer to human language. Human languages (English, French, Spanish, Japanese, etc.) are inherently flexible and often ambiguous, but higher-level computer languages are quite rigid in their form and composition rules. Nonetheless, higher-level languages remove much of the drudgery associated with assembly language programming. Consider figure 1.2 comparing a section of C++ code to its equivalent assembly code for two different CPUs. (The word *code* used in the context of programming has both a noun and verb form. The noun refers to programs or sections of a program written in a particular programming language; thus, a C++ programmer writes in C++ code which is eventually translated into low-level machine language code. The act of programming is sometimes called *coding.*)

Both assembly language code sequences were adapted from the assembler output from C++ compilers designed specifically for each system. Whereas the C++ code is the same for both systems, the actual machine language code is very different. The 80x86 code is for a complex instruction set computer (CISC) processor. CISC processors contain many different machine language instructions in their set of usable instructions. The PowerPC is a reduced instruction set computer (RISC). RISC

```
_SUM_LIST:
     PUSH BP
     MOV  BP,SP
     PUSH SI
     PUSH DI
     XOR  SI,SI
     XOR  DI,DI
     JMP  SL2
SL1:
     MOV  AX,SI
     SHL  AX,1
     LES
BX,[BP+06]
     ADD  BX,AX
     MOV  AX,DI
     ADD
AX,ES:[BX]
     MOV  DI,AX
     MOV  AX,SI
     INC  AX
     MOV  SI,AX
SL2:
     CMP
SI,[BP+0A]
     JL   SL1
     MOV  AX,DI
     POP  DI
     POP  SI
     POP  BP
     RETF
```

Intel 80×86 Assembly
Language

```
..LL33:
        .globl  sum
sum:
        ori     %r10,%r3,0
        addi    %r9,%r0,0
        addi    %r3,%r0,0
        cmp     0,%r9,%r4
        bge     ..LL34
..LL35:
        mulli   %r12,%r9,4
        lwzx
%r12,%r12,%r10
        addc    %r3,%r12,%r3
        addic   %r9,%r9,1
        cmp     0,%r9,%r4
        blt     ..LL35
..LL34:
        bclr    20,0
```

PowerPC Assembly Language

```
int sum_list(int list[], int
size)
{
    int index = 0, sum = 0;

    while ( index < size ) {
        sum = sum +
list[index];
        index = index + 1;
    }
    return sum;
}
```

C++ Language

Assembly Language vs. C++
Figure 1.2

machines employ a small number of highly optimized instructions to attempt to achieve greater processing speed. Higher-level languages, which are easier to use due to their proximity to natural languages and mathematical expression, provide another, perhaps more important, advantage. A program written in C++ can easily be adapted to execute on any computer system (PC, Macintosh, DEC VAX minicomputer, IBM mainframe, etc.); however, an assembly language program written for one kind of machine would need to be completely rewritten to work on a different kind of machine. i486 assembly language (PC) is much different from either 68040 (Macintosh) or PowerPC (Macintosh) assembly languages. (This fact should not be minimized—some programs require years of development by scores of programmers.) Higher-level languages include *C++, C, BASIC, Pascal, FORTRAN, COBOL, Ada, Modula-2, Lisp,* and *Prolog.*

Since the processor only understands its own machine language and cannot interpret any higher-level language, all higher-level languages must be translated into the machine language of the particular processor. A special program called a *compiler* converts the higher-level program text

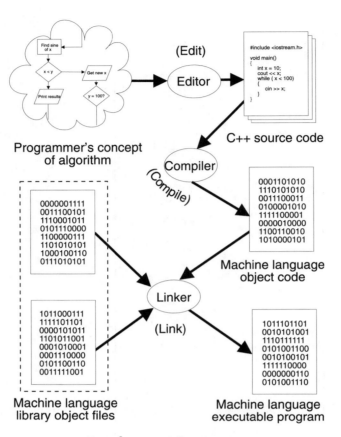

Development Sequence
Figure 1.3

into machine language. Figure 1.3 illustrates the development process. The C++ language source code is typed in with an editor (a program that works like a simplified wordprocessor) and stored in a file. Different systems use different naming conventions. Throughout this text we will assume that the C++ source files are named with a `.cpp` extension. Some development environments prefer `.C`, `.c`, `.CXX`, `.cxx`, or perhaps some other filename extension. The compiled machine language code file, here given an `.obj` extension, may instead use `.o`. The executable program file is here assumed to have an `.exe` extension, but other systems may have other preferences (or none at all). Some systems, like Unix, distinguish between upper- and lowercase (capitalized and uncapitalized) characters in file names. Some systems, like DOS, treat both the same. All references to filenames in this book will be of the form `filename.ext` in all lowercase (uncapitalized) small font.

Exercises

1. Define the following terms: *ALU, compiler, hardware, software, bus, input, output, algorithm, higher-level language, RAM, ROM, code,* and *operating system.*

2. List the steps in the translation of a C++ program into a computer's native machine language.

3. What are the major components in any computer system?

4. How is a higher-level computer programming language different from a lower-level computer programming language?

5. List some examples of *applications software.* List some examples of *systems software.*

6. What commands must you follow on your system to invoke the (1) editor, (2) compiler, and (3) the linker?

7. What filename extension for C++ source programs is preferred by your development environment?

1.4 THE STORY OF C++

C++ is an extension of C, a higher-level computer language developed by Dennis Ritchie in the early 1970s at AT&T Bell Laboratories. C++'s genealogy is shown in figure 1.4. C was first designed to run on a PDP-11 minicomputer. The C language made possible the implementation of the Unix operating system as it is known today. More than 90 percent of Unix was written in C (the remainder was written in assembly language). By the late 1970s, C began to gain widespread popularity and support and became available for commercial use outside of AT&T Bell Labs.

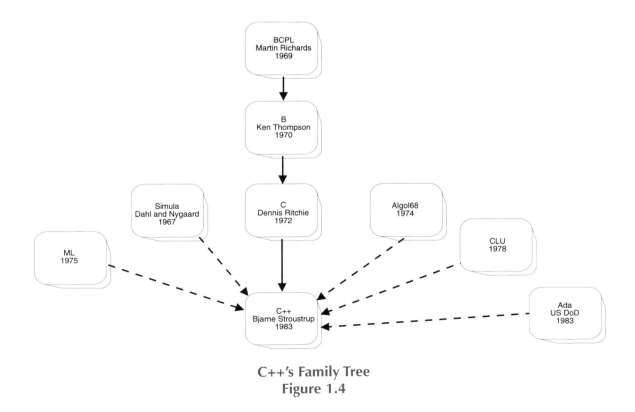

C++'s Family Tree
Figure 1.4

In the early 1980s, the American National Standards Institute (ANSI) formed a committee to study the standardization of the C language. By 1989 the committee released the specifications for ANSI C, a standard by which all companies that write C compilers should follow.

The "bible" for C has for years been the book *The C Programming Language* by Brian Kernighan and Dennis Ritchie (1977). With the advent of the ANSI standard C, the second edition of the book (1988) is now available.

In the early 1980s, Bjarne Stroustrup of AT&T Bell Labs began work on a significant evolutionary enhancement of C. Originally called *C with Classes* it quickly took the name *C++*. Its development was influenced by *Simula, CLU, Algol 68, ML*, and eventually *Ada*. C++ supports an *object-oriented* programming style as well as other features that are helpful in constructing large, complex programs. It is almost entirely a superset of C, and regular C programs (especially ANSI C programs) can be written in C++ with few, if any, changes. Currently, an ANSI committee, in conjuction with the International Standards Organization (ISO), is working on a C++ standard. We will be using C++ as our programming language, but many of our earlier programs will emphasize the features that it shares with regular C. (A C++ compiler is necessary to run all of the programs presented, however.) A beginning programmer should consider the advanced features of C++ only after becoming very comfortable and quite proficient in the features it has in common with C. We will identify the differences between C++ and regular C as the need arises. Books containing examples in ANSI C (like Kernighan and Ritchie's Second Edition) can be useful to further illustrate the basic concepts of C++ that are shared with C.

1.5   C++'s Virtues

When a beginning programming class was first taught, most colleges and universities used FORTRAN as the language medium. FORTRAN was the only higher-level language that readily supported mathematical and scientific calculations, and most students in the 1960s that registered for programming classes were likely scientists or engineers. Business data processing students most likely enrolled in COBOL classes. As time passed, the language of choice changed. BASIC was used because it was simpler than FORTRAN and was widely available. In the late 1970s Pascal became the dominant language for teaching programming. Many institutions still use Pascal in their introductory programming courses. Its use is only natural; Pascal was designed primarily to teach good programming practices. It offers the features required for modern structured programming, and its rigid form dictates that the programmer *will* construct programs in a certain way, or the program will not compile; however, because it is primarily a teaching language, Pascal has some limitations that have prevented its widespread use in the real world.

C++ is a language very similar to Pascal. It supports all of the features of modern structured programming. It is a higher-level language with lower-level capabilities. Since it was conceived to develop the Unix OS, C was originally a systems software development tool. Twenty years has seen it evolve into one of the most popular general-purpose languages used to develop many applications software packages. C/C++ is said to be the primary programming language for product development at Microsoft and Lotus. C was used to develop Unix, MS-DOS, all of the recent dBASE versions, Microsoft Excel, Microsoft Word, PageMaker, Paradox (and countless others); it was used in the development of the special effects for the films in the *Star Wars* and *Star Trek* motion picture series. C++ is popular on microcomputers and minicomputers and is rapidly gaining acceptance on mainframes as well. It is slowly eroding FORTRAN's dominance on supercomputers used for advanced scientific and engineering research. Many programs are written in C or C++ with small, time critical sections written in assembly language. When compared to other programming languages, C is often described as being efficient and portable. These adjectives have little meaning to the beginning programmer, but the implication is that when writing the same program in C, Pascal, BASIC, COBOL, etc., C will most likely produce the smallest, fastest program. A C++ program written using only features available in C will be just as efficient as the same program written in C. One of C++'s design goals was to provide more powerful features without sacrificing efficiency. It is evident that a knowledge of C/C++ is desirable when facing a sophisticated software project, whether it is systems or applications directed.

As stated, C++ is the next step in the evolution of the C language. In the past several years, it has become increasingly popular. It supports an object-oriented programming style that is useful for constructing very complex programs. It retains all of the advantages of regular C. In fact, its object-oriented features can be ignored, and because of its improved syntax, it can easily be used as a "better" C. C++ is a relatively young language. Consequently, programmers are even now gaining experience using its advanced features and determining good and bad programming techniques in C++. One might be concerned that pursuing a brand new language might be dangerous; that is, it is unproven and may turn out to be a "bad" language. Fortunately, at the foundation of C++ is C—a mature, well-understood, and highly respected language. This fact makes C++ an exciting, yet safe (in terms of investing the time to learn it), programming language. It can readily be used for developing traditional programming skills as well as providing access to state-of-the-art software development methods.

1.6   C++'s Pitfalls

As with most things, C++ has its disadvantages. It is based on C, and C has some quirks that mystify beginning programmers. C is sometimes referred to as a "programmer-friendly" language because, it seems, only people intimately familiar with computers and programming understand its behavior. A beginner will write a section of code that appears as if it should work perfectly. When it doesn't work, it is easy to blame the compiler or the C++ language when, in fact, there is a subtle problem with the code itself. Other languages such as Pascal and BASIC are less likely to foster these kinds of problems so we will take special care to point out possible problems and examine techniques that can be used to avoid these pitfalls. Knowing why the problems arise will make us better programmers. Remember, C++ is not problematic; it is programmers' incorrect assumptions about how C++ works that generate the problems.

One way to avoid many of the previously mentioned problems is to write C++ programs in a very precise, rigid fashion similar to the way a Pascal program must be written. Fortunately, C++ addresses some of the shortcomings of C. In many areas C++ is a stricter language than C and thus offers many of the advantages of Pascal. In fact, C++'s advanced features allow construction of programs that closely resemble the problems they are to solve. Using C++ as our development language will afford us many of the pedagogical advantages of Pascal and yet will familiarize us with a more powerful and much more marketable and practical language.

Exercises

1. Why is C sometimes called a "programmer-friendly" language?

2. What language was the immediate predecessor of C?

3. Who created the C++ language?

4.   What language was created for the sole purpose of teaching structured programming?

5.   How are C and C++ related?

6.   The C language was developed in which decade?

7.   What operating system was developed in the early 1970s using C?

Assignment

Type in the last paragraph of section 1.6 using the editor. Save your work to a file called PARA-GRAF.TXT. Leave the editor or development environment. Re-enter the editor, load in PARA-GRAF.TXT. Change every occurrence of the word C into Pascal and every occurrence of the word C++ into Ada. Save the changed paragraph to a file called PARANEW.TXT. Obtain a printout of both files.

CHAPTER 2

VARIABLES, ASSIGNMENT, AND SIMPLE I/O

2.1 THE FIRST C++ PROGRAM

We will write, compile, link, and execute the following C++ program (program 2.1):

```
#include <iostream.h>

void main()
{
    cout << "Hello, world!" << "\n";
}
```

Program 2.1

At this point you shouldn't be concerned about why and how it works; just type it in exactly as it appears. This exercise will familiarize you with your particular C++ working environment.

Enter the C++ development environment and, using the editor, type in the text exactly as it appears above. Compile, link, and execute the program. It should print the message "Hello, world!" on the screen. You can say that you have just written your first successful C++ program.

In the beginning all of our programs will have the following general form:

```
void main()
{
        .
        .
        .
}
```

On some systems, the following program skeleton is preferred:

```
int main()
{
        .
        .
        .
    return 0;
}
```

The C++ statements that make up your program will be found between the curly braces {} in the order you would like them executed. The word `void` is known as a *reserved* word (or *keyword*), and it indicates that when the program executes it won't return any special message to the operating system when it is finished. All programs have the name `main` indicating this is the main part of the program. As you might guess, we will eventually write programs that have multiple parts, or functions, with different names, but there must always be a function called `main` that will be executed when the program begins running. The `#include` line just before `main` will be explained below.

The program `first.cpp` contains only one line of code (code means one or more C++ statements that make up a program). It makes use of an output stream `cout`, pronounced *see-out*. A stream corresponds to a flow of information from one place to another. In this case, `cout` is a stream that connects messages and data within your program to the display screen. Other output streams might direct a program's data to a printer, a disk file, a particular window in a graphical environment, or a sound generator. The display screen is the only destination for output streams that we will consider at present. The << symbol is called the *insertion operator*. (The exact definition of the term *operator* will not be given here.) Sometimes it is referred to as the *put to* operator. It indicates that a data element, a message, or some kind of control information is to be inserted into the stream. In this case, the statement

```
cout << "Hello world!" << "\n";
```

uses << to insert two things into the `cout` stream, thereby displaying them on the screen. The first item is a string, *"Hello world!"*. A string is a collection of characters enclosed within quotes. The characters within the quotes of a string will be printed exactly as they appear with a few exceptions. The next item, also a string, contains a control code called the *newline* character. It moves the cursor down to the beginning of the next line after the message is displayed. Notice that the line ends with a semicolon. All C++ statements are terminated with a semicolon.

The details that go into the making of streams will be covered after C++ classes are introduced later in the text. For now, streams can be used without worrying about *how* they work. Streams are not part of the C++ language proper; they were created with the features provided by C++. In a sense, they work like small, independent C++ programs within the C++ programs that we'll write. Since `cout` is not part of the actual C++ language, the compiler does not understand its usage unless it is defined someplace before it is used. The line `#include <iostream.h>` inserts the definitions for `cout` and << (along with many other I/O related functions and classes, many of which we will eventually use) into your C++ source code. You can't see it in the editor, but the compiler sees it when compiling your program. The definitions are in the file called `<iostream.h>`, which is located in a subdirectory of your development environment. (All standard include files will be listed within angle brackets, just as they are written in a program.) Since the compiler knows the definition of `cout` when the `#include` is used, you may legally use it in the programs you write. If you omit the `#include`, you will receive an error message from the compiler. Errors cause the compiler to stop. When errors are present, the compiler can't figure out how to generate machine language from the C++ code provided. Most systems also produce less fatal messages called *warnings*. In a warning situation, the compiler indicates that the situation will not prevent machine code generation, but the programmer is likely doing something wrong. Modify `first.cpp` and marvel at the errors and warnings that the compiler produces.

Notice that C++, unlike commands given to some operating systems (like DOS), is *case sensitive*. A language is case sensitive when capitalized and uncapitalized letters are treated differently. Whether or not capital letters are used is important. The names `main`, `Main`, and `MAIN` all represent different names. Using `Cout` or `COUT` instead of `cout` will produce an error, since only `cout` is defined in the `#include` file `<iostream.h>`, not either of the variations.

2.2 Variables

Variables in C++ are used in a similar way to those found in algebra. *Variables* represent values. As in mathematics, variables only have meaning within a specified domain. In algebra we might say:

$$\{x \mid x \in \mathbf{R} \text{ and } -10 \leq x \leq 10\}$$

which says that x represents an element of a set that holds real numbers that can take on any value between −10 and 10, inclusive.

In C++, a variable is *declared* by specifying its *type*. The range of values is determined by the type specified. For example, in program 2.2:

```
#include <iostream..h>

void main()
{
        int x;

        x = 10;
        cout << "x has the value " << x << "\n";
}
```

Program 2.2

x is declared to be an *int* variable. The statement

```
int x;
```

declares to the compiler that a variable named x will be used in the program, and it will be of type `int`. An int can represent integer values (positive and negative whole numbers) of limited range. On some microcomputers (16-bit systems), the range is often −32,768 to +32,767. The reason for the restriction in the range of integer values will be explained in chapter 3. All variables must be declared *before* they are used within a program. The compiler will generate an error message when a variable is used without being declared. The compiler needs to know the type of the variable so that it can set aside enough room in memory to store the variable's value. (Different variable types require different amounts of memory.) The statement

```
x = 10;
```

is slightly different from the same statement in algebra. In algebra you could just as easily say

```
10 = x
```

because algebraic equality has the property of symmetry. In C++, the = symbol is an *operator* called the *assignment operator*. The left-side argument must be a variable. = may be read "takes on the value of." The expression `x = 10;` means "x takes on the value of 10." 10 is a constant, so the statement `10 = x;` would generate a compiler error since you can't change the value of a constant (10 is always 10, and common sense would indicate that it can't take on any other value and still be called 10).

Variables must be given names. x is the name of the variable in the previous program. Variable names are called *identifiers* and are constructed from letters (A...Z or a...z, case is important), digits (0...9), and the underscore character (_). No other symbols are allowed in identifiers. The first character in a variable name must be a letter or the underscore. The number of characters that make up the name is compiler specific but usually it is around 32. Some older compilers allow names only eight characters long. The following represent valid variable names:

```
x
number1
number_2
grand_total
GrandTotal
GRANDTOTAL
xyz4abc2
```

The following would be invalid variable names:

```
3number          (Begins with digit)
Grand Total      (Space between Grand and Total)
you_lose!        (Special character !)
```

A small collection of words are reserved as parts of the C++ language itself and cannot be used as variable names. These reserved words are listed in table 2.1.

The names of variables should be carefully chosen. Any name that satisfies the above rules is legal to use; however, the name for a variable should as closely as possible represent how it is used within the program. Names such as x, y, a, b, and θ are used frequently in mathematics, but in computer programming, more descriptive names such as grand_total, temp_value, initial_reading, slope, vertex, and attack_angle, when used appropriately, make programs more readable and understandable.

Variable names are best kept typographically distinct; that is, two variables used in the same section of the program should immediately look different. Variables named vector and Vector are separate variables, but if both were declared to the compiler, one of them could easily be typed accidentally in place of the other causing the program to produce erroneous results. Better names might be based on the nature of the different vectors, maybe in_vector and adjacent_vector. The use of variable names that are too similar makes proofreading a program tedious and error prone.

In some languages (notably BASIC), variables do not need to be declared before they are used. The compiler (or interpreter as in the case of BASIC) creates the variables as they are used within the program. Far from a convenience, this feature could not, for example, indicate when vector is used accidentally in place of Vector (if the programmer is following the practice of keeping variable names distinct).

To aid program readability, we will adopt the convention that variable names will not typically contain any capitalized letters. Capitalized letters will be used in other special identifiers (constants and defined types to be examined later). By adopting this convention, when we see an object in a program that is not a reserved word and whose letters are all lowercase, we can assume that it is a variable.

The terms *identifier* and *variable* name will be used interchangeably, although identifier means something more. The rules given actually cover more than just variable names. Variable names, function names, labels, programmer-defined type names, and preprocessor defined constants are all classified as identifiers. The rules given above cover all identifiers, not just variable names.

Reserved words (or keywords) cannot be used as variable names or identifiers; thus, `void` (the only reserved word we've seen so far) cannot be used as a variable name. The following is a list of reserved words. We will eventually discover the meaning of most of them, but for now you should become familiar with them so you *don't* use them as variable names. Table 2.1 lists C++'s reserved words.

Table 2.1 C++ Reserved Words

auto	else	operator*	template*
break	enum	private*	this*
case	extern	protected*	typedef
catch*	float	public*	union
char	for	register	unsigned
class*	friend*	return	virtual*
const	goto	short	void
continue	if	signed	volatile
default	inline*	sizeof	while
delete*	int	static	
do	long	struct	
double	new*	switch	

The starred items are reserved words unique to C++ and are not reserved words in standard C. The following are C++'s built-in types. Variables can be declared to be any of the types shown in table 2.2, which is a subset of table 2.1.

Table 2.2 C++ Data Types

int	float	unsigned char
long	double	unsigned long
short	long double	
char	unsigned	

The types `long` (or `long int`), `short` (or `short int`), `unsigned` (or `unsigned int`), and `unsigned long` (or `unsigned long int`) are all integer types differing only in their range of possible values and amount of the computer's memory they require. The types `float`, `double`, and `long double` are known as *floating point* numbers. They are the computer representations of mathematical real numbers; that is, numbers that have fractional parts. A complete discussion of these data types, including their capabilities and limitations, appears in chapter 3. Some programmers (or, more likely, organizations that employ the programmers) have precise rules for naming variables that include an indication of the variable's type. The so-called *Hungarian notation* (named for its inventor, Microsoft's Hungarian-born Charles Simonyi), adopted by Microsoft Windows developers, is one style. The name chosen is not only descriptive of the variable's purpose, but it is also a prefix that identifies the variable's type. The prefix `n` means int, `f` means float, `ch` means char, etc. The following variables make use of Hungarian notation:

```
nCount    (integer for counting)
fSum      (float used for summing up a list of values)
chKeyIn   (character corresponding to the key the user pressed)
```

The compiler associates a variable's name with a location in memory. A memory location is referenced by its *address*. The programmer does not need to worry about where in memory the variable resides; he or she need only use its name to reference its value.

Exercises

1. Classify each of the following words as *I* for valid identifier (variable name), *R* for reserved word, or *N* for neither:

I R N	hello	I R N	gross-pay	I R N	fred!
I R N	x	I R N	Return	I R N	plus_two
I R N	Four4	I R N	estimate	I R N	23go
I R N	letter count	I R N	who_done_it	I R N	z1
I R N	printf	I R N	main	I R N	variables

2. How is a reserved word different from an identifier?

3. What control character sent to the output stream indicates that the cursor should move to the beginning of the next line?

4. All C++ statements are terminated with what symbol?

5. What symbol is the *assignment operator*?

6. List four *types* that variables can have.

7. What does the #include directive do?

8. What is the maximum int value for your particular compiler?

9. What does the symbol << do?

2.3   EXPRESSIONS

Consider the following C++ program (program 2.3):

```
#include <iostream.h>
void main()
{
        int x;
        x = 2;
        cout << x << " + " << 3 << " = " << x + 3 << ".\n";
}
```

Program 2.3

Here a variable called x is declared, assigned the value of 2, and the following message is displayed:

```
2 + 3 = 5.
```

The value of x is printed, followed by the string containing the plus sign. Then the value of the constant 3 is displayed, followed by the equals sign and the value of the arithmetic *expression* x + 3. Finally, the period is printed and the cursor moves to the beginning of the next line. An expression combines variables and/or constants using operators. The + operator is the familiar addition operator. The arithmetic operators are

+ addition
− subtraction
* multiplication
/ division
% modulus (remainder after division, useful for integer types only)

These operators, when acting only on integer operands, produce integer results. If either operand is a floating type, they (except for % that is only used for integer types) will produce floating results. The +, −, *, and % operators act as expected. Since division is not closed under the integers, the / operator, when used with two integer operands, produces a whole number quotient with the fractional part, if any, discarded. The following illustrates:

```
5/3 = 1
3/5 = 0
```

The division operator works as expected when at least one of its operands is a floating type:

```
3.0/5 = 0.6
```

The modulus operator returns the remainder after division of two integers:

```
5 % 3 = 2
3 % 5 = 3
```

Expressions can occur on the right side of the assignment operator but generally *not* on the left-hand side:

```
2 + 3 = x;    /*  Wrong  */
```

Here x gets the value of 5:

```
x = 2 + 3;
```

As in algebra, parentheses can be used to group elements of an expression. Consider program 2.4:

```cpp
#include <iostream.h>

void main()
{
        int grade_avg;
        int grade1;
        int grade2;
        int grade3;

        grade1 = 5;
        grade2 = 7;
        grade3 = 6;
        grade_avg = (grade1 + grade2 + grade3)/3;

        cout << "The average of " << grade1 << ", " << grade2;
        cout << ", and " << grade3 << " is " << grade_avg << "\n";
}
```

Program 2.4

Here `grade_avg`, `grade1`, `grade2`, and `grade3` are declared to be integers by the declaration `int`, and `grade1`, `grade2`, and `grade3` are assigned the values 5, 7, and 6, respectively. The value of `grade_avg` is calculated from these values. Notice that the calculation is done outside of the output statement but could have just as easily been done within:

```
#include <iostream.h>

void main()
{
        int grade1, grade2, grade3;

        grade1 = 5;   grade2 = 7;   grade3 = 6;
        cout << "The average of " << grade1 << ", " << grade2
             << ", and " << grade3 << " is " << ((grade1 + grade2 + grade3)/3)
             << "\n";
}
```

Program 2.5

Program 2.5, an alternate version of program 2.4, illustrates C++'s *free-form* property. Multiple statements can be placed on one line; the semicolon indicates where the statement ends, not the end of the line of text. If many variables are declared of the same type, the type may be used once, and the variables of that type follow separated by commas. Also, variables can be given values at the time of their declaration:

```
#include <iostream.h>
  void main()
  {
        int grade1 = 5, grade2 = 7, grade3 = 6, grade_avg;

        grade_avg = (grade1 + grade2 + grade3)/3;
        cout << "The average of " << grade1 << ", " << grade2
             << ", and " << grade3 << " is " << grade_avg <<
                 "\n";
  }
```

Program 2.6

Here in program 2.6 `grade1`, `grade2`, and `grade3` are said to be *initialized* at the time of declaration. This means each is given an *initial* or beginning value. Variables that are declared but not given a value have *undefined* values; that is, their values are random values that cannot be determined at any given time the program is executed. All variables should be given values either through initialization or assignment.

The statement

```
grade_avg = (grade1 + grade2 + grade3)/3;
```

becomes an instruction to the computer; it is *not* an attempt to define what `grade_avg` is. The variables `grade1`, `grade2`, and `grade3` must be given their values before this calculation statement appears in the program. Some make the mistake of placing the calculation statement first (thinking that it describes to the computer how to find `grade_avg`), then assign values to each of the variables and assume the computer then has the necessary information to find `grade_avg` and thus perform the calculation. The calculation is performed when it appears in the program. If variables appearing in the calculation have yet to be given values, then many compilers (if all the compiler error and warning messages are active) will issue a warning (something to the effect of "variable used before definition," that is, before it has been given a well-defined value).

The above programs are limited in that they execute exactly the same way each time they are run. The following program is a bit more useful:

```
#include <iostream.h>
void main()
{
        int grade1, grade2, grade3, grade_avg;

        cout << "Please enter three integer values: ";
        cin >> grade1 >> grade2 >> grade3;
        grade_avg = (grade1 + grade2 + grade3)/3;
        cout << "The average of " << grade1 << ", " << grade2
                << ", and " << grade3 << " is " << grade_avg << "\n";

}
```

Program 2.7

cin (pronounced *see-in*) is a standard C++ stream as is cout. cin is defined in the <iostream.h> header file just as is cout. It allows the user of the program to enter values for variables directly from the keyboard. The "stream" of data for cin flows from the keyboard to the program. Whereas programs 2.1–2.6 execute exactly the same way each time since the variables are always assigned the same values, in program 2.7 the values of the variables will likely vary each time the program is run. Program 2.7 is said to be more *general purpose* than any of programs 2.1–2.6; it will calculate the average of any three integers instead of specific integers. (A program that would be even more general purpose than program 2.7 would allow the user to find the average of *any number* of integers, not just three. The curious can peek at chapter **5** to see such a program.)

When running the program, the user could press the return key after typing each number. As an alternative, all the numbers could be entered at once, each separated by at least one space, with the return key being pressed only after all the numbers are typed in.

The input stream cin provides for an indirect way of assigning values to variables. Variables that are given values through cin before they are used in a calculation or some other expression don't need to be given initial values.

Programs should be made as readable and understandable as possible. Someone other than the actual author of the program will be able to read and understand a well-written program more quickly than a poorly written program that works identically. Since most important software today is created by teams of programmers, this clarity in program composition is important. Programmers may change jobs or be transferred from one section of a company to another and be placed in the middle of a development project. Again, the readability of the previously developed code determines the difficulty level of the transition. Finally, one programmer writing a nontrivial program can find his/her own code difficult to understand if the need arises to fix an error or extend its capabilities. This situation will become apparent as we progress through this course and begin to write more sophisticated programs. Writing readable code from the start makes the inevitable program modifications less painful.

How can C++ code be made more readable? Style guidelines will be provided as new concepts are introduced throughout this book. The importance of well-chosen variable names has already been emphasized.

C++ is a free-form language. This means that spaces and indentations can be used many places to make the code more visually appealing. Consider the following two programs:

```
#include <iostream.h>
void main(){int number;cin>>number;cout
<<number;cout<<"All done now.";}
```

Program 2.8

```
#include <iostream.h>
void main()
{
        int number;

        cin >> number;
        cout << number;
        cout << "All done now.";
}
```

Program 2.9

As far as the compiler is concerned, programs 2.8 and 2.9 are identical. Most humans would consider program 2.9 to be the more readable and visually appealing. It is less bunched up, and it is clearer at first glance where one statement ends and another begins. The variable declaration part is visually separate from the statement part of the program. Imagine how these differences would be magnified in a program that contained 100,000 lines of code.

Any part of the C++ language can be classified as one of the following:

reserved word	(int, void, etc.)
identifier	(variable names, function names, etc.)
operator	(=, +, -, etc.)
separator	(curly braces, parentheses, semicolon, etc.)

Blank spaces, newlines (ending a line and returning to the beginning of the next), and tabs are classified as *white space* (since on a white sheet of paper nothing appears). White space, when used as a separator, is ignored by the compiler. White space should be used liberally to make programs more readable. White space must be used to separate reserved words from identifiers as in the declaration:

```
int number;
```

When run together, it looks to the compiler like a single identifier:

```
intnumber;
```

which has not been declared anywhere and has been used improperly anyway since a variable all by itself is not a useful C++ statement.

White space cannot be used to split up individual reserved words or identifiers; they must stay together as units:

```
int num ber;
```

Recall that a variable cannot have any spaces within it. The compiler can't decide whether the programmer really meant a single variable

```
int number;
```

or perhaps two different variables

```
int num, ber;
```

We will adopt the style that always places at least one blank space after all commas. We will usually not place more than one statement on one line. We will place one space before and after binary operators like =, +, - , *, etc. (A binary operator is an operator that has two arguments [operands]—one on the left and another on the right.) The statement

```
grade_sum = grade1 + grade2 + grade3;
```

is preferred to

```
grade_sum=grade1+grade2+grade3;
```

Remember the compiler sees no difference; the advantages are to the human reader. When the additive operators (+ and −) are combined with the multiplicative operators (*, /, and %), the whitespace is sometimes *omitted* to improve readability. The operator precedence in C++, when it comes to the arithmetic operators, is identical to standard arithmetic rules: in mixed expressions the multiplicative operators are applied before the additive operators. For example:

```
3 + 2 * 4 = 3 + (2 * 4) = 3 + 8 = 11      (Correct)
```

not

```
3 + 2 * 4 = (3 + 2) * 4 = 5 * 4 = 20      (Wrong!)
```

Many programmers don't put white space around the multiplicative operators, especially when additive operators appear in the same expression. Although the following statements are all the same to the compiler,

```
x = a + b * c;
x = a+b * c;
x = a + b*c;
```

the last statement most accurately reflects operator precedence rules of arithmetic. The first statement is certainly not wrong (the reader should know the precedence rules), but the middle statement is downright misleading because upon casual reading it appears the addition is supposed to be performed before the multiplication, since the a and b are "bound" more closely together. If it is desired that the addition be performed first, parentheses must be used:

```
x = (a + b)*c;
```

Consider a frequent calculation mistake:

```
grade_avg = grade1 + grade2 + grade3 / 3;
```

Due to operator precedence, `grade3` will be divided by 3 and *then* added to `grade1` and `grade2` yielding an incorrect result. Following the above style guidelines for white space (once the habit is formed), the statement would be written:

```
grade_avg = grade1 + grade2 + grade3/3;
```

It may be (a little) more obvious from this statement that parentheses are needed to correct the calculation, since the 3 appears more closely bound to only `grade3`.

Exercises

1. What value does a variable have if it is not initialized when it is declared?

2. Why is the following statement incorrect?

   ```
   x + 5 = y;
   ```

3. Which arithmetic operator has higher precedence in C++, + or *?

4. Why is the following statement syntactically correct but misleading?

   ```
   a = b+c * d;
   ```

5. How are `cout` and `cin` different?

2.4 REDIRECTION AND FILE ACCESS

Some operating systems such as DOS and Unix allow the standard input device (keyboard) and standard output device (screen) to be *redirected* to other devices and files. In DOS, for example, the command `dir` displays a list of all the files on the default disk drive. At the command line prompt, one could type

```
dir > prn
```

(The command under Unix would be `ls`, and the printer device would be different.) Instead of the disk directory appearing on the screen, it is printed on a printer (assuming a printer is attached to the system, is powered up, is on line, has paper, etc.). The > symbol redirects information from the screen to another device, in this case the printer. The command

```
dir > temp.out
```

creates a file called `temp.out`. Using the `type` command under DOS (or the `more` command under Unix or loading the file into the editor), it can be seen that its contents are what would have been printed on the screen using `dir`.

If the executable file for program 2.7 is named `grades.exe`, it can be run using redirection so that the average of the grades is not printed on the screen but instead is printed to a file or printer:

```
grades > prn
grades > output.dat
```

The ability to redirect output provides a means for keeping a permanent record of the program's runtime behavior. Anything that is normally displayed on the screen by `cout` can be stored on a disk file or printed on a printer using redirection.

Using your editor, type in the following numbers and save them to a file called NUMBERS.DAT:

```
88
83
73
```

Again, if the executable file for program 2.7 is named `grades.exe`, it can be run using redirection so that `cin` grabs its data from the file `numbers.dat` instead of the keyboard as follows:

```
grades < numbers.dat
```

The program runs as if 88, 83, and 73 were typed in by a user. This technique of redirecting input is useful when testing predefined data sets. Most often a program will not be correct the first time it is written, and the programmer must make changes to the program in an attempt to correct it. Testing the program for correctness might require the programmer to type sets of values over and over again. Not only is this repetitive task boring and time consuming, it can be error prone. Redirection automates this testing process and insures that the data given to the program is consistent for each test.

Typing

```
grades < numbers.dat > output.dat
```

not only redirects `cin`, but also redirects `cout` to print to the file `output.dat` instead of the screen.

2.5 COMMENTS

Comments, or *remarks,* are notes to the human reader that are completely ignored by the compiler. Comments comprise what is known as the program's *internal documentation.* Comments consist of any text that is enclosed within the symbols /* and */. These symbols enclose the comment in the same manner as parentheses or curly braces, but they do *not* nest within themselves as do curly braces and parentheses. The symbol // signifies a comment that continues until the end of that line of text. (This // style of comments is new to C++ and is not available in C.) The average program written with comments might appear as follows:

```
/*   Grade Average                                        */
/*   Programmer:  Richard Halterman                       */
/*   Last modified: 5/4/94                                */
/*   Purpose:  To calculate the integer average of three integer */

grades as entered by the user  */
#include <iostream.h>   //  For cin and cout streams
void main()
{
        int grade1, grade2, grade3;  // The individual scores
        int grade_avg;               // The average of the scores
        /*  Prompt the user for the values  */
        cout << "Please enter three integer values: ";
        /*  Read in the values from the keyboard  */
        cin >> grade1 >> grade2 >> grade3;
        /*  Calculate the average of the scores  */
        grade_avg = (grade1 + grade2 + grade3)/3;
        /*  Display the result on the screen  */
        cout << "The average of " << grade1 << ", " << grade2 << ", and ;
            << grade3 << " is " << grade_avg << "\n";
}
```

Program 2.10

To be honest, program 2.10 is actually *overcommented.* Simple direct lines of code usually do not need to be commented. A reasonably experienced programmer will understand what we're doing by reading the statement itself. Writing C++ code in a simple, direct, and readable style with well-chosen variable names renders the code "self-documenting." Comments should include at least the programmer's name, the purpose of the program (really unnecessary for this particular program, since it's so simple), and the date last modified (Is this program the one I wrote yesterday or the one I wrote last week? They look so similar . . .). Particularly crucial sections of code generally warrant commenting. Usually, a sequence of individually simple instructions that together accomplish a more sophisticated task are preceded by a single comment that explains their corporate activity. In general, if the programmer can't decide if a comment is necessary, it is most likely necessary.

2.6 ERRORS

When writing programs, errors inevitably arise. If the program will not compile successfully because some language rule of C++ is broken, the error is called a *syntax* error. For example, forgetting to put the closing curly brace at the end of the program constitutes a syntax error. For students learning any programming language, syntax errors are very common in the early stages. At first, the syntax errors are hard to fix because the language is new and unfamiliar. The compiler does provide messages that are sometimes helpful in diagnosing the problem, and with time syntax errors become less frequent. For someone very experienced in programming a particular language, syntax errors arise mainly from typographical errors and carelessness and can be quickly corrected looking at the compiler messages.

The second type of error is much more severe than a syntax error. A program can be easily written that compiles and runs but does not produce the intended results. The program is said to contain a *logic* error (or, more likely, several logic errors). It could be that the programmer does not completely understand the problem; thus, the program is designed incorrectly. It may be that a statement was typed incorrectly—perhaps the programmer used a variable named x in an expression when y was actually intended (and both variables are properly declared). Two or more statements could be placed out of order. Logical errors are also known as *bugs*. Bugs are harder to fix than syntax errors because the compiler cannot even hint at the problem. The compiler only enforces language rules; it does not understand what the programmer is attempting to do with a program. Bugs are particularly insidious because in complex programs some logic errors may only become apparent under certain rare circumstances. The program is thought to work perfectly and is shipped to the user only to crash (fail) or give faulty results in actual use.

Logic errors are perpetuated by the human capacity for making mistakes (quite high). Programs are complex entities that require careful attention. All programming languages instruct the computer to "do as I say," not "do as I intend." We will investigate ways to reduce bugs and examine some common problems that arise in program development, but our attempts at bug prevention will fall far short. Ultimately, it is the individual programmer's ability to understand the problem, design a suitable algorithm that represents its solution, and implement the algorithm with the given language tools that determines the success of a program. Clear, logical thinking is required. Unfortunately, the process is not easy, and there are no shortcuts.

Compiler Errors

Logical Errors

Caution

Poor Style or Approach

"Bad" Program Icons
Figure 2.1

Throughout this book, a variety of programs will be examined. Some of the programs will contain errors to illustrate common programming problems. To assist the reader, figure 2.1 lists the symbols that appear to the left of programs that have a problem. The "compiler curses" balloon indicates that the program, as it appears, will generate compiler errors and/or warnings. The program will not be able to be compiled as executed until the errors are remedied. The bug symbol appears beside programs that contain one or more logical errors (bugs). The program should compile and run under most systems, but it will not perform as expected. The caution sign means that the program should be scrutinized closely because it may act differently than expected from a casual reading. (It's the exception in this group, since the program or piece of the program may not necessarily be "bad.") The "thumbs down" icon is placed beside programs that contain no syntax or logical errors but exhibit stylistic errors or can otherwise be improved in some way. This would include misleading variable names, improper indentation, overly complex logic for the given problem, and so forth. The thumbs down icon is also used to highlight programs that may not be as efficient as they could be.

Exercises

1. What are the two ways in which comments can be placed within a C++ program?

2. How can the output stream of a program be redirected to a file called "myout"?

3. List several things that can be done with redirection that make it so useful.

4. What is the difference between a syntax error and a logic error?

5. What is a bug?

Assignments

1. Write a small C++ program that displays your initials on the screen. These initials will be *large* letters that you must construct. Each letter is created by composing many smaller "normal" characters into the shape of the desired letter:

```
RRRRRRRRRR          LLLL              HHHH        HHHH
  RR      RR         LL                HH          HH
  RR      RR         LL                HH          HH
  RR      RR         LL                HH          HH
  RR      RR         LL                HH          HH
  RRRRRRRRR          LL                HHHHHHHHHHHH
  RR   RR            LL                HH          HH
  RR    RR           LL                HH          HH
  RR     RR          LL        LL      HH          HH
  RRRR    RRR        LLLLLLLLLLLLLL    HHHH        HHHH
```

Don't be afraid to be creative. For example, you may prefer more flair:

```
    RRRRR                L    LLLL          HHHHH                H
  RR   RRRRRRR          LL   LL  LL         HH   HH            HH
  R  RR      RR         LL   LL    LL       H      HH          HH
     RR      RR         LL LL       LL             HH          HH
    RR         RR       LLLLLLLLL              HH          HH
    RR         RR         LL                   HH          HH
  RRRRRRRRRRRR            LL              HHHHHHHHHHHH
    RR     RR           LLLLLLLL              HH          HH
    RR      RR          LL  LL LL        L    HH          HH
  R   RR      RR    R   LL   LL   LL        LL  HH        HH   H
 RR   RR        RR  RR  LL LL   LL    LL   HH          HH  HH
    RRRR          RRRR   LLL        LLLLLL    H        HHHHH
```

You need do only *your* initials, not all the letters in the alphabet.

This program uses only the stream cout, and its main purpose is to provide practice using the text editor and compiling and running C++ programs in your particular development environment. Use redirection to make a hard copy with a printer.

2.   Write a C++ program that draws the following picture on the computer's screen:

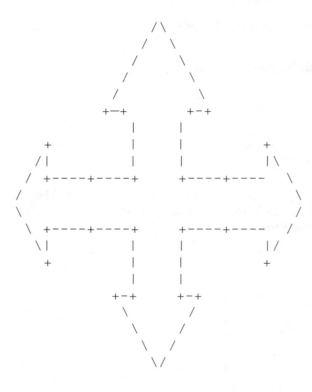

This assignment, like #1, provides practice using your development environment.

3.   Write a program that calculates the sum and average of five values entered by the user. Your program should work in a fashion similar to the examples in this chapter.

4.   Write a program that allows the user to type in a number and then displays the number's square and cube.

5.   Write a program that allows the user to type in a value that represents his or her age in years. The program then displays the number of days that the user has been alive (not counting fractions of a year).

CHAPTER 3

CHARACTERISTICS OF C++ DATA TYPES

3.1 INTRODUCTION TO DATA TYPES

Recall C++'s rich number of built-in data types reproduced here in table 3.1.

Table 3.1   C++ Data Types

int	float	unsigned char
long	double	unsigned long
short	long double	
char	unsigned	

Of these, `int`, `long`, `short`, `char`, `unsigned`, `unsigned char`, and `unsigned long` are called *integral types* and `float`, `double`, and `long double` are called *floating point types* (or just *float types*). The integral types all consist of values that have no decimal, or fractional, part. These are whole number types, with some allowing negative values. The floating types correspond roughly to mathematics' real numbers. They all may be positive or negative and have fractional parts. Each type is slightly different in terms of range and precision. The programmer's choice of data type for a particular application depends on the kind of data to be processed balanced with the program's performance needs.

3.2 THE INTEGRAL TYPES

The `int` is the "most natural" data type in C++. *Most natural* means the `int` is represented by the fundamental *word size* of the computer system being used. To explain, we will digress momentarily into a discussion of computer hardware.

Recall that the processor (microprocessor) contains a few memory locations called *registers*. The amount of register memory is negligible compared to the amount of memory in RAM. These registers, since they are located within the processor (remember RAM memory is apart from the processor), are very fast. Many times data from RAM memory must pass through a register before it can be manipulated by the ALU. Each register can hold one machine *word*.

Data is stored in memory (RAM or register) as a sequence of electrical impulses. In simple terms, these electrical impulses can either be "on" or "off." "On" corresponds to the value 1, and "off" corresponds to the value 0. Each 0 or 1 in the sequence is called a *bit*. Bit is short for *binary digit*, since in the binary number system the only digits used are 0 and 1. (By contrast, the decimal number system, with which we are all familiar, uses ten digits: 0, 1, 2, 3, 4, 5, 6, 7, 8, and 9 to form any number.) The first few binary numbers are shown in table 3.2.

Table 3.2   Binary Numbers

Binary (Base 2)	Decimal (Base 10)
0	0
1	1
10	2
11	3
100	4
101	5
110	6
111	7
1000	8
1001	9
1010	10

In the decimal system, the place value of digits within a number is based on powers of ten:

$$23,752_{10} = 2 \times 10^4 + 3 \times 10^3 + 7 \times 10^2 + 5 \times 10^1 + 2 \times 10^0$$

The same is true for a binary number, except that powers of two are used:

$$
\begin{aligned}
10101_2 &= 1 \times 2^4 + 0 \times 2^3 + 1 \times 2^2 + 0 \times 2^1 + 1 \times 2^0 \\
&= 16_{10} + 0_{10} + 4_{10} + 0_{10} + 1_{10} \\
&= 21_{10}
\end{aligned}
$$

A sequence of eight bits form a *byte*; thus, when a byte represents nonnegative numbers, its values range from 00000000_2 to 11111111_2. Therefore, the values that a byte can assume are:

$$
\begin{aligned}
00000000_2 &= 0_{10} \\
00000001_2 &= 1_{10} \\
00000010_2 &= 2_{10} \\
00000011_2 &= 3_{10} \\
&\;\;\vdots \\
11111101_2 &= 253_{10} \\
11111110_2 &= 254_{10} \\
11111111_2 &= 255_{10}
\end{aligned}
$$

A byte can represent a nonnegative integer in the range 0 to 255 (256 different values; note 2^8 = 256). Whereas a byte is always eight bits, the size of a word varies from machine to machine. Two bytes form a machine word on 16-bit machines. Most modern PC computer systems use 32-bit processors, in which case machine words (and, therefore, registers) are 32 bits (four bytes) wide. For a 16-bit word, the range of values is

$$00000000\ 00000000_2 \text{ to } 11111111\ 11111111_2$$

or

$$0_{10} \text{ to } 65{,}535_{10}$$

which is 65,536 different values. 32-bit machines can represent over 4 billion different integral values.

$$00000000\ 00000000\ 00000000\ 00000000_2 \text{ to } 11111111\ 11111111\ 11111111\ 11111111_2$$

or

$$0_{10} \text{ to } 4{,}294{,}967{,}295_{10}$$

More advanced processors use 64-bit registers for even greater ranges of integer values. Since negative numbers also need to be represented, the range of values for normal ints on a 16-bit machine is

$$-32768 \text{ to } 32767$$

which is still 65,536 different values. On a 32-bit machine, the range is

$$-2{,}147{,}483{,}648 \text{ to } 2{,}147{,}483{,}647$$

Why is there one more negative value than positive value? In order for the number of positive and negative values to be the same, one would need to omit one legal number (wasteful) or allow both +0 and − 0 (again wasteful). The reason that there is one additional negative number is based on the system for representing negative numbers called *two's complement* representation.

Two's complement will be illustrated using a reduced size 4-bit system. The left-most bit indicates whether the number is positive or negative. If the left-most bit is 0, the number is positive; if the left-most bit is 1, the number is negative. Consider the positive numbers shown in table 3.3.

Table 3.3   4-bit Integers

Two's Complement	Decimal
0000	0
0001	1
0010	2
0011	3
0100	4
0101	5
0110	6
0111	7

There are no surprises here. The negative numbers require a little manipulation. To convert a negative two's complement number into its decimal equivalent, the following algorithm can be used:

```
1.  Ignore the left-most bit. Remember, it only serves to indicate that
    the number is negative.
                  1101   -> 101
2.  Swap all the bits in the number; that is, change each 0 to a 1 and
    each 1 to a 0.
                  101 -> 010
3.  Add one to the result. Convert directly to decimal form remembering to
    put a negative sign in front.
                  011 -> 3 -> -3
```

Adding one to a binary number means using *binary addition*. Consider the binary addition provided in table 3.4.

Table 3.4   Binary Addition

+	0	1
0	0	1
1	1	10

$1 + 1 = 0$ with a carry of 1. Two binary numbers are added:

```
    1011        (-5)
   +0011        (+3)
    1110        (-2)
```

Notice that in two's complement arithmetic the additions work out correctly when adding negative numbers. The complete range of our 4-bit values is shown in table 3.5.

Binary addition (as well as subtraction, multiplication, and division), using two values whose sum (difference, etc.) is within range, yields the correct result.

Our 4-bit system expanded to 16 bits explains the behavior of a 16-bit compiler forced to "extend" the range of `int`s. Consider this section of C++ code compiled on a 16-bit system:

```
x = 32767;
cout << (x + 1);
```

The value −32768 is printed when the answer should be +32768. The novice programmer may make several erroneous conclusions:

```
1.   addition is not working properly
2.   the cout stream is not displaying properly
3.   the compiler has a bug in it
```

None of these conclusions is correct. Recall the range of `int`s is −32768 to +32767. Attempting to add one to 32767 will generate a number out of range that still has a 16-bit representation. Consider what happens in our 4-bit system. The addition of 7 + 1 is performed as follows:

$$
\begin{array}{r}
0111_2 \\
+\ 0001_2 \\
\hline
1000_2 \ = \ -8_{10}
\end{array}
$$

When a number is added to an `int` value to cause it to go out of range (either too large or too small), the value "wraps around." Some more examples include:

```
-32768 - 1 = +32767
 32767 + 2 =  32767
 32767 + 3 =  32766
```

What would 20,000 + 20,000 yield?

This wrap around phenomenon can catch unwary programmers by surprise and cause otherwise correct programs to produce erroneous results. One solution is to increase the range of values. For example, many 16-bit compilers for PCs use four bytes to represent the type `long`, or `long int`. Normally, a 16-bit compiler would use two bytes for each `int`. The range is increased dramatically:

$$- 2,147,483,648 \text{ to } +2,147,483,647$$

This range is equivalent to the standard `int`s on a 32-bit machine. The penalty to pay for this greater range is that twice as much memory is needed to store a `long`. Also, all arithmetic on `long`s takes a little longer to perform. Since `long`s, unlike `int`s, are not a "natural" type (fitting conveniently within a machine register with direct machine language manipulation of the data), the processor has to do more work when handling `long`s. Many times, however, this additional overhead is negligible, and increased range is necessary. On 32-bit machines, of course, 32-bit calculations (with 32-bit `int`s, no less) are just as efficient as 16-bit calculations.

For many applications, negative values are not needed. In which case the type `unsigned`, or `unsigned int`, can be used. An `unsigned`, when stored in 16 bits like an `int`, ranges from 0 to 65535.

The `long` and `unsigned` type can be combined into the `unsigned long` (also called `unsigned long int`). The values for this type on a 16-bit machine that uses four bytes to store `long`s would range from 0 to 4,294,967,295 (the same number of individual values afforded by 32-bit `long`).

Table 3.5 4-bit Signed Values

Two's Complement	Decimal
1000	-8
1001	-7
1010	-6
1011	-5
1100	-4
1101	-3
1110	-2
1111	-1
0000	0
0001	1
0010	2
0011	3
0100	4
0101	5
0110	6
0111	7

The type `short`, or `short int`, is available to represent integer values in possibly less space than regular `int`s. On some systems, `short`s and `int`s, as well as `unsigned short`s and `unsigned`s, are identical.

For `unsigned` integral values (`unsigned` and `unsigned long`), the range can be easily determined if the number of bits making up the type is known. If `b` is the number of bits, the range is

$$0 \text{ to } 2^b - 1$$

For `signed` integral values, the range is

$$-2^{b-1} \text{ to } 2^{b-1} - 1$$

The number of bytes used to store each of these types can be found using the `sizeof` operator. This operator looks like a function (see chapter 6), since it has a word for a symbol. When given a variable or type as an argument, it returns an `unsigned` result indicating the number of bytes of storage the variable or type requires. On a 16-bit machine, `sizeof(int)` would evaluate to two, and `sizeof(long)` would probably be four.

None of the sizes (and consequently none of the value ranges) listed above are specified in C++. C++ does guarantee that the following relationships hold for all systems and all implementations of the language:

```
sizeof(short) ≤ sizeof(int) ≤ sizeof(long)
sizeof(int) = sizeof(unsigned)
```

Integral *constants* are written as whole numbers, with no decimal points or fractional parts. Integers with no qualifying suffix are treated as `int`s; the suffixes u and L are appended to indicate `unsigned` and `long` constant values:

```
3         int constant
3u        unsigned constant
3L        long constant
3uL       unsigned long constant
```

Actually, either upper- or lowercase u and L can be used. The lowercase u is used here so at a quick glance it is distinguishable from a digit (since all digits are tall). The uppercase L is used almost universally, since the lowercase l looks almost exactly like the digit one.

Consider the following output statement:

```
cout << 21 << "\n" <<  4 << "\n" << 18231 << "\n" << 450 << "\n";
```

It produces the less than attractive list of numbers on the screen:

```
21
4
18231
450
```

Usually a column of numbers is right justified; that is, the numbers are lined up on the right side instead of the left side. With `cout`, this can be acomplished using the `setw()` manipulator:

```
cout << setw(6) << 21 << "\n" << setw(6) <<  4 << "\n" << setw(6) << 18231
     << "\n" << setw(6) << 450 << "\n";
```

The resulting display

```
    21
     4
 18231
   450
```

is more pleasing to the human observer. Notice that `setw()` must be sent to the stream before each value that requires right justification is sent to the stream.

Exercises

1. List all the *integral* types in C++.

2. What is meant by the *word* size of a processor?

3. Express the following `int`s in two's complement binary form:

    5, -6, 345, -250, 0.

4. Express the following two's complement `int`s in decimal form:

    00000000 01010011, 10000000 10000010, 11111111 11111111, 01111111 11111111.

5. How many bits make up one byte?

6. How many bytes are required to store an `int` on your system?

7. What does the `sizeof()` operator do?

3.3 THE FLOATING POINT TYPES

Many applications demand the ability to represent numbers with fractional parts. The *floating point types* (`float`, `double`, and `long double`) provide for such a representation. They are similar to mathematical real numbers. The floating types have only a finite precision representation; hence, they only approximate mathematical real numbers. Recall using *scientific notation* to represent numbers.

$$23{,}317 = 2.3317 \times 10^4$$
$$0.000\ 000\ 004\ 124 = 4.124 \times 10^{-9}$$

In the first example, 2.3317 is called the *mantissa*, and 4 is the associated whole number *exponent*. This form is also known as *exponential notation*.

Most compilers support the standard floating point number representation for digital computers created by the Institute of Electrical and Electronics Engineers in the 1980s. This IEEE standard is supported by microprocessors that contain internal circuitry designed to perform floating point calculations very quickly and precisely. Sometimes a *math coprocessor* can be installed on machines that lack the built-in floating point capability. Most compilers support floating point computations on machines that lack math coprocessors or internal floating point circuitry. In these cases extra machine language code must be inserted into the compiled program to emulate the operations that a math coprocessor would perform. Floating point math emulation is much slower than direct floating point calculations done by a dedicated math hardware unit. Software applications that are heavily graphics oriented like computer-aided design (CAD) packages often require millions of floating point calculations to display the projection of a complex three-dimensional object on the computer's display.

On many C++ systems, the `float type` corresponds to the IEEE single precision floating point number. It requires four bytes of storage. These four bytes, or 32 bits, are broken down into three parts:

```
1 bit for the sign of the mantissa
8 bits for the exponent (biased by 127 to account for
     its sign)
23 bits for the mantissa
```

Figure 3.1 shows how a `float` value is stored internally. Obviously, the floating point type is more complicated than even the two's complement form for the integral types. The value of a `float`, based on its bit pattern, is interpreted by consulting figure 3.1 in conjunction with the equations described in figure 3.2.

The NaN in the equations stands for "Not a Number;" that is, a sequence of bits that does not represent a valid `float`. The machine arithmetically manipulates `float`s similar to the way numbers in exponential notation must be done by hand without a calculator. To add two `float`s, the exponents must be the same. If they differ, one of the numbers must be adjusted so that the exponents are the same, then they can be added.

$$
\begin{array}{cc}
\begin{array}{r}
2.3 \times 10^3 \\
+\ 3.4 \times 10^5 \\
\end{array}
& \longrightarrow &
\begin{array}{r}
0.023 \times 10^5 \\
+\ 3.400 \times 10^5 \\
\hline
3.423 \times 10^5 \\
\end{array}
\end{array}
$$

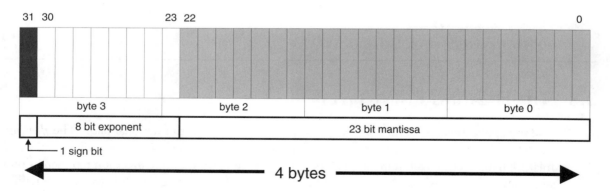

Internal Representation of a `float`
Figure 3.1

To multiply, recall that one need only multiply the mantissas and add the exponents.

$$
\begin{array}{r}
2.3 \times 10^3 \\
\times\ 3.4 \times 10^5 \\
\hline
(2.3 \times 3.4) \times 10^{3\,+\,5} \quad =\quad 7.82 \times 10^8 \\
\end{array}
$$

```
If 0 < exponent < 255,
  then value = (-1)^sign × 1.mantissa × 2^(exponent -127)
If exponent = 0 and mantissa ≠ 0,
  then value = (-1)^(sign × 0.mantissa) × 2^(-126)
If exponent = 0 and mantissa = 0,
  then value = 0
If exponent = 255 and mantissa = 0,
  then value = (-1)^sign × ∞
If exponent = 255 and mantissa ≠ 0,
  then value is a NaN
```

Floating Point Representations
Figure 3.2

The main difference is that the numbers are represented in binary scientific notation instead of decimal.

A float's range, as represented above, is approximately $\pm(3.4 \times 10^{-38}...3.4 \times 10^{38})$ with seven digits of precision. The type double stands for *double-precision* floating point. A double, according to the IEEE standard, requires eight bytes of storage. Its range is approximately $\pm(1.7 \times 10^{-308}...1.7 \times 10^{308})$ with 15 digits of precision. If a double's range is insufficient, the long double type is available. The long double's range and precision is more than adequate for most applications; on some systems, it takes up ten bytes of memory and ranges from $\pm(3.4 \times 10^{-4932}...1.1 \times 10^{4932})$ with 19 digits of precision. These ranges are provided for relative comparisons; the exact ranges are system-specific.

As you might imagine, floating point manipulations require the machine to do much more work than with integral types. Not only must the mantissas be dealt with, but exponents are also involved. Floating point arithmetic is much slower than integer arithmetic (even with a math coprocessor or built-in floating point unit), and these "real" types require more storage. Floating types should be avoided when not absolutely necessary. On the small programs that we write, the time penalty for using floating point values is usually not apparent, and the issue is not so important.

Because of the finite representation of floating point types, the number of decimal places (actually, binary places) is limited. This means rounding occurs quite frequently. Rounding introduces a small amount of error. In a complicated calculation, these errors can become compounded to produce a result that is nowhere near the correct answer. Floating point arithmetic does not adhere to many of the important real number properties we've grown to trust. For example, it is *not* associative:

Associative Property

```
    (a + b) + c = a + (b + c)
Let   a = 1.0004 x 10³        With five digits of
      b = 1.0004 x 10³        precision
      c = 1.0001 x 10⁴
      (a + b) + c = (1.0004 × 10³ + 1.0004 × 10³) + 1.0001 × 10⁴
                  = 2.0008 × 10³ + 1.0001 × 10⁴
                  = 0.2001 × 10⁴ + 1.0001 × 10⁴
                  = 1.2002 × 10⁴
```

$$a + (b + c) = 1.0004 \times 10^3 + (1.0004 \times 10^3 + 1.0001 \times 10^4)$$
$$= 1.0004 \times 10^3 + (0.1000 \times 10^4 +$$
$$1.0001 \times 10^4)$$
$$= 1.0004 \times 10^3 + 1.1001 \times 10^4$$
$$= 0.1000 \times 10^4 + 1.1001 \times 10^4$$
$$= 1.2001 \times 10^4$$

Because of the rounding error in conversion to identical exponents, notice that the two answers are different; both differ from the actual answer of 1.20018. The first result is a reasonable approximation (rounded off version) of the actual answer. That result is the best that can be expected with only five digits of precision. The second answer introduces a greater error than the first. The first answer has a relative error of about 0.002 percent, while the second has a relative error of about 0.007 percent. Both are small errors, but their effects can accumulate over successive calculations sometimes producing errors in the final result of over 100 percent!

Floating point numbers are distinguished from mathematical real numbers in another way. Mathematical real numbers are said to be *infinitely dense*. This means that given any two real numbers, another real number can be found that fits between the first two real numbers. For example, consider the two real numbers 12.022034 and 12.022035. In this case, just take the smaller number, extend the decimal places by one, and add a nonzero digit in the last decimal position. The number 12.0220345 happens to be exactly halfway between the original two values. (You can always easily find the number halfway between by adding the two numbers together and dividing the sum by two.) As in our four-bit integer example, consider a scaled-back floating point number that has a three-bit mantissa and two bit exponent. (The signs of the mantissa and exponent will be ignored here for simplicity, but the argument will still be valid for signed representations.) In the decimal number system, the value 0.842 can be written in expanded form as:

$$0.842 = \left(8 \times \frac{1}{10} \right) + \left(4 \times \frac{1}{100} \right) + \left(2 \times \frac{1}{1000} \right)$$

For our experiment here, the three-bit binary mantissa 0.101 would correspond to

$$0.101 = \left(1 \times \frac{1}{2} \right) + \left(0 \times \frac{1}{4} \right) + \left(1 \times \frac{1}{8} \right)$$

Just as decimal places divide by ten each step moving from left to right (1, 1/10, 1/100, 1/1000, etc.), binary places divide by *two* (1, 1/2, 1/4, 1/8, 1/16, 1/32, etc.) A mantissa of $.101_2$ and exponent of 10_2 would yield:

$$.101_2 \times 2^{10}{}_2 = \left(\frac{1}{2} + \frac{1}{4} \right) \times 2^{2_{10}} = \frac{3}{4} \times 4 = 3$$

Table 3.6 shows all the possible values that can be represented in this limited system:

Table 3.6   Small Floating Point Values

Exponent	Mantissa							
	.000	.001	.010	.011	.100	.101	.110	.111
00	0	1/8	1/4	3/8	1/2	5/8	3/4	7/8
01	0	1/4	1/2	3/4	1	5/4	3/2	7/4
10	0	1/2	1	3/2	2	5/2	3	7/2
11	0	1	2	3	4	5	6	7

Since a finite number of digits must be used to represent the values of the mantissa and exponent, the hope of infinite density is surely lost. Another undesirable effect is the duplication of values. Out of 32 table entries only 20 are unique. Perhaps a more surprising consequence becomes apparent when the numbers in the table are plotted on the number line. On figure 3.3, the arrows point to values that are represented.

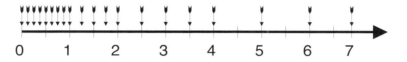

"Real" Numbers in the Small Floating Point System
Figure 3.3

Not only are the values not infinitely dense, but they are also not even uniformly dense. There are more representable numbers closer to zero and fewer as the distance from zero becomes greater. This effect, while not as severe, also occurs in the standard floating point implementations due to the nature of the representation. On most systems, the following code can produce unexpected results:

```
float x;
cin >> x;
cout << x;
```

The value in decimal form typed in might not be exactly representable as a binary decimal. Rounding will occur and the displayed number may differ in the last decimal place from the number typed in. Fortunately, it will be close, as close as the implementation allows.

These examples (i.e., nonassociativity and imprecise representation) illustrate some potential problems with floating types; there are many other types of problems that can occur. Most are due to allowing values to get out of range, allowing values to get close to (but not exactly) zero, or combining numbers of vastly different magnitudes. Floating point calculations are essential in many applications. As you can see, however, they should be handled, and their results interpreted, with care. Chapter 5 provides an example of how the imprecision of floating point numbers can cause problems for the unwary programmer when comparing two `float`s. A solution to this problem is discussed there as well.

The arithmetic operators, when given floating point operands, produce floating point results; thus, / will produce an answer with fractional parts. Thus,

```
5.0/3.0 = 1.666666
3.0/5.0 = 0.600000
```

Notice that 5.0 was written instead of just 5. Floating point constants are numbers written with an explicit decimal point. The default type, interestingly enough, of floating point constants is `double`:

```
3.0           double constant
3.0f          float constant
3.0L          long double constant
```

As with the integral types above, the case of the prefix is not critical; however, the lowercase `L` should be avoided for the reason given above.

Floating point constants can be written in *exponential,* or *scientific,* form. Since superscripts are rare on character based displays, the value 2.3×10^3 is written

2.3e3

Floating point numbers can be printed in exponential (or scientific) form using `cout` as follows:

```
cout.setf(ios::scientific, ios::floatfield); // Display in exponential form
cout << 3012.4;      //   Prints 3.0124E3
```

As with integral types, the numerical width can be specified. In addition, the number of decimal places to display can be set as follows:

```
cout.setf(ios::showpoint);          //   Show decimal point
cout.precision(4);                  //   Always show four decimal places
cout << 3012.4;                     //   Prints 3012.4000
```

The qualifier `unsigned` may not be used with a floating type. Also, `short` may not be used in combination with any floating type. The `long` qualifier is used only with `double`. In C++ there is no such thing as a `long float` type. (This is true for ANSI C as well. Some older C compilers may allow a `long float` and treat it as a `double`.)

Exercises

1. List all the floating point types in C++.

2. How is the exponential expression 2.34×10^{-4} expressed in C++?

3. List three shortcomings that floating point numbers have compared to mathematical real numbers.

4. How can a floating type's precision and width be set?

5. What three distinct parts make up the internal representation of a floating point type?

6. Why might the following two statements present surprising results?

    ```
    cin  >> f;  //  f, a float
    cout << f;
    ```

3.4 CHARACTER DATA TYPE

The type char is used to represent a single character. A char is most often stored in one byte of memory; thus, because of its eight-bit representation, the char type assumes the values −128 to +127 unsigned chars fall in the range of 0 to 255.

All computers have a *character set*. The character set is the set of all characters that the computer system can display. All popular microcomputers and many minicomputers have character sets based on a standard set called the *ASCII* character set. ASCII stands for American Standard Code for Information Interchange. Most microcomputers use an extended ASCII character set that contains additional characters not found in the standard ASCII set. As an example, the IBM PC-extended ASCII set can be found in the appendix.

ACSII codes range from 0 to 255, and each code has an associated character. The ASCII code 65 corresponds to the character A. Characters can be treated as numbers or literal characters:

```
void main()
{
        char ch1, ch2;

        ch1 = 'C';
        ch2 = 77;
        cout << ch1 << ch2 << "\n";
}
```

Program 3.1

Literal characters (character constants) are enclosed within single quotes. In program 3.1, ch1 is assigned the ASCII value of the character C which, consulting the ASCII chart, is 67. ch2 is given the value 77, which corresponds to the character M. Since both are declared as chars, their character interpretations are printed. The type char can be treated very comfortably as a small integer value and can participate in arithmetic expressions. Some characters correspond to special control codes—'\n' is the newline character, '\b' is the backspace character, '\t' is the tab character, '\f' is the form feed character (when sent to a printer), and '\a' is the alert character (causes the computer to beep). Notice that the backslash symbol emphasizes the fact that these are special control characters instead of printable characters. Both the backslash and letter that follows constitute one character; it is not correct to place more than one actual character within the single quotes.

When a character is read from the keyboard through cin using the extractor (<< operator), whitespace (made up of spaces, tabs, and newlines) is ignored. This is generally desirable, but if whitespace characters, in addition to other characters, need to be extracted, the cin.get() function can be used as follows:

```
cin >> ch;          //  Ignores whitespace characters
ch = cin.get();     //  Will get any character typed in, including white space
```

The character data type is very valuable, especially when used in a special structure known as a string. We examine strings in more detail in chapter 7.

3.5 MIXED ARITHMETIC EXPRESSIONS AND TYPE CASTING

As we've seen, the arithmetic operators produce integral results with integral operands and floating point results with floating point operands. Nothing was mentioned about mixing int and long, much less int and double. C++'s rules for mixed expressions are very strict but, fortunately, also very straightforward.

An arithmetic expression using one or more of the binary operators +, −, *, /, % is evaluated as follows:

1. The standard conversions—for the purposes of the calculation:
    *   any `char`, `unsigned char`, or `short` is promoted to an `int`
    *   any `unsigned short` is promoted to `unsigned`

2. If an operator has operands of mixed type, then the "weaker" type is promoted to the dominant type according to the scale:

    ```
    int < unsigned < long < unsigned long < float < double < long double
    ```

Promotion means temporarily treating the value of a variable or constant to be a higher type for the *purpose* of the calculation. The actual variable is unchanged; its value is just interpreted differently than usual. Promotion also goes by the names *conversion, coercion,* or *widening.* Notice that any floating point type dominates any integral type. The hierarchy chain was designed to attempt to do the right thing in most circumstances. Information is less likely to be lost promoting values in this direction.

Older versions of C always promoted `float`s to type `double` before they were used in an expression. C++ and ANSI C do not perform this standard conversion.

Recall that all expressions have an associated value. They also have an associated type that can be determined by the previous rules. Consider the following declarations:

```
char c = 'A';                  int i = 200, j = 3;
long L = 100;                  unsigned u = 50;
float f = 5.0, g = 3.0;        double d = 10.0;
long double LD = 25.0;
```

Expression	Value	Type
i + L	300	long
i + c	265	int
c + c	130	int
f + c	70.0	float
LD + c + u	140.0	long double
i/j	66	int
j/i	0	int
i/g	66.66667	float
g/i	0.015	float
1/2*f	0.0	float
1.0/2*f	2.5	double
6L + c	71	long
3.0 + c	68.0	double
3.0f + c	68.0	float
3.0Lf + c	68.0	long double

Promotion occurs across assignment:

```
f = i;    /*  f is assigned the value 200.0f  */
```

Values can also be *demoted* in assignment:

```
f = 5.5;
i = f;    /*  i is assigned the value 5  */
```

Here, the fractional part of `f` is lost when assigning its value to an `int` variable. This demotion is also known as *narrowing,* since approximately the same value is attempting to be squeezed into a representation using fewer bits or less precision. Obviously, not all narrowing conversions will produce valid results. Consider

```
i = 3.2e+8
```

Printing out the value of i after this assignment will produce a value totally unrelated to reality. Many systems will issue a warning in this case but are powerless to do so if the same value is assigned through a floating point variable, instead of a constant.

The above examples illustrate *implicit* conversion. It is done automatically because of the way the expression within the C++ statement is formed. These automatic conversions may be overridden by using *explicit* conversions known as *type casting* (or just *casting*). A value can be forced to be treated as a different type by merely placing it within parentheses and preceding it by the desired type name. For example:

```
c = 'A';
cout << int(c);
```

Here 65 is printed instead of A. An alternate syntax for type casting is

```
cout << (int)c;
```

This style of type casting will work in both C and C++. C++ allows the use of the more attractive *function style type casting*, shown in the previous example, whereas C compilers do not.

Consider the following scenario:

```
i = 5;
j = 10;
f = i/j;
```

Since f is a float, it is expected that it should be assigned the value 0.5, but because of the operator precedence rules, the assignment is equivalent to

```
f = (i/j);
```

The operator / has two int operands, i and j. The integer division yields zero, and f is assigned the value zero. To fix the situation, one might try

```
f = float(i/j);
```

but this merely casts int zero to be float zero. The correct approach is one of

```
f = float(i) / j;
```

or

```
f = i / float(j);
```

A cast is actually a unary operator and has very high precedence. The spacing above illustrates the precedence; therefore,

```
f = (float) i/j;
```

is equivalent to

```
f = ((float) i))/j;
```

and not

```
f = (float) (i/j);
```

Exercises

1. What is the ASCII code?

2. What is a type cast?

   For questions 3–14, indicate both the value and the type of the expression given the declarations:

   ```
   char c = 'A';            int i = 10, j = 3;
   long L = 10;             unsigned u = 10;
   float f = 10.0;          double d = 5.0;
   long double LD = 2.0;
   ```

   3. `i + j`   4. `f + i`   5. `j/i`   6. `j/f`

   7. `c + 5`   8. `f + 2.0`   9. `1/2*LD`   10. `LD*1/2`

   11. `c + c`   12. `char(L)`   13. `L + L`   14. `float(i/j)`

15. What is the difference between implicit and explicit type conversions?

16. What is an alternative to using `<<` to extract a character from the input stream?

17. What is the range of a `char`?

3.6 ENUMERATED TYPES

C++ allows the creation of simple integral types with associated programmer-defined values. These *enumerated* types are given names, and the legal values that the types can assume are listed (enumerated).

```
enum Color { red, orange, yellow, green, blue, brown, black, white };
```

The `enum` reserved word creates a new data type. Variables of type `Color` can be declared and assigned values:

```
Color hue, tint; //  Two variables of type Color

hue  = red;      //  value red is assigned to hue variable
tint = brown;    //  value brown is assigned to tint variable
hue  = tint;     //  hue is given value of tint (hue becomes brown)
```

The words listed in the `enum` list are identifiers (i.e., they follow identifier naming rules) that represent values that a variable of that `enum` type can assume. `enum` types are integral types (i.e., compatible with `int`s, `long`s, `char`s, etc., with the restrictions listed below) and can be used as arguments to `case` labels within `switch` statements (chapter 4), as array subscripts (chapter 7), and anywhere else integral types must be used. Enumerated types can also be passed to, and returned from, functions (chapter 6).

The compiler actually associates each `enum` constant with an integer value. In the previous `Color` example, the `enum` constants have the following values:

```
red = 0,   orange = 1,   yellow = 2,   green = 3,...
```

The compiler begins at zero and numbers each constant in sequence. This numbering can be overridden, however:

```
enum Color { red = 5, orange, yellow, green = 44, blue, brown, black, white };
```

Here `red = 5`, `orange = 6`, `yellow = 7`, `green = 44`, `blue = 45`, `brown = 46`, etc. Enumerated types are particularly useful when representing sequential values.

Even though enumerated types are new, user defined integral types, they are not freely interchangeable with `int`s. Enumerated types are automatically promoted to ints when necessary, but the opposite conversion is not done:

```
Color c = red;
  int   i =   3;

  i = c;          //  Ok
  c = i;          //  Illegal
  c = Color(i);   //  Legal, an explicit cast must be used
```

Arithmetic cannot be performed on `enum` types:

```
  c = red*blue;  //  Illegal
  c = c + 1      //  Illegal
```

since `enum` types can't be automatically converted from the `int` result across assignment. The result is likely to be outside the enumerated type's range anyway. A programmer that feels the need to do arithmetic on `enum`s needs to re-evaluate his or her reason for using enumerated types in the first place—they are likely inappropriate for the particular program.

Exercises

1. What is an enumerated type?

2. How are enumerated types defined and used?

3. What advantages do enumerated types have over simple `unsigned types`?

Assignments

1. Write a program that asks the user for a temperature in degrees Celsius and then displays the temperature in degrees Fahrenheit. The program should then ask for a temperature in degrees Fahrenheit to be converted to degrees Celsius. The respective conversion formulas are:

$$F = \frac{9}{5}C + 32$$

$$C = \frac{5}{9}(F - 32)$$

2. Write a program to display the size (in bytes) of every data type mentioned in this chapter. A sample run would begin:

```
Data sizes for this C++ system:
Type:           Size in bytes:

char:               1
short:              2
int:                2
long:               4
(etc...)
```

3. It has been said that the typical American consumes about 4,000 calories at the main Thanksgiving meal. Running or walking burns off about 100 calories per mile. Write a program to calculate how many miles you would have to run or walk to burn off the Thanksgiving meal (assuming you ate the typical amount). Your program should calculate the answer, not just print a precalculated value.

4. Consult table **3.7**. Running or walking burns off about 100 calories per mile. Write a program to calculate how many miles you would have to run or walk to burn off the burritos, salads, and shakes that you consume. The program would likely run as follows:

```
How many bean burritos, bowls of salad, and milk shakes did you
     consume?  3 2 1
You ingested 1829 Calories.
You will have to run 18.29 miles to expend that much energy.
```

Table 3.7 Mexican Food Calorie Chart

Food	Calories
Bean burrito	357
Salad w/dressing	185
Milk shake	388

CHAPTER 4

CONDITIONAL EXECUTION

4.1 INTRODUCTION

Computer programs "flow"; that is, their execution begins at the first statement and then each succeeding statement is executed in turn until the last statement is performed. With this concept in mind, the programs we've seen so far are simple streams (not to be confused with I/O streams) flowing downhill. Some streams, however, branch out and follow different courses; there may be more than a single channel carrying the water downstream. Programs can be written that execute differently (flow proceeding one way or another) based upon certain conditions. *Conditional* statements can be used to change the flow of a program. Programs can be written that execute certain sections of code over and over again. This is known as *iteration* and is introduced in the next chapter. Iteration corresponds to an eddy or whirlpool within a stream in which the water swirls around and around without moving downstream. Extremely powerful programs can be written using the concepts of conditional and iterative execution.

4.2 RELATIONAL OPERATORS

Relational operators are used to indicate whether or not two values are related in a particular way. They essentially indicate "yes" or "no." The relational operators are

$<$	is less than?
$>$	is greater than?
$<=$	is less than or equal to?
$>=$	is greater than or equal to?
$==$	is equal to?
$!=$	is not equal to?

Technically, $==$ and $!=$ are *equality* operators, and the other four inequality operators are relational operators, but for the sake of this discussion they will all be lumped into the general category of relational operators. The answer "yes" or "true" is indicated by the integer value 1. A "no" or "false" response generates the integer value 0. An expression that involves a relational operator always has the value of 0 or 1. Consider the expressions and their associated values in table 4.1 (not all are relational expressions):

Table 4.1 Simple Expression

Expression	Value
3 + 4*10	43
(2 + 3 + 1)/2	3
5 < 10	1
5 > 10	0
5 > (2 + 3+ 1)/2	1
(2 + 3 + 1)/2 > 5	0

With the introduction of the relational operators, we need to determine how they interact with the other operators when parentheses are not present. We will begin to build an operator hierarchy chart that will grow as new operators are explored. Operators have two important properties that dictate how they interact with other operators—*precedence* and *associativity.*

We've discussed operator precedence. It involves the order of application of different operators. Associativity concerns the direction of operator application when several identical operators are applied in sequence. Operators associate either left to right, or they associate right to left. Consider the statement:

```
x = a + b + c + d;
```

and especially the expression that comprises the right-hand side:

```
a + b + c + d
```

In algebra, the associative property of addition dictates that since the only operation occurring is addition, it is safe to add in either direction—adding a to b first, then c and finally d; or adding c and d first then b and finally a. In C++, the + operator always associates left to right; that is, in the absence of parentheses, the expression is evaluated as if parentheses were placed as follows:

```
((a + b) + c) + d
```

This "associativity" is certainly acceptable, since it does produce mathematically correct results, and the compiler can generate machine code in a regular fashion. The original statement is equivalent to

```
x = ((a + b) + c) + d;
```

The assignment operator has a lower precedence than the arithmetic operators so that the statement is literally evaluated as if parentheses were placed as follows:

```
x = (((a + b) + c) + d);
```

The assignment operator associates right to left; therefore, the expression on the right is evaluated first and the overall value is assigned to x. In C++, "chained" assignments are not uncommon:

```
x = a = b = c = d;
```

Because of assignment's right to left associativity, this is interpreted as

```
x = ((a = (b = (c = d)));
```

This statement may look a bit strange so let's carefully examine it. The expression c = d is evaluated first because it is in the innermost set of parentheses. All expressions in C++ have a value associated with them. The value of an assignment expression (which, recall, can be a stand alone C++ statement itself) is the same as the value that is assigned; thus, the value of the expression c = d is d. Since the next outer most set of parentheses consist of the assignment b = (c = d), and since c = d has the value of d, b is given the value of d. The overall effect is that in a chained assignment statement all the variables take on the value of the right-most value; thus, the statement

```
a = b = c = d = e = 99;
```

assigns the value 99 to each of the variables a, b, c, d, and e.

The precedence rules for our limited knowledge of C++'s operators can be summarized in table 4.2:

Table 4.2 Operator Precedence

Operators	Associativity
* / %	L to R
+ -	L to R
< <= > >=	L to R
== !=	L to R
=	R to L

The arithmetic operators have higher precedence than the relational operators, and assignment has the lowest precedence possible of the operators we've seen.

Exercises

1. What int value does *false* have?

2. What two critical properties do all operators possess?

3. What C++ operator indicates the remainder after integer division?

4. How is the = operator different from the == operator?

5. What is a chained assignment?

4.3 CONDITIONAL STATEMENTS—IF

The relational operators have limited application apart from *conditional statements*. Relational and logical expressions, in fact, form the conditions to check within conditional statements. A conditional statement allows part of the program to be executed or ignored depending on the circumstances. The programs we've considered so far exhibit what can be called *linear flow*; that is, the first statement in the program is executed, followed by the second, then the third, and so forth, until the last statement within the program is carried out. No statement is omitted, and none is performed more than once (unless, of course, the exact statement is duplicated elsewhere in the program). Recall program 2.7 reproduced here as program 4.1.

```
#include <iostream.h>

void main()
{
    int grade1, grade2, grade3;
    int grade_avg;
    cout << "Please enter three integer values: ";
    cin >> grade1 >> grade2 >> grade3;
    grade_avg = (grade1 + grade2 + grade3)/3;
    cout << "The average of " << grade1 << ", "
         << grade2 << ", and "
         << grade3 << " is " << grade_avg << "\n";
}
```

Program 4.1

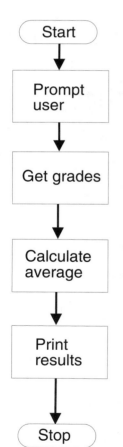

Flowchart for a Linear Program Figure 4.1

The program's *flow*, or sequence of execution, can be represented pictorially with a *flowchart* as shown in figure 4.1.

The slanted parallelogram represents a statement within the program that performs input or output, in this case printing something to cout or reading data from cin. A rectangle within a flowchart represents a process that the program is to perform, such as a calculation or assignment. The other flowchart symbols that we'll use here are defined in figure 4.2. Flowchart symbols usually contain simplified English descriptions instead of C++ language statements. Flowcharts are language independent and are used to describe algorithms, which may be implemented in the programmer's language of choice. Some programmers can better construct the solution to a programming problem (i.e., the algorithm) using a flowchart. This may be related to research that has found that some individuals are visually oriented and better understand concepts when presented with graphs or diagrams as opposed to reading the same information in textual form. In the 1960s and 1970s, flowcharts were routinely used to teach programming concepts. The advent of the structured programming revolution in the early 1970s and 1980s led to their temporary demise. Now, as we will see, the disciplined use of *structured* flowcharts can be a significant programming aid. To those more visually than textually oriented, flowcharts can be very enlightening.

Consider a simple situation that involves *conditional execution. Conditional execution* means certain parts of the program may or may not be performed, depending on a particular condition. A rather simple program must be written to ask the user for a number. If the number entered has the appropriate value, a message will be displayed indicating the successful entry of the correct number. Otherwise, this message will not be printed. A variation of this program could be incorporated into a larger program to provide passworded access to some of the larger program's features. The flowchart that represents this program appears in figure 4.3.

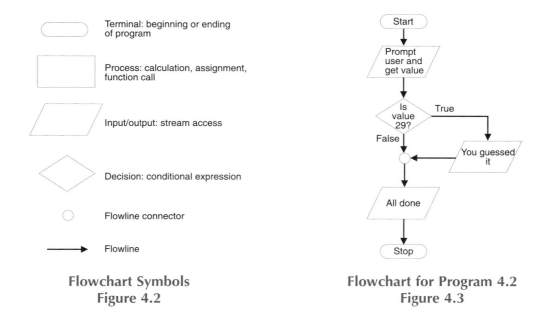

Flowchart Symbols
Figure 4.2

Flowchart for Program 4.2
Figure 4.3

Notice the flowlines coming out of the diamond (conditional) symbol. Based on the condition described in the conditional symbol, the flow of the program may optionally take a different path. The C++ implementation of figure 4.3 is program 4.2.

```
#include <iostream.h>
void main()
{
    int in_value;
    cout << "Enter the secret number: ";
    cin >> in_value;
    if ( in_value == 29 )
        cout << "You guessed the secret number!\n";
    cout << "Program completed, thank you.\n";
}
```

Program 4.2

Every line of the program is always executed except for the output statement that displays "You guessed the secret number!" This statement is only done when the user types in the number 29. Note the == operator is used to check for equality instead of the = operator which would assign 29 to in_value, not the intended operation. A line of the program is executed or ignored based upon the value of the variable in_value. The *general form* of the if statement is

```
if ( condition )
    statement;
```

where *condition* is a relational and/or logical expression and *statement* is any C++ statement (even another if statement). The generalized if statement can be illustrated by the flowchart in figure 4.4.

The reserved word if and the parentheses around the condition must always be present. A group of statements surrounded by curly braces is called a *compound statement* and is considered one statement; thus, the if statement could have been written:

```
if ( in_value == 29 )
{
  cout << "You guessed the secret number!\n";
  cout << "The value you entered was "
      << in_value << "\n";
}
```

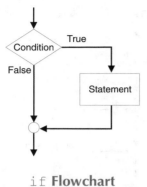

if Flowchart
Figure 4.4

in which case both output statements within the curly braces would be either executed or ignored depending on in_value. Notice that a semicolon need not terminate a compound statement outside the curly brace. The statement (or compound statement) within the if statement is sometimes referred to as the *body* of the if.

Notice that the line of code containing the if is not terminated with a semicolon. The end of the line in this case does not indicate the end of the if statement. The if statement includes the body. The following section of code

```
if ( in_value == 29 );
    cout << "Right!\n";
```

will always print "Right!" even though the intention is to only print it if in_value is 29. Properly indenting to portray the actual meaning above, the following is how the compiler interprets the stray semicolon:

```
if ( in_value == 29 )
    ;  /*   Empty body  */
cout << "Right!\n";
```

The semicolon terminates the if, so its body must be empty.

Frequently, the programmer needs to choose between two mutually exclusive courses of action. What if the program is to provide negative feedback if the incorrect number is typed in? The program flow is illustrated in figure 4.5.

For choosing between two courses of action, doing one or the other, the if...else statement is useful:

```
if ( in_value == 29 )
    cout << "You guessed the secret number!\n";
else
    cout << "You guessed incorrectly, sorry!\n";
cout << "Program completed, thank you.\n";
```

Here, as shown in figure 4.6, the last statement is always executed, but only one of the other two output statements will be performed.

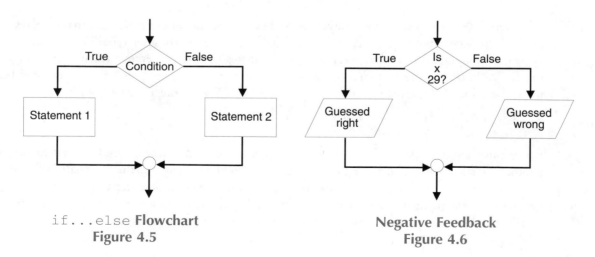

if...else Flowchart
Figure 4.5

Negative Feedback
Figure 4.6

4.4 LOGICAL OPERATORS

Logical expressions are constructed with the *logical operators* &&, | |, and !. && represents logical *and*. The following section of a program illustrates its usage. (For small examples, only sections of a program will be shown to save space; however, their placement inside of main(), variable declarations, #include, etc. would be required to test them out.)

```
//  x is an int with its value already assigned
if ( x > 10  &&  x < 100 )
    cout << x << " is within the proper range.\n";
```

For the message to be printed, x must be both greater than 10 and less than 100 (expressed mathematically $10 < x < 100$). If either subcondition is not true, the whole condition involving the && is considered false.

The operator | | represents logical *or*. In an *or* situation, if either operand is true or both operands are true, the *or* expression is true.

The ! is the unary *logical* not (also known as *logical negation*). All of the operators so far have been binary operators; that is, they have two associated operands. A unary operator acts on only one operand. The *not* operator reverses the logical value of its operand. Some examples appear in table 4.3.

Table 4.3 Logical Expressions

Expression	Value	Interpretation
10 < 100	1	True
!(10 < 100)	0	False
10 == 100	0	False
!(10 == 100)	1	True

Notice that the following expressions are equivalent:

```
x != y          →    x not equal to y
!(x == y)       →    It is not true that
                     x is equal to y
```

Other unary operators include *unary plus* and *unary minus*:

```
x = -3;
x = +3;
x = -(3 + 4);
```

As you might expect, the unary + is basically ignored by the compiler since x = 3; and x = +3; are equivalent statements (unary + is interpreted exactly as it is in algebra).

Notice the use of parentheses when negating a whole expression. Unary operators have very high precedence and are therefore applied to the operand immediately to their right. (They also all associate right to left like assignment.) The expression

```
!10 < 100
```

is interpreted as

```
(!10) < 100
```

What does !10 mean? Remember that 0 represents false and 1 stands for true. All relational and logical expressions evaluate to either 0 or 1; therefore, !10 must be either 0 or 1. Recall !0

means not false; thus, `!0` means true. When any of the relational operators are involved, the result of the expression is either `0` or `1`, and so `0!` is ultimately `1`. Similarly, `!1` is not true, which is false, or `0`. To recap, `!0` is `1`, and `!1` is `0`. When evaluating an expression for its truth value, the `int 0` is false, and any other `int` value is considered true. The value `10` is considered true, so `!10` would be false; thus, `!10` is `0`. It follows that the expression `!10 < 100` is true, whereas `!(10 < 100)` is false.

With the addition of the new operators, the operator chart expands to table 4.4.

Table 4.4 Expanded Operator Chart

Operator	Associativity
`! (unary)` `+ (unary)` `- (unary)`	R to L
`*` `/` `%`	L to R
`+` `-`	L to R
`<` `<=` `>` `>=`	L to R
`==` `!=`	L to R
`&&`	L to R
`||`	L to R
`=`	R to L

`&&` has precedence over `||` in the same way that multiplication has precedence over addition. Operators that consist of more than one character, such as `&&` and `<=`, may not include any intervening spaces (`< =` is interpreted as the less than operator followed by the assignment operator, which is an error). When the two characters that make up the operator are different, they must appear in the proper order (`=<` is incorrect, `<=` must be used).

The application of the `&&` and `||` operators is summarized by table 4.5 (used like a multiplication table).

Table 4.5 Logical AND/OR

`&&`	0	1
0	0	0
1	0	1

`||`	0	1
0	0	1
1	1	1

The operators `&&` and `||` are applied to their operands using *short-circuit* evaluation. This means that if the value of the expression can be determined by evaluating the first operand, then the second operand is not evaluated. In the `&&` situation, if the first operand is `0`, no value for the second operand can make the result anything other than `0` so the second operand is ignored. For `||`, if the first operand is `1`, then the result is `1` without the second operand being consulted. This short-circuit evaluation can be exploited to produce short, elegant, and efficient sections of programs, but it also can be used incorrectly to introduce errors that are hard to find.

Logical expressions can be made very complicated and tricky. This is especially true when ! is used in conjunction with the other logical operators. Many beginning programmers use && when || is what is really needed or vice versa. Consider the following conditional statements that are all logically equivalent:

```
if ( x > 10   &&   x < 100 )
      cout << "ok";
else
      cout << "bad";
if ( !(x <= 10)   &&   !(x >= 100) )
      cout << "ok";
else
      cout << "bad";
if ( !(x <= 10   ||   x >= 100) )
      cout << "ok";
else
      cout << "bad";
if ( x <= 10   ||   x >= 100 )
      cout << "bad";
else
      cout << "ok";
/*  etc...  */
```

Errors arise many times because of the imprecision of the English (or any) language. Suppose, as above, the user must enter a value, and for a certain action to be performed, the value must be within the range 10...100, exclusive. In English we may sloppily say, "if x is greater than 10 or it's less than 100, then [do something]." *And* and *or* are very different operators, however. Translating that English statement directly into C++ yields:

```
if ( x > 10   ||   x < 100 )
      /*  Do something here...  */
```

What happens if the user provides the value 250? 250 should be out of range, so the statements within the body of the if are ignored. It is indeed true that 250 < 100 is false, but 250 > 10 is true. In the || situation, if either operand is true, the || expression is true. The sloppy English statement does not accurately describe what is intended.

Beginners also attempt the direct translation of "if x is greater than 10 and less than 100 then [do something]." This English statement is correct in its construction but does not translate "word for word" into C++:

```
if ( x > 10   &&   < 100 )
      /*  Do something here...  */
```

Since both && and < are binary operators, they must have operands (either variables, constants, or properly formed expressions that have values) immediately to their left and right. The && has the < operator immediately to its right, and the < has the && immediately to its left; thus, the condition has been constructed improperly. Fortunately, the compiler can easily see the problem and an error message will be given. Consider the situation, however, that arises upon translating "if x is equal to either 10 or 100, then [do something]." Here, two values of x will cause an action to be taken, any other values won't. Again, the English statement is perfectly valid. The direct translation:

```
if ( x == 10 || 100 )
      /*  Do something here...  */
```

will not even get a rise out of the compiler (both binary operators are surrounded by operands). It appears to represent the idea of "only do something if x is equal to 10 or 100"; however, under careful scrutiny using the operator precedence rule table above, it can be shown that the compiler interprets the condition quite differently than was intended:

```
if ( (x == 10) || 100 )
        /*  Do something here...  */
```

The == operator has precedence over the ||. So overall the condition is an *or* expression involving the result of x == 10 and the value 100. But 100 is a nonzero constant which is always interpreted as true. In an *or* expression, if either operand is true, the expression is true. The expression

```
x == 10   ||   100
```

is always true, no matter what value x has. Would parentheses help?

```
x == (10 || 100)
```

Since 10 || 100 means *true* OR *true*, the parentheses do not solve the problem. One correct representation is:

```
if ( x == 10   ||   x == 100 )
        /*  Do something here...  */
```

Other correct constructions are possible. Translating the C++ code directly into English yields "If x is equal to 10 or x is equal to 100, then [do something]." This English statement is a bit wordy and really no better than the abbreviated one above, as far as the English language goes. Due to the operator rules, however, the C++ condition must be represented more explicitly.

The variety of equivalent logical expressions can be demonstrated with the simple example x == y:

Equivalent statements representing x equal to y

```
x == y
!(x != y)
x - y == 0
!(x - y)
```

Table 4.6 recaps the relational and logical operators.

Table 4.6 Relational and Logical Operator Examples

Expression	Value
45	45
45 + 1	46
45 < 46	1
45 < 46 && 19 > 4	1
1 == 0 || 1 > 0 || 1 < 0	1
1 == 0 && 1 > 0 && 1 < 0	0
!3	0
!(!3)	1

Exercises

1. If x is to be checked to see if it is equal to either 10 or 20, why is the condition in the following if statement incorrect, and how can it be correctly rewritten?

    ```
    if ( x == 10 || 20 )

        //  Do something...
    ```

2. What is a simpler way to write the following expression?

    ```
    !(x > y)
    ```

3. Why is the condition within the following if statement superfluous?

    ```
    if ( x > 10  ||  x < 100 )

        //  Do something...
    ```

4. Why is the condition within the following if statement faulty?

    ```
    if ( x < 10  &&  x > 100 )

        //  Do something...
    ```

5. Write the section of code (using if-else statements) that will determine the largest of three int numbers.

6. What shape is used within a flowchart to indicate a decision?

4.5 NESTED if STATEMENTS AND OTHER ifs WITHIN ifs

The if...else construct allows the program flow to branch one way or the other. What if three or more paths are necessary instead of two? if statements may be placed inside of other if statements to provide a multiway branch:

```
if ( number == 1 )
      cout << "First";
else
      if ( number == 2 )
            cout << "Second";
      else
            if ( number == 3 )
                  cout << "Third";
            else
                  cout << "Fourth (or higher)";
```

Here, one of four messages will be printed based upon the value of the variable number. Notice that the code tends to creep over the right. As the number of choices increase, the code will eventually "run off" the right side of the screen or paper printout. Since this overrunning looks bad, most programmers indent a complicated if statement like this one as follows:

```
if ( number == 1 )
     cout << "First";
else if ( number == 2 )
     cout << "Second";
else if ( number == 3 )
     cout   << "Third";
else
     cout << "Fourth (or higher)";
```

Since the C++ compiler is oblivious to indentation, the compiler treats the code the same. The second version is easier to read, however, especially when the number of cases increase. Notice the alignment of the initial `if`, the internal `else  if`s, and the final `else`. The experienced C++ programmer will immediately recognize this construct as a multiway branch. When reading this section of code from top to bottom, the indented body of the first true condition encountered will be executed. Exactly one path will be taken; it is not possible for more than one body to be performed with this nested `if` construct.

Program 4.3 uses this multiway branch to add, subtract, multiply, or divide two numbers based on the user's choice. The corresponding flowchart is given in figure 4.7.

```
#include <iostream.h>

void main()
{
     float number1, number2;
     int choice;

     //  Get numbers for calculation
     cout << "Please enter the numbers you "
             "wish to calculate with ==> ";
     cin >> number1 >> number2;

     //  Print menu and get user's choice
     cout << "\n\n\n        Menu\n\n"
             " 1.     Add\n"
             " 2.     Subtract\n"
             " 3.     Multiply\n"
             " 4.     Divide\n"
             "     Please enter choice ==> ";
     cin >> choice;

     //  Decide what to do and print results
     if ( choice == 1 )
          cout << number1 << " + " << number2 << " = "
               << number1 + number2 << "\n";
     else if ( choice == 2 )
          cout << number1 << " - " << number2 << " = "
               << number1 - number2 << "\n";
     else if ( choice == 3 )
          cout << number1 << " x " << number2 << " = "
               << number1 * number2 << "\n";
     else if ( choice == 4 )
          cout << number1 << " / " << number2 << " = "
               << number1 / number2 << "\n";
     else
          cout << "You made an incorrect choice!\n";
}
```

Program 4.3

(Note how strings may be divided between lines by closing them off with the close quote and then beginning on the next line with a new open quote. No intervening punctuation is used. The compiler treats the string

```
"  2.    Subtract\n"
"  3.    Multiply\n"
```

as if it were

```
"  2.    Subtract\n 3.    Multiply\n"
```

In the output statement displaying the menu, `cout` is being sent only one string, even though it is divided over several lines. Taking advantage of this feature can make your program more

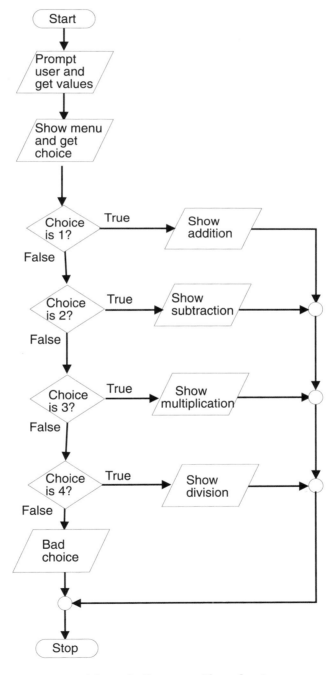

Arithmetic Program Flowchart
Figure 4.7

readable and visually appealing and easier to edit.) Another approach, which looks equally readable, would be

```
cout << "\n\n\n        Menu\n\n";
     << " 1.   Add\n";
     << " 2.   Subtract\n";
     << " 3.   Multiply\n";
     << " 4.   Divide\n";
     << "     Please enter choice ==> ";
```

This nested if construct is not always what is needed. Consider the problem of making change given a certain amount of money. The following program (4.4) accepts a floating point number representing a dollar amount between $0.00 and $5.00. It then prints what currency would need to be disbursed, in the largest denominations possible, to total this amount. For example, if $4.82 is entered, the program would indicate that four $1 bills, three quarters, one nickel, and two pennies constitute this much money.

```
#include <iostream.h>

void main() {
     float money;       //  Amount of money input by the user, in dollars
     int   cents,    //  Amount of money input by user, in cents
           dollars,  //  Number of dollar bills
           quarters, //  Number of quarters
           dimes,    //  Number of dimes
           nickels,  //  Number of nickels
           pennies;  //  Number of pennies

     //  Get amount from user
     cout << "Please enter the amount in dollars ==> $";
     cin >> money;

     //  Only process value that is in range
     if ( money < 0.0  ||  money > 5.00 )
          cout << "I'm sorry, you entered an amount I "
                  "am unable to process\n";
     else {  //  Value in range, continue
          //  Calculate in whole number cents; take into account
          //  imprecision of floats, otherwise sometimes pennies will
          //  be lost.
          cents = 100*(money + 0.0001);

          //  Partition the cents into largest denominations possible
          dollars = cents/100;
          cents   = cents % 100;
          quarters  = cents/25;
          cents   = cents % 25;
          dimes   = cents/10;
          cents   = cents % 10;
          nickels = cents/5;
          cents   = cents % 5;
          pennies = cents;

          //  Print grammatically correct answer
          if ( dollars > 0 ) {
               cout << dollars;
               if ( dollars == 1 )
                    cout << " dollar\n";
               else
                    cout << " dollars\n";
          }
          if ( quarters > 0 ) {
               cout << quarters;
               if ( quarters == 1 )
```

```
                    cout << " quarter\n";
            else
                    cout << " quarters\n";
        }
        if ( dimes > 0 ) {
            cout << dimes;
            if ( dimes == 1 )
                    cout << " dime\n";
            else
                    cout << " dimes\n";
        }
        if ( nickels > 0 ) {
            cout << nickels;
            if ( nickels == 1 )
                    cout << " nickel\n";
            else
                    cout << " nickels\n";
        }
        if ( pennies > 0 ) {
            cout << pennies;
            if ( pennies == 1 )
                    cout << " penny\n";
            else
                    cout << " pennies\n";
        }
    }
}
```

Program 4.4

Notice the "fudge factor" used in the assignment of `cents`. Since floating point numbers do not have exact representations (as opposed to integers which do), this adjustment makes sure that cents are not lost when converting to an integer representation. For example, 4.82 may be represented as 4.8199999 internally; thus, 4.81999999 × 100 = 481.99999, and, when it is assigned to an `int`, the decimal places are truncted, and so 481 will result. The program will use this value in its calculations and ultimately come up a penny short. When 0.0001 is added to 4.8199999, the result is 4.8200999 which truncates to 4.82. This is a simple program that illustrates one of the problems arising from the floating point number representation.

Program 4.4 contains a sequence of `if`s. They are not nested, as no `else if` combinations appear. Each top level `if` statement must be checked, even if the conditions within one or more of the earlier `if`s were found to be true. Also notice the `if...else`s within the top level `if`s. These are used to insure that the plurals of the words are formed properly, if necessary.

Since indentation is a style issue, and not a language dictate, which of the following "interpretations by indentation" will the compiler actually choose?

```
/*  Interpretation #1  */

if ( x > 10 )
     if ( y > 100 )
          cout << "Passed";
     else
          cout << "Failed";
/*  Interpretation #2  */

if ( x > 10 )
     if ( y > 100 )
          cout << "Passed";
else
     cout << "Failed";
```

Recall that the if...else construct is itself a statement, just like the if without the else. In #1, an if...else statement makes up the body of the first if. In #2, the second if statement constitutes the body of the if...else statement. Of course, since the compiler ignores indentation, both sections of code are identical. To the reader, however, indentation implies the body of the if statement. To the casual reader these two sections of code mean different things. For example, in #1, if x is 3, then nothing should be printed. In #2, if x is 3, then the message "Failed" should be printed. This situation is called the *dangling else* problem. Which is the correct way to indent in this situation? The rule is simple: an else is associated with the nearest preceding if unless curly braces override this association. Interpretation #1 is the correct way to express the C++ code visually. Beginning programmers sometimes wish to write code that performs as #2 looks and become frustrated when it fails to do as they expect. If the indentation in #2 really portrays what is intended, it must be written as follows:

```
if ( x > 10 ) {
        if ( y > 100 )
                cout << "Passed";
}
else
        cout << "Failed";
```

The curly braces around the inner if statement force the else to be associated with the first if.

Exercises

For questions 1–7, indicate what is printed by the following section of code (all variables are declared to be ints):

```
if ( x > y )
        if ( x < z )
                y = z;
        else
                z = y;
else
        if ( y < z )
                y = x;
        else
                x = z;
cout << x << ' ' << y << ' ' << z;
```

1. What is printed when x = 5, y = 10, and z = 7?

2. What is printed when x = 7, y = 5, and z = 10?

3. What is printed when x = 10, y = 7, and z = 5?

4. What is printed when x = 7, y = 10, and z = 5?

5. What is printed when x = 5, y = 7, and z = 10?

6. What is printed when x = 10, y = 5, and z = 7?

7. What is printed when x, y, and z are all equal to 5?

4.6 THE switch STATEMENT

The switch statement is like an extended if statement with some restrictions. The following if will be rewritten as a switch:

```
/*  if version  */
if ( x == 1 )
    cout << "x is 1\n";
else if ( x == 2 )
    cout << "x is 2\n";
else if ( x == 3 ) {
    cout << "x is 3, ";
    cout << "that's three\n";
}
else if ( x == 4 )
    cout << "x is 4\n";
else
    cout << "x is a weird number\n";

/*  switch version  */
switch ( x ) {
  case 1  : cout << "x is 1\n";
            break;
  case 2  : cout << "x is 2\n";
            break;
  case 3  : cout << "x is 3, ";
            cout << "that's three\n";
            break;
  case 4  : cout << "x is 4\n";
            break;
  default : cout << "x is a weird number\n";
}
```

The flowchart for the if...else version as well as the switch version is shown in figure 4.8.

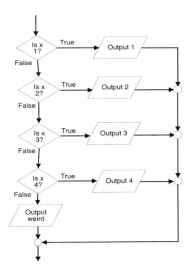
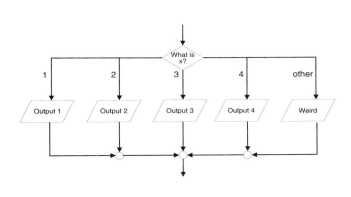

Conditional Flowcharts
Figure 4.8

The reserved words used are `switch`, `case`, and `break`. `switch` begins the construct, and each optional branch is indicated by a `case` label. `break` ends the optional path of execution that the `case` label begins. The body of the `switch`, which includes the `case` labels and `break`s, is enclosed within curly braces. Using a `switch` in place of an `if` in certain situations can make the program more readable and produce more efficient code. The reason for the increased efficiency is due to restrictions on the `switch`. The expression within the parentheses directly following the reserved word `switch` must evaluate to an *integral* type. The value directly following the reserved word `case` must be an integral *constant*; thus, the following translation of an `if` is not possible:

```
/*  x, y, and z are declared somewhere above  */
if ( x == y )
        x = y + 5;
else if ( x == z )
        cout << x;
else
        x = 5;

/*  Illegal switch construct   */
switch ( x ) {
  case y  :   x = y + 5;       break;
  case z  :   cout << x;       break;
  default :   x = 5;  break;
}
```

@%#&!

Here y and z are variables, not constants; hence, they *cannot* be used as `case` labels. Symbolic constants (defined as `const int MAX = 100;`, see chapter 5), literal constants (like 45), and enumerated type values can be used as case labels.

Program 4.3 from above can be modified so that a `switch` is used instead of the nested `if`s. Program 4.5 shows the slightly cleaner looking result.

```
#include <iostream.h>

void main()
{
      float number1, number2;
      int choice;

      //  Get numbers for calculation
      cout << "Please enter the numbers you wish to calculate with ==> ";
      cin >> number1 >> number2;

      //  Print menu and get user's choice
      cout << "\n\n\n        Menu\n\n";
             << " 1.    Add\n"
             << " 2.    Subtract\n"
             << " 3.    Multiply\n"
             << " 4.    Divide\n"
             << "     Please enter choice ==> ";
      cin  >> choice;

      //  Decide what to do and print results
      switch ( choice ) {
          case 1:
              cout << number1 << " + " << number2 << " = "
                  << number1 + number2 << "\n";
              break;
          case 2:
              cout << number1 << " - " << number2 << " = "
                  << number1 - number2 << "\n";
              break;
```

```
               case 3:
                     cout << number1 << " x " << number2 << " = "
                          << number1 * number2 << "\n";
                     break;
               case 4:
                     cout << number1 << " / " << number2 << " = "
                          << number1 / number2 << "\n";
                     break;
               default:
                     cout << "You made an incorrect choice!\n";
        }
   }
```

Program 4.5

The switch version avoids the use of the == operator in multiple comparisons.

The default clause is optional and may be omitted. If none of the case labels match the integral expression and no default is present, then none of the statements in the body of the switch is executed. Once a case label is selected, all the statements that *follow* that case label are executed until the reserved word break is encountered. Most often, break is used at the end of each statement sequence associated with a particular case label. It is frequently omitted when multiple case labels are associated with identical statement sequences:

```
cin >> ch;   //  ch is declared to be a char
switch ( ch ) {
     case   'a':
     case   'A':   cout << "An A was entered";   break;
     case   'b':
     case   'B':   cout << "A B was entered";    break;
     case   'C':
     case   'c':   cout << "This is the weird one, no break";
     case   'Q':
     case   'q':
     case   'X':
     case   'x':   cout << "Do you want to quit?";
   }
```

Here, if either an upper- or lowercase A is entered, the message "An A was entered" will be printed. If either upper- or lowercase B is entered, a similar message will be printed for B. If any one of the letters Q, q, X, or x is entered, the quit message will be printed. If C or c is entered, the message "This is the weird one, no break" will be printed, and the "Do you want to quit?" message will be printed, since the statement in option C is not followed by a break statement to exit the switch body.

4.7 THE CONDITIONAL OPERATOR

Another conditional construct provided by C++ is the *conditional expression.* It involves C++'s only *ternary* operator; that is, an operator that requires three operands. It is an expression; therefore, it has an associated value. Its general form is

condition ? *expression1* : *expression2*;

If the condition evaluates to nonzero, then expression1 becomes the value of the conditional expression; otherwise, expression2 becomes the value of the conditional expression. Usually the condition is placed in parentheses to aid readability. (Precedence rules generally don't require the parentheses for proper evaluation.)

It is often used in an assignment statement:

```
z = (y == 0) ? 0 : x/y;
```

Here z is to be assigned x/y, except in the case of y = 0 where the quotient would be undefined (and produce a runtime error). z is assigned 0 in the case of attempted division by zero. (A more reasonable option might be to assign to z the maximum value of its type—to approximate infinity.) The same assignment could be performed within an if...else construct:

```
if ( y == 0 )
    z = 0;
else
    z = x/y;
```

Although the indiscriminate use of the conditional operator can lead to obscure and possibly error-prone code, it is quite handy when used in a simple, straightforward manner. Consider the awkward and wordy alternative of using an if in place of the conditional operator in the following situation:

```
/*  Assign to x the absolute value of y  */

if ( y < 0 )
    x = -y;
else
    x = y;
```

compared to

```
/*  Same assignment using a conditional expression  */

x = (y < 0) ? -y : y;
```

Exercises

1. Rewrite the following if-else construct so that the switch is used instead:

    ```
    if ( x == 1 )
        x = y;
    else if ( x == 4 ) {
        cin >> x;
        y = x + 5;
    }
    else if ( x == 19 )
        cout << y;
    else
        cout << y + 5;
    ```

2. How is the switch statement restricted in ways the if-else statement is not?

3. Rewrite the following conditional expression so that if-else is used instead:

    ```
    new_val = ( x > y) ? 200 : y - x;
    ```

4.8 FORMATTING COMPOUND STATEMENTS

Program readability is aided by the disciplined formatting of structured statements such as `if` and `switch`. The principles in this section also apply to the iterative structures examined in the next chapter. The bodies of `if...else` and `switch` constructs are optionally executed; therefore, the bodies are indented to indicate visually within the program source text the program's departure from strictly linear flow. Reconsider program 4.3 from above *without* the indentation of the `if`. It is presented in program 4.6.

```
#include <iostream.h>

void main()
{
    float number1, number2;
    int choice;

    // Get numbers for calculation
    cout << "Please enter the numbers you wish to calculate with ==> ";
    cin >> number1 >> number2;

    // Print menu and get user's choice
    cout << "\n\n\n      Menu\n\n";
        << " 1.   Add\n"
        << " 2.   Subtract\n"
        << " 3.   Multiply\n"
        << " 4.   Divide\n"
        << "      Please enter choice ==> ";
    cin >> choice;
    // Decide what to do and print results
    if ( choice == 1 )
    cout << number1 << " + " << number2 << " = " << number1 + number2 << "\n";
    else if ( choice == 2 )
    cout << number1 << " - " << number2 << " = " << number1 - number2 << "\n";
    else if ( choice == 3 )
    cout << number1 << " x " << number2 << " = " << number1 * number2 << "\n";
    else if ( choice == 4 )
    cout << number1 << " / " << number2 << " = " << number1 / number2 << "\n";
    else
    cout << "You made an incorrect choice!\n";
}
```

Program 4.6

Visually, the alignment of the last part of program 4.6 implies sequential execution or linear program flow; however, because of the way program 4.3 is visually composed with text, one can tell immediately that the last part of it is not a simple sequentially flowing program. Control structures are emphasized by indenting their bodies. This indentation provides a visual cue that program flow is somehow special in that area of the program. The original code better portrays the conditional nature of this section of the code.

How should curly braces be arranged around compound statements? There are several acceptable indentation conventions for compound statements with curly braces. The `if` statement is shown illustrating the different styles:

```
/*  The begin...end "Pascal" style  */
if ( condition )
{
    statement1;
    statement2;
    statement3;
}
```

```
/*  The Kernighan and Ritchie style  */
if ( condition ) {
      statement1;
      statement2;
      statement3;
}

/*  The Plum style  */
if ( condition )
      {
      statement1;
      statement2;
      statement3;
      }

/*  The hybrid K & R and Plum style  */
if ( condition ) {
      statement1;
      statement2;
      statement3;
      }
```

The Pascal style is based on the way most Pascal programmers align the `begin` and `end` Pascal reserved words that are used like C++'s curly braces. The K & R style was made popular by the original book coauthored by C's creator, Dennis Ritchie. The Plum style was popularized by Thomas Plum in a book that outlines a standard style for C programs. You should choose one of these four styles as your personal convention. Whichever style is chosen, it should be used consistently throughout a program. You'll find that the Kernighan and Ritchie style and the hybrid style will leave fewer "empty" lines that add to the length of program listings. The Pascal and Kernighan and Ritchie styles are the most popular styles found in currently published C++ code.

Assignments

1. Extend the change making program:

    ☐ Allow the user to type in the cost of the entire purchase (subtotal)

    ☐ Calculate the sales tax based on 7.75 percent

    ☐ Calculate the total due (subtotal + sales tax)

    ☐ Allow the user to type in the amount tendered (amount of money given to pay the total due)

    ☐ Calculate the change due back (amount tendered – total due)

    ☐ Allow dollar amounts (total and change) up to $500

    ☐ The largest denomination to be used in making change is a $20 bill.

    Retain the ability to print out grammatically correct (plural/singular) descriptions of the money to return.

2. Write a program that allows the user to type in exactly five floating point values. The largest and smallest of these values should be displayed, along with the median value. Ties should be properly processed. For example, the values:

    23.4, 0.3, 0.2, 100.3, 88.2

would yield

```
High: 100.3, Low:  0.2, Median: 23.4
```

and the values

```
44.0, 22.0, 22.0, 10.0, 44.0
```

would yield

```
High:44.0, Low:10.0, Median: 22.0
```

3. Write a C++ program that allows the user to type in an integer. The English word for that integer should then be displayed. For example, a sample program run might look like the following:

```
Please enter an integer:      67          (User types in 67)
sixty-seven                               (Program displays "sixty-seven")
```

Zero should be the lowest integer displayed. *One hundred* should be the largest printed. All integers less than zero should result in the message "Value less than zero." When a number above 100 is entered, the message "Value greater than one hundred" should be displayed.

Do not use a hundred conditional statements to decide what should be printed! That is, don't include code like

```
    .
    .
    .
if ( in_value == 88 )         //      Do
    cout << "eighty-eight\n"; //      NOT
else if ( in_value == 87 )    //      do
    cout << "eighty-seven\n"; //      it
else if ( in_value == 86 )    //      this
    cout << "eighty-six\n";   //      way!
    .
    .
    .
```

Instead, factor out common properties to reduce the number of `if` statements required. For example, a value between 81 and 89 inclusive would result in the phrase "eighty-" being printed, and the value of its one's digit (acquired by modulus 10) could be determined from a different conditional statement. In this way, 97, 87, 77, 67, 57, 47, 37, 27, and 7 would all have only one `if` statement decide that "seven" should be displayed (see the advice about the value 17 below).

Hints:

☐ Treat the values 10. . .19 as special cases since their English words are irregular compared to 20. . .99. The number 13 is "thirteen," not "ten-three," for example.

☐ Treat zero and one hundred as special cases.

☐ Handle multiples of ten (10, 20, 30, etc.) separately. While 21 is displayed as "twenty-one" and 22 is "twenty-two," don't print 20 as "twenty-zero."

CHAPTER 5

ITERATION

5.1 INTRODUCTION

The previous chapter showed how the linear flow of a program could be altered with conditional statements. In this chapter iteration, or looping, is examined.

5.2 ITERATION

Programs that have strictly linear flow are typically not very useful. Using conditional statements like `if` makes for more interesting programs. *Iteration*, the ability to repeat sections of the program an arbitrary number of times, provides even more power and flexibility. We will modify program 4.2 to illustrate iteration. This is shown in figure 5.1.

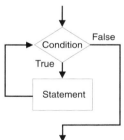

General Form of
`while` **Loop**
Figure 5.1

```
#include <iostream.h>
void main()
{
    int in_value;

    cout << "Enter the secret number: ";
    cin >> in_value;
    while ( in_value != 29 ) {
    cout << "You have guessed incorrectly, please try again: ";
        cin >> in_value;
    }
    cout << "You guessed the secret number!\n";
    cout << "Program completed, thank you.\n";
}
```

Program 5.1

The statements within the curly braces after the line containing the reserved word `while` will be executed over and over until the condition in the parentheses following the `while` becomes false. As long as the user continues to enter values other than `29`, he or she will be asked repeatedly to enter more numbers until the correct value is entered (which may be a long time). The general form of the `while` statement is

```
while ( condition )
      statement;
```

The expressions *condition* and *statement* have identical meanings to their counterparts in the `if` statement. Figure 5.1 shows the corresponding flowchart for the `while` construct. Figure 5.2 shows the flowchart for program 5.1.

As with `if`, the statement within the `while` is sometimes called the *body* of the `while` statement. The condition can be made as complicated as necessary using the logical connectives mentioned above. When the `while` statement is encountered for the first time, its condition is checked. If the condition is false, the body of the `while` is not executed. Program flow proceeds directly to the statement following the `while` statement (i.e., the statement that follows the *body* of the `while` statement). If the condition is true, the body is executed, and the condition is rechecked. If the condition is still true, then the process is repeated; if not, the loop terminates.

The `do...while` is a similar construct to the regular `while`, except that the condition is checked after the body is executed. Its general form is:

```
do
      statement;
while ( condition );
```

Since the condition is checked after the body in the `do...while`, the body is always executed once. In the `while` statement, the body may not be executed at all (if the condition is not true to start with). Compare the `while` flowchart in figure 5.1 to the `do...while` flowchart in figure 5.3.

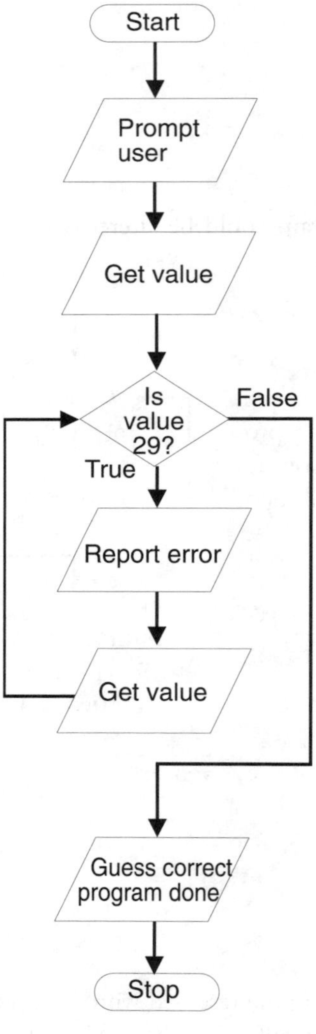

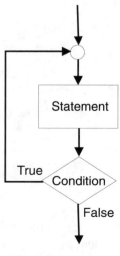

Flowchart for Program 5.1
Figure 5.2

General Form of
`do..while`
Figure 5.3

Program 5.1 will be modified so that a do...while is used. A counter variable will also be added:

```
#include <iostream.h>
void main()
{
    int count = 0, in_value;
    do {
        count = count + 1;
        cout << "Enter the secret number (Attempt #"
            << count << "):";
        cin >> in_value;
    } while ( in_value != 29 );
    cout << "You guessed the secret number, and it "
            "only took " << count << " tries!\n";
    cout << "Program completed, thank you.\n";
}
```

Program 5.2

The if, while, and do...while constructs are sometimes called *control structures*, since they control the flow of the program. The program flow is nicely represented with a flowchart. The flowchart for program 5.2 is shown in figure 5.4.

This program displays how many numbers the user has entered so far and, when done, how many attempts were necessary to guess the right number. Consider the statement

```
count = count + 1;
```

The variable count is said to be *incremented* by one. Since assignment has such low precedence, the statement works by adding 1 to the current value of count and then modifying count to have the new value; thus, count counts 0, 1, 2, 3, ... until 29 is entered. Since incrementing is done so frequently in programming, C++ has some syntactical shortcuts:

```
count += n;    /*  Means count  = count + n;  */
count++;       /*  Means count  = count + 1;  */
++count;       /*  Means count  = count + 1;  */
```

Decrementing involves subtracting a value from a variable.

```
count -= n     /*  Means count  = count - n;  */
count--;       /*  Means count  = count - 1;  */
--count;       /*  Means count  = count - 1;  */
```

There is actually a subtle difference between count++ and ++count, as well as between count-- and --count, and we will examine the differences later. For now, as long as the ++ and -- unary operators are not used in an expression involving other operators, they act identically.

These abbreviations are more than a syntactical and typographical convenience. Most compilers can generate more efficient machine language code with the abbreviated statements. In fact, on most systems, the performance difference among several logically equivalent statements can be surprising. On one particular

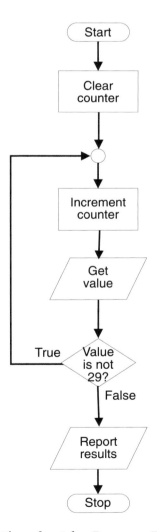

Flowchart for Program 5.2
Figure 5.4

platform, the following results were found (a byte is a measurement of memory; ML means machine language; cycles means the number of actual processor clock cycles needed to carry out the ML instruction):

```
x = x + 1;   /*  3 bytes of ML code, 6 cycles  */

x += 1;      /*  3 bytes of ML code, 4 cycles  */

x++;         /*  1 byte of ML code, 2 cycles  */
```

The actual results will vary on different computer systems and on the same systems with different compilers. Some good compilers will optimize the code so that all the above statements generate the same efficient code.

```
#include <iostream.h>
void main() {
    int total_count = 0, in_value, range_count = 0;
    do {
        total_count++;
        cout << "Enter the secret number, "
                "please only choose values "
                "between 1 and 100, inclusive "
                "(Try #" << total_count << "):";
        cin >> in_value;
        if ( in_value < 1  ||  in_value > 100 ) {
            cout << "Not even in the proper range!\n";
            range_count++;
        }
    } while ( in_value != 29 );
    cout << "You guessed the secret number, and it "
            "only took " << total_count << " tries!\n";
    cout << range_count << " times you submitted "
    cout << "a value out of range.\n";
    cout << "Program completed, thank you.\n";
}
```

Program 5.3

The `while` statement is used more often than the `do...while`, since in most situations it is desirable that the condition be checked before the body of the loop is executed.

Since a control structure is itself a statement, it can appear within the body of another similar or different control structure. Consider program 5.3; notice that an `if` statement is embedded in the `do...while`.

One enhancement to program 5.3 is the expression of the constant values 29, 1, and 100 by symbols instead of actual numbers. Program 5.4 shows how program 5.3 can be better written by defining constants at the top of the program. If the range of legal values or numbers to guess needs to be changed, then the only modification to the program needs to take place at the very top of the program. There are several advantages to this approach. Since these constants will be defined at the top of the program, they are immediately visible and easily modifiable. If the program becomes several thousand lines long, and these values are sprinkled throughout the program, every occurrence of each constant can be changed by changing one line at the top of the program. For this program, the benefit is not very apparent, but for a 500,000 line program, it could save hundreds of changes. The problem is not so much making the changes but making *all* the changes, since every appearance of the numeric constant must be changed. You might ask: "So what? Why not use the actual numbers and use the editor's global *search and replace* feature to change them when needed?" The problem with this approach arises when two constants representing different concepts initially have the same values and later need to be changed.

What if the `MAGIC_NUMBER` was 100, the same as the `HIGH` value in the range? Using defined constants, it is no problem giving two different constants the same value:

```
const int HIGH         = 100,
          LOW          =   1,
          MAGIC_NUMBER = 100;
```

If the literal value of 100 was used throughout the program for both quantities, and the time came to change one or both of the values associated with the high range and/or magic number, an editor's search and replace feature could not distinguish between them and could not make the correct textual substitutions.

Notice that the definitions are similar to variable declarations, except that they are preceded by the reserved word `const`, and initial values must be given to the objects being defined. These constants can be used in many places where variables can be used. The exceptions: constants cannot be modified like variables can. The following is illegal:

```
//  x is defined as const int x = 10;
x = 22;
```

Also, the constants are defined outside of `main()`'s curly braces instead of inside. Constants can be defined inside as well, but for now we will define all of our constants outside of `main()` at the top of the program. In chapter 6 we will examine the differences between declaring objects inside or outside of `main()`.

Constants should be used liberally as they aid in the readability and modifiability of programs. Physical and mathematical constants should be defined instead of using literal values. Consider the definition

```
const double pi = 3.1416;
```

Instead of using the literal value `3.1416` hundreds of places throughout a large geometrical calculation program, the constant `pi` would be used. Not only would the program be more readable and less cluttered but also, when more accuracy is needed in the future, the constant can be changed

```
const double pi = 3.1415926536;
```

easily at the top of the program instead of making possibly hundreds of changes throughout the program (and possibly missing only a few of the changes—leading to obscure accuracy problems that can be very difficult to find and repair).

Constant names are identifiers so they follow the same naming rules as variables. One convention uses no lowercase letters within constant names; thus, they are quickly visually distinguishable from variables.

```
#include <iostream.h>

const int HIGH         = 100;
          LOW          =   1;
          MAGIC_NUMBER=  29;

void main()
{
    int total_count = 0, in_value,
        range_count = 0;

    do {
        total_count++;
        cout << "Enter the secret "
                "number, please only "
                "choose values between "
             << LOW << " and " << HIGH
             << ", inclusive (Attempt # "
             << total_count << "):";
```

```
        cin >> in_value;
        if ( in_value < LOW  ||
            in_value > HIGH ) {
        cout << "Not even in the "
                "proper range!\n";
        range_count++;
            }
    } while ( in_value != MAGIC_NUMBER );
    cout << "You guessed the secret "
            "number, and it only took "
        << total_count << " tries!\n";
    cout << range_count << " times you submitted a value"
            " out of range.\n";
    cout << "Program completed, thank you.\n";
}
```

Program 5.4

The flow of control is clear from the flowchart in figure 5.5. However, because of the way program 5.4 is visually composed with text, one can tell immediately that it is not a simple sequentially flowing program. As with the `if` statements from the previous chapter, control structures are emphasized by indenting their bodies. This indentation provides a visual cue that program flow is somehow special in that area of the program. Either the code is repeated (as in the case of iteration) or optionally executed (as in the case of a conditional construct).

Exercises

1. What is meant by the word *iteration*?

2. List all the differences between a `while` statement and a `do-while` statement.

3. List three different ways to write the statement `x = x + 1;` .

4. How can symbolic constants be defined in C++?

5. Can conditional statements be used within iterative statements?

5.3   INFINITE LOOPS

In order for a program to work correctly, the control statements that constitute the program must be constructed correctly. The task of building these control structures is not automatic or simple. Loops can be placed within other loops, conditional statements (`if`, `switch`) can be involved, and the conditions for loop termination can be quite involved with multiple `&&` operators and/or `||` operators. Consider the following small section of a program that asks the user to enter a menu choice. If a character is typed in that is not a menu choice, the menu is printed again, and the user is forced to choose again.

```
//  ch is declared to be a char
do {
    cout << "  Menu \n\n"
         << "P  Print\n"
         << "O  Open\n"
         << "S  Save\n"
         << "Q  Quit\n\n"
         << " Please enter selection: ";
    cin >> ch;
} while ( ch != 'P'  &&  ch != 'O'  &&  ch != 'S'  &&  ch != 'Q' );
```

As mentioned in the previous chapter, combining logical operators and negative conditions (in this case !=) can be tricky. Many students will first provide the following for the last line in the above code:

```
} while ( ch != 'P'  ||  ch != 'O'  ||  ch != 'S'  ||  ch != 'Q' );
```

Their reasoning, which sounds somewhat convincing, often follows along these lines:

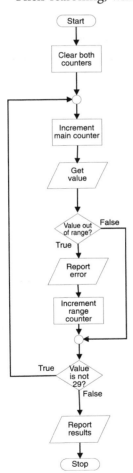

Flowchart for Program 5.4 Figure 5.5

1. Ponder the problem. The program must loop until the user enters the 'P', 'O', 'S', or 'Q' character. This involves checking several things in the negative sense, using !=.
2. Consider the opposite situation. Loop while the user types in a 'P', 'O', 'S', or 'Q'. This situation is correctly implemented as

```
} while ( ch == 'P' || ch == 'O' || ch == 'S' || ch == 'Q' );
```

3. Since the opposite is actually needed, replace all the == operators with !=.

This approach is not bad, but the final step is faulty. The negation of the expression

```
ch == 'P'  ||  ch == 'O'  ||  ch == 'S'  ||  ch == 'Q'
```

is

```
!(ch == 'P' || ch == 'O' || ch == 'S' || ch == 'Q')
```

which is equivalent to the first example above, which is correct. To show why it is correct, consider the simpler situation of negating two *OR*-ed equalities:

```
!(x == 2  ||  y == 3)
```

This says that the statement "x equals two or y equals three" is not true. For an *OR* statement to be false, both arguments must be false; therefore, both substatements "x equals two" *and* "y equals three" must be false or, said another way, "x does not equal two *and* y does not equal three." Symbolically, this is expressed as

```
x != 2  &&  y != 3
```

or, in a sentence, "The negation of a disjunction (*OR*) is equivalent to the conjunction (*AND*) of the negations." A complimentary rule states that "The negation of a conjunction (*AND*) is equivalent to the disjunction (*OR*) of the negations." The rules come from the study of Boolean logic and are called deMorgan's Laws.

Reconsider the incorrect line from above

```
} while ( ch != 'P'  ||  ch != 'O'  ||  ch != 'S'  ||  ch != 'Q' );
```

This expression is always true. No matter what character is entered, at least three of the four subexpressions will be true. What if `'P'` is entered? The first subexpression is false (ch != 'P'), but all the others are true. The characters 'O', 'S', and 'Q' cause similar results. If none of these letters are used, then all of the subexpressions are true, and the problem remains. The loop cannot be exited; it will continue until the user takes extraordinary measures by pressing the *break* key or other such action required to stop an unruly program. A loop that has no way to terminate is called an *infinite* loop. It is obvious that the programmer meant for the loop to terminate under certain conditions because an infinite loop could have been more easily written as

```
do {
        /*  Whatever...  */
        .
        .
        .
} while ( 1 );
```

Unquestionably, the condition of the `while` is always true.

Infinite loops are sometimes designed, but beginning programmers usually create them by accident. Any time the program "hangs" and does nothing or does the same thing over and over with no way to quit (except for the aforementioned *break* key), and a loop of some kind is being used in the program, an infinite loop should be suspected. It is surprisingly easy to accidentally generate terminating conditions that can never be met.

The following simple counting program (program 5.5) has a subtle error.

```
#include <iostream.h>

void main() {
        float sum = 0.0;
        while ( sum != 1.0 ) {
                cout << sum << "\n";
                sum += 0.0001;
        }
}
```

Program 5.5

One would expect 10,001 numbers to be displayed 0, 0.0001, 0.0002, 0.0003, . . . , 1. On most systems, this code results in an infinite loop. Due to the imprecision of `float`s and the differences between their displayable decimal representations and their internal binary representations, the value 0.0001 is not represented exactly. It might actually be stored as 0.0000997 or 0.0001002. Successively adding this slightly inexact value can lead to a larger and larger accumulated error. The value 1 can be represented exactly in both decimal and binary exponential form, but after 10,000 additions of this inexact increment, the sum may not add up to exactly 1. The program can be fixed as shown in program 5.6:

```
#include <iostream.h>

const float difference = 0.0001;

void main() {
        float sum = 0.0;
        cout.precision(5);
        while ( (1.0 - sum) > difference ) {
                cout << sum << "\n";
                sum += 0.0001;
        }
}
```

Program 5.6

Here, equality between two numbers x and y would be determined not from the fact that x − y == 0 but that their difference is so small that they are close enough in value to be considered equal.

One way to help track down logic errors is to use *debugging statements* within the program. A debugging statement can be as simple as an output statement that prints the value of a variable. The source of the infinite loop in the menu program above could have been diagnosed by inserting the following statements right before the condition is checked at the bottom of the loop:

```
cout << "The condition is \n"
    << "ch == 'P' : " << (ch == 'P') << '\n'
    << "ch == 'O' : " << (ch == 'O') << '\n'
    << "ch == 'S' : " << (ch == 'S') << '\n'
    << "ch == 'Q' : " << (ch == 'Q') << '\n'
    << "Combined expression :   "
    << (ch == 'P'  &&  ch == 'O'  && ch == 'S'  &&  ch == 'Q') << '\n';
```

This displays the state of all the subexpressions within the condition, as well as the overall condition itself.

Debugging statements are often not as elaborate. For example, the statement

```
cout << "{" << ch << "} was entered";
```

could be placed right after the character is gotten from the input stream. This is known as *echoing* the input and is useful for verifying that the program got the value from the stream that you think you gave it. The common beginning mistake of placing a semicolon right after the condition of a while, do...while, or if can be discovered by using a debugging statement that simply indicates what part of the program is currently being executed:

```
while ( x < 10 );      /*  Accidental ;  */
{
        cout << "Now in \"while ( x < 10 )\" loop.\n";
        /*  Rest of body here... */
}
```

Debugging statements are used only in development; they are removed when the section of the program is known to be correct.

Most modern development environments provide powerful tools for program debugging, eliminating the need for some debugging statements. *Source level debuggers* allow the programmer to see what statements within the source code are being executed as the program is simultaneously running. The programmer can select variables from the source code and see their current values updated as the program executes.

5.4 THE for STATEMENT

Another iterative control structure is the for statement. The for statement has the form

```
for ( initialization; condition; modification )
     statement;
```

for statements are used most often as counters:

```
int i;
for ( i = 0;  i < 10;  i++ )
     cout << i << '\n';
```

The above for loop displays the numbers 0. . .9. i = 0 is the initialization expression. It initializes i to 0. The expression i < 10 is the condition. The loop continues while i is less than 10. i++ is the modification expression. The variable i is incremented each time through the loop.

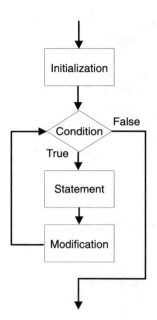

General `for` **Flowchart**
Figure 5.6

When a `for` loop is encountered, the following steps take place:

1. The initialization is done
2. The condition is checked:
   if true, do step 3
   if false, do step 6
3. The body of the loop is performed
4. The modification is done
5. Go to step 2
6. Loop is finished

Figure 5.6 shows the general `for` flowchart.

The above counting code could be rewritten with a `while` instead of a `for` as follows:

```
int i;

i = 0;
while ( i < 10 ) {
        cout << i << '\n';
        i++;
}
```

In fact, a `while` loop can be easily rewritten in an equivalent `for` loop by omitting the initialization and modification expressions:

```
for ( ; x < 10; )       /*  while ( x < 10 )  */
```

Most programming languages have their own version of the `for` statement. C++'s `for` is quite unrestricted compared to other languages. Pascal, for example, restricts the counter variable to integral (whole number) types that can only be incremented or decremented by one each time through the loop. The following section of code allows the user to enter the starting value, ending value, and increment value of the counter variable (which can be negative):

```
int count, start, stop, inc;
cout << "Enter beginning value, ending value, and amount of change: ";
cin >> start >> stop >> inc;
for ( count = start;  count <= stop;  count += inc )
     cout << count << '\n';
```

The variable used as the counter variable within a `for` statement is often declared during the initialization step:

```
for ( int i = 1;  i <= 100;  i++ ) {
    /*  Do something  */
}
```

In C++, unlike most other languages, the condition section of the statement can be quite complex:

```
//  y given a value somewhere above
for ( i = 100;  i > 0  &&  y != STOP_VAL;  i--)
     //  Do something in the loop...
```

The condition not only checks the counter variable, but it also compares y to some predefined constant. Also notice that this `for` loop counts down instead of up. The rarely used *comma operator* can also be used to perform multiple initializations and multiple modifications within the parentheses of the `for`. Consider:

```
for ( x = 0, y = 100;  x < 100  &&  y > 0;  x++, y-- )
        cout << x << '  ' << y << '\n';
```

Here, the two variables `x` and `y` are simultaneously counting. `x` is counting up from 0 to 99, and `y` is counting down from 100 to 1. This type of complicated loop is rarely needed and should be avoided. Making the `for` overly complex can lead to code that is difficult to understand and much more difficult to write so that it executes correctly. The rarely used *comma operator* is used to chain together separate statements into one statement; the value of the overall statement is the same as the *right-most* expression (in this case `a++`):

```
x = 3, y = z + 1, a++;
```

This single statement is a combination of three separate statements, and the overall value of the statement is the value of the variable `a`. The comma operator has the lowest precedence of any C++ operator and, to re-emphasize, is almost never used.

Exercises

1. Rewrite the following `for` statement so a `while` is used instead:

    ```
    for ( i = 100;  i > 25;  i-- )
            cout << "i has the value " << i << '\n';
    ```

2. How many times will "Hi" be displayed?

    ```
    for ( i = 0;  i < 2450;  i++ )
            cout << "Hi\n";
    ```

5.5 LOOP TERMINATION: `break, continue, goto`

Both `for` and `while` are *top exiting* forms of iteration; the `do...while` statement is a *bottom exiting* loop. Actually, any of these loops may be exited at any time by using the `break` statement:

```
while ( x != MAGIC_NUMBER ) {
    cin >> x >> y;
    if ( y == SECRET_NUMBER )
        break;      /*  Exit the while loop now  */
    x *= y;
    z = x + PI;
}
```

The `break` transfers control of the program to the statement that follows the body of the loop (`while, do...while,` or `for`) in which the program is executing. The behavior of the `break` statement within a loop is similar to its behavior in a `switch` statement—it transfers control out of the structured statement. `break` allows *middle exiting* loops to be created. Figure 5.7 illustrates the process.

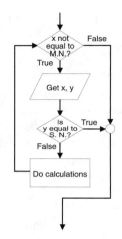

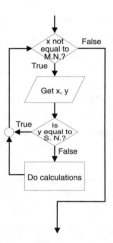

The break **Statement**
Figure 5.7

The continue **Statement**
Figure 5.8

Related to the break statement is the continue statement. When continue is encountered within a loop body, the flow of control is transferred immediately to the top of the loop for possibly another iteration; thus, continue skips the rest of the statements in the body of the loop. Consider the above code modified so that a continue is used instead of the break:

```
while ( x != MAGIC_NUMBER ) {
    cin >> x >> y;
    if ( y == SECRET_NUMBER )
        continue;
    x *= y;    // These two statements are skipped
    z = x + PI; //  if y is SECRET_NUMBER
}
```

Its flowchart appears in figure 5.8. The continue is less useful than the break because code using it can easily be rewritten to exclude it. The above code is trivially changed to:

```
while ( x != MAGIC_NUMBER ) {
    cin >> x >> y;
    if ( y != SECRET_NUMBER ) {
        x *= y;     // These two statements are skipped
        z = x + PI; // if y is SECRET_NUMBER
    }
}
```

The condition for the if was logically negated, and in the body of the if the continue was replaced with the rest of the body of the while.

The break construct is much more valuable. Any loop containing a break can also be rewritten without it. Unlike in the case of continue, however, often more complex and less clear code results when avoiding the break statement. The sample code above using the break could be changed to

```
done = 0;
while ( !done  &&  x != MAGIC_NUMBER ) {
    cin >> x >> y;
    if ( y == SECRET_NUMBER )
        done = 1;
    else {
        x *= y;
        z = x + PI;
    }
}
```

Few would argue that the logic in the `break`-less version is easier to follow. An additional variable was introduced, the condition of the `while` was made more complicated, and the `if` statement was extended to include an else clause with a compound statement for its body. All of these modifications introduce the risk of errors. The cleaner and simpler the logic of a section of code, the easier it is to make it work correctly. In general, however, the fewer the possible exit points from the loop, the better. Multiple `breaks` within an iterative statement tend to make the logic difficult to understand. Before using a `break` or `continue` statement, ask yourself the question "Can this loop be rewritten to do the same thing without using the special exit statements and without overly complicating the logic?" If the answer is "yes," then the `break` or `continue` should be avoided.

Loops can be *nested*; that is, one loop can be enclosed within another loop. The following section of code prints a portion of the multiplication table:

```
for ( row = 1;   row < 5;   row++ ) {
    for ( column = 1;   column < 5;   column++ )
        cout << "\t" << row * column;
    cout << '\n';
}
```

The inner loop is executed four times every time the outer loop is executed. The outer loop is executed four times as well, and so the output statement inside the inner loop is performed sixteen times.

A `break` (or `continue`) statement encountered within an inner loop in a nested loop will only affect the loop in which it is found; it will not jump out of (or skip the rest of) more than one level of nesting. If the flow of control of a program must be passed from deep inside several nested loops to the outside of all the loops, one simple option is available: the `goto` statement. The `goto` statement causes an unconditional jump to another portion of the program. The statement that is "gone to" must be preceded by a *label*, that is, an identifier followed by a colon. For example, the following code illustrates two different ways to construct a counting loop. One uses a familiar `while`, and the other uses the less desirable `goto` statement.

```
i = 0;                              i = 0;
while ( i < 10 ) {            loop: if ( i < 10 ) {
    cout << i;                          cout << i;
    i++;                                i++;
}                                       goto loop;
                                    }
```

The `goto` version is no more efficient than the `while` version, and it is more difficult to read, especially as the program logic becomes more complex.

The `goto` statement should be avoided at all costs. In fact, in the 1970s a move was made by several prominent computer scientists to ban the `goto` statement from all future programming languages. The use of `goto`s tend to make programs more difficult to read and understand, especially as the programs become larger. A program longer than 20 lines that contains many `goto`s becomes very difficult to modify. The unstructured flow of program control throughout the program (jumping all over the place in the program) has been called "spaghetti code" after the way spaghetti noodles become intertwined and convoluted when cooked. Program logic is much clearer if entry into loops is restricted to the top of the loop, and loop exit is restricted to the top or bottom of the loop. The issue of multiple exit points from a loop has been examined in the discussion about `break`. What is worse about the `goto` statement is that it provides a means to also have *multiple entry points* into a loop. Unfortunately, there is no "came from" statement. When examining a single statement within a program that has a `goto` label attacted to it and many `goto`s spread around elsewhere, it may be a very difficult task to determine which `goto` jumped to this particular statement.

The break statement is quite mild compared to goto; it jumps to the statement immediately following the loop. A goto can jump as far ahead or as far backwards in the code as its limits allow (it cannot jump into or out of a function, thankfully). Writing correct code with structured statements is difficult enough; a generous dose of gotos in a complex program greatly magnifies the difficulty. An unescapable curse is placed upon the programmer that "inherits" someone else's code to fix or extend and that code happens to be sprinkled with many gotos.

The complete banishment of the goto statement is considered too harsh an action by most programmers; however, with C++'s break and continue statements, the need for a goto is mainly limited to the aforementioned exit from the middle of a nested loop. Realize that even in this situation the goto statement can be avoided, but doing so makes the logic a bit more complicated as well as obscure:

```
//   Nested loop three levels deep that must be abandoned in a
       particular situation

//   goto version
for ( i = 0;   i < 100;   i++ )
    for ( j = 0;   j < 100;   j++ )
        do {
            cout << "Enter value: ";
            cin >> in_value;
            if ( i*j + in_value == BAD_VAL )
                goto exit;        //   Get out of loops
            cout << "Calculated value is: " << i*j + in_value << '\n';
        } while ( in_value >= 0  &&  in_value < 10 )
exit:   cout << "All done with calculations\n";
        //   goto-less version
done = 0;   //   Not done yet
for ( i = 0;   i < 100  &&  !done;   i++ )
    for ( j = 0;   j < 100  &&  !done;   j++ )
        do {
            cout << "Enter value: ";
            cin >> in_value;
            if ( i*j + in_value == BAD_VALUE )
                done = 1;   //   Get out of loops
            else
                cout << "Calculated value is: " << i*j +in_value
                     << '\n';
        } while ( in_value >= 0  &&  in_value < 10  &&  !done );
cout << "All done with calculations\n";
```

The goto-less version requires the use of an accessory variable done that keeps track of the entry of a "bad" value. The status of done must be checked in the conditions of each of the loops as well as in the body of the innermost loop. This makes each condition more complicated and less efficient. The goto version implies that a premature exit from the loop is an extraordinary situation (known as an *exception*), and the loop conditions should not be obscured by checking a situation that is unlikely to occur most of the time.

In keeping with C++'s structured nature, some restrictions are placed on the goto statement. A goto statement cannot transfer control into or out of a function or into or out of a block (see chapter 6).

When reading published C and C++ programs, the goto statement is almost never seen. This fact is a testimony not only to its dispensability, but also to the quality of code that is routinely produced without it (not to mention the programmers' inevitable tribulations when it is used).

One "middle exit" from a loop is performed often enough to warrant attention. Many times a list of values must be entered with the end of the list indicated by entering a special value. For example, if a list of integers is to be entered to be averaged, the value 999 might indicate the end of the list (also called a *sentinel*). The while version could be written as in program 5.7.

```
#include <iostream.h>
const int Sentinal = 999;
void main() {
        int in_val, sum = 0, count = 0;
        cin >> in_val;
        while ( in_val != Sentinal ) {
                sum += in_val;
                count++;
                cin >> in_val;
        }
        cout << sum /count;
}
```

Program 5.7

Program 5.8 contains the do..while version.

```
#include <iostream.h>
const int Sentinal = 999;
void main() {
        int in_val, sum = 0, count = 0;
        do {
                cin >> in_val;
                if ( in_val != Sentinal ) {
                        sum += in_val;
                        count++;
                }
        } while ( in_val != Sentinal );
        cout << sum /count;
}
```

Program 5.8

Both versions seem to have more code baggage than is needed conceptually. Program 5.7 duplicates the input statement. Program 5.8 contains the conditional statement within the loop, which would be required even if break or continue were employed. The comma operator, introduced in the previous chapter, can be used to produce simpler code as in program 5.9.

```
#include <iostream.h>

const int Sentinal = 999;

void main() {
        int in_val, sum = 0, count = 0;
        while ( cin >> in_val, in_val != Sentinal ) {
                sum += in_val;
                count++;
        }
        cout << sum /count;
}
```

Program 5.9

The expression

```
cin >> in_val, in_val != Sentinal
```

is evaluated left to right, with the value of the right-most subexpression (in_val != Sentinal) being the value of the overall expression. The comma operator allows us to "cheat" and execute one or more statements within the while condition. In this case, the while is not a top exiting loop at all; it can only exit after one statement has been executed.

Sometimes a sentinel value is not practical; every possible integer value is considered acceptable input. In these cases, a noninteger must be entered instead. Any character would work fine to quit (such as 'Q'). The following while condition would work:

```
while ( cin >> in_val, cin.good() ) {
```

The status of a stream can be checked with its good() function. If a requested input value cannot be extracted from the stream, the cin.good() function will return a zero. In the previous example, if the user does not type in a sequence of characters that can be interpreted as a valid number, then the loop will terminate. (The cin.good() function will indicate that the stream is in an error state by returning 0.)

In this program, testing the state of the stream for loop termination works fine because the program is finished immediately after exiting the loop; however, if a program must use the stream later, the stream's error state must be cleared. Since there is no built-in, standard function for clearing the stream (also known as *flushing* the stream), the following code can be used to flush the cin stream:

```
//  Flush the cin stream
cin.clear();  //  Clear the error status
char ch;
do {
  ch = cin.get(); // Grab a character, no matter what it is, and ignore it.
                  // Keep going until newline or end-of-file is reached.
} while ( ch != '\n'  &&  ch != EOF );
cin.clear();   //  Clear the status again
```

After executing this sequence of code, cin's error status will be cleared, and any keys typed in to the input stream's buffer will have been flushed out. cin is as good as new to use elsewhere in the program. The next chapter will incorporate this code into a convenient function.

Exercises

1. Rewrite the following loop so that the continue is not used (do not use goto):

```
while ( x > MIN_VALUE ) {
    cin >> in_value;
    x += in_value;
    if ( x == CODE )
        continue;
    cout << "No code yet.\n";
    cin >> in_value;
    x -= in_value;
}
```

2. Give an example of nested loops.

3. Rewrite the following loop so that the gotos are not used:

```
          cin >> in_value;
loopentry: if ( in_value == 10 )
              goto loopend;
          x = in_value + delta;
          cin >> in_value;
          goto loopentry;
loopend:  cout << "All done.\n";
```

4. Why should the `goto` statement not be used?

5.6 Efficiency in Iteration

The more statements a program must perform, the longer it takes to run. Statements within loops are executed multiple times. In fact, whenever programs are *optimized* (i.e., made to run faster), loops are particularly scrutinized. If the body of an iterative statement can be made simpler and still work correctly, the time savings will be much more dramatic than the same improvement on code that has linear sequencing. The linear sequence of code is executed once, but the loop body might be executed 10,000 times. The easiest improvement to make is to move any calculations that can be done outside the loop from inside the loop:

```
/*  Print risk factors for cases 0 through 10,000  */
for ( i = 0;  i < 10000;  i++ ) {
    age_factor = age + 215*omega;
    genetic_factor = gene_rating + 661*theta;
    risk_factor = age_factor*i + genetic_factor*i;
    cout << "Risk factor #" << i << ": " << risk_factor << '\n';
}
```

In the body of the loop the variables `age`, `omega`, `age_factor` (since it is calculated from values that are not changing), `gene_rating`, `theta`, and `genetic_factor` (since it is being calculated from values that are not changing) have constant values. Each time through the loop, in addition to access to the `cout` stream and the calculations required to manage the `for` loop itself, three additions, three assignments, and four multiplications are performed. For the duration of the loop, 30,000 additions, 30,000 assignments, and 40,000 multiplications are done. Each of these operations by itself may be quite fast, but tens of thousands of them may amount to a lot of time (a second is gone before you know it, but 10,000 seconds is over two hours and 45 minutes). Here, multiplications are performed the most and, unfortunately, are much more time consuming than either assignment or addition. Using the distributive property from mathematics in a straightforward manner, the expression

```
age_factor*i + genetic_factor*i
```

can be rewritten as

```
(age_factor + genetic_factor)*i
```

which involves one addition and one multiplication versus one addition and two multiplications (a great savings due to the expense of multiplication). Most of the work may be moved out of the loop body:

```
/*  Print risk factors for cases 0 through 10,000  */
age_factor = age + 215*omega;
genetic_factor = genetic_rating + 661*theta;
combined_factor = age_factor + genetic_factor;
for ( i = 0;  i < 10000;  i++ ) {
    risk_factor = combined_factor*i;
    cout << "Risk factor #" << i << ": " << risk_factor << '\n';
}
```

In this version, before the loop is entered, three assignments, three additions, and two multiplications are done. In the loop, one assignment and one multiplication are performed 10,000 times making the total number of operations (again excluding `cout`'s access and the `for` management operations which are identical to the above version): 10,003 assignments, 3 additions, and 10,002 multiplications. The overall number of operations is reduced from 100,000 to 20,008 (an 80 percent reduction), and the extravagant multiplications have been reduced from 40,000 to 10,002 (a 75 percent reduction). The speed of the loop is dramatically affected.

Both versions do the job. Which version is better?

Exercise

1. What principles should be followed when trying to improve the efficiency of loops?

5.7   SOME SIMPLE EXAMPLE PROGRAMS

Now the grade averaging program from chapter 2, program 2.9, will be expanded to accept any number of grades. It appears in program 5.10. As indicated above, the cin stream object can be checked to see if a legitimate value was entered. (Remember that if the stream cin must be used later in the same program, it must be flushed to clear its error state.) The loop continues until a non-number is entered. The check for count > 0 prevents a possible division by zero in the average calculation. Division by zero is just as undefined in C++ as it is in mathematics. The compiler can't check for division by zero when a variable is used as a divisor, since the compiler doesn't know that when the program is running the variable will indeed be equal to zero.

```
#include <iostream.h>
void main() {
        int total = 0, count = 0, in_grade;
        cout << "Enter the grades to average. Type [Q] to quit. \n";
        cin >> in_grade;
        while ( cin.good() ) {
                total += in_grade;
                count++;
                cin >> in_grade;
        }
        if ( count > 0 )
                cout << "The average of " << count
                        << " grades is " << float(total)/count << '\n';
        else
                cout << "No grades were properly entered.\n";
}
```

Program 5.10

Division by zero will thus produce a *runtime* error. A message will be displayed and the program will terminate. It is the programmer's responsibility to check all variable divisors if there is any chance that they can be zero. Runtime errors are the manifestations of a program's logical errors. Notice that, if the check for division by zero were removed, the program would execute perfectly in almost all cases. (When would it fail?) Note that the comma operator could have been used within the while condition to avoid the duplicated stream extraction; it was omitted here for increased clarity.

Program 5.11 reads in characters until the end-of-file character is entered. (On many systems, the end-of-file character can be entered by entering CONTROL-Z.) The characters entered are displayed as is, unless the letter 'A' is entered. Instead of displaying the 'A', an asterisk will be displayed in its place.

```
#include <iostream.h>
void main() {
      char ch;
      while ( ch = cin.get(), !cin.eof() )
            if ( ch == 'A' )
                  cout << '*';
            else
                  cout << ch;
}
```

Program 5.11

If the characters

```
WGH$7&AQwgha76@AAHIK
```

are entered, then

```
WGH$7&*Qwgha76@**HIK
```

will be displayed. The function `cin.eof()` is similar to the expression `cin.good()`. `cin.eof()` evaluates to 1 if the end-of-file character has been extracted from the stream; it returns 0 otherwise. Because of the test for the end-of-file character, this program can be used with redirection to manipulate textfiles. If the program 5.11 can be executed from the command line by typing `atostar`, then

```
atostar < file1.dat > file1.new
```

will copy every character in `file1.dat` to `file1.new` exchanging every occurrence of 'A' within `file1.dat` with '*' in `file1.new`.

5.8   A MORE COMPLEX EXAMPLE PROGRAM

Iteration and conditional execution are powerful programming concepts. Program 5.12 is about as complicated a `main()` function as we'll see in this class. Our programs will become much more sophisticated than program 5.12, but we'll manage the complexity of large programs by decomposing them into a collection of smaller, simpler functions that do most of the work so that `main()` does not have to do the whole job itself. This process of functional decomposition is examined in chapter 6. For now, program 5.12 serves to illustrate the power of combining C++'s control statements.

Program 5.12 is used to tabulate the votes for three candidates running for office. The contenders are Fujimoto, Jones, and Alvarez. An election official starts the program by entering a secret password that begins the vote tallying process. Voters can then come and cast their vote by typing an appropriate choice: 1 for Fujimoto, 2 for Jones, and 3 for Alvarez. When the poll is to be closed, the election official then enters another secret number to end the vote collection portion of the program. The program then tallies the votes for each candidate, prints the results along with percentages, and declares a winner (or indicates a tie, if appropriate). The program attempts to be *robust* by disallowing illegal input. A program is considered to be robust when it gracefully handles improper user interactions instead of terminating with a runtime error or producing erroneous results.

```
#include <iostream.h>
const int START_PASSWORD = 3265,
          END_PASSWORD  = 1193;
void main() {
      int fujimoto_votes = 0,
          jones_votes   = 0,
          alvarez_votes= 0,
```

```
        vote, password, total_votes;
//   Initiate voting program
do {    //   Repeat until correct password is entered
        cout << "Please enter password to begin program.\n";
        cin >> password;
} while ( password != START_PASSWORD );
do {
        do {
                cout << "Please cast your vote: \n"
                    << "1   Fujimoto \n"
                    << "2   Jones \n"
                    << "3   Alvarez \n";
                cin >> vote;
        } while ( vote != 1 && vote != 2 && vote != 3 && vote !=
                END_PASSWORD );
        if ( vote == 1 )
                fujimoto_votes++;
        else if ( vote == 2 )
                jones_votes++;
        else if ( vote == 3 )
                alvarez_votes++;
} while ( vote != END_PASSWORD );
//   Tabulate and report results
total_votes = fujimoto_votes + jones_votes + alvarez_votes;
cout << "Fujimoto received " << fujimoto_votes
        << " votes (" << 100.0*fujimoto_votes/total_votes << "%)\n";
cout << "Jones     received " << jones_votes
        << " votes (" << 100.0*jones_votes/total_votes << "%)\n";
cout << "Alvarez   received " << alvarez_votes
        << " votes (" << 100.0*alvarez_votes/total_votes << "%)\n";
if ( fujimoto_votes > jones_votes  &&  fujimoto_votes > alvarez_votes )
    cout << "Fujimoto won the election.\n";
else if ( jones_votes > fujimoto_votes  &&  jones_votes > alvarez_votes )
    cout << "Jones won the election.\n";
else if ( alvarez_votes > fujimoto_votes && alvarez_votes > Jones_votes )
    cout << "Alvarez won the election.\n";
else if ( fujimoto_votes == jones_votes )
    if ( fujimoto_votes == alvarez_votes )
            cout << "There is a three way tie for first place.\n";
    else    //   Already determined that Alvarez did not win
            cout << "Fujimoto and Jones tied for first place.\n";
else if ( jones_votes == alvarez_votes )
    //   Already determined that Fujimoto did not win
    cout << "Jones and Alvarez tied for first place.\n";
else
    cout << "Fujimoto and Alvarez tied for first place.\n";
}
```

Program 5.12

Exercise

1. Draw a flowchart for the voting program (program 5.12).

Assignments

1. Write a program that emulates a simple voting machine. The program should print the message "Enter 1 for Smith or 2 for Jones." The user would type 1 to vote for Smith or 2 to vote for Jones. Any values other than 1 and 2 are ignored, with the exception of 999. Typing 999 ends the program by printing the number of votes each candidate received as well as the integer (truncated) percentage of the votes that they received. Indicate who won the election. Use only the int data type for this assignment.

2. Write a program that allows the user to enter in any number of int test scores (a non-number terminates the loop). As each score is entered, not only is it used to calculate the average at the end, but it is also used to determine a letter grade and an associated grade point number based on the scale:

   ```
   90+.........A    (4 points)
   80-89.......B    (3 points)
   70-79.......C    (2 points)
   60-69.......D    (1 points)
    0-59.......F    (0 points)
   ```

   The average of the test scores should be calculated, along with the class GPA for the test.

3. Write a program that reads in letter grades for a class. Keep track of the number of students that passed (D or above), and the number that failed (F). No plus or minus should be attached to a letter grade. Entering a Z indicates end of input. Be sure that Z is not counted as a grade! Calculate and print the percentage of students passing and failing, as well as the class GPA (A = 4.00, B = 3.00, C = 2.00, D = 1.00, and F = 0.00).

   Example:

   ```
   Enter a grade: C
   Enter a grade: F
   Enter a grade: A
   ...(etc.)

   12 students passed:  80.00 percent
    3 students failed:  20.00 percent

   Overall class GPA:    2.84
   ```

   passed / total × 100 =

   14/5

4. On the average, a person watches three hours of TV per day over the course of his or her lifetime. Write a program that has the computer print the number of hours in a person's life which he/she will have spent watching TV given his/her date of birth and today's date. Use 365 days in each year and 30 days in each month to simplify your calculations. Use the type long instead of int for your calculations.

   Example run:

   ```
   Enter your birthday:   9 27 68
   Enter today's date:   10 26 92

   You have been alive 6599 days.

   If you are a typical person, you have watched 52792 hours of TV!
   ```

5. Write a simple cash register program. Your program should allow the entry of the prices of any number of items (enter a non-number to exit loop), provide a subtotal for the items entered, calculate and display the appropriate sales tax (at 7.75 percent), display the total amount due, allow entry of money tendered, and display the amount of change to return. The program is designed to be used by people with limited change-making skills; hence, in addition to displaying the amount of change to return, it indicates the number of twenties, tens, fives, ones, quarters, dimes, nickels, and pennies that should be handed to the customer. Return the fewest number of bills and coins possible (don't return 57 pennies, for example). Don't display a money unit if it is not to be given back (don't say Tens: 0, for example).

A sample run might appear as:

```
* * * * * * * * * * * * * * * * * * * * * * * * * * * * * * * * * * * * * * * * * * * * * * * * * * * * * * * * * *
Begin Transaction:
                  12.99
                   1.50
                   0.95
                   0.95
                  21.99
                  _____

Subtotal          38.38
Sales Tax          2.97
Total             41.35

Tendered          50.00
Change             8.65

Change Summary:
    Fives: 1,  Ones: 3,  Quarters: 2,  Nickels: 3.

* * * * * * * * * * * * * * * * * * * * * * * * * * * * * * * * * * * * * * * * * * * * * * * * * * * * * * * * * *
Begin Transaction:
```

Your program should continue to run for multiple customers until a non-number is entered as the first value in a transaction. Since the program deals with money, two decimal places should be displayed for all values except the quantity of each type of money to return.

6. Write two programs that read textfiles (using redirection). One program should encrypt the characters in the file based on the following "secret" code:

the alphabetic characters are scrambled as follows:

```
A B C D E F G H I J K L M N O P Q R S T U V W X Y Z
| | | | | | | | | | | | | | | | | | | | | | | | | |
Z Y X W V U T S R Q P O N M L K J I H G F E D C B A
```

the digits are scrambled as follows:

```
0 1 2 3 4 5 6 7 8 9
| | | | | | | | | |
9 8 7 6 5 4 3 2 1 0
```

all other characters are to be left unchanged. The other program should decrypt or decode an encrypted file performing the reverse translation. For example, consider the following textfile MARY.TXT which contains

```
Mary had 420 little lambs.  She was a busy person!
```

The command

```
encrypt < mary.txt > mary.enc
```

would produce a new textfile called `MARY.ENC` that contains

```
Nzib szw 579 orggov oznyh.   Hsv dzh z yfhb kvihlm!
```

(Notice that upper- and lowercase is preserved.)

The command

```
decrypt < mary.enc > mary.dec
```

would produce a textfile called `MARY.DEC` that contains

```
Mary had 420 little lambs.  She was a busy person!
```

that is, the contents of the original file.

CHAPTER 6

FUNCTIONS

6.1 INTRODUCTION

All of the programs we've seen so far contain only one programmer written function—`main()`. As our programs get larger, expressing them in one function will become increasingly inconvenient. Consider one person assigned to do some simple tasks at a job. As the demands of the workplace increase, this person is assigned more and more tasks to do. Eventually, the number of tasks, no matter how simple each might be, will overwhelm the worker. The solution is to provide assistants so that the person can manage the tasks and assign them to the assistants to be performed. What if the company becomes so large that the number of tasks that this person must manage becomes too large to handle? You guessed it—provide another level of management so that each manager's management duties are not overwhelming.

As our programs grow in length and logical complexity, they suffer the same management problems as the growing company. When a programmer has too many details to worry about at one time, the code he or she produces will take longer to write and be more error prone. Clearly it is easier to write short, simple sections of code. This is the purpose of functions in C++. The `main()` function becomes merely the top-level manager that delegates duties to other functions to perform. It may be that these delegated duties are still so complex that the functions that serve `main()` must use their own "servant" functions to perform their tasks. A large program may have scores of these levels of functionality.

6.2 PARAMETER PASSING AND RETURN VALUES

Program 6.1 illustrates a user written function.

```
#include <iostream.h>
int twice(int x)
{
    return 2*x;
}
```

```
                          void main()
                          {
                               int number, doubled_number;
                               cout << "Please enter a number to be doubled: ";
                               cin >> number;
                               doubled_number = twice(number);
                               cout << "Twice " << number << " is " << doubled_number <<
'\n';
                          }
```

Program 6.1

The name of the function is *twice*. Function names are identifiers; hence, functions follow the same name composition rules as variables. When discussing a function, we will place empty parentheses after its name to indicate that it is a function and not a variable. The *definition* of twice() is given right above main(). The definition includes the *header* (the first line of the definition) and the *body* of the function (the code within the curly braces). The header declares to the compiler how the function should be used. twice() is declared to accept an int value as a parameter and return an int value. Parameter(s) are enclosed within the parentheses in the header, and the type of the return value immediately precedes the function's name. A function may have any number of parameters but only one return value. The parameters' types must be specified in the parameter list because functions can accept all of the built-in data types as well as programmer-defined types. Since function names are identifiers, the rules for naming functions are the same as the rules for naming variables.

main() is the function that is always executed first. The main() function in program 6.1 uses, or *calls*, the function twice(). Since main() calls twice(), main() is said to be a *client* of twice(). The variable number is given a value and then *passed*, or *sent*, to twice(). The value of the parameter x within twice() is assigned the value passed. The value of the expression that follows the reserved word return is returned to the calling function (main(), in this case). twice()'s return value is assigned to the variable doubled_number, and then both number and doubled_number are displayed.

The parameter x in the definition of twice() is called the *formal parameter* of twice(). When the function is called in main(), the variable number which is passed to twice() is called the *actual parameter* in that call of twice(). The function call consists of copying the value of the actual parameter into the formal parameter and then executing the body of the function. When the function is finished, control is passed back to main() at the point directly following the function call. A function is finished when a return statement is encountered or, if no return is present (as is often the case in void functions), when the close curly brace for the function body is reached.

The two statements within program 6.1

```
        doubled_number = twice(number);
        cout << "Twice " << number << " is " << doubled_number << '\n';
```

could be replaced with one statement

```
        cout << "Twice " << number << " is " << twice(number) << '\n';
```

thus eliminating the need for the variable doubled_number. This is an example of using the return value of a function (twice()) directly as a parameter to another function, since the << operator is a special kind of function associated with the cout stream object. The following is certainly possible:

```
        number_X_16 = twice(twice(twice(twice(number))));
```

Here, the result of one function call (the innermost twice(number)) is used as the actual parameter to another call, and that return value is being used as the actual parameter for the next outermost call of twice().

The type of the actual parameter passed does not have to match the formal parameter type exactly as long as a standard conversion (see chapter 3) can be used to convert the actual parameter to the specified type. The same holds true for return type. For example, consider the code

```
float f;
double d;
d = twice(f);
```

Even though `twice()`, as defined, expects an `int` parameter and returns an `int` result, a `float` can be converted to an `int` (with the same perils noted in chapter 3 when the conversion occurs over assignment). The `int` return type can always be safely converted to a `double`. In fact, if one type can be implicitly converted to another type across assignment, the same conversion is performed when an actual parameter is passed to a formal parameter of a different, but compatible, type.

The return types and parameter types are not limited to `int`s. Functions can accept any of C++'s data types as parameters and also return any data type. Because the types of each parameter and the type of return value are declared before the function is called, the compiler can perform the necessary automatic conversion to make sure the correct type of value is sent to the function. Program 6.2 illustrates.

```
#include <iostream.h>
double sum_of_squares(double x, double y) {
     return x*x + y*y;
}
void main() {
     double d;
     int i;
     cout << "Enter a double and an int: ");
     cin >> d >> i;
     d = sum_of_squares(d, d);
     d = sum_of_squares(i, d);
     i = sum_of_squares(i, d);
     i = sum_of_squares(i, i);
}
```

Program 6.2

Here, both the arguments and return value are double precision floating point numbers. Of course, any data type compatible to a `double` (`int`s, `char`s, `float`s, etc.) can be passed.

Program 6.3 will be expanded to include an additional function.

```
#include <iostream.h>
int twice(int x)
{
     return 2*x;
}
void display_results(int x, int y)
{
     cout << "Twice " << x << " is " << y << '\n';
}
void main()
{
     int number, doubled_number;

     cout << "Please enter a number to be doubled: ";
     cin >> number;
     doubled_number = twice(number);
     display_results(number, doubled_number);
}
```

Program 6.3

The reserved word `void` preceding the function `display_results()` indicates, as in `main()`, that no value is going to be returned by the function. `display_results()` accepts two `int` parameters. No `return` statement is needed since nothing is returned. The function automatically returns to `main()` after executing the output statement.

The following function accepts an integer parameter and displays a message only if the parameter is one of three values: 1, 2, or 3:

```
void print_at_most_three(int x)
{
    if ( x >= 1 )
        cout << "Once ";
    if ( x >= 2 )
        cout << "Twice ";
    if ( x >= 3 )
        cout << "Thrice";
}
```

The `return` statement may appear more than once anywhere within a function. In a function returning `void`, `return` is used all by itself, without arguments; thus, an alternate form of the `print_at_most_three()` function could be written:

```
void print_at_most_three(int x)
{
    if ( x < 1 )
        return;
    cout << "Once ";
    if ( x < 2 )
        return;
    cout << "Twice ";
    if ( x < 3 )
        return;
    cout << "Thrice";
}
```

It is considered good programming practice to limit the number of `returns` used within a function. Ideally, a function should have one entry and one exit point. (Multiple exit points within a function sometimes make its logic difficult to follow.) The first formulation with one `return` (by default, a `void` function returns at the end even if a `return` statement is not explicitly provided) is therefore preferred to the second version with the multiple `returns`.

None of the functions examined thus far have been very useful. Let's look at a *little* more useful function:

```
/*
 *   Divides
 *      Programmer: Rick Halterman
 *      Last modified: 5/8/94
 *        Purpose:  Determines if divisor divides evenly into number.
 *        Returns 1 if so, 0 otherwise.
 */
int divides(int number, int divisor)
{
    if ( number % divisor == 0 )
        return 1;
    else
        return 0;
}
```

This function accepts two `int` parameters and returns an `int` result. `divides()` is called a *Boolean* function (after the British mathematician George Boole, a founder of mathematical logic) because it actually returns an indication of truth value—0 (false) or 1 (true). It could easily be used within a conditional statement:

```
if ( divides(12, 4) )
    cout << "4 evenly divides 12\n";
```

Functions need not accept any parameters. Up to this point `main()` has not been passed any arguments. An empty parameter list indicates no parameters are to be sent to the function:

```
char do_menu() {
    char choice;
    cout << "         Enter your choice (1-4)\n"
         << "\n"
         << "W.   Go to work\n"
         << "B.   Go back to bed\n"
         << "A.   Ask someone else what to do\n"
         << "Q.   Quit\n"
         << "\n"
         << "Choice-> ";
    cin >> choice;
    return choice;
}

void main() {
    char response;
    response = do_menu();
    switch ( response ) {
        case 'W': /*  Do something here ... */
                break;
        case 'B':  /*  Do something else here ...  */
                break;
        .
        .
        .   /*  Etc.  */
    }
}
```

When the function is defined (or declared as a prototype), an empty parameter list indicates that no parameters are to be passed to the function. When the function is called, the parentheses are left empty. In old C, the reserved word `void` must be used within the parentheses in the definition (and declaration, if used). If the parentheses are left empty in a C function definition, the compiler will not do parameter checking when the function is called. This means that you may call the function with as many parameters of any type you wish. This "feature" is provided to ensure compatibility with older, non-ANSI compilers. In general, it is a dangerous practice to limit the compiler's type-checking ability in this way. Since C++ strictly checks function parameters and return types, many problems that made programming in old C so tedious are caught at compile time.

Notice that the variable `choice` is declared within `do_menu()`. It is called a *local* variable and can only be used privately within `do_menu()`. In fact, any variable declared within the curly braces of a function can only be used within that function. The variable `response` can only be used within `main()`. If `choice` is used in `main()`, the compiler will issue an error message saying `choice` is an undeclared variable (within `main()`). The variable `response` in `main()` could be named `choice`, and it would be a separate variable from the `choice` in `do_menu()`, even though the names would be identical. It would occupy a different memory location. This concept of *locality* is crucial to the development of complex programs. When a function is written, the programmer need not look through a list of all the variables in a program to see if a particular name is already being used. The parameter names and local variable names used in a function definition represent new, temporary memory locations that remain in effect only as long as the body of the function is being executed.

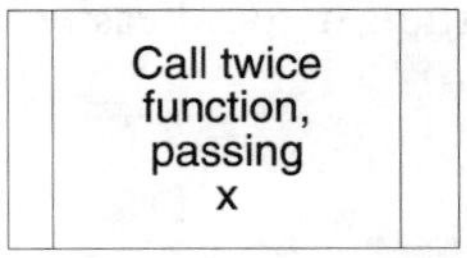

```
┌─────────────┐
│ Call twice  │
│ function,   │
│ passing     │
│     x       │
└─────────────┘
```

The flowchart symbol for a function call is shown in figure 6.1. The code for the actual function body is a separate flowchart with its own start and stop symbols. This agrees with the idea that functions are little programs executed within larger programs.

Function Call
Figure 6.1

Exercises

1. What are the four parts of a function definition?

2. What is the difference between *actual* parameters and *formal* parameters?

3. Ideally, how many `return` statements should appear within a function?

4. How are local variables different from parameters?

5. What type is a function that returns no value?

6. What is a *Boolean* function?

    For questions 7–11, refer to the following functions:

    ```
    int f(int x, int y) {
         int a = 2*x;
         return a + y;
    }

    int g(int x) {
         return x - 235;
    }

    int h(int a) {
         return a + g(a);
    }
    ```

7. Which of the functions uses local variables?

8. Evaluate `f(10, 20)`.

9. Evaluate `f(g(1000), h(1000))`.

10. Evaluate `h(h(g(h(1))))`.

6.3 CALL-BY-VALUE VS. CALL-BY-REFERENCE

It is important to note that a formal parameter used within the function body is a separate variable from the actual parameter passed by the calling function. They have the same values but refer to separate memory locations. Consider program 6.4.

```cpp
#include <iostream.h>

void twice(float x)
{
        cout << "x = " << x << '\n';
        x = 2*x;
        cout << "x = " << x << '\n';
}

void main()
{
        float number = 10.0;

        cout << "number = " << number << '\n';
        twice(number);
        cout << "number = " << number << '\n';
}
```

Program 6.4

When the program is run, it produces:

```
number = 10.00000
x = 10.00000
x = 20.00000
number = 10.00000
```

Notice that when this program is executed the value of `number` is not permanently modified by `twice()`. Only a copy of `number` is modified. This principle of functions working on copies of actual parameters and not the actual parameters themselves is called *call-by-value*. The call-by-value process means that if the programmer wants to modify the value of a variable through a function call, he or she must use the return value of a function in an assignment statement. Most functions in C++ follow the call-by-value protocol.

At times, it is convenient for the programmer to write a function that can modify the actual parameter(s) sent to it. The call-by-value protocol only allows the function to have access to a copy of an actual parameter so that any modification that the function makes on the parameter does not affect the actual parameter. C++ uses *reference parameters* to allow functions to modify permanently parameters passed to them. (C programs must perform call-by-reference another way, since reference parameters are not part of the C language. Old C's call-by-reference requires the introduction of pointers and is outlined in chapter 9.) Program 6.5 is updated here to work as expected:

```cpp
#include <iostream.h>

void twice(float &x)
{
        cout << "x = " << x << '\n';
        x = 2*x;
        cout << "x = " << x << '\n';
}

void main()
{
        float number = 10.0;

        cout << "number = " << number << '\n';
        twice(number);
        cout << "number = " << number << '\n';
}
```

Program 6.5

This program produces the expected output:

```
number = 10.00000
x = 10.00000
x = 20.00000
number = 20.00000
```

The ampersand (&) is used to declare that the parameter is a `float &` (read as "`float ref`"). Any modification of the formal parameter x within `twice()` now modifies the actual parameter (the variable `number` used within `main()`), even though their names are different. In effect, x in `twice()` becomes an *alias* for `number` in `main()`.

How would one write a function to interchange the values of two variables?

```
/*  Faulty swap routine  */
void swap(int x, int y)
{
        int temp;
        temp = x;
        x = y;
        y = temp;
}
```

This indeed interchanges the values of the value parameters x and y, but the call in the following client code

```
int val1 = 10, val2 = 12;

swap(val1, val2);
```

does not affect `val1` or `val2`, since only their *copies* were switched. The correct `swap()` is

```
/*  Correct swap routine  */
void swap(int &x, int &y)
{
        int temp;

        temp = x;
        x = y;
        y = temp;
}
```

The call to `swap()`:

```
swap(val1, val2);
```

now correctly interchanges the values of the two variables.

A more practical example is found in a function used to reduce a fraction. Recall from mathematics that a fraction, or rational number, is the ratio of two integers, where the bottom number cannot be equal to zero. The most common approach to reducing a fraction to lowest terms first finds the largest integer that is a factor of both the numerator and denominator. This number, called the *greatest common factor* or *greatest common divisor*, is divided into both the numerator and denominator to complete the reduction. A function to reduce a fraction could be written as:

```
void reduce_fraction(int &numerator, int &denominator) {
    int gcf;
    gcf = greatest_common_factor(numerator, denominator);
    numerator   /= gcf;
    denominator /= gcf;
}
```

The function `greatest_common_factor()` would need to be written for this function to work. (It is left as an assignment.) The following `main()`

```
void main() {
    int a = 12, b = 36;
    cout << a << '/'  << b << '\n';
    reduce_fraction(a, b);
    cout << a << '/'  << b << '\n';
}
```

would print

```
12/36
1/3
```

thus illustrating that the actual variables a and b are modified.

Functions that use reference parameters are not required to modify them. If parameters are not to be modified, the call-by-value protocol should be used. (An exception to this rule will be seen in chapter 8 with programmer-defined types.) This prevents an error in a function that accidentally modifies the parameter from disturbing the actual parameter. Errors of this nature can be difficult to track down. Functions that modify their arguments are said to cause *side effects*. In complex programs, it can take some work to determine if errors in a program's behavior are the result of undesirable side effects in functions or errors in the client code that calls them.

Using the reduce_fraction() function from above, what would the following code do?

```
reduce_fraction(12, 36);
```

Since the parameters passed are constants, not variables, they can't be modified. The function has no effect. Most compilers will generate a warning message if this statement is used, but it does not technically violate any rules of the language. Since the built-in data types should be passed by value unless the explicit aim is to modify them, the rationale of sending constants to call-by-reference functions is questionable.

The automatic parameter type conversions described above for call-by-value do not hold for call-by-reference. Consider:

```
#include <iostream.h>
void re_init(int &i) {
    i = 5;
}
```

```
void main() {
    unsigned number = 2;
    cout << "Number = " << number << '\n';
    re_init(number);
    cout << "Number = " << number << '\n';
}
```

In this case, the compiler should issue a warning about a *temporary* being generated for the parameter in the call to re_init(). Temporaries will be discussed more fully in chapter 11, but for now it is important to understand that the call-by-reference effect does not occur here. Since the actual parameter did not exactly match the formal parameter and a reference parameter was used, a temporary, new unsigned object was allocated, and its address was passed to re_init(), not number's address. Behind the scenes, the compiler generates code that acts like the following:

```
re_init(number);
```

is changed to

```
int temp = number;
re_init(temp);
```

`number` itself was not changed. The temporary object was changed, but it cannot be accessed by the programmer. (The compiler uses it "in secret.") It suffices to remember that in call-by-reference parameter types should match exactly.

Some languages, such as FORTRAN, use call-by-reference as their standard means of passing parameters to functions. C++ uses call-by-value as its default mode. It is considered good programming practice to use call-by-value whenever possible. That way, any damage a faulty function does will be limited to the body of that function, and it can only corrupt the rest of the program through an incorrect return value.

The code presented in the previous chapter to flush `cin` will now be incorporated within a function called `inflush()`. The input stream is passed into the function by reference, and the stream is returned as a reference value. The effect of returning a reference will be discussed in later chapters; for now, it (like streams objects themselves) can be used without understanding all of the details that make it work:

```
istream &inflush(istream &is) {
    // Flush the cin stream
    is.clear();  // Clear the error status
    char ch;
    do {
        // Grab a character, no matter what it is, and ignore it.
        ch = is.get();
        // Keep going until newline or end-of-file is reached.
    } while ( ch != '\n'  &&  ch != EOF );
    is.clear();   // Clear the status again
    return is;
}
```

`cin` is of type `istream`. This function can be used to flush any `istream` object, including input files (chapter 7). Due to the nature of streams objects, this function can be used one of two ways; namely, like a normal function call—

```
inflush(cin);
```

or as a stream *manipulator*—

```
cin >> inflush;
```

Both work identically. A manipulator is a message sent to a stream to alter its state (such as `setw()` or `setprecision()` seen in chapter 3). The reason for this flexibility in expression is discussed in chapter 11.

6.4 ARRANGEMENT OF FUNCTIONS WITHIN A PROGRAM

Many C++ programmers prefer to have `main()` appear at the top of their program and have all the other functions follow. This is natural, since `main()` is the function that is always executed first. The problem is that if the compiler encounters a function call before it has seen the definition of that function, it does not know whether or not the function is being used correctly (correct return type and correct number and types of parameters). Recall that the header of the function definition serves to declare the function to the compiler. Using a function before its declaration is like using a variable before its declaration—a compile error will be generated. In C++, functions can be *declared* one place and *defined* elsewhere. Consider program 6.6:

```
#include <iostream.h>

int twice(int);
void display_results(int, int);
```

```
void main()
{
     int number, doubled_number;

     cout << "Please enter a number to be doubled: ";
     cin >> number;
     doubled_number = twice(number);
     display_results(number, doubled_number);
}

int twice(int x)
{
     return 2*x;
}

void display_results(int x, int y)
{
     cout << "Twice " << x << " is " << y << '\n';
}
```

Program 6.6

This modification of program 6.3 lists `main()` first. The other functions used within `main()` are declared above `main()`. They could have also been declared within `main()`:

```
void main()
{
     int number, doubled_number, twice(int);
     void display_results(int, int);
     .
     .
     .
}
```

The function *declaration* of return type and parameter types without the body is also known as a *function prototype*. When a function is declared at the top (right after the `#include`), it can be used anywhere in the program (`main()` and the other functions). When a function is declared within a function, it can be used within that function and the functions that follow its *definition* (remember the definition includes the body of the function). A function can always be used in parts of the program that follow its definition. The convention normally used here will be the one first explored; that is, `main()` will be last, and function definitions will appear before they are called. Except for rare cases (when function `A()` calls function `B()` and function `B()` also calls function `A()`), this eliminates the need to declare functions apart from their definitions. The bottom line is functions must be declared before they are called.

Older C compilers did less strenuous checking and would allow the use (call) of a function before its definition or declaration. The compiler would assume the number and types of parameters used during the call were correct. This led to many errors that were difficult to track down, since the compiler kept silent about the improper function calls. The newer ANSI C compilers do more extensive checking but have options for reduced checking to be compatible with older code. C++ requires that the parameter types and return value be known before the function is used. Except in rare, special situations, it is best to let the compiler check the code as exhaustively as possible. Although compiler error messages may not always be welcome, at least they provide some guidance as to where a problem occurs in the program. A program that does not work and does not give an indication as to the location and nature of the problem is usually much more difficult to fix.

Generally, the issue of where to place the *call* of a function depends solely on what the program is attempting to accomplish. As long as the function's declaration precedes the first call of the function, the compiler can determine the correctness of the call and will be able to generate machine language code properly. Sometimes the judicious placement of a function call can make a big difference in a program's efficiency. Consider the following section of code:

```
if ( do_extreme_things_to(x)  &&  x < 10 )
      /*  Use x in some calculation...  */
```

The function `do_extreme_things_to()` returns a Boolean result of 0 or 1. In the course of its activity, the `do_extreme_things_to()` function does some complex number crunching and time-consuming processing, possibly evolving loops within loops. In short, getting the result of the function takes about 3,000 times longer than getting the result of x < 10. Due to the short-circuit evaluation that C++ performs on Boolean expressions, it would be best to rewrite the code as

```
if ( x < 10  &&  do_extreme_things_to(x) )
      /*  Use x in some calculation...  */
```

Here, the cheap comparison of x < 10 may produce 0, in which case the expensive function `do_extreme_things_to()` would not even be called. Except in the cases where logical errors would be introduced, the easiest conditions to check should be placed first in logical expressions containing && and ||.

Exercises

1. Describe the normal call-by-value process of parameter passing.

2. Describe the process through which an actual parameter may be modified by a function.

3. Write a function called `make_max()` that accepts two integer parameters and forces both actual parameters to be equal to the larger of the two parameters. The following code:

    ```
    int x = 2, y = 4;
    make_max(x, y);
    cout << x << ' ' << y << '\n';
    ```

    would display 4 4.

4. What is a function prototype?

5. What is the difference between a function *declaration* and a function *definition*?

6. Why would a programmer want to locate `main()` above all of the other functions within the program?

7. Why would a programmer want to locate `main()` after all of the other functions within the program?

8. If `twice()` is defined as

    ```
    float twice(float x) {
        return x * 2.0;
    }
    ```

and `y` is declared to be an `int`, is the following call legal or illegal?

```
y = twice(y);
```

6.5 EXAMPLE OF FUNCTIONAL DECOMPOSITION

The process of breaking a larger problem up into smaller problems and constructing functions to solve those smaller problems is called *functional decomposition*. To illustrate functional decomposition, program 5.12, the voting program from chapter 5, will be decomposed into a collection of simpler functions. `main()` will become uncluttered, and the complexity of the program will be managed by simple, single purpose functions that do work that `main()` used to do. Program 6.7 contains the improved version.

```cpp
#include <iostream.h>
const int START_PASSWORD = 3265,
          END_PASSWORD   = 1193;

void wait_for_official_start() {
    int password;
    do {   //  Repeat until correct password is entered
        cout << "Please enter password to begin program.\n";
        cin >> password;
    } while ( password != START_PASSWORD );
}

int get_vote() {
    int vote;
    do {
        cout << "Please cast your vote: \n"
                "1   Fujimoto \n"
                "2   Jones \n"
                "3   Alvarez \n";
        cin >> vote;
    } while ( vote != 1 && vote != 2 && vote != 3 && vote != END_PASSWORD );
    return vote;
}

void poll_voters(int &fv, int &jv, int &av) {
    int vote;
    //  Clear all votes to begin session
    fv = 0;   jv = 0;   av = 0;
    do {
        //  Loop until poll closes and all votes are in
        vote = get_vote();
        if ( vote == 1 )
            fv++;
        else if ( vote == 2 )
            jv++;
        else if ( vote == 3 )
            av++;
    } while ( vote != END_PASSWORD );
}

void print_results(int fv, int jv, int av) {
    //  Tabulate and report results
    int total_votes = fv + jv + av;
    cout << "Fujimoto received " << fv
```

```
                  << " votes (" << 100.0*fv/total_votes << "%)\n";
         cout << "Jones     received " << jv
                  << " votes (" << 100.0*jv/total_votes << "%)\n";
         cout << "Alvarez   received " << av
                  << " votes (" << 100.0*av/total_votes << "%)\n";

         if ( fv > jv  &&  fv > av )
              cout << "Fujimoto won the election.\n";
         else if ( jv > fv  &&  jv > av )
              cout << "Jones won the election.\n";
         else if ( av > fv  &&  av > jv )
              cout << "Alvarez won the election.\n";
         else if ( fv == jv )
              if ( fv == av )
                   cout << "There is a three way tie for first place.\n";
              else   //  Already determined that Alvarez did not win
                   cout << "Fujimoto and Jones tied for first place.\n";
         else if ( jv == av )
              //  Already determined that Fujimoto did not win
              cout << "Jones and Alvarez tied for first place.\n";
         else
              cout << "Fujimoto and Alvarez tied for first place.\n";
}
void main() {
     int fujimoto_votes, jones_votes, alvarez_votes;

     wait_for_official_start();
     poll_voters(fujimoto_votes, jones_votes, alvarez_votes);
     print_results(fujimoto_votes, jones_votes, alvarez_votes);
}
```

Program 6.7

One of its functions, `poll_voters()`, uses call-by-reference. The logic in `main()` is now so simple it would be difficult to get it wrong:

```
1.   Wait for voting official to start polling process
2.   Poll all the voters
3.   Report the results
```

`main()` no longer contains any loops or `if-else` statements. The more difficult tasks of controlling loops and making decisions based on the values of variables is delegated to other small functions that may be debugged on their own merits without worrying about any other part of the program interfering. In general, all functions should be kept as simple and straightforward as possible. Complicated and/or long functions should be analyzed for ways to be decomposed further. When done properly, functional decomposition results in programs consisting of independent *modules* (functions) that can be isolated for error detection and correction and that can be reused in other programs where applicable. `main()`'s logic is much simpler, and its collection of local variables has been reduced. It almost reads like plain English and is much more self-documenting.

6.6 FUNCTION OVERLOADING

In C++ (but not C), functions may be *overloaded*. Two or more functions are said to be overloaded when their names are identical, but their argument lists are different. Many of C++'s (and C's) operators are overloaded. The + operator is used for adding `int`s, `float`s, `double`s, etc., as well as all types of pointers (see chapter 9). The following `print()` function is overloaded:

```
int print(int);
int print(int, int);
int print(float);
int print(int, float);
```

print() is an overloaded function, since the four separate functions above differ only in the number or types of parameters they accept. The return values may be different for overloaded functions; however, it is an error for two functions to have identical names and parameter lists but differ only in the types that they return. The definitions for the functions must be provided somewhere:

```
int print(int i) {
     if ( i > 0 ) {
          cout << i;   //  Print only if positive
          return 1;
     }
     return 0;  //  Zero indicates nothing was printed
}
int print(int i, int j) {
     if ( i < j ) {          //  Print only if first argument < second
          cout << i << ' ' << j;
          return 1;
     }
     return 0;   //  Zero indicates nothing was printed
}
int print(float f, int i) {
     if ( f > 0.0001  &&  i < 999 ) {
          cout << f;  // Only print float argument under certain conditions
          return 1;
     }
     return 0;    //  Zero indicates nothing was printed
}
//   Etc....
```

With the statement

```
float a;
int   b;
       .
       .
       .
if ( print(a, b) == 1 )
    b = do_something(a);
```

the compiler knows the types of the variables a and b; thus, the proper function call can be used (print(float, int)). The compiler actually generates a slightly different name for each overloaded function instance. How the name is modified is implementation dependent, but the above functions could be renamed as the following:

```
print(int)          becomes   @prnt$qi   (the linker sees this name)
print(int, int)     becomes   @prnt$qiqi
print(float)        becomes   @prnt$qf
print(float, int)   becomes   @prnt$qfqi
```

This process of assigning unique names to overloaded functions is known as *name mangling*. Of course, this renaming is done behind the scenes, and the programmer is unaware of (and need not be concerned with) the compiler's name mangling. The idea is that even though the four functions have the same names in the source code, they are four separate functions as far as the compiler is concerned.

6.7 DEFAULT ARGUMENTS

C++ (but not C) provides a convenient way for programmers to indicate that functions can receive default arguments.

```
int print(int = 0);
void main() {
    print(19);
    print();
}
int print(int i) {
    cout << i;
}
```

The declaration of `print()` indicates that an `int` type will be passed. If *no* parameter is passed, the compiler will pass a zero by default; thus, `print(19)` will print out 19, and `print()` will print out 0.

Notice that the declaration (prototype) indicates the default values, not the definition. Default values may be placed in the header of the definition only when definition and declaration are one and the same.

Only trailing parameters may be defaulted. The function prototype

```
void display(int, float, int = 100);
```

is legal, but the prototype

```
void display(int = 100, float, int);
```

is illegal because the default is followed by parameters that are given no default values. Care should be taken when mixing overloaded functions and functions with default arguments:

```
void print(int);
void print(int, double = 0.0);
```

Would a call of `print(3)` use `print(int)` (since no `double` is provided) or substitute 0.0 as the default `double` parameter in `print(3, 0.0)` (again since no `double` is provided)? The compiler can't decide (can you?), so it generates an error about an ambiguous function declaration.

Exercises

1. What is function overloading?

2. How does the compiler separate two functions of the same name with different parameter lists?

3. What advantage does the ability to overload functions provide?

4. How can default arguments be used in functions?

5. What restrictions are placed on the ordering of default arguments?

6.8 TOP-DOWN DESIGN

Program development is simplified by the liberal use of functions. The functions end up doing the bulk of the work in the program. If each function is kept fairly simple, the hard task of solving a big, difficult problem is converted into a more manageable task of solving many, simpler problems.

This process of decomposing a program into a series of functions is best done in an organized manner. Haphazard program decomposition and function creation can lead to programs that are difficult to understand and impossible to modify easily. Over the years, a process known as *top-down design* has emerged as the dominant method of program design.

The top-down design process begins with a general statement of the overall problem. This initial problem is decomposed into smaller subproblems. Each subproblem itself is then decomposed into even smaller subproblems (sub-subproblems?). This process of breaking down subproblems continues until a subproblem is simple enough to be solved by a short (no more than about 50 lines of C++ code) function.

Consider the problem of developing a fairly sophisticated program like a wordprocessor or text editor. We will limit our discussion to a program that has only some simple capabilities: save, retrieve, set margins, set font, set line spacing, print to file, and print to disk file. (The editor is of limited use since no part of the program allows for text entry!)

**The Problem
Figure 6.2**

The problem can be illustrated in the block diagram of figure 6.2. This main problem can be divided into the distinct tasks in figure 6.3.

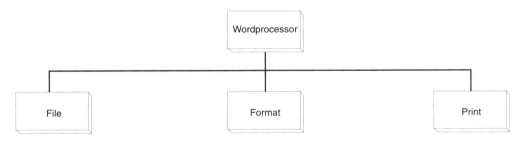

**First Refinement
Figure 6.3**

This decomposition of a block into several simpler blocks is known as *step-wise refinement*. Some of the tasks can be further subdivided as shown in figure 6.4.

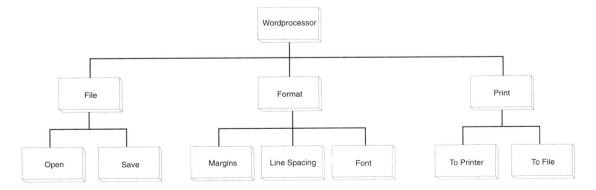

**Second Refinement
Figure 6.4**

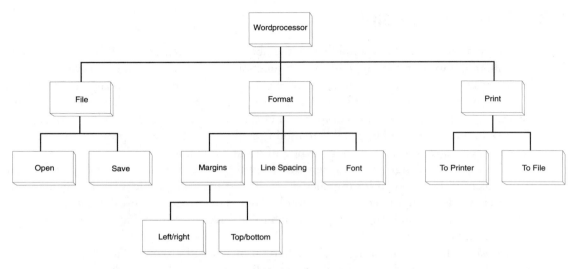

Third Refinement
Figure 6.5

Finally, the `margin` block will be divided into two as in figure 6.5.

Whereas a flowchart as seen in chapter 4 is used to illustrate the logic of statements within an individual function, this *structure chart* can be used to show the relationships between functions within a program. One can quickly see that the function that implements the `format` portion of the program depends on the functions that implement the `margins`, `line spacing`, and `font` portions.

When all of the subtasks at the lowest level can be implemented with simple functions, the design is complete. The overall problem is addressed by `main()`. Each block in the diagram is represented by a function. These functions may, in turn, call other functions to get their jobs done. `main()` may contain a menu that allows the user to make several choices:

```
void main()
{
    int choice;

    do {
      cout << "\n    Main Menu\n"
           << " 1.    File Commands\n"
           << " 2.    Format Commands\n"
           << " 3.    Print Options\n"
           << " 4.    Quit\n"
           << " Enter your selection ==> ";
      cin >> choice;
      if ( choice == 1 )
          do_file_stuff();
      else if ( choice == 2 )
          do_format();
      else if ( choice == 3 )
          do_print();
    }  while ( choice != 4 );
}
```

One of the choices is "Format Commands" which could be implemented by a function named `do_format()`. `do_format()`, in turn, uses several functions called `set_margins()`, `set_spacing()`, and `set_font()`:

```
void do_format()
{
    int choice;

    cout << "\n    Format Menu\n"
         << " 1.   Set Margins\n"
         << " 2.   Set Line Spacing\n"
         << " 3.   Change Character Font\n"
         << " Enter your selection ==> ";
    cin >> choice;
    if ( choice == 1 )
            set_margins();
    else if ( choice == 2 )
            set_spacing();
    else if ( choice == 3 )
            set_font();
}
```

The function `set_margins()` works by calling two other functions—`set_leftright()` and `set_topbottom()`:

```
void set_margins()
{
    int choice;

    cout << "1. Left/right    2. Top/bottom\n";
    cin >> choice;
    if ( choice == 1 )
        set_leftright();
    else if ( choice == 2 )
        set_topbottom();
}
```

If `set_leftright()` and `set_topbottom()` can be implemented as simple, direct functions, then there is no need to decompose them further. Perhaps `set_spacing()` is also simple enough so that no further functional decomposition is necessary.

As our programs become more complex, the top-down design philosophy will become more useful and natural. Top-down design is part of a larger philosophy called *structured programming*. Structured programming concepts began in the late 1960s. Attacking program development in an organized manner leads to code that is more correct and reliable. C++ and C fully support the concepts of structured programming. C++ goes one step further by also providing a means to do *object-oriented* programming, which will be introduced in chapter 8. In object-oriented programming, the task of program development is approached slightly differently. The principles of structured programming are not abandoned, although they are used on a somewhat different scale.

Exercises

1. What is top-down design?

2. How is a structure chart different from a flowchart?

3. What is step-wise refinement?

4. Why should a programmer consider using functions?

6.9 STANDARD LIBRARY FUNCTIONS

Properly written functions are self-contained units that can be inserted and used within a wide variety of different programs. All the information that a function needs to do its job is communicated to the function via the parameter list. Values can be returned through the function return mechanism. Actual parameters can be modified in the case of call-by-reference. Well-written functions do not depend on the outside world to do their job. If a complete, self-contained, and robust function is general enough to be used in a wide variety of programs, it might become part of a *library* of functions. *Library functions* are software tools that can be pulled out and used when needed. They work as is off the shelf. They do not require any additional programming to work with a new program.

Actually, we have been using functions (other than `main()` itself) since the very first program, because the `<<` and `>>` operators associated with the `cout` and `cin` stream objects are special types of functions. They are so special that discussion of them is deferred until chapter 11. Standard functions will be introduced throughout the text as needed. For now, the following collection of functions might prove useful and readily applicable to the tasks at hand.

A variety of mathematical functions are available for mathematical, scientific, and engineering calculations. The prototypes for these functions are found in `<math.h>`, which must be `#included` in programs that use these functions. Table 6.1 includes many of the functions found in `<math.h>`. In each case x and y represent `double` values and a result of type `double` is returned. They all use call-by-value protocol; therefore, both constants and variables can be passed to them, and the variables passed to them are guaranteed not to be modifed.

Table 6.1   Mathematical Functions

`acos(x)`	arccosine of x
`asin(x)`	arcsine of x
`atan(x)`	arctangent of x
`ceil(x)`	ceiling of x
`cos(x)`	cosine of x
`cosh(x)`	hyperbolic cosine of x
`exp(x)`	e^x
`fabs(x)`	absolute value of x
`floor(x)`	floor of x
`fmod(x, y)`	x modulus y
`log(x)`	$\log_e x$
`log10(x)`	$\log_{10} x$
`pow(x, y)`	x^y
`sin(x)`	sine of x
`sinh(x)`	hyperbolic sine of x
`sqrt(x)`	square root of x
`tan(x)`	tangent of x
`tanh(x)`	hyperbolic tangent of x

Program 6.8 uses some well-known formulas from algebra. If P_1 is a point at (x_1, y_1) and P_2 is a point at (x_2, y_2), then the distance between the points is found by

$$d\left(P_1, P_2\right) = \sqrt{\left(x_1 - x_2\right)^2 + \left(y_1 - y_2\right)^2}$$

The midpoint is found by averaging the x and y values.

The slope, m, of the line passing through P_1 and P_2 is found by

$$m = \frac{y_2 - y_1}{x_2 - x_1}$$

Given the slope and one point, the equation for the line can be found by the point-slope equation

$$y - y_1 = m(x - x_1)$$
$$y = mx - mx_1 + y_1$$
$$y = mx + (y_1 - mx_1)$$

```
#include <iostream.h>
#include <math.h>

void print_point(double x, double y) {
    cout << '(' << x << ',' << y << ')';
}

double distance(double x1, double y1, double x2, double y2) {
    return sqrt( (x1 - x2)*(x1 - x2) + (y1 - y2)*(y1 - y2) );
}

void print_midpoint(double x1, double y1, double x2, double y2) {
    cout << "The midpoint between ";
    print_point(x1, y1);
    cout << " and ";
    print_point(x2, y2);
    cout << " is ";
    print_point((x1 + x2)/2, (y1 + y2)/2);
    cout << '\n';
}

double slope(double x1, double y1, double x2, double y2) {
    if ( x2 - x1 == 0 ) {
        cout << "Warning!  Undefined slope.\n";
        return 1.0e30;  /*  High slope!  */
    }
    return (y2 - y1)/(x2 - x1);
}

double y_intercept(double x1, double y1, double x2, double y2) {
    return y1 - slope(x1, y1, x2, y2)*x1;
}

void print_equation(double x1, double y1, double x2, double y2) {
    cout << "The equation for the line passing through the points\n ";
    print_point(x1, y1);
    cout << " and ";
    print_point(x2, y2);
    cout << " is:\n y = " << slope(x1, y1, x2, y2)
        << "x + " << y_intercept(x1, y1, x2, y2) << '\n';
}

void main() {
    double x_1, y_1, x_2, y_2;
```

```
cout << "Please enter the coordinates of the two points: ";
cin >> x_1 >> y_1 >> x_2 >> y_2;
cout << "The distance between the points ";
print_point(x_1, y_1);
cout << " and ";
print_point(x_2, y_2);
cout << " is " << distance(x_1, y_1, x_2, y_2) << '\n';
print_midpoint(x_1, y_1, x_2, y_2);
print_equation(x_1, y_1, x_2, y_2);
}
```

Program 6.8

<math.h> is included so that the square root function can be used. Some systems require special instructions to the linker to allow programs to use these library functions.

Often characters need to be manipulated to determine if they are alphabetic characters (letters) or digits or something else. Lowercase letters need to be capitalized, or maybe just classified as being upper- or lowercase. The functions listed in table 6.2 and declared in <ctype.h> are handy for character processing. The following are some C++ character routines that could be useful to us. Since they are declared in the file <ctype.h>, this file must be #included in any programs that use them. The parameter x is officially an int. Recall that the int is the most "natural" type on any given machine; a char value is automatically promoted to an int for purposes of evaluating an expression. In this case, a char passed to any of these routines will be cast automatically to an int, so both chars and ints work equally well. Each also officially returns an int value.

Table 6.2   Character Functions

Boolean Functions (Return 1 or 1)

isalnum(x)	is x alphanumeric?
isalpha(x)	is x alphabetic?
isdigit(x)	is x a digit?
islower(x)	is x lowercase?
isprint(x)	is x printable?
ispunct(x)	is x punctuation?
isspace(x)	is x white space?
isupper(x)	is x uppercase?

Character Conversion Functions

tolower(x)	returns the lowercase version of x
toupper(x)	returns the uppercase version of x

The latter two routines in table 6.2 can simplify code like the following:

```
if ( ch == 'Q'  ||  ch == 'q' )
    do_quit_routine();
```

The programmer makes sure that both upper- and lowercase Q lead to the call of the function do_quit_routine(). A shorter, clearer way could be

```
if ( toupper(ch) == 'Q' )
    do_quit_routine();
```

We could write our own `toupper()` function. Consulting the ASCII chart in the appendix, we see that the letters `'A'` through `'Z'` have the ASCII values of 65 through 90. The letters `a` through `'z'` correspond to the values 97 through 122. `toupper()` could be written:

```
int my_toupper(int c) {
    if ( c >= 65  &&  c <= 90 )
        return c + 32;
    else
        return c;
}
```

This works fine, but if a given library function is available to do the job, it should be used instead. Programs that use standard library routines are more portable to other platforms. Compiler vendors normally provide standard library routines with their development environment. `my_toupper()` works well on most systems, but some mainframe computers use a character code known as EBCDIC (Extended Binary Coded Decimal Interchange Code). The characters in EBCDIC are arranged differently than in ASCII; therefore, the function `my_toupper()` would have to be modified to work correctly on an EBCDIC system. The better approach, including `<ctype.h>` and using its `toupper()` function, relies on the compiler vendor's library to contain `toupper()` code that works correctly for that platform's particular character set.

A second reason for using library routines is that there is a chance that they are optimized for that particular system. The library functions are likely to have been developed by the same company (maybe even some of the same programmers) that built the compiler; thus, they may take advantage of features that are handled particularly well by that compiler. This "inside" information about how the compiler works may be undocumented or unknown to the typical C++ programmer. Some of the functions may actually be totally or partially written in assembly language to make them as fast as possible.

The third reason is that there is some assurance that the function has been thoroughly tested to become a part of a commercial library. With more exciting problems to solve, programmers do not need any more code to anguish over, especially when off-the-shelf solutions may be readily available.

Exercises

1. What are the consequences of not using a standard library function, if one exists to do the job?

2. What types are the parameters and return values for most of the `<math.h>` functions?

3. What types are the parameters for most of the `<ctype.h>` routines?

4. What is the difference between the `toupper()` and `isupper()` routines?

6.10 STORAGE CLASSES

In program 6.7, the voting program, all of the functions had their own local variables. Local variables are declared within the curly braces that delimit the body of a function. For example, the function `wait_for_official_start()` contains a local integer called `password`. This variable has meaning only within `wait_for_official_start()`. No other variable named `password` is declared in any of the other functions. Even if another function within the same program declared a local variable named `password`, this variable would be distinct from the `password` in `wait_for_official_start()`. The functions `poll_voters()` and `get_vote()` both contain a local variable named `vote`. In both functions it is declared to be of type `int`. These variables are different; they occupy different memory locations and have different lifetimes. As mentioned previously, this concept of locality is crucial to modern computer programming.

In chapters 2 and 3, variables were seen to possess several properties. Every variable has a name, a type, a value, and a storage location in the computer's memory. The name is used by the programmer to reference the variable with the program. The variable's type dictates what operations may be performed on the variable and what range of values it can assume. A variable has a value because the value of a variable is the binary pattern of 0s and 1s that are found in its storage location in memory. When the only variables used were local to `main()` and other functions were not written, this picture of variables was adequate. We now see that variables also have a *scope* and a *lifetime*.

The *scope* of a variable refers to the portion of the source code within which the variable's name has meaning. A variable can be accessed (i.e., be assigned, participate in a calculation, be sent to a function, etc.) within its scope, and it cannot be accessed outside of its scope. In the voting program, the scope of `password` is the body of `wait_for_official_start()`, after the point of its declaration. The scope of the `START_PASSWORD` and `END_PASSWORD` constants is the whole program, since they are declared outside of and above all of the functions within the program. Any of the functions can use either of these constants. Local variables are known as *automatic variables* because memory is allocated for them automatically at the point of declaration within the function and deallocated automatically when the function is finished. The reserved word `auto` can be used to indicate that the variable is an automatic variable:

```
void sum_account(float pmt, int time) {
    auto float sub_total;
    .
    .           // Rest of body follows...
    .
```

but in practice, this is never done. The `auto` specifies that the variable is of `auto` *storage* class. A variable's *lifetime*, or persistence, is determined by its storage class. The storage class determines how long the memory space allocated for the variable is kept. The memory occupied by a variable declared within a function can be released when a particular function call is finished. The variable is said to *go out of scope* since the scope of the local variable (the function) is gone. Since `auto` variables for a particular function are created at their point of declaration within the function and destroyed when the function exits, the local variables may be created and destroyed many times over if the function is called multiple times in the course of the program's execution. The variables local to `main()` are in existence from their point of declaration for the remainder of the life of the program, since `main()` is the first function executed when the program begins executing. When `main()` calls another function (such as `poll_voters()` above), `main()` is *not* finished executing, it is merely temporarily passing control (and possibly some information) to another function that will eventually return back to `main()`. `main()`'s auto variables "live" for the whole program. In program 6.7, when `poll_voters()` is called from `main()`, space for `vote` is allocated. The variable `vote` within the function `get_vote()` does not exist until `get_vote()` is called, at which time both `poll_voters()`'s `vote` and `get_vote()`'s `vote` exist in memory. Then the space allocated for `vote` in `get_vote()` is deallocated and thus freed up for possible use by other functions' local variables. The space could also be used again by `get_vote()`, when it is called again. It would be purely accidental if the actual memory location used to store `vote` was identical in multiple calls of `get_vote()`, but sometimes it happens, especially if calls to the same function are made one right after another. Eventually, the `vote` inside of `poll_voters()` will also be released.

`auto` variables and function parameters are allocated in a portion of memory known as the *stack*. A piece of data stored in the stack area of memory is said to be *pushed* onto the top of the stack, since access to the stack is limited to a last-in, first-out sequence. The inverse of pushing something onto the stack is *popping* an object off the top of the stack. Interaction with the stack can be demonstrated with the call of the function `dummy_calc()`:

```
float dummy_calc(int x, double y)
{
    int a = 45;
    float b = 10.0;

    return (x + a)/(y + b);
}
```

When the statement `number = dummy_calc(5, 2.0);` is encountered in a program, the following events occur:

1. The space for the function's return value, if any (here a float), is allocated on the stack.
2. The program's current position (return address for the program) is pushed onto the stack.
3. The parameters (here, the values of 5 and 2.0) are copied onto the stack (exact order is unspecified by the language).
4. The `auto` variables a and b within `dummy_calc()` are created on the stack.
5. The function body is executed.
6. The value of the expression for the return is copied into space reversed in step 1.
7. The auto variables are popped off the stack and lost.
8. The parameters are popped off the stack and lost.
9. The return address is popped off the stack and used to return to the client function (without the return address the function would not know which of possibly many client functions called it and would not know where to go back to).
10. The return value is popped off the stack and used by the client function.

These events are generally followed, but actual details vary from system to system. (For example, some compilers on certain systems might communicate the return value back to the client function through a register instead of using stack space.) The steps listed above are meant to outline the typical function call protocol.

You've been using functions without knowing that all of this was going on behind the scenes. The compiler generates the proper code to make sure the interaction with the stack is done properly. In general, the programmer does not need to worry about the low-level details. This outline provides a look into the life of `auto` variables.

Objects of storage class `auto` are created within *blocks*. The only blocks we've encountered so far have been function bodies. In C++, blocks are created any time variables are declared within curly braces. Program 6.9:

```
void main() {
    int x = 1, y = 2;
    cout << x << ' ' << y '\n';
    {
        int x = 10, a = 20, b = 30;
        cout << x << " << y << " << a << " << b << '\n';
    }
    cout << x << ' ' << y '\n';
}
```

Program 6.9

contains two blocks: the body of the function `main()` declaring the variables x and y, and the inner block declaring the variables x, a, and b. The inner block is defined by the two statements within the inner curly braces. The variables x, a, and b declared within the inner block cannot be used outside of that block or before their point of declaration within that block. Variables declared in an outer block can be freely used in an inner block unless the inner block declares a variable with the same name as a variable in the outer block. If a variable in an inner block is given the same name as a variable in an outer block, the variable in the outer block cannot be accessed in the inner block. The variables with the same name are distinct entities occupying different areas of storage. The above code will print:

```
1  2
10  2  20  30
1  2
```

The outer x is inaccessible from within the inner block. The inner variables do not exist in memory until the inner block is entered. The variables cease to exist upon block exit. Blocks can be indefinitely nested—it is permissible to have blocks within blocks, within other blocks, within other blocks, . . .

Said another way, the scope of a variable declared somewhere within a pair of curly braces (like the body of a function, inside the compound statement of an `if`, `while`, `do...while`, etc. body, or arbitrarily placed curly braces as in program 6.9) extends from the point of the definition to the close curly brace that matches its level of nesting. (`auto` variables exist from their point of declaration within a block to the end of that block.) Consider the following code fragment:

```
void f() {
    //   x and y are NOT accessible
    int x;  //   Now x can be used, but NOT y
    //   Etc. (do some stuff...)
    do {
        //   x can still be used, but NOT y
        int y;  //   Now both x and y can be used
        cin >> x;
        //   Etc. (do some stuff...)
    } while ( x != 999 );
    //   Etc. (do some stuff...)
    //   x still accessible, but NOT y
}   //   Now both x and y are again NOT accessible
```

After the body of the loop, y is inaccessible since the close curly brace before the while matches the open curly brace after which y was declared. Notice that x is visible in both the outer scope and inner scope. It is not until the end of the function that the close curly brace is found that matches the open curly brace that precedes x's declaration.

Variables can be declared outside of all functions, similar to the way the constants START_PASSWORD and END_PASSWORD were declared:

```
#include <iostream.h>

int n;

void f(int x) {
    n = x + n;
}

void main() {
    int a;
    cin >> a >> n;
    f(a);
    cout << n;
}
```

In this example, n is an *external* variable. It has `extern` storage class. `extern` means the variables are not declared within any function, including `main()`. Many times these `extern` variables are declared at the top of the program source code. They are visible (i.e., their scope is valid) from where they are defined to the end of the source code. When external variables are declared at the top of the file, they are known as *global variables*. Global variables can be used anywhere in the file, in any function. Some might be tempted to rewrite program 6.7 as program 6.10.

```cpp
#include <iostream.h>

const int START_PASSWORD = 3265,
          END_PASSWORD  = 1193;
//  Global variables
int password, in_vote, fujimoto_votes, jones_votes, alvarez_votes, total_votes;

void wait_for_official_start() {
     do {    //  Repeat until correct password is entered
          cout << "Please enter password to begin program.\n";
          cin >> password;
     } while ( password != START_PASSWORD );
}

void get_vote() {
     do {
          cout << "Please cast your vote: \n"
                  "1  Fujimoto \n"
                  "2  Jones \n"
                  "3  Alvarez \n";
          cin >> current_vote;
     } while ( in_vote != 1 && in_vote != 2 && in_vote != 3 && in_vote !=
               END_PASSWORD );
}

void poll_voters() {
     //  Clear all votes to begin session
     fujimoto_votes = 0;  jones_votes = 0;  alvarez_votes = 0;
     do { //  Loop until poll closes and all votes are in
          get_vote();
          if ( in_vote == 1 )
             fujimoto_votes++;
          else if ( in_vote == 2 )
             jones_votes++;
          else if ( in_vote == 3 )
             alvarez_votes++;
     } while ( in_vote != END_PASSWORD );
}

void print_results() {
     //  Tabulate and report results
     total_votes = fujimoto_votes + jones_votes + alvarez_votes;
     cout << "Fujimoto received " << fujimoto_votes
          << " votes (" << 100.0*fujimoto_votes/total_votes << "%)\n";
     cout << "Jones     received " << jones_votes
          << " votes (" << 100.0*jones_votes/total_votes << "%)\n";
     cout << "Alvarez   received " << alvarez_votes
          << " votes (" << 100.0*alvarez_votes/total_votes << "%)\n";
     if ( fujimoto_votes > jones_votes  &&  fujimoto_votes > alvarez_votes )
         cout << "Fujimoto won the election.\n";
     else if ( jones_votes > fujimoto_votes  &&  jones_votes > alvarez_votes )
         cout << "Jones won the election.\n";
     else if ( alvarez_votes > fujimoto_votes  &&  alvarez_votes > jones_votes )
         cout << "Alvarez won the election.\n";
     else if ( fujimoto_votes == jones_votes )
```

```
        if ( fujimoto_votes == alvarez_votes )
                cout << "There is a three way tie for first place.\n";
        else   //  Already determined that Alvarez did not win
                cout << "Fujimoto and Jones tied for first place.\n";
    else if ( jones_votes == alvarez_votes )
            //  Already determined that Fujimoto did not win
            cout << "Jones and Alvarez tied for first place.\n";
    else
            cout << "Fujimoto and Alvarez tied for first place.\n";
}
void main() {
    wait_for_official_start();
    poll_voters();
    print_results();
}
```

Program 6.10

In program 6.10, no parameters, no return values, and no local variables are used. All information is communicated to the functions through shared global variables. The novice programmer might remark "Global variables are great. Now I don't need to type in all those confusing parameters."

As it turns out, global variables are more of a curse than a blessing. As soon as global variables appear in a function, that function immediately becomes *unreuseable* in another program. The function only works in one particular program for a particular set of global variables. Reusing it in another program means forcing a set of global variables into the new program in possibly an awkward fashion. Convenient library functions written with global variables would be impractical to use.

Using global variables is dangerous when constructing nontrivial programs. In general, it is good programming practice to write functions as independent from each other as possible. This means that modifying function a() should not "break" a perfectly performing function b(). When the function parameter passing/return protocol is breached by using global variables, functional independence is undermined. Function a() may be modified so that it appears to be fixed, but it inadvertently modifies a global variable that b() uses. Function b() no longer works (although it's still correct, a() is the problem), and unnecessary time is spent trying to "correct" a correctly written function. Consider the small example:

```
/*  Global variables  */
int maxtime;
int overtime;
int comptime;
    .
    .     /*  Numerous other globals declared */
    .

void a()
{
int temptime, counter = 0;
    .
    .     /*  Lots of convoluted code here...  */
    .
overtime = 0.3*(overtime + temptime) + basesal;

/*  Oops, programmer meant to assign to comptime but
    accidentally typed overtime instead.  The variable overtime
    is not even supposed to be involved in a().
    Unfortunately, global variables are public to all
    functions.  Testing that is far from exhaustive indicates
    that a() looks like it's working ok.  */

        .
        .     /*  More convoluted code ...  */
        .
}
```

```
void b()
{
    int fltsde, dser;
    .
    .          /*    Some complex code goes here  */
    .
    basesal = overtime + comptime - fltsde;
     /*  b() using overtime global messed up by a()
         and produces an immediately noticeable error  */
    .
    .          /*   Some more complex code goes here  */
    .
}
```

When parameters are passed to functions, the names of the formal parameters are separate from any global names. Parameter names and local variable names override global variable names and render global variables of the same name invisible in that section of code. If no global variables are used, the function parameter/return protocol is used, and b() is known to work correctly, then a typographical error in a() will only affect a()'s parameters and return values, not any unrelated stray global variables.

Global variables do offer some advantages. It is faster to use global variables in functions because values of parameters need to be copied onto the stack in order to be passed, and the stack needs to be cleaned up (the parameters popped off) when the function is done. All this stack interaction takes time to perform. Also, stack space is not taken up by global variables. Space for extern variables is allocated at the beginning of the program execution in a place in memory (usually called *static memory*) separate from the stack. Whereas auto variables are not initialized (they are created on the stack, and their value becomes whatever was left on the stack in the position they acquire) and contain garbage upon creation, extern variables are automatically initialized to zero, unless initialized with another value. For most programs, the advantages of *not* using global variables (greater programming productivity and program correctness) far outweigh the slight efficiency advantage they provide.

The lifetime of extern variables is the same as the program itself. auto variables are created upon function entry and destroyed upon function exit. extern variables tie up a piece of memory for the life of the program, and auto variables dynamically allocate and deallocate memory as needed.

C++ provides the means to declare variables local to a particular function that have storage characteristics similar to externs. The class static can be used with local variables:

```
int keep_track(int sightings) {
    static int count = 0;
    return count += sightings;
}
```

Here, count is declared to be a static int variable. It is not created on the stack like an auto variable. Instead, it is placed in memory that is reserved for the life of the program, similar to the way externs are allocated. Its value is retained between calls to the function keep_track(). Normal auto variables are lost between function invocations. The initialization setting count to zero is done only once, at the beginning of the program's execution. Unlike an extern variable, however, a static variable declared within a function is still local to that function. It enjoys the same privacy benefits as auto variables and cannot interfere with other functions or be changed accidentally by other functions. Variables of class static used within functions are not used that often. Generally, it is better for space to be allocated and deallocated on the stack as needed instead of tying up memory for the duration of the program's execution.

The `static` specifier has additional meanings that are examined in future chapters.

One additonal storage class is notable. The storage class `register` attempts to store values in one of the processor's registers:

```
register int i;
```

Here `i` is declared to be an `int`, and the `register` specifier is a suggestion to the compiler that space for `i` should not be allocated on the stack or any part of RAM. The request is to store `i`'s value within a register. Since the machine has only a small number of registers, and since many of these registers are being used by the program at runtime for other purposes, the compiler may not grant the request. If a register is unavailable, the default storage class is `auto`; thus, `register` variables can only be used as local variables in functions. Also, not all data types can be of `register` class. Some processors cannot store floating point types in `registers`. Some compilers can be set up to use register variables when possible, even if the `register` storage class is not specified.

Registers can be accessed much more quickly than RAM. Programmers often use `register` variables to improve the program's execution speed, especially in time-critical sections of code. Often variables used as counters within loop statements are designated as class `register` to speed up the loops. For example:

```
register int i;
for ( i = 0;  i < 100;  i++ )
    . . .
```

Since the variable `i` is continuously being compared to 100 and incremented, it might be advantageous to make its storage class `register`.

Exercises

1. Why are `auto` variables often called local variables?

2. In what special part of memory are `auto` variables stored?

3. Why are variables of `extern` storage class often called global variables?

4. Why is the unrestrained use of global variables dangerous?

5. How do `static` variables declared within functions behave differently from `auto` variables?

6. Why is the `register` specifier merely a suggestion to the compiler and not an order that must always be followed?

7. What storage class is a `register` variable if the compiler decides not to place it in a register?

6.11 INLINE FUNCTIONS

Writing large programs without the ability to create functions would be a very difficult task indeed. Not only do functions provide a means of avoiding code duplication, but they also aid in organizing a program and localizing errors. The proper use of functions greatly speeds up the program development process.

The small price to pay for the use of functions is *function call overhead*. Function call overhead is the amount of work that must be done to call and return from the function. Consider the following function:

```
void increment(int &x, int val) {
    x += val;
}
```

Calling the function as

```
increment(number, 10);
```

accomplishes the same thing simply

```
number += 10;
```

except it is restricted to `int`s. The machine code that the compiler generates to call the function, perform the calculation, and return the result is larger than the code required to use the += operator. For example, on one system, the function call code required 29 bytes. Using the += operator in the same situation required only four bytes. In this case, it is inappropriate to create such an `increment()` function. The code produced is larger and takes much longer to execute. The function produces slower, larger code, and it is not as obvious to use as the += operator.

For functions with more than about three lines of code, the function call overhead is considered acceptable. A larger function will be less dominated by the overhead. Does this mean that small functions (consisting of three lines or less) should not be written? C++ provides a way to help overcome the function call overhead problem by making available `inline` functions. The reserved word `inline` is placed before the return type of the function. An `inline` function call may not actually result in a real function call. The compiler may duplicate the body of the function with appropriate substitution of parameters at each call to the function. As in the case of `register` variables, the compiler may choose to ignore the `inline` directive and produce a normal function call. When the above function is made inline:

```
inline int increment(int &x, int val) {
    return x += val;
}
```

The compiler produces the same code as if the += operator had been used. Consider the following `skewed_sum_of_squares()` function:

```
inline int skewed_sum_of_squares(int x, int y) {
    int offset = x + y - 5.221;
    return x*x + y*y + offset;
}
```

When a call to the function is made

```
z = skewed_sum_of_squares(a, 9);
```

the compiler might not produce a function call but instead may produce code equivalent to

```
z = a*a + 9*9 + (a + 9 - 5.221);
```

thereby avoiding the function call overhead. This process is called *inline expansion*.

The disadvantage of `inline` functions is that (if the compiler chooses to make them `inline`) their code is duplicated every place they are used. That is why `inline` functions are usually kept to three lines or less. If a large function were made `inline` and called many times in different places within a program, the program's compiled size would be much larger than if the function were not `inline`.

`inline` functions are always faster than non-`inline` versions. `inline` functions provide all the good programming features of regular functions (local variables, call-by-value, modularization, conceptual simplicity, etc.) without the overhead but should only be used for functions of around three lines or less. Even when `inline` functions are kept small, programmers should be careful. Sometimes `inline` function code secretly gets big:

```
inline void f1() {
    // Do something...
}

inline void f2() {
    // Do something...
    f1();
    // Do something else...
}

inline void f3() {
    // Do something...
    f2();
    // Do something else...
}
```

Every call to `f3()` not only duplicates `f3()`'s code, but also `f2()`'s code and `f1()`'s code. If `f1()` is three lines long, `f2()` is five lines long, and `f3()` is five lines long, then each call of `f3()` will generate the 13 lines of the combined `inline` code.

Some compilers place additional restrictions on `inline` functions. For example, `inline` functions contained within loops or called more than once in the same statement may not be compiled as `inline`. The compiler might produce machine code that generates normal function calls instead.

Exercises

1. What is function call overhead?

2. What does the `inline` specifier mean?

Assignments

1. Write a function called `gcf()` which has the following prototype:

    ```
    int gcf(int, int);
    ```

    `gcf()` accepts two `int` parameters and returns their greatest common factor. For example, `gcf(12, 18)` would return 6, since the greatest common factor of 12 and 18 is 6. One approach to writing this function is to try all the numbers from 1 to the smaller argument and find the largest of these numbers that will divide evenly (with no remainder) into both arguments. (1 will divide evenly into all integers.) Provide a small `main()` function that can be used to test your `gcf()` function. Do *not* do any I/O inside of the `gcf()` function.

2. Write a pair of functions `f_to_c()` and `c_to_f()` whose prototypes are:

```
double f_to_c(double);
double c_to_f(double);
```

The function `f_to_c()` converts its double precision floating point argument from degrees Fahrenheit to Celsius and returns the result. `c_to_f()` provides the inverse conversion. The formulas (from chemistry) are:

$$F = \frac{9}{5}C + 32 \qquad\qquad C = \frac{5}{9}\left(F - 32\right)$$

Provide a small `main()` function that tests your conversion routines. Do *not* do any I/O inside of the conversion functions.

3. A *prime* number is any integer greater than one that is evenly divisible only by itself and 1. For example, the numbers 2, 3, 5, and 7 are prime while 9, 10, and 15 are not. Write a function called `is_prime()` that accepts an integer greater than 1 and returns 1 if the integer is prime or 0 if it is not. The computer can test an integer by repeatedly dividing it by integers smaller than itself but larger than 1 and checking whether the quotient is a whole number. If so, the number is not prime. Your program should call `is_prime()` for all the integers between 2 and 100 and print those numbers that are indeed prime. The prototype for the function is

```
int is_prime(int);
```

Do *not* do any I/O inside of the function.

4. Two integers greater than 1 are said to be *relatively prime* to each other if they have no common factor other than 1. For example, 40 and 49 are relatively prime to each other because the factors of 40 are 1, 2, 4, 5, 8, 10, 20, and 40, whereas the factors of 49 are 1, 7, and 49. Their only common factor is 1. 12 and 15 are not relatively prime because 3 is a factor of both 12 and 15. Write a function called `are_relatively_prime()` that accepts two integer values and returns 1 if the two values are relatively prime and returns 0 if the two values are not relatively prime. One way to do this is to see if 2 divides evenly into the smaller value. If so, divide it into the larger value. If it goes into the larger value evenly, return 1; otherwise, continue by adding 1 to the original number (in this case 2) and repeating the process. If you try all the numbers up to and including the smaller value and have found none that divide both values evenly, then return 0. The function's prototype is:

```
int are_relatively_prime (int, int);
```

Do *not* do any I/O inside of the `are_relatively_prime()` function.

5. Write a function called `least_common_multiple()`. Its prototype is

```
int least_common_multiple(int, int);
```

It returns the least common multiple of the positive parameters `x` and `y`. Recall that the least common multiple (LCM) is used to find common denominators when adding fractions. The LCM of 8 and 12 is 24:

```
8, 16, 24, 32, 40, 48, ...
12, 24, 36, 48, 60, ...
```

If one wanted to add the fractions 1/8 + 1/12, the common denominator 24 would be used: 3/24 + 2/24 = 5/24.

The following algorithm can be followed to find the LCM of positive integers x and y:

1. Are x and y the same? If so, return x (or y, it doesn't matter—they're the same). Proceed with step 6.
2. Use four accessory variables min (for current minimum), min_inc (for minimum increment), max (for current maximum), and max_inc (for maximum increment). Let both max and max_inc be the larger of x and y, and let both min and min_inc be the smaller of the two (step 1 guarantees they're not the same).
3. Repeat steps 4 and 5 until min is greater than or equal to max:
4. Keep increasing min by min_inc until min is greater than or equal to max.
5. If min and max are equal, then return min (or max—they're the same) and proceed with step 6; otherwise, increase max by max_inc and proceed with step 3.
6. You're all done!

Translate the above algorithm into the C++ function least_common_multiple(). Use the following main() to test your function:

```
void main() {
    int val1, val2;
    cout << "Enter values to test <Q> quits.\n";
    while ( cin >> val1 >> val2, cin.good() )
        cout << "The LCM of " << val1 << " and " << val2 << " is "
            << least_common_multiple(val1, val2) << '\n';
}
```

6. Write a function called is_vowel() that returns 1 if the char argument passed is a vowel (A, E, I, O, or U); or zero if any other character is passed. Write a small main() to test your function. The function's prototype is

```
int is_vowel(char);
```

7. Write a program that uses redirection to read in a textfile and count the number of vowels ('A', 'a', 'E', 'e', 'I', 'i', 'O', 'o', 'U', 'u'), consonants, and digits ('0'–'9') contained in that file. Other punctuation marks or characters are ignored. You may use the standard routines defined in <ctype.h> (isalpha(), isdigit(), toupper(), etc.) but also write the functions isvowel() and isconsonant() to assist your program. isvowel() expects a char parameter and returns 1 if the character passed is a vowel, 0 otherwise. isconsonant() works in a similar fashion indicating whether or not the character passed to it is a consonant.

You should make up a small textfile with the editor to test your program. For example, scanning the file containing:

```
Mary (don't know her last name) had 125
little lambs. So what?
```

would result in the following output:

```
Number of vowels:    13
Number of consonants: 30
Number of digits:     3
```

8. Write a function called reduce_fraction() with the following prototype:

```
void reduce_fraction (int numerator, int denominator, int &red_num,
                      int       &red_dem);
```

which produces `red_num/red_dem`, the reduced form of `numerator/demoninator`. The following code:

```
reduce_fraction(12, 36, x, y);
cout << x << '/' << y;
```

would print 1/3. Write a small `main()` routine to test your function.

9. A rational number, you recall, can be expressed as the ratio of two integers `a/b`, where `b` is not equal to `0`. Write a program that performs addition, subtraction, multiplication, and division on rational numbers. The program should display the results reduced to lowest terms (do *not* make improper fractions into mixed numbers). The input should be natural. One should be able to type in the following:

```
1/4+2/3
```

The result should be displayed:

```
11/12
```

You should construct separate functions to handle the adding, subtracting, multiplying, and dividing. A separate function should reduce the result (see assignment 8). Another function should be used to print a rational number. The program should continuously request expressions to evaluate until the user terminates the program by entering a non-number where a number is expected.
Sample run:

```
Enter expression: 1/2+1/3
1/2 + 1/3 = 5/6
Enter expression: 3/4/5/3
3/4 / 5/3 = 9/20
```

It will be very helpful to devise a function called `lcm()` (see assignment 5) which finds the least common multiple of two integers (so that you can find the least common denominator when adding and subtracting). Another helpful function is `gcf()` (see assigment 1) that finds the greatest common factor (or greatest common divisor) of two integers (so that you can easily reduce any fraction to lowest terms). Since a rational number is, by definition, the ratio of two integers, you will have no need of floating types anywhere in your program. Remember that no function in your program should exceed one printed page in length.

10. Recall the elementary length conversion equations:

```
2.54 cm = 1 in    12 in = 1 ft    5280 ft = 1 mi

100 cm = 1 m   1000 m = 1 km
```

Write a program that displays a menu that prompts the user to select a conversion to be performed. The user is then asked for the value to be converted, and the result is calculated and then displayed. The following menu should be used:

```
Conversion Program

1.  miles to kilometers
2.  kilometers to miles
3.  Quit

Choice? ==>_
```

Your `main()` should appear as follows:

```
void main() {
    int choice;
    double value;
    do {
        choice = menu(); // menu() prints the menu and returns value chosen
        value = getvalue();
        if ( choice == 1 )
            cout << value << " mi = " << mi_to_km(value) << '\n';
        else if ( choice == 2 )
            cout << value << " km = " << km_to_mi(value) << '\n';
    } while ( choice != 3 );
}
```

Using *only* the conversion factors listed above create the following conversion functions (prototypes listed here):

```
double cm_to_in(double cm);
double in_to_ft(double in);
double ft_to_mi(double mi);
double cm_to_m(double cm);
double m_to_km(double m);
double in_to_cm(double in);
double ft_to_in(double ft);
double mi_to_ft(double mi);
double m_to_cm(double m);
double km_to_m(double km);
```

After writing these functions, write the functions needed by `main()`:

```
int menu();    //  Prints the menu, returns the menu option number chosen
double getvalue();   // Gets the value to be converted
double mi_to_km(double mi);   //  Does the conversion
double km_to_mi(double km);   //  Does the conversion
```

These last two functions should *not* use the conversion factors directly; they should use the appropriate function(s) from the group of ten above to do their work. For example, to convert from miles to kilometers, the following sequence must be followed:

```
miles –> feet –> inches –> centimeters –> meters –> kilometers
```

Each of the intermediate steps in the conversion can (and must) be performed by one of the ten functions above. Also, observe that none of the functions except `menu()` and `getvalue()` do any I/O (that is, do not access the `cout` and `cin` streams in any of the conversion functions).

CHAPTER 7

ARRAYS AND STRINGS

7.1 INTRODUCTION

All of the data types discussed so far represent simple, atomic entities. A variable represents a value, one number or one character. In this chapter we introduce an *aggregate* or *composite* type—the *array*. The array structure allows many values to be manipulated using only one name. We'll see how many useful programs would be inconvenient, if not impossible, to construct without arrays.

Reconsider program 2.10, from chapter 2. It allows the user to enter three grades and then prints the grades entered and their average. What if the user's needs change so that the average of four grades must be calculated, instead of three? Fortunately, the program is easily modified because it is so short. A variable called `grade4` is added to the declaration statement. Unfortunately, every executable statement in the program must be changed in some way. If the program were larger (say 1,250 lines instead of 6 lines), the prospects might be grim. Nonetheless, the modifications are completed correctly, and the program again works well for the satisfied user.

Several months later, when an additional grade must be considered, the work to add `grade4` is duplicated to add `grade5`. Eventually, 15 grades are going to be averaged. The program looks ugly with all the different variables, and work that should have been done only once has to be repeated many times. Surely, the programmer's productivity is plummeting. The worst news finally arrives: the program that averages 15 grades must now average 500 grades. There must be a better way to extend the program than adding 485 new variables (with their declarations) and modifying all the I/O and calculation statements.

Some will suggest program 5.8, from chapter 5, as a possible solution. However, program 2.10 and program 5.8 are fundamentally different programs. In program 2.10, any individual grade, through its variable, can be displayed and possibly modified at any time after it is entered. The value is stored in its own unique memory space. In program 5.8, once a grade is entered and its value contributes to the developing calculation, it can no longer be displayed or modified because all the grades use the same temporary memory location for storage.

C++'s array facility answers both concerns. A group of similar data values can be stored in unique memory locations, and each can be accessed through a single name. An *array* is a collection of *homogeneous* data values; that is, it contains elements that are all the same type. It is not possible to have a single array that contains both `int`s and `float`s simultaneously. A value in an array can be accessed given the array name and the item's *position* within the array.

7.2   ARRAY DECLARATIONS AND ASSIGNMENT

A collection of 100 `float`s named `num_list` can be declared

```
float num_list[100];
```

`num_list` is the *name* of the array, `float` is the *type* of its members, or elements, and 100 is the number of elements it contains. It is referred to as a one-dimensional array, since one value is used to access a position within the array. The following program declares an array, fills it with values, and then displays its contents:

```
#include <iostream.h>

void main()
{
     float num_list[3];
     int i;

     num_list[0] = 2.3;
     num_list[1] = 0.234;
     cout << "Enter a number: ";
     cin >> num_list[2];
     for ( i = 0;   i < 3;   i++ )
          cout << num_list[i] << ',';
     cout << "\b\n";  /*  backspace erases last comma  */
}
```

Program 7.1

Borrowing terminology from vectors and matrices in mathematics, the value within the square brackets is called a *subscript*. (The subscript is indicated in square brackets instead of a literal subscript, since most text-based displays and printers won't display literal subscripts.) The expression `num_list[2]` is read "num_list sub two," indicating position number two in the array. Since the first position in the array is position number zero, position number two would actually be the third position in the array. The subscript can be a constant or a variable, but it must be an integral value. In the declaration, the subscript indicates the size of the array. The last element in an array is actually one less than the array's declared size (since numbering begins at zero instead of one). A beginner often commits the error:

```
int a[10];
a[10] = 5;
```

Position 10 in array `a` is just past the array's end. `a[9]` is the array's last value.

In program 7.1, `num_list` is an array of `float`s, and `num_list[0]` is itself a `float`; thus, as illustrated above, the individual `float` element can be assigned, printed, read in from the keyboard, and participate in any activity that any normal `float` value can.

Arrays can be initialized when they are declared:

```
int    a[5] = { 12, 34, 22, 51, 10 };
char   c[4] = { 'a', 'b', 'c', 'd' };
float  f[2] = { 2.0, 3.4e-4 };
int    b[]  = { 12, 13, 14, 15, 16 };
```

The elements with which to initialize the array are enclosed in curly braces and separated by commas (like mathematical set notation). When the contents of the array are known before program execution, this initialization is much more convenient than initializing each element individually through its subscript. As illustrated by array `b` above, the subscript can be omitted because the compiler can calculate the size based on the number of elements listed in the initialization list.

Exercises

1. What are the three components of an array declaration?

2. How is an individual element accessed from an array?

3. What restrictions should be placed on an array subscript?

4. How can arrays be initialized when they are declared?

5. If an array is declared to hold 100 items, what is its *last* position?

7.3 ARRAYS AND FUNCTIONS

When passing arrays to functions, the size of the array does not need to be specified. Program 7.2, which follows, shows how arrays can be passed to functions.

```cpp
#include <iostream.h>
const int ARRSIZE = 10;

void get_array(float n_list[]) {
    int i;
    cout << "Please enter " << ARRSIZE << " values: ";
    for ( i = 0;  i < ARRSIZE;  i++ ) {
        cout << "Item number " << i + 1 << ": ";
        cin >> n_list[i];
    }
}

void show_array(float n_list[]) {
    int i;
    for ( i = 0;  i < ARRSIZE;  i++ )
        cout << n_list[i] << ',';
    cout << "\b\n";  //  Backspace to remove final comma
}

void main() {
    float values[ARRSIZE];
    get_array(values);
    show_array(values);
}
```

Program 7.2

Notice the syntax of the empty square brackets that indicate that the parameter is an array, but no size is given. This is only legal for describing function parameters; it cannot be used when defining actual array variables (unless an initialization list is provided).

The syntax can be made a little cleaner by using the `typedef` feature as shown in program 7.3.

```
#include <iostream.h>
const int ARRSIZE = 10;

typedef float NumberList[ARRSIZE];

void get_array(NumberList n_list) {
    int i;
    cout << "Please enter " << ARRSIZE << " values: ";
    for ( i = 0;   i < ARRSIZE;   i++ ) {
        cout << "Item number " << i + 1 << ": ";
        cin >> n_list[i];
    }
}

void show_array(NumberList n_list) {
    int i;
    for ( i = 0;   i < ARRSIZE;   i++ )
        cout << n_list[i] << ',';
     cout << "\b\n";   //  Backspace to remove final comma
}
void main() {
    NumberList values;
    get_array(values);
    show_array(values);
}
```

Program 7.3

The C++ `typedef` statement allows the programmer to create a new type name. The new type name can be used to declare variables of that type, just as one does with C++'s built-in data types. The statement

```
typedef float NumberList[ARRSIZE];
```

looks almost like it is declaring a variable called `NumberList`, which is an array of `ARRSIZE` `float`s. The `typedef` directive in front signifies that `NumberList` is *not* a *variable* name but is a *type* name. `NumberList` can now be used as a type name to declare variables of type array of `float`s throughout the program. Notice how it is used in the function headers to declare array parameters and in `main()` to declare the local variable. Our convention will be to capitalize the first letter of defined types. If the name is constructed from multiple words, the first letter in each of the words will be capitalized (as in the case of `NumberList`). Again, these visual differences between variable, constant, and defined type names greatly aid program readability.

Without the `typedef`, the function headers are

```
void get_array(float n_list[])
```

and

```
void show_array(float n_list[])
```

instead of

```
void get_array(NumberList n_list)
```

and

```
void show_array(NumberList n_list)
```

The `typedef` simplifies the syntax but renders the function less self-documenting. To a programmer familiar with arrays, it is obvious that the non-`typedef`-ed version does process an array of floating point numbers. The second version cannot be readily interpreted unless the definition of `NumberList` is well known or close at hand.

A natural question is "Why can the sizes of arrays be omitted in function parameter lists?" Another question might be "How does `get_array()` work in the call-by-value parameter passing scheme?"

Both questions can be addressed with one response. Arrays are the exception to the default call-by-value rule. C++ passes all arrays by reference; thus, when an array is passed to a function, all of its values are not copied to new locations. The address of the array, which is its starting point in memory, is passed. Any modification to the contents of the passed array within the function body will modify the contents of the array in the client function. The function does not need to know the size of the array, since the compiler does not need to allocate new space to store copies of all the values. The size of the array may be enclosed in the square brackets when the array parameter is declared in the parameter list of a function, but it is not required by the compiler and is ignored.

By not copying all the individual elements of an array to a new location (as is normally done in call-by-value), C++ keeps function calls with array parameters very efficient. It is possible that the amount of space required to hold the array might exceed the size of the space used to transfer parameters to functions (typically the stack), especially if the array is large. Even if enough space could be found, the amount of time required to copy all the elements of a large array to this new location might be significant.

7.4 INTERNAL REPRESENTATION

The elements of an array must occupy contiguous memory locations. Assume for the sake of discussion that integers (`ints`) on a particular system require two bytes of storage (a common size for integers for many C++ compilers on microcomputers). That means that if an array A of five `ints` (each two bytes) is located at address 2350 in memory, `A[0]` is located at 2350, `A[1]` is at 2352, `A[2]` is at 2354, `A[3]` is at 2356, and `A[4]` is at 2358. See figure 7.1. There can be no gaps between elements. This is because the compiler uses the expression `A[x]` to calculate the member's literal memory location. The array name, in this case A, is actually the address of the array's starting point in memory. `A[0]` is zero bytes from the starting position (or at the starting position), `A[1]` is two bytes away (since A contains two byte `ints`), `A[2]` is four bytes from the start, and so forth. Given an array's name and a subscript, the compiler can calculate the position of the array's element by the formula

$$e = A + si$$

where e is the address of the array element, A is the starting address of the array, s is the size in bytes of the array's component type, and i is the index or subscript.

It is the programmer's responsibility to make sure subscripts are within the bounds of the array. Given the declaration

```
int A[5];
```

The following statement is syntactically legal but can be disastrous:

```
A[5] = 3;
```

The last position in the array is `A[4]`, not `A[5]`. `A[5]` is the next position in memory past the end of the array. Of course, `A[6]`, `A[7]`, etc. would also be syntactically legal but logically erroneous. The statement

```
A[-1] = 2;
```

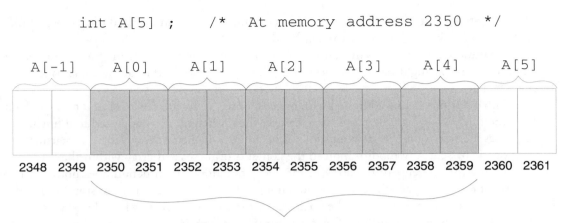

An Array's Internal Representation
Figure 7.1

can also be attempted. It places the value 2 just before the beginning of array A. Remember, the compiler uses the subscript to calculate a position in the array using the formula above. Any integral value subscript can be legally used in the formula.

What happens if one attempts `A[30] = 5;` when the array A was declared to hold only five `int`s? A position in memory outside the array is modified. It could be a memory location that contains a part of the program that is finished executing, and thus no ill effects are seen. It most likely corrupts another variable being used by the program. It could overwrite the stack where some local variable is stored. It could corrupt memory that contains part of the program that has yet to execute or part of the operating system, in which case the computer could lock up or do all kinds of interesting (but undesirable) things. Many multitasking operating systems won't allow programs to access memory beyond a small area allocated specifically for that program. In this situation, a program that goes outside of an array's bounds can hurt nothing else in the system but itself. The operating system may issue a warning that an attempt was made to access an illegal address (an address that was not reserved for that program to use). This is the best possible situation as far as the programmer is concerned, since an experienced programmer would immediately suspect (among a few other things) the possibility of exceeding the range of an array.

On many microcomputer systems that lack a protected operating system, the problem can be serious. This kind of bug is insidious because its results are often nonreproducible from one program run to another on the same machine, or it may usually work on one computer but usually not work on another. Array subscripts should be handled with extreme care.

Why doesn't the compiler check the subscript? For one reason, the subscript is often a variable, in which case its value at runtime is unknown to the compiler at compilation time. Since the compiler has had the size declared, it could generate code that, in effect, checks the range:

```
if ( i >= 0  &&  i < 5 )
     A[i] = 2;
else
     exit_error("Array subscript out of range");
```

Here, `exit_error()` is a function that would print a message and then terminate the program. The designers of the C++ language deemed this conditional expression, that would need to be used every time an array element is accessed, too inefficient. Since array elements may be accessed frequently in sophisticated programs, the overhead of checking each subscript could slow down the program significantly. Often, adept programmers can write code that checks for proper subscripting once for several array accesses, thus saving considerable time compared to checking the subscript at each access. In many situations, access to the array is done through a loop with a fixed beginning and ending value (like show_array() in program 7.2), and no check is needed. A variable subscript should be checked in any situation where its value is not guaranteed to be in the proper range, as in cases when it is retrieved from the user from the input stream cin.

Exercises

1. What is the purpose of a typedef statement?

2. Is a typedefed identifier a variable?

3. What kind of arithmetic does the compiler perform to access a[i]?

4. What is wrong with the following function that places zeroes in every position in an int array?

```
void initialize_array(int a[], int size) {
    //  size is number of elements in array a
    int count = -1;  //  So count starts at zero inside loop
    do {
        count++;
        a[count] = 0;
    } while ( count < size );
}
```

7.5 SAMPLE PROGRAM

Program 7.4 is the synthesis of programs 2.10 and 5.8. Here any number of grades can be entered, all the grades are displayed after the last grade is entered, and their average is calculated and displayed.

```
#include <iostream.h>
const int MAXGRADES = 100;
typedef int GradeList[MAXGRADES];


/*
 *      Get_grades
 *          Allows user to enter up to max_size
 *          grades into array g.  Returns the
 *          actual number of grades entered.
 */
```

```
int get_grades(GradeList g, int max_size)
{
    int count = 0;

    //  Loop until maximum size is attained or user types a
    //  non-number
    while ( count < max_size  &&  cin.good() ) {
        cin >> g[count];
        if ( cin.good() )  //  Increment count unless non-number
            count++;       //  non-number entered
    }
    return count;
}
/*
 *    Print_grades
 *    Displays the array of grades.
 */
void print_grades(GradeList g, int size)
{
    int count;
    for ( count = 0;  count < size;  count++ )
        cout << g[count] << '\n';
}

/*
 *    Avg_grades
 *        Returns the arithmetic mean of the grades
 *        stored in array g.
 */
double avg_grades(GradeList g, int size)
{
    int count;
    double sum = 0.0;

    for ( count = 0;  count < size;  count++ )
        sum += g[count];
    return sum/count;  /*  Division by zero unchecked  */
}

void main()
{
    GradeList grades;
    int numgrades;

    cout << "Enter the grades to average [Q] quits:\n";
    numgrades = get_grades(grades, MAXGRADES);
    cout << "The average of the grades\n";
    print_grades(grades, numgrades);
    cout << "is " << avg_grades(grades, numgrades) << '\n';
}
```

Program 7.4

The identifier GradeList is the programmer-defined type for an array of up to 100 ints. In main(), the statement

```
GradeList grades;
```

allocates space for 100 ints. When the program is actually executed, however, not all of that space may be needed. The constant MAXGRADES should be chosen carefully to be big enough for the largest anticipated usage, but not too big as to waste memory unnecessarily.

The variable numgrades is used to keep track of the actual size of the array. Only the first numgrades spaces of the allocated array will be used during any given execution. In a sense, the array grows or shrinks depending on the need at a particular time. Remember, the memory space allocated is constant, but the array's logical size depends on `numgrades` which is assigned by the return value of `get_grades()`. The code within `get_grades()` limits the number of grades entered to the maximum number allowed. The program may be modified to allow more or fewer grades by merely changing the `MAXGRADES` constant. The condition of the `while` within `get_grades()`

```
count < max_size && cin.good()
```

guarantees that the loop will terminate if the array is filled to maximum capacity or if a non-number is entered.

Often large arrays are defined external to functions. Recall from chapter 6 that `auto` variables are allocated on the stack. Usually, the amount of memory reserved for the stack is very small compared to the rest of memory. A large array declared local to a function may be too big for the stack. If `main()` declares a medium or large array and it calls another function that uses a local array, and that function calls another function that uses its own local array, etc., the stack can be filled up rather quickly. Remember that the stack is also used to transfer parameters and return values during function calls. Having `grades` be local to `main()` is nice, but having it tie up stack space is undesirable. Fortunately, two solutions are available. One is shown in program 7.5, which is a modification of program 7.4:

```
//   All the other functions appear above this point in the program
     .
     .
     .
GradeList grades;

void main()
{
        int numgrades;

        cout << "Enter the grades to average [Q] quits:\n";
        numgrades = get_grades(grades, MAXGRADES);
        cout << "The average of the grades\n";
        print_grades(grades, numgrades);
        cout << "is " << avg_grades(grades, numgrades) << '\n';
}
```

Program 7.5

Here, `grades` is of storage class `extern`, but since it is defined after all of the functions in the program except for `main()`, its scope is limited to `main()`. It is not a global variable, since it is not accessible by any function other than `main()`.

The second approach simply declares grades to have `static` storage:

```
void main()
{
        static GradeList grades;
        int numgrades;

        cout << "Enter the grades to average [Q] quits:\n";
        numgrades = get_grades(grades, MAXGRADES);
        cout << "The average of the grades\n";
        print_grades(grades, numgrades);
        cout << "is " << avg_grades(grades, numgrades) << '\n';
}
```

`grades`, therefore, will not be allocated on the stack but will occupy static memory, just as if it were declared `extern`.

7.6   SEARCHING AND SORTING

Many times it is necessary to find an element within an array. If the array's elements are not arranged in any particular order, a *linear search* is the most straightforward means of locating the element. Our function `find()` will return the position of the element sought or −1 if the element is not in the array:

```
/*
 *    find()
 *          Accepts an array of doubles, the size of the array, and
 *          the element sought.  Returns the position of the element
 *          within the array or -1 if it is not present.
 */
int find(double list[], int size, double seek)
{
    int i;

    for ( i = 0;  i < size;  i++ )
        if ( list[i] == seek )
            return i;
    return -1;
}
```

It is often convenient to order the elements within an array. The process of ordering the elements of an array is called *sorting*. There are several elementary sorts; we will consider the *selection sort*, because it is simple. The selection sort works as described by the following informal algorithm:

1. Compare the 0th element to the 1st element. If they are out of order, interchange their values. If they are already in the proper order, leave them alone.
2. Compare the 0th element to the 2nd element as in step 1. Then do the same with the 3rd, 4th, etc. until the 0th and the last element have been compared and possibly swapped. At this point it is guaranteed that the element in position 0 is in its proper place.
3. Repeat steps 1 and 2 using the 1st element in place of the 0th element. The element in position 1 is now in its proper place.
4. Repeat step 3 using the 2nd, 3rd, etc. elements until the next to the last element is compared to the last element.
5. All the elements are in their proper places and the sort is complete.

The C++ code follows:

```
/*
 *    select_sort()
 *          Arranges the element in array list in ascending order.
 *          The array contains size elements.
 */
void select_sort(double list[], int size) {
    int i, j;
    double temp;
    for ( i = 0;  i < size - 1;  i++ )
        for ( j = i + 1;  j < size;  j++ )
            if ( list[i] > list[j] ) {
                temp = list[i];
                list[i] = list[j];
                list[j] = temp;
            }
}
```

If descending order is required, replace the > in the `if` condition with <.

A sorted array looks more attractive when printed, compared to an array whose elements are in random order. An ordered array can also speed up the searching process. The linear search above becomes slower and slower as the size of the array grows. However, in an ordered array, the information about its ordering can be exploited to speed the search. In the linear search above, the array is searched all the way to its end if the element sought is not present. For an array arranged in ascending order, one need only look until either the value sought is found or an element larger than the element sought is encountered. Since the array is ordered, one need not search all the way to the end of the list (unless the element sought is larger than all the elements currently in the array). The modified search follows:

```
/*
 *      ordered_find()
 *          Accepts an array of doubles, the size of the array, and
 *          the element sought.  Returns the position of the element
 *          within the array or -1 if it is not present.  Note:
 *          only works for arrays that are arranged in ascending
 *          order!
 */

int ordered_find(double list[], int size, double seek)
{
    for ( int i = 0;  i < size  &&  list[i] <= seek;  i++ )
        if ( list[i] == seek )
            return i;
    return -1;
}
```

An even better search on an ordered array is the *binary search*. It is called a binary search because at each step it cuts in half the size of the array that needs to be searched. The algorithm is roughly described:

1. Let A be the array. Its first position (FIRST) is 0, and its last position (LAST) is the last item in A. X is the element sought.
2. Calculate M, the middle position: $M = $ (FIRST + LAST)/2
3. If $A[M] = X$, then go to step 4.
    If $A[M] < X$, then
        if LAST = FIRST, then go to step 5,
        otherwise go to step 2 using $M-1$ as the new *LAST* position of A.
    If $A[M] > X$, then
        if LAST = FIRST, then go to step 5,
        otherwise go to step 2 using $M + 1$ as the new *FIRST* position of A.
4. Return M, the position of X within A.
5. Report failure to find X in A.

Each time step 3 cuts in half the remaining array that needs to be searched. What is the maximum number of comparisons that must be done in the standard linear search of an array containing 100 elements? If the element is not found, it would compare all 100 elements to the item sought before it signals failure. A binary search would look at the middle of the 100 elements, then the middle of 50 elements, then the middle of 25 elements, then the middle of 13 elements, then the middle of seven elements, then the middle of four elements, then the middle of two elements, then one element, and then respond unsuccessfully. This amounts to seven comparisons. In fact, the number of comparisons required for the linear search is proportional to the number of elements in the array. Due to its "dividing by two" nature, the number of comparisons required by the binary search is proportional to $\log_2$ of the number of elements in the array. The statistics on worst case behaviors of the two search techniques in table 7.1 shows the dramatic difference.

Table 7.1

Number of Comparisons Required		
Array Size	Linear Search	Binary Search
100	100	7
1,000	1,000	10
10,000	10,000	14
100,000	100,000	17
1,000,000	1,000,000	20

Each comparison takes a small but measurable amount of time. Notice that the time to linearly search 1,000,000 elements takes 1,000 times as long as linearly searching for 1,000 elements. In a binary search, however, it takes only twice as long to search 1,000,000 elements as it does 1,000.

In actual practice, the simpler linear search is better for small arrays. The binary search requires a bit of overhead to do its work (the time-consuming division) and only becomes faster than the linear search in arrays with more than about 100 elements.

The binary search can be coded in C++ as follows:

```
/*
 *      binary_search()
 *         Searches for item seek in array list.  list must be
 *         arranged in descending order.  list is size large.
 *         The position of seek is returned or -1 if it is not present.
 */
int binary_search(double list[], int size, double seek) {
     int first = 0, last = size - 1, middle;
     while ( first <= last ) {
          middle = (first + last)/2;
          if ( list[middle] == seek )
               return middle;
          else if ( list[middle] > seek )
               last = middle - 1;
          else
               first = middle + 1;
     }
     return -1;
}
```

Exercises

1. How is a linear search performed on an array?

2. How is a binary search performed on an array?

3. What restrictions must be placed on an array if a binary search is to be performed?

For questions 4–15, assume the following declarations:

```
int a[10] = { 23, 5, 16, -2, 3, 0, 99, 2, 2, 5 }, x = 4, y = 8;
void print_array(int a[], int size) {
    int i;
    for ( i = 0;  i < size;  i++ )
      cout << a[i] << ' ';
}
```

Indicate whether the following statements are syntactically illegal, legal but contain a logic error, or, if totally correct, what would be printed by `print_array(a, 10)` after their execution. Each statement should be considered separately; that is, each statement starts fresh with the original definitions above (Question 5 does not depend on Question 4, etc.).

4. `a[0] = x;`

5. `a[] = x;`

6. `x = a[3];`

7. `a[x] = 10;`

8. `a[x] = a[x + 1];`

9. `a[x] = a[x] + 1;`

10. `a[x + 1] = a[x];`

11. `a[x] + 1 = a[x];`

12. `a[a[x]] = a[a[y]];`

13. `a[a[3]] = 5;`

14. `a[x + y] = x + y;`

15. `a = y;`

7.7 STRINGS

Strings are one-dimensional arrays of characters with one distinguishing feature; namely, the last valid element of a string array is always the character zero. This is the ASCII code 0, which can be written explicitly as the character `'\0'`. It is often called the *null character* or *null byte*.

A string could be declared and initialized as follows:

```
char str[6] = { 'h', 'e', 'l', 'l', 'o', '\0' };
```

or the equivalent

```
char str[] = { 'h', 'e', 'l', 'l', 'o', '\0' };
```

Neither of these forms is commonly used, since a more convenient syntax can be used with strings:

```
char str[6] = "hello";
```

or

```
char str[] = "hello";
```

Note that when using the double quote initialization, the terminating '\0' character is not listed; it is included implicitly in the string literal form. Even though it is not listed explicitly, the '\0' character is still part of the array and space must be allocated for it; thus, "hello" must be allocated six character places and not five.

Of course, strings may be declared without being initialized:

```
char str[30], word[10];
```

Null-terminated character string variables can be freely printed through cout:

```
char str[] = "world";
cout << "Hello " << str << '\n';
```

In the above output statement, "Hello" is called a *string literal* (or *string constant*) and str is called a *string variable*.

Strings can be read in from the keyboard via the cin stream:

```
char word[20];
cin >> word;
```

A word of caution: the user could type in 25 characters and the extractor would blindly cram 26 characters (remember the null character) into the space reserved for 20 characters. This action would overrun the end of the array corrupting memory the string does not own. A safer approach will be examined shortly. If "dog" is entered, then word[0] would contain a 'd', word[1] would contain an 'o', word[2] would contain a 'g', word[3] would contain the null byte, and word[4] through word[19] would contain whatever they contained before cin was accessed. Whitespace is used to delimit strings in when reading them from the keyboard; thus, strings that contain spaces, tabs, or newlines cannot be completely entered through cin using the extractor. The getline() function, associated with the cin object, can be used to grab all characters, including whitespace characters, up to the '\n' character. It is used as follows:

```
char word[20];
cin.getline(word, 20);
```

The second parameter indicates the maximum number of characters (less one) to read into the word string.

Because of the unique structure of C++ strings (with their null terminating byte), simple, elegant string routines are easy to write. One useful operation is determining the length of a string. This would be useful when working on the screen-formatting function for a wordprocessor or when simply copying one string to another.

```
/*
 *      str_len()
 *        Returns the length of string s, excluding
 *        the terminating null byte.
 */
int str_len(char s[]) {
    int length = 0;
    while ( s[length] != '\0' )
      length++;
    return length;
}
```

Consider several versions of `str_cpy()` that copies the contents of one string to another (the space for the destination string *must* be big enough; no error checking is done):

```
int str_len(char s[]);  /*  From above  */

void str_cpy(char dest[], char source[]) {
    int length = str_len(source), i;
    for ( i = 0;  i <= length;  i++ )
      dest[i] = source[i];
}
```

This makes use of `str_len()` defined above, but the length really does not need to be known up front. A more efficient version could be

```
int str_cpy(char dest[], char source[]) {
    int i = 0;
    while ( source[i] != '\0' ) {
      dest[i] = source[i];
      i++;
    }
    dest[i] = '\0';
}
```

`str_cpy()` is potentially unsafe. Consider the section of code:

```
char d[5], s[10] = "abcdefg";

str_cpy(d, s);
```

Ten bytes are allocated for `s` even though only the first eight bytes are occupied with characters of a valid string. The string copy operation crams eight characters into space reserved for only five bytes. String `d` is overrun and memory somewhere (possibly even string `s`) is corrupted.

Some languages, such as many implementations of Pascal and BASIC, represent strings in a different way. Since the first element in a BASIC array is in position one, not position zero as in C++, BASIC strings, which are one-dimensional character arrays also, reserve position zero for the length of the string. Although Pascal allows general array subscripts to vary (a beginning index of -50 is possible), those language implementations that support built-in string types usually use the same representation scheme as BASIC. The advantage of having the size immediately available is that routines such as `strlen()` would be faster. The disadvantage is that since the range of unsigned characters is 0 to 255, strings are limited to 255 characters or fewer. With C++'s null-terminated representation, strings can be as long as is necessary (with some system imposed contraints).

7.8 STANDARD STRING ROUTINES

The header file `<string.h>` contains declarations for some standard string functions. These string functions are found in table 7.2.

All of the string functions work properly only on null-terminated character strings. Generally, these functions should be used instead of writing custom routines (as we did for `str_len()` and `str_cpy()`) that do the same thing. The same arguments for using the standard string functions apply that were provided in chapter 6 when discussing the standard mathematical and character-processing functions. These standard routines are well documented; hence, their behavior is quite predictable. A programmer using these functions can consult a standard reference in the event a question arises concerning their use. Custom functions may have idiosyncrasies that produce unpredictable results. In the worst case, the custom functions may not be totally correct. Also, the library functions may be optimized in low-level code to take advantage of some special feature of the system that the compiler may neglect.

Table 7.2 Standard String Functions

Parameters s and t are strings; n is an int; c is a char

strcpy(s, t)	Copies t to s
strncpy(s, t, n)	Copies first n characters of t to s
strcat(s, t)	Appends t onto the end of s
strncat(s, t, n)	Appends first n characters of t onto end of s
strcmp(s, t)	If s < t returns < 0, if s == t returns 0, if s > t returns > 0
strncmp(s, t, n)	Does strcmp() on first n characters of s and t
strchr(s, c)	Returns pointer to first occurrence of c in s (or NULL if not found)
strstr(s, t)	Returns pointer to first occurrence of t in s (or NULL if not found)
strlen(s)	Returns length of s, excluding null byte

It may be that the programmer can write a more efficient routine that works the same as a library routine. If the conditions warrant it, the more efficient routine should be used. Care should be taken to verify that it indeed works correctly in all situations. Of course, custom functions must be written when there are no library functions that do exactly what is needed.

7.9 STRING EXAMPLE

Program 7.6 reads in a textfile (perhaps using redirection), and it places the individual words making up the text into an array of strings. The array is then sorted, and finally the words are printed along with their associated lengths. In addition, if a word appears more than once in the textfile, it is placed in the array only once; thus, no duplicate words are found in the array of words. To simplify the word extraction process, no words in the file have apostrophes, and no word is hyphenated; thus, white space (spaces, tabs, and newlines) and punctuation are used to delimit the words in the file.

```
#include <iostream.h>
#include <ctype.h>
#include <string.h>

typedef char String[20];        //  A string
typedef String WordList[100];   //  An array of strings

/*
 *    Getword
 *       Grabs a word delimited by white space and punctuation from cin
 *       Returns 1 if end-of-file is encountered, 0 otherwise.
 */

int getword(String s) {
    char ch;
    int  pos  = 0,
    done = 0;
    do {
        ch = toupper(cin.get());  //  Get a single character
        if ( cin.eof() || isspace(ch) || ispunct(ch) ) {
            s[pos] = '\0';  //  Properly terminate the string;
            if ( cin.eof() )
                return 1;   //  End-of-file
            done = 1;       //  End of word; quit
        }
```

```
                    else
                         s[pos++] = ch;
                    if ( s[0] == '\0' ) {
                         pos = 0;    //  Reset to beginning of word
                         done = 0;
                    }
        } while ( !done );
        return 0;    //  Not end-of-file
}


/*
 *  Find
 *      Searches an array of strings (w) for a particular string (s).
 *      Returns the position s if within w or -1 if s is not in w.
 */

int find(WordList w, int size, String s) {
    int i;
    for ( i = 0;  i < size;  i++ )
        if ( strcmp(w[i], s) == 0 )
            return i;       //  string s found in position i in w
    return -1;    // string s not found in w
}


/*
 *  Loadlist
 *      Calls getword() and fills up the WordList with individual words.
 */

void loadlist(WordList w, int &size) {
    String buffer;
    int done = 0;
    size = 0;
    do {
        done = getword(buffer);
        if ( !done ) {
            if ( find(w, size, buffer) == -1 ) {
                strcpy(w[size], buffer);
                size++;
            }
        }
    } while ( !done );
}


/*
 *  Sortlist
 *      Sorts the array of strings into lexicographical order.
 */

void sortlist(WordList w, int size) {
    //  Selection sort on an array of Strings
    int i, j;
    String temp;
    for ( i = 0;  i < size - 1;  i++ )
        for ( j = i + 1;  j < size;  j++ )
            if ( strcmp(w[i], w[j]) > 0 ) {
                strcpy(temp, w[i]);
                strcpy(w[i], w[j]);
                strcpy(w[j], temp);
            }
}
```

```
/*
 *    Printlist
 *        Prints the contents of the array of words.
 */
void printlist(WordList w, int size) {
    int i;
    for ( i = 0;  i < size;  i++ ) {
    cout << "[" << w[i] << "]";
    if ( i % 10 == 9 )   //  Newline every 10 words
        cout << '\n';
    }
    cout << '\n';
}

WordList list;

void main() {
    int list_size;
    loadlist(list, list_size);
    sortlist(list, list_size);
    printlist(list, list_size);
}
```

Program 7.6

This program is a good example to lead into the next section. We can think of the structures involved (strings and an array of strings) as two one-dimensional arrays when, in fact, the array of strings is actually a *two-dimensional* array of characters.

Exercises

1. How is a string different from a standard array of `chars`?

2. In what two ways can strings be initialized when declared?

3. What is the ASCII value for the *null* character?

4. How is the null character expressed as a character literal?

5. What special function can be used for string input, and how is it properly used?

6. Does `strlen()` count the null character in its length determination?

7. What do the standard string routines `strlen()`, `strcpy()`, `strcmp()`, and `strcat()` do?

8. What happens when a standard string routine like `strcpy()`, `strcmp()`, or `strlen()` is sent an array of `chars` that is not null terminated?

9. What value would be returned by the call `strcmp("ABC", "XYZ");`?

7.10 MULTIDIMENSIONAL ARRAYS

One-dimensional arrays can be extended to two and higher dimensions. These higher-dimensional arrays can conveniently represent tabular data and can be used in modeling advanced problems in the sciences, engineering, and business. C++ provides a natural and simple syntax for implementing multidimensional arrays. Consider the following code that uses a `typedef`:

```
const int ARRSIZE = 100;

typedef int List[ARRSIZE];

void main() {
    List lst;
    List table[25];
        .
        .
        .
}
```

`lst` is an array of 100 `int`s, and `table` is an array of 25 arrays of `int`s—each holding up to 100 characters; thus, `table` is an *array of arrays.* `table` could have been declared without the `typedef` as

```
int table[25][100];
```

The dual subscripts explicitly indicate a two-dimensional array. The subscripts are best read left to right; that is, `table` is an array of 25 arrays of 100 `int`s each. By contrast, it is *not* an array of 100 arrays of 25 `int`s each. Two-dimensional arrays are like tables having rows and columns. Each row is a one-dimensional array. All the rows are collected into another one-dimensional array (of rows). The first subscript references a particular row in the table. The second subscript references a particular column within the table. In the `table` array, changing the value in column two (actually the third column) of row fifteen (actually the sixteenth row) to 19 can be accomplished by the following statement:

```
table[15][2] = 19;
```

The ultimate size of a two-dimensional array (its total number of elements) is determined by multiplying the number of rows by the number of columns; thus, `table` contains 2,500 elements. Since each element is of type `int`, it requires 2,500 × `sizeof int` bytes of storage. On a system that stores integers in two bytes:

$$\#rows \times \#columns \times \text{size of each element} = 25 \times 100 \times 2 = 5,000 \text{ bytes}$$

Two-dimensional arrays may be initialized when declared, but as you might imagine, this is only practical for small arrays:

```
float num_list[3][4] = { { 1.0, 2.0, 0.0, 3.1 },
                         { 0.0, 0.0, 5.1, 9.2 },
                         { 6.3, 0.0, 0.0, 1.0 } };
```

Notice how the individual rows are grouped within nested braces. The elements are listed in *row order*, which means all elements in the zeroth row are grouped in braces, then all the elements in the first row, and so forth.

`num_list` could be displayed with a pair of nested `for`s:

```
for ( row = 0;  row < 3;  row++ ) {
    for ( col = 0;  col < 4;  col++ )
        cout << num_list[row][col] << ' ';
  cout << '\n';
  }
```

The newline character is displayed at the end of each row, so each new row begins on a new line.

When passing a two-dimensional array to a function, the use of `typedef` is most convenient. The syntax of the defined type makes the parameter list much more attractive. Consider:

```
/*  Typedef at top of program:
    typedef int Table[MAXROW][MAXCOL];   */
int table_sum(Table t)
{
    int row, col, sum = 0;

    for ( row = 0;  row < MAXROW;  row++ )
        for ( col = 0;  col < MAXCOL;  col++ )
            sum += t[row][col];
    return sum;
}
```

versus

```
int table_sum(int t[][MAXCOL])
{
    /*  Body same as above...  */
}
```

In two-dimensional arrays, the first subscript may be omitted but the second must be explicitly given its proper size when used to declare a function parameter. The `typedef` syntax is arguably the cleaner approach.

Computer memory is inherently linear. The first address is 0, the second is 1, the third 2, and so forth. The last (highest) address depends on the amount of memory in the system. Two-dimensional arrays are planar but must be stored in linear memory. C++ stores arrays in *row major order*. This means that memory is occupied one row at a time, similar to the way arrays are initialized above. Figure 7.2 shows the layout of an array in memory.

```
int A[2] [4];    /*  Located at memory address 2350  */
```

Conceptual layout:

A[0][0]	A[0][1]	A[0][2]	A[0][3]
A[1][0]	A[1][1]	A[1][2]	A[1][3]

Actual arrangement in memory:

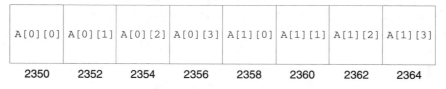

A[0][0]	A[0][1]	A[0][2]	A[0][3]	A[1][0]	A[1][1]	A[1][2]	A[1][3]
2350	2352	2354	2356	2358	2360	2362	2364

Internal Storage of a 2-D Array
Figure 7.2

Arrays of strings are two-dimensional arrays of characters in which each row is null-terminated. Figure 7.3 shows how an array of strings is represented.

Given the declaration

```
char wordlist[4][5];
```

the expression `wordlist[2][3]` refers to a single character (string in position 2, character at position 3 within that string). The expression `wordlist[2]` refers to the entire string in row 2; thus, `wordlist[2]` could be passed to any string function and treated exactly like any other simple string.

```
char words[4][5] = { "abc", "xyz", "", "1234" };
```

'a'	'b'	'c'	'\0'	???
'x'	'y'	'z'	'\0'	???
'\0'	???	???	???	???
'1'	'2'	'3'	'4'	'\0'

```
words[0][0] == 'a'              words[0] == "abc"
words[1][2] == 'z'              words[2] == ""
words[2][2] == unknown          words[3] == "1234"
```

Array of Strings
Figure 7.3

7.11 SAMPLE PROGRAM: IMAGE PROCESSING

The following program reads in data redirected from a file and displays an image on the screen. Different characters have different visual densities. For example, the @ symbol is denser and darker than the O symbol which is darker than the . symbol.

So as to be implemented on a wide variety of workstations, the program here uses the following symbols:

```
WHITE  = '.'
LIGHT  = '-'
GRAY   = '+'
DARK   = '#'
BLACK  = '@'
```

The program will assume that the file contains 16 characters or ASCII codes stored in row-major order representing a picture four characters by four characters. The file containing

```
@@@@@..@#++#####
```

would be displayed as

```
@@@@
@..@
#++#
####
```

Each character block that makes up the image is called a *picture element* or *pixel* for short. The image data is stored in a two-dimensional array so that it can be manipulated easily. One task that must be performed is *filtering*. Filtering involves removing certain types of pixels. The above image can be filtered to remove the + pixels and appear as

```
@@@@
@..@
#..#
####
```

This filtering process can be useful if some pixels represent possible errors in the data. The removed pixel is replaced with the WHITE pixel ('.').

Another task is *image inversion*. An image is inverted if all dark pixels are made light and vice-versa. Using the above pixels, the conversion is straightforward:

```
'.' --> '@'
'-' --> '#'
'+' --> '+'    (Middle shade, no change)
'#' --> '-'
'@' --> '.'
```

The original image above could be inverted to

```
....
.@@.
-++-
----
```

Program 7.7 implements our image processing program:

```cpp
#include <iostream.h>

const int SIZE = 4;

const char WHITE = '.',
           LIGHT = '-',
           GRAY  = '+',
           DARK  = '#',
           BLACK = '@';

typedef unsigned char Image[SIZE][SIZE];


void get_image(Image pic) {
    int row, col;
    for ( row = 0;  row < SIZE;  row++ )
        for ( col = 0;  col < SIZE;  col++ )
            cin >> pic[row][col];
}

void show_image(Image pic) {
    int row, col;
    cout << '\n';
```

```
            for ( row = 0;  row < SIZE;  row++ ) {
                for ( col = 0;  col < SIZE;  col++ )
                    cout << pic[row][col];
                cout << '\n';
            }
        }
    void filter(Image pic, char pixel) {
        int row, col;
        for ( row = 0;  row < SIZE;  row++ )
            for ( col = 0;  col < SIZE;  col++ )
                    pic[row][col] = (pic[row][col] == pixel)?
                                    WHITE: pic[row][col];
    }
    void invert(Image pic) {
        int row, col;
        for ( row = 0;  row < SIZE;  row++ )
            for ( col = 0;  col < SIZE;  col++ ) {
                    if ( pic[row][col] == WHITE )
                        pic[row][col] = BLACK;
                    else if ( pic[row][col] == LIGHT )
                        pic[row][col] = DARK;
                    else if ( pic[row][col] == BLACK )
                        pic[row][col] = WHITE;
                    else if ( pic[row][col] == DARK )
                        pic[row][col] = LIGHT;
                    //   else don't change GRAY
            }
    }

    Image picture;   //  Extern, but local to main()
    void main() {
        get_image(picture);
        show_image(picture);
        filter(picture, GRAY);
        show_image(picture);
        invert(picture);
        show_image(picture);
    }
```

Program 7.7

7.12 SAMPLE PROGRAM: SIMPLE ANIMATION

Program 7.8 illustrates simple animation using text "graphics." A ball moves within a box as shown in figure 7.4 bouncing off of its walls in a regular fashion. The number of times the ball travels through a particular portion of the box is recorded in a two-dimensional frequency array.

This program does not take advantage of any system-specific screen functions; it is done using the output stream. Therefore, it merely redraws the entire screen each time the ball is moved. To redraw the screen, the current display is scrolled up until a blank screen is available on which to draw. Since this constant scrolling would be distracting, the next frame is not displayed until the user presses the enter key. Any other key entry terminates the program.

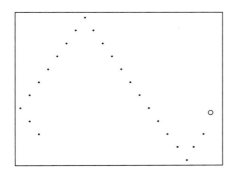

**Ball in a Box Animation
Figure 7.4**

```
#include <iostream.h>

const char BLOCK = 'O',
           BALL  = 'o',
           EMPTY = ' ';
const int  XHI     =  60,
           XLO     =  20,
           YHI     =  18,
           YLO     =   5,
           MAXROWS =  24,
           MAXCOLS =  79;

typedef char ScreenArray[MAXCOLS][MAXROWS];

/*
 *      initialize()
 *          Clears the screen array, frequency array, positions the walls and
 *             ball, and draws the screen.
 */

void initialize(int &x, int &y, ScreenArray screen, ScreenArray freq) {
    int row, col;

    //    Center ball in box
    x = (XHI + XLO)/2;
    y = (YHI + YLO)/2;

    //   Initialize the screen array...
    for ( row = 0;  row < MAXROWS;  row++ )
        for ( col = 0;  col < MAXCOLS;  col++ )
            if ( ((row == YLO  ||  row == YHI)  &&  col >= XLO
                && col <= XHI)
                || ((col == XHI  || col == XLO)  && row >= YLO
                &&  row <= YHI) )
                screen[col][row] = BLOCK;
            else if ( row == y  &&  col == x )
                screen[col][row] = BALL;
            else
                screen[col][row] = EMPTY;

    //   Clear frequency array...
    for ( row = 0;  row < MAXROWS; row++ )
        for ( col = 0;  col < MAXCOLS;  col++ )
            freq[col][row] = 0;
}


/*
 *      update_position()
 *          Moves the ball within the box.  Changes the ball's direction
 *          if a wall is encountered.
 */

void update_position(ScreenArray screen, int &x, int &y) {
    static int dx = 1, dy = 1;
    /*  Static so values are retained between function calls  */

    //  Check for collision...
    if ( x + dx >= XHI  ||  x + dx <= XLO )
        dx = -dx;         //  Collision with left or right wall
    if ( y + dy >= YHI  ||  y + dy <= YLO )
        dy = -dy;         //  Collision with ceiling or floor
    //  Erase ball in old position
    screen[x][y] = EMPTY;
    //  Update ball's position
    x = x + dx;  y = y + dy;
```

```
                //   Draw ball in new position
                screen[x][y] = BALL;
      }
/*
 *      update_frequency()
 *              Increments the table at the ball's current position.
 */
  void update_frequency(ScreenArray f, int x, int y) {
        f[x][y]++;
  }
/*
 *      scroll_up()
 *              Clears the screen by scrolling it up one frame.
 */
  void scroll_up() {
        //  "Clear" screen by scrolling it up one frame
        for ( int row = 0;   row < MAXROWS;   row++ )
              cout << '\n';
  }

/*       report_frequency()
 *              Displays a map of the ball's travels.
 */
  void report_frequency(ScreenArray f) {
        int i, j;
        scroll_up();
        for ( j = 0;   j < MAXROWS;   j++ ) {
              for ( i = 0;   i < MAXCOLS;   i++ )
                    if ( f[i][j] > 3 )
                          cout << '@';
                    else if ( f[i][j] > 2 )
                          cout << 'O';
                    else if ( f[i][j] > 1 )
                          cout << 'o';
                    else if ( f[i][j] > 0 )
                          cout << '.';
                    else
                          cout << ' ';
              cout << '\n';
        }
  }

/*
 *    draw_screen()
 *            Draws the current configuration—the walls and the ball
 */
  int draw_screen(ScreenArray screen) {
        int row, col;

        scroll_up();
        //  Draw the borders or ball
        for ( row = 0;   row < MAXROWS;   row++ ) {
              for ( col = 0;   col < MAXCOLS;   col++ )
                    cout << screen[col][row];
              cout << '\n';
        }
        // Wait for enter key
        return   cin.get() != '\n';
  }
```

```
ScreenArray scrn, freq;      // Declared extern to save stack space
void main() {
    int xpos, ypos, done = 0;
    initialize(xpos, ypos, scrn, freq);
    while ( !done ) {
         update_position(scrn, xpos, ypos);
         update_frequency(freq, xpos, ypos);
         done = draw_screen(scrn);
    }
    report_frequency(freq);
}
```

Program 7.8

This program's graphics effects are meager by today's standards, but the program will run fine on just about any text-oriented display or terminal. It can even send its output to a line printer or file using redirection. The poor graphics can be improved by using some system-specific routines that take advantage of the screen's capabilities instead of going through `cout`. Most C++ development systems provide libraries that offer access to system-specific functions that can position the cursor at a particular (x,y) location on the screen; thus, instead of storing the walls and ball in a display array, the walls may be drawn once, and the ball may be erased literally on the screen and redrawn in its updated position. This effect is far superior to the frame-by-frame generic approach. System-specific special characters (like the half-tone characters mentioned), if available, can be used to improve the frequency array map. Even better results can be achieved on bitmapped graphics displays that can display many shades and/or colors at a finer resolution.

Exercises

1. In the expression `a[i][j]`, which subscript indicates the row, and which subscript indicates the column?

2. Is it legal to have an array of arrays?

3. How can two-dimensional arrays be initialized when declared?

4. Explain what is meant when it is said that C++ stores 2-D arrays in *row-major* order in memory.

5. Given the following declaration:

    `int a[20][20];`

    what is meant by the expression `a[2][3]` and the expression `a[2]` ?

6. How many bytes of memory are required to store the array declared as follows:

    `int a[10][25][15];`

7. What is the limit to the number of dimensions that can be represented in a C++ array?

7.13 FILE STREAMS

Arrays are useful for storing collections of homogeneous types. The grading program introduced early in this chapter has one glaring flaw that would not be found in a commercial electronic gradebook program. When the program is finished, all of the data painstakingly entered into the array is lost. When the program is to be executed again, the grades must be entered (or re-entered, as the case may be) from scratch. Fortunately, the streams library provides a means to write data to and read data from a disk file just about as easily as using the standard `cout` and `cin` streams. The following function saves an array of integers to a file named `data.tmp`:

```
int array_save(int a[], int size) {
    ofstream out_file("data.tmp");
    if ( !out_file )
        return 1;  //  Error indication
    for ( int i = 0;  i < size;  i++ )
        out_file << a[i] << ' ';
    return 0;  //  Success
}
```

The statement

```
ofstream out_file("data.tmp");
```

declares `out_file` (a variable name created by the programmer) to be a stream object of type `ofstream` and connects this stream to the diskfile `data.tmp`. The name stands for output file stream. The `!` operator is used to test whether there was an error opening the file. The `out_file` is local to the function `array_save()`. When the function is finished, the file connected to `out_file` will be closed and updated. While connected to the file, `out_file` can be used just like `cout`; data will be stored in a textfile in exactly the same form as it would have been displayed on the screen. Add this function to one of your array-processing programs and try it out. Load `data.tmp` into a text editor and examine it. It should contain exactly those integers that were in the array passed to it. All the values will be separated by single spaces as was dictated by the function (any white space will do—tabs or newlines could also have been used as delimiters). The function returns a non-negative value for failure and a zero value for success. While this return protocol may seem odd, many functions that interact with the operating system or directly with the hardware act similarly. Consider that there is only one way to accomplish the job perfectly but many ways in which to fail. The function could be modified in the future to differentiate among several possible errors. It could return 1 indicating disk full, 2 indicating drive door not closed, 3 indicating disk write protected, and so forth. The calling function needs to check only for a zero result to determine success. A more general function would allow the filename to be passed in as a string variable:

```
int array_save(int a[], int size, char filename[]) {
    ofstream out_file(filename);
    //  Rest remains the same...
```

Here, the function call might be

```
if ( array_save(list, current_size, "grades.dat" )
    cout << "Error writing data to file.\n";
```

While the same file could have been created using redirection, this approach has the advantage of keeping `cout` available for screen display at the same time. When redirection is used, `cout` is tied to the output file until the program finishes.

A complementary function allows the data stored on disk in the fashion described above to be read into an array:

```
int array_load(int a[], int &size, int maxsize, char filename) {
    ifstream in_file(filename);
    if ( !in_file )
        return 1;  //  Cannot open file
    size = 0;
    while ( size < maxsize  &&  !in_file.eof() ) {
        in_file >> a[size];    //  Read in an item into the array
        if ( !in_file.eof() )
            size++;            //  Only increment size if end-of-file not
                              //  reached
    }
    return 0;  //  Success
}
```

The `ifstream` class allows data to be retrieved from a file. Since the file may contain more data than the array has space allocated, the parameter `maxsize` is used to limit the number of values read. Values are read into the array until the size limit is reached or the end-of-file character is read. The end-of-file condition is checked with the `eof()` function, as is done with the `cin` stream. The actual number of values read in is stored in the `size` parameter which is passed in by reference. This function will overwrite the contents of an existing array (unless the file access is unsuccessful), so it should be used with care.

Exercises

1. How would one associate the `ofstream` variable f with the diskfile `zdata.dta`?

2. What does the ! operator do when applied to `ofstream` and `ifstream` variables?

3. What is the rationale behind writing a function that returns zero (false) if it successfully completes its task?

Assignments

1. Write a simple statistics package with the following features:

   - Can store up to 100 floating point numbers in an array
   - Can display the contents of the list [`Print`]
   - Can insert new values at the end of the list (don't add more than the maximum allowed!) [`Insert`]
   - Can delete values (delete the first occurrence of the number in the array sliding the valid numbers that follow the deleted number forward; don't delete anything if the number is not in the list) [`Delete`]
   - Can display the number of items in the list [`Count`]
   - Can add up all the valid items in the list and print the sum [`Total`]
   - Can calculate and display the average of the valid items in the list [`Average`]
   - Can display the maximum value in the list [`maXimum`]
   - Can display the minimum value in the list [`miNimum`]
   - Can clear the entire list (make it empty) [`Erase`]

- Can arrange the values in the list in ascending order [Sort]
- Can gracefully exit the program [Quit]

Your program should be menu driven with the options:

```
Erase Print Insert Delete Total Average Count maXimum miNimum Sort Quit
```

The capitalized letter of the menu option indicates which key should be pressed to perform the task. (Allow either the upper- or lowercase version of the character to be entered for the menu choice.)

2. One limitation of ints is that they have a maximum representable value. (For example, 16-bit integers have a maximum value of 32,767.) This limitation can be overcome on some systems by using longs and unsigned longs, but a new, higher limit is eventually reached.

   To illustrate one technique for circumventing these limitations, write a program that represents unsigned ints as arrays of normal unsigneds. These extended ints are typedefed as:

   ```
   typedef unsigned ExtendedInt[10];
   ```

An ExtendedInt represents a ten-digit non-negative integer. The number 34,453,789 would be stored in an ExtendedInt array as

0	0	3	4	4	5	3	7	8	9

(Note the leading zeroes in the 0th and 1st positions.) The 9th position is the ones place, the 8th position is the tens place, the 7th position is the hundreds place, ..., the 0th position is the billions place.

   Write the following routines to manipulate ExtendedInts:

   ```
   void getExtInt(ExtendedInt i);
   void printExtInt(ExtendedInt i);
   void addExtInt(ExtendedInt x, ExtendedInt y, ExtendedInt result);
   void subExtInt(ExtendedInt x, ExtendedInt y, ExtendedInt result);
   ```

getExtInt() allows the user to type in the characters for the big integer. These characters are converted into their corresponding integer values and stored in the proper place in an ExtendedInt array. As indicated, zeroes should be placed at the beginning of the array as necessary. printExtInt() displays an ExtendedInt as if it were a normal everyday integer. addExtInt() does a componentwise addition of the corresponding digits of two ExtendedInts (x and y) and places the result of the addition into a third ExtendedInt (result). Don't forget to carry when the sum of the two digits exceeds nine! For example, 267 + 188 = 455:

   subExtInt() works like addExtInt(), except subtraction is performed instead of addition. With subtraction, borrowing frequently must be done to properly implement the componentwise digit subtraction. Even though a carry "array" is shown in the diagram for convenience, it is not necessary. A single variable called carry may be used.

   Provide a small main() function that tests your routines.

3. Write a function with the following prototype:

   ```
   char menu(char *menu_str);
   ```

   Calling the function

   ```
   ch = menu("Erase Clear Average Sum eXecute Quit");
   ```

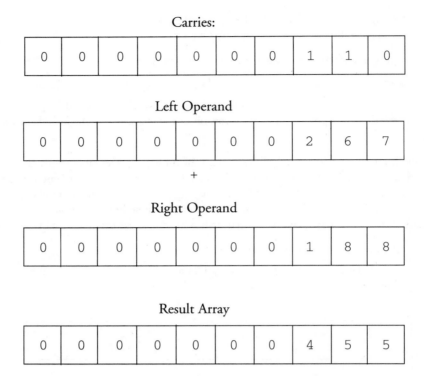

Carries:

| 0 | 0 | 0 | 0 | 0 | 0 | 0 | 1 | 1 | 0 |

Left Operand

| 0 | 0 | 0 | 0 | 0 | 0 | 0 | 2 | 6 | 7 |

+

Right Operand

| 0 | 0 | 0 | 0 | 0 | 0 | 0 | 1 | 8 | 8 |

Result Array

| 0 | 0 | 0 | 0 | 0 | 0 | 0 | 4 | 5 | 5 |

will result in a menu bar being displayed across the screen with the options included. It will also result in ch being assigned the uppercase character corresponding to the key entered by the user. The only characters that should be returned are those that are capitalized letters in the string passed to the function. If the user, in the example above, enters any character other than *E, C, A, S, X,* or *Q,* the menu will continue to be displayed, and nothing will happen (until the user enters one of the proper keys). (Experiment with strchr().) Write several different main() programs to test your function. Note that the string passed should be short enough to fit across the screen without running over into the next line; a string that is too long should be truncated. Also, note that each choice must have a unique capital letter so that each item is able to be chosen.

A typical usage:

```
switch ( menu("    Yes          No          Maybe") ) {
      case 'Y':  do_proc();     break;
      case 'N':  return NULL;   break;
      case 'M':  do_help();     break;
}
```

4. Write a C++ program that reads in *words* from a textfile and places them into an array. When the entire file has been read, the words should be sorted lexicographically (alphabetically) and printed out in order, along with their length. Finally, the following statistics should be displayed:

a. Number of words
b. Longest word in file (if there are ties, just list one of the longest words)
c. Shortest word in file (if there are ties, just list one of the shortest words)
d. Average length of a word in the file
e. Number of sentences in the file

For example, the following textfile

```
Mary had a little lamb. Its fleece was white as snow.
```

would yield

```
A         1
AS        2
FLEECE    6
HAD       3
ITS       4
LAMB      4
LITTLE    6
MARY      4
SNOW      4
WHITE     5
WAS       3

Number of words:      11
Longest word:      FLEECE
Shortest word:        A
Average word length:  3
Number of sentences:  2
```

5. Computers are quite useful in the analysis of data from scientific experiments. Scientific visualization is a field of study that encompasses computer science, mathematics, and a scientific area of application. Data from an experiment or simulation are stored in a textfile as integers between 0 and 4, inclusive. These numbers could represent a picture of a planet as transmitted from a distant space probe, ozone levels in the stratosphere over a rectangular area in the western United States, or temperatures in degrees K as modelled in a rectangular region near a black hole. Your job is to take the sequence of numbers and produce a corresponding picture.

   The numbers received represent levels of brightness as perceived by the camera on some remote sensing device. A crude picture can be printed with text by printing a lighter, less dense character (like a '.') when the brightness level is high and print a darker, denser character (like a '@') when the brightness level is represented by a lower number. Use appropriate symbols available on your particular .

   Unfortunately, errors (such as errors in transmission from a distant space probe) sometimes occur. It is generally the case that these errors are rare and occur randomly. Your program should attempt to locate and correct these errors and eventually print a corrected picture on the screen. Assume a picture element (or pixel, call it P) is in error if 1) all eight of P's neighboring pixels have the same brightness value, and 2) the unanimous value of P's neighbors is different from P itself by more than 2 units of brightness. Correct the "bad" P value by giving it the value of its neighboring picture elements. Example:

```
4 4 4      The 1 would be regarded as an error and
4 1 4      would be given a corrected value of 4.
4 4 4
```

   This simple scheme is not very effective for general use, but it is easy to understand and implement. Do not do any error correcting to positions on the borders of the picture. The picture consists of an array of 80 by 24 pixels chosen from the above five possibilities. Your program must 1) read in the 1,920 values from the data file (redirected from disk), 2) display the noisy (error containing) picture, and 3) display the enhanced (error corrected) picture. Your program should also report the number of pixels that were classified as having erroneous values and therefore changed in the enhanced image.

6. The game of Life was devised by John H. Conway in 1970. It is a simple example of a computer simulation. It represents the interactions among artificial organisms whose reproduction, sustenation, and

death is dictated by simple rules. The world of Life as created by Conway is a checkerboard in which each square may contain 0 or 1 cells. The starting pattern is chosen by the user or generated at random. The game proceeds in generations, with the pattern of each succeeding generation determined by the pattern of the preceding generation by very simple reproduction rules:

a. If a cell has exactly two neighbors, then it remains the same in the next generation
b. If a cell has exactly three neighbors, then it is on (lives) in the next generation
c. If a cell has fewer than two or more than three neighbors, then it is off (dies of loneliness or overcrowding) in the next generation

Each cell on the interior of the Life board has eight neighboring cells. If a neighboring cell is on, it is said to be a neighbor. Thus a cell that has three of its eight neighboring cells turned on is said to have three neighbors.

Write a program that plays the game of Life. You are free to make up your own rules about how cells on the border are treated (they really have only five screen neighbors). The board should be displayed on the screen and updated each generation. Provide a way for the user to enter an initial configuration. It may be as simple as entering pairs of numbers indicating which cells are on; it may be as elaborate as using the cursor keys to move around on the screen and thereby turning on and off cells interactively. The latter approach would require access to a library that allows such powerful I/O methods—but most implementations provide such support. Observe the complex and interesting patterns that develop from various initial conditions.

The following points outline the task:

a. Represent the game board by an 80 x 24 array of integers (the exact dimensions of most PC text screens, minus one row to prevent scrolling)
b. Use a value of 1 to indicate an active cell and 0 to indicate a nonliving cell
c. In a suitable loop, calculate the board configuration of the next generation by the following rules given above
d. Devise an output routine to display the board (you will likely print a certain character if the cell is alive and not print a character if the cell is nonliving)
e. Devise an input routine whereby the user can enter the initial board configuration

Cells labelled N are neighbors of cell X

N	N	N
N	X	N
N	N	N

7. The word find or word search puzzle is popular. In this type of puzzle, words are hidden in a block of random letters. The player attempts to find all the words provided in an accompanying list. The letters within individual words may be arranged left-to-right or right-to-left horizontally; they may appear from top-to-bottom or bottom-to-top vertically; they may also appear diagonally forwards or backwards. The player circles each word as it is discerned from the background clutter of the random letters. The game is over when all the words have been found.

Write a program that produces such a puzzle. Allow the user to enter a list of words. Place the uppercased words into a 20 by 20 block filled with random uppercase letters. The number of words and length of each word should be restricted (such as ten words of up to ten characters each). Produce a copy of the puzzle and an answer key. Words should be placed randomly forwards and backwards, vertically, horizontally, and diagonally in the grid. Be careful that words overlap properly. (Hint: Have two copies of the puzzle—the puzzle itself and its key. Place the words and produce the key first then trivially construct the puzzle from the key by filling in the remaining empty spots with randomly chosen uppercase letters.)

```
M H G S N S K Y X Z Q A E T I N X L L C
L F R U O B E B P Z E D D E V D J J Z W
T B W Q Y K E R R O R U B Q J V Q S A D
B N W K W V O Z D T I P X J S G K R A D
Z D M E V G J U L V U I W Q D H I S E I          COMPUTER
O Z C V R R N X W O Z P C M D T E G N S          PROGRAM
Y I P A L Q E I B M Z T X B C Z Z O G K          KEYBOARD
O G M L F V J E G L T L O H X Q I E L E          DISKETTE
T S S F X I V N P Y E H I S V T A G W T          ALGORITHM
G M Y H H J W C O O H E X X C H U Q P T          TECHNOLOGY
R H F Y D P T Y W O C C F N O K O V Z E          ERROR
L T F E Q X Q F M Y M O U O O W W S S D          FUNCTION
T I G F G B O Z B Y C F M B G O W J G V          ARRAY
W R T W I H V R J Z B N R P A B U G I I          BJARNE
O O H U Z C L C I K X U E U U Y P P D T
E G T N B W Y L Q P T N N E G T S E Q E
C L A O T O M K F W G K V X O J E H E D
T A D R A O B Y E K V Q I K W H W R G R
L X X N I I L X X W R M O D N X B U G D
O B W T S A Y G O L O N H C E T Y I O S
```

```
                      P
              E R R O R
                  O                                 D
              G                                     I
          R                           A   N         S
        A                           R   O           K
      M                           R   I             E
                                A       T           T
      M                       Y       C             T
      H                     C       N       E       E
      T                       O   U   N
      I                         F M R
      R                         A P
      O                       J       U
      G                     B               T
      L                                   E
      A D R A O B Y E K               R

          Y G O L O N H C E T
```

COMPUTER
PROGRAM
KEYBOARD
DISKETTE
ALGORITHM
TECHNOLOGY
ERROR
FUNCTION
ARRAY
BJARNE

8. Add to assignment 1 the ability to save and load files.

9. Combine assignments 1, 3, and 8 into one program.

10. Add to assignment 5 the ability to save the corrected image back to an image data file.

CHAPTER 8

STRUCTS, CLASSES, AND OBJECT-ORIENTED PROGRAMMING

8.1 INTRODUCTION

Today, sophisticated software is being used to tackle a multitude of complex problems. Software routinely manages billions of dollars in financial transactions, controls the air traffic at major airports (it even controls many of the aircraft directly), oversees the operation of nuclear power plants, and makes sure automobile brakes don't lock up during panic stops. Such software must be highly reliable. So far, all the programs we have developed have been trivial. The larger ones have contained fewer than a couple hundred lines of source code, none of them have done anything exciting enough to cause people to stand in line to buy them, and no one's life has been in jeopardy just because they might have contained errors.

Very little of today's marketable software is written by one person. Each of the large software packages for microcomputers—like Microsoft Windows, IBM's OS/2, WordPerfect's word processor, or Borland's Quattro Pro spreadsheet—was developed over a course of years by scores of experienced and talented programmers. It has been reported that Microsoft Windows 3.1 is built from about 5,000,000 lines of source code; its successor, Microsoft Windows '95, a true 32-bit operating system with a graphical user interface and multimedia capabilities, tips the scales at around 20,000,000 lines. With an understanding of the complexities and difficulties of building small programs, imagine what it must be like to work several years or so with scores (possibly hundreds) of other programmers on a single multimillion line software project. Its success or failure in the marketplace means a multimillion dollar gain or loss for the company. Taking more time to make sure the job is totally correct may be an unavailable luxury. Time is important, since a good idea realized six months late in the software industry may be obsolete. Having lots of programmers helps, but often the inherent human problems of poor communication and personality conflicts add to the difficulty of the task at hand.

Software is hard to write, as beginning programmers can attest. Complicated, powerful software is even harder to write. Tools are desperately needed that can make the task of software development easier and make programmers more productive. As the demands on software have grown, programming languages have evolved to address the challenge of producing ever increasingly complex software that at the same time must be more reliable. The late 1960s and 1970s produced the structured programming revolution. This revolution produced the structured statements, the concept of locality, and the functional independence that we've been utilizing throughout. These features made complicated software easier to write with fewer errors.

The modern software revolution is object-oriented programming (OOP). Its goal is to allow programmers to concentrate more on the problem at hand by modeling the objects that exist in the problem domain. OOP also promotes *software reuse*, not by simply using library functions as is, but by extending library objects (classes) or customizing them to the problem at hand. The programmer can customize the behavior of these classes in original ways even if the details of how they work is unknown. Structured objects, `structs` and `classes`, make OOP possible.

8.2 STRUCTS

Arrays are aggregate data types that hold homogeneous data. C++ `structs` are aggregate data types that can hold *heterogenous* data types. `structs` are useful for modeling many real word problems where objects made up of diverse components need to be represented in a computer program. `structs` also provide a means for building elaborate data structures that can be used to represent relationships among complex objects or improve the efficiency of some algorithms.

Suppose an employee record needs to be represented in a program. The record contains the following pertinent information:

Employee ID Number
Last Name
First Name
Age
Salary
Seniority

These data items could be represented by separate variables:

```
typedef char String[25];

void main()
{
        unsigned ID_number;      /*  Value 0...9999  */
        String last_name;
        String first_name;
        unsigned age;
        float salary;
        int seniority;           /*  Value -3...120  */

        /*  Process employee record...  */
        .
        .
        .

}
```

The seniority value can be negative to represent employees hired on a probationary status; the value increases by one each month up to a maximum of 120 (ten years). All other whole numbers are unsigned because negative values are not needed.

This is a reasonable implementation, but it has some drawbacks. An employee record is conceptually a unit. It should be treated as one item until its contents need to be examined. At this point, passing an employee record to a function requires the passing of six separate variables. Ideally, it would be better to somehow pass only one item—the record itself. Also, if three employee records are going to be represented in a program, three sets of employee information variables must be used. Since each variable must have a unique name, there will be names such as last_name1, last_name2, last_name3, first_name1, first_name2, first_name3, etc. If an array of employee records is desired (as is likely, if a database is being constructed), then six separate arrays must be used:

```
unsigned ID_number[SIZE];
String last_name[SIZE];
String first_name[SIZE];
unsigned age[SIZE];
float salary[SIZE];
int seniority[SIZE];
```

Besides being inconvenient, this representation is conceptually inappropriate. This represents arrays of six separate kinds of items. We want an array of one type of item, each item of which has six component parts. Forcing the solution to a problem to conform to the features of a programming language in an unnatural way slows development, since the programmer must then transform the solution to the real world problem into the solution for the computer. Performing this transformation process is just another layer of effort for the programmer and another opportunity for errors and inconsistencies to creep into the program. A struct is what we need.

The following declaration can be used for our employee record function:

```
typedef char String[25];

struct EmpRec {
        unsigned    ID_number;
        String      last_name;
        String      first_name;
        unsigned    age;
        float       salary;
        int         seniority;
};

void main()
{
    EmpRec r;
    /*  Process r...  */
    .
    .
    .
}
```

The reserved word struct is followed by the *structure name* EmpRec. The record structure is defined within the curly braces. A variable of this structure type can be declared—as r is in main():

```
EmpRec r;
```

EmpRec is treated as a type name and can be used to declare variables. r is not a simple variable as is a built-in numeric or character type; it is a composite type that contains six different *fields*. A *field* is a component of the struct and can be accessed with the structure member (dot) operator:

```
r.ID_number = 2341;
r.salary = 35000.00;
```

r.ID_number is read "r dot ID_number." struct fields can consist of any type, including arrays and even other structs. structs cannot be *recursive* in nature; that is, a struct cannot have a field that is a struct exactly like itself. For example:

```
struct EmpRec {
        String name;
        EmpRec boss;    /*  Recursive definition, illegal  */
};
```

is not legal.

A function can receive a struct as a parameter or return a struct:

```
EmpRec process_record(EmpRec x) {
        EmpRec temp;

        temp = x;   /*  Copies the whole struct  */
        cout << "Enter new ID number: ";
        cin >> temp.ID_number;
        return temp;
}
```

structs can be initialized when declared in a fashion similar to arrays:

```
EmpRec r = {
        1324,
        "Doe",
        "Jane",
        24,
        25000.00,
        12
};
```

Each field does not need to appear on its own line. This convention is used to improve readability, since it emphasizes the diverse nature of the struct's components. By contrast, array elements in an array initializer usually appear all on the same line (as much as possible) emphasizing their type uniformity.

Figure 8.1 shows how structs are stored in memory on one particular system. On some systems, more efficient code can be generated if the struct's individual components are each stored

Memory layout for object **r** located at address 250:

Internal Arrangement of a struct
Figure 8.1

beginning at even addresses. This will leave some small, unused portions of memory tied up by each `struct`. These "holes" are small and their presence is invisible to the C++ programmer.

For assignment or call-by-value parameter passing, a simple *bit copy* of memory is done (although the actual activity of the copy can be altered; see chapter 11). All the bits in one part of memory are copied without interpretation or translation to another part of memory. Since this copying can take a long time, especially for large `structs`, originally C did not allow `structs` to be passed by value. Recall that arrays are not passed by value because of the unreasonable overhead that can occur from copying all of their elements. However, unlike arrays, `structs` have to be passed explicitly by reference to avoid the overhead. In general, it is best to pass large `structs` by reference, not only to avoid the copying overhead, but also to lessen the possibility of running out of stack space. Instead of copying each component of the `struct` onto the stack, only the address of the `struct` needs to be copied onto the stack. The disadvantage of the call-by-reference technique for passing `structs` to functions is obvious—accidental side effects are possible. Fortunately, the efficiency of call-by-reference and the safety of call-by-value can be achieved by specifying the reference parameter to be `const`:

```
EmpRec process_record(const EmpRec &x) {
    EmpRec temp;
    temp = x;   /*  Copies the whole struct  */
    cout << "Enter new ID number: ";
    cin >> temp.ID_number;
    return temp;
}
```

In this version of `process_record()`, an `EmpRec` is efficiently passed-by-reference, but it is illegal to attempt to modify the formal parameter within the function. The `const` specifier makes parameters "read-only," like the global constants introduced in chapter 5.

8.3   EXAMPLE: SIMPLE DATABASE

Program 8.1 illustrates the use of `structs` in a simple database program. The type `EmpRec` defined above will be used in an array that holds information concerning all the employees for a particular company.

```
#include <iostream.h>
#include <ctype.h>

const int MAX_STR_LEN   =  25,
          MAX_EMPLOYEES = 100;
typedef char String[MAX_STR_LEN];

struct EmpRec {
    unsigned   ID_number;
    String     last_name;
    String     first_name;
    unsigned   age;
    float      salary;
    int        seniority;
};

struct DataBase {
    EmpRec emp_list[MAX_EMPLOYEES];
    int    size;
};
```

```cpp
int more_records() {
      char in_ch;
      int done = 1, response;
      do {
         cout << "Enter another record <Y>es or <N>o?";
         cin >> in_ch;
         switch ( toupper(in_ch) ) {
               case 'N': response = 0;
                          done = 1;
                          break;
               case 'Y': response = 1;
                          done = 1;
                          break;
               default : done = 0;
          }
      } while ( !done );
      return response;
}

void get_record(EmpRec &r) {
      cout << "Enter Employee ID number: ";
      cin  >> r.ID_number;
      cout << "Enter last name: ";
      cin  >> r.last_name;
      cout << "Enter first name: ";
      cin  >> r.first_name;
      cout << "Enter age: ";
      cin  >> r.age;
      cout << "Enter salary: ";
      cin  >> r.salary;
      cout << "Enter seniority:";
      cin  >> r.seniority;
}

void insert_database(DataBase &d) {
      int more = 1;
      while ( d.size < MAX_EMPLOYEES  &&  more ) {
            get_record(d.emp_list[d.size]);
            d.size++;
            more = more_records();
      }
}

void clear_database(DataBase &d) {
      d.size = 0;
}

char do_menu() {
      cout <<  "****************************************************\n"
               "*                  Database Menu                   *\n"
               "****************************************************\n"
               "*          I          Insert                       *\n"
               "*          P          Print                        *\n"
               "*          C          Clear                        *\n"
               "*          Q          Quit                         *\n"
               "****************************************************\n";
      char ch;
      cin >> ch;
      return toupper(ch);
}
```

```
void print_rec(const EmpRec &r) {
    cout << "ID: " << r.ID_number << "\nLast: " << r.last_name
        << "\nFirst: " << r.first_name << "\nAge: " << r.age
        << " Salary: " << r.salary << " Seniority: "
        << r.seniority << '\n';
}
void print_database(const DataBase &d) {
    int i;
    cin.get();    //  Remove "enter" character from menu selection
    for ( i = 0;  i < d.size;  i++ ) {
        print_rec(d.emp_list[i]);
        cout << "[Enter] continues...\n";
        cin.get();
    }
    cout << "No more records.\n";
}


DataBase base;  //  External

void main() {
    int done = 0;
    clear_database(base);
    while ( !done )
        switch ( do_menu() ) {
            case 'I': insert_database(base);  break;
            case 'C': clear_database(base);   break;
            case 'P': print_database(base);   break;
            case 'Q': done = 1;
        }
}
```

Program 8.1

Observe that a DataBase object is a *big* object. If, for example, the integer fields (both signed and unsigned) require two bytes each (a conservative estimate these days) and the float is stored in four bytes, then each EmpRec requires 60 bytes of storage. A DataBase holds an array of 100 EmpRecs plus the size of the array. Based on these values, a DataBase object requires 6,002 bytes of storage. It definitely should *not* be passed by value to any of the functions, since that is a lot of stack space to consume (it might overflow the stack on some systems). Even if the stack were large enough, the time it would take to copy a complete DataBase onto the stack would take much longer than simply copying its address, as is done in call-by-reference.

It has been said that the creation of Unix was made possible when Dennis Ritchie added the struct feature to his infant programming language C. Unix is a multiuser, multitasking operating system of great complexity. structs provide the means to organize data and manage complexity, allowing a programmer to be more productive.

Exercises

1. When discussing structs, what is a *field?*

2. What is the structure member operator?

3. How can a struct be initialized when it is declared?

4. Can one `struct` be contained within another `struct`?

5. Explain why it is possible for the size of a `struct` to be larger than the sum of its component parts.

> For questions 6–22, assume the following declarations. Indicate whether the following expressions are syntactically legal or illegal. If an expression is illegal, indicate why it is illegal. If it is legal, interpret its meaning.

```
enum Gender { female, male };

enum Status { probationary, standard, elite, retired, deceased };

struct Date {
     int year, month, day;
};

struct EmpRec {
     char lastname[20];
     char firstname[20];
     char middleinitial;
     int  ID_number;
     Date DOB;
     Gender sex;
     float salary;
     Status stat;
};

EmpRec r[100], record;
Date d;
char word[20], ch;
int i;
Gender g;
Status s;
```

6. `r[3].sex = male;`

7. `r.middleinitial = 'K';`

8. `record.ID_number = 45;`

9. `r[2].lastname = word;`

10. `r[4] = record;`

11. `s = i;`

12. `i = s;`

13. `d.month = i;`

14. `i = d.year;`

15. `EmpRec.ID_number = 49;`

16. `g = s;`

17. `record.DOB = d;`

18. `r.middleinitial = 'E';`

19. `record.middleinitial = word[2];`

20. `record.d = DOB;`

21. `r[3].lastname[3] = word[3];`

22. `i = strlen(r.lastname);`

8.4   AN INTRODUCTION TO OBJECT-ORIENTED PROGRAMMING

An essential idea in OOP is that an object should be able to perform operations on itself. This means that an object is not sent off to a function so that the function can manipulate the data within the object. Instead, the object is "told" to manipulate its own data. In traditional OOP terminology, an object is *sent a message* to perform some task, and the object chooses its own *method* (from a collection of methods it has at its disposal) to carry out this task. This is the essence of OOP.

Since the mid-1980s, the OOP style has been gaining momentum among developers as well as increased attention from the popular computer press. The ideas of OOP are not new; indeed, OOP languages have been around for over 25 years. The recent advent of modern OOP languages (including C++), a better understanding of OOP techniques, as well as a need to conquer large software projects in a reasonable way have all led to OOP's current popularity.

As alluded to in the introduction, the history of computer programming is a progression from total obsession with "thinking like the hardware works" to solving the problem "conceptually, in human terms." Higher-level languages have almost completely unshackled programmers from the tyranny of meeting the needs of specific hardware in order to get the job done. Assembly language was dominated by languages like FORTRAN, COBOL, and BASIC that allow programmers to think in more symbolic terms as is done in mathematics. Structured languages such as Pascal, Modula-2, Ada, and C arose adding sanity to the organization of the program's component parts. All of these aforementioned languages are known as *procedural languages*. Procedural languages accomplish their tasks by applying algorithms (procedures) to passive data. Data (i.e., the elements in an array, for example) get modified (sorted) because an algorithm (i.e., a selection sort routine) is applied to them. The data have no choice but to be manipulated by whatever procedures the programmers wish to impose upon them.

OOP techniques view the situation from a different perspective. The problem to be solved involves a collection of real world or abstract *objects*. These objects can interact with each other and perform certain tasks. Instead of applying procedures to passive data as in the procedural paradigm, the data themselves contain procedures to modify themselves based on messages that other objects may send them. The methods of program design introduced in chapter 6 are not as useful in OOP. The overall solution to the problem is not envisioned as a hierarchical structure chart of functions and modules—a program designed top-down through step-wise refinement. The problem is solved by identifying the components (objects) of the problem domain and determining how these components interact and are related. OOP takes a bottom-up approach to development. The correct specification of the details of the objects that make up the system allows the overall structure of the system to evolve into the final solution. Object relationships are emphasized over functional decomposition. The OOP paradigm appears well suited for large projects that must change over time, where the prime players are cursed by the *software crisis*—the paradoxical need to develop more complex programs in a shorter period of time with fewer errors.

A good programmer has a thorough knowledge of the principles of good *data structure construction*. This knowledge is critical to the development of sophisticated programs. The types `EmpRec` and `DataBase` were data structures used within program 8.1. The proper marriage of data structures (such as `DataBase`) and their associated algorithms (such as `insert_database()`) yields programs with substantial power. However, program 8.1 uses data structures in a non-OO fashion. A `DataBase` object is a passive entity that is sent off to the `insert_database()` function to be processed. The OO approach sends a message to the `DataBase` object telling it to apply its "insert into the database" method. In C++, this process is accomplished through a *member function*.

The definition of DataBase from above will be modified:

```
struct DataBase {
    EmpRec emp_list[MAX_EMPLOYEES];
    int size;
    void insert();
    void print();
    void clear();
};
```

Notice that three functions have been added as fields of the `DataBase` structure. These are called member functions of the class. When some new records are to be inserted into a `DataBase` object `base`, instead of passing `base` to a function, the member function for `base` is called:

```
base.insert();
```

The member function is defined as follows:

```
void DataBase::insert() {
    int more = 1;
    while ( size < MAX_EMPLOYEES  &&  more ) {
        get_record(emp_list[size]);
        size++;
        more = more_records();
    }
}
```

The *scope resolution operator* (`::`) is used to associate the member function properly with a `DataBase` structure. Another structure type could have a member function with the same name, and the scope resolution operator distinguishes been the two. Notice that a local variable, `more`, is used as in any normal function. Also, observe the identifiers `size` and `emp_list`. These are the fields within the object for which the member function was evoked. For example, if two `DataBase` objects have been defined:

```
DataBase base1, base2;
base1.insert();  //  Call to function uses base1.size and base1.emp_list
base2.insert();  //  Call to function uses base2.size and base2.emp_list
```

Consider the following potential problem. The `Database::clear()` method is provided to clear the database `base`. It merely sets the `size` field of `base` to zero. The programmer does not need to know how it does it, just that the database will be empty as far as the other member functions are concerned. The programmer merely sends a message to the database object to clear itself, and it does whatever is necessary to get the job done. The problem is that the programmer could have accomplished that same feat with the statement:

```
base.size = 0;
```

This circumvents the message passing philosophy. Ideally, objects should be self-contained, robust units that are accessed only through member functions. That programmers can write code to manipulate the internals of an object violates the principles of OOP. This unlimited ability to access the details of a data structure often leads to problems in large programs, especially if multiple programmers are involved. It would be beneficial to be able to hide the internal details of a data structure so that access to the data structure is limited to a fixed number of specific operations (the member functions). This process of restricting access to data structures is called *encapsulation*. The internal details of the data structure are encapsulated by an interface that provides a set of legal operations on that data structure. The data structure thus becomes an *abstract data type* (ADT).

`int`s are built-in data types. Access to the `int` type is normally restricted to assignment, addition, and so forth. Many of C++'s operators can use `int`s as operands. Normally, a programmer does not go in and try to change the individual bits that make up an `int` (although the programmer could—see chapter 15). Most applications work quite well with access to `int`s being restricted to normal assignment, addition, and so forth.

In general, it is best for the author of a module that defines a data structure to be able to limit the access to a client programmer. This encapsulation ability limits errors that can be introduced by client code. The ADT becomes a black box that *must* be used as intended. Any misuse could (and should) be handled gracefully by the black box.

C++ provides the ability to create ADTs with its `class` feature.

8.5 CLASSES

A `class` is defined in C++ in a similar fashion to a `struct`:

```
class DataBase {
    EmpRec emp_list[MAX_EMPLOYEES];
    int size;
    void insert();
    void print();
    void clear();
};
```

The difference is that the fields of a `class` are, by default, not directly accessible to the user of the `class`:

```
DataBase base;
base.size = 10;   //  Illegal, data field is not accessible.
base.clear();     //  Illegal, member function is not accessible
```

Parts of a `class` can be made accessible with the reserved word `public`:

```
class DataBase {
    EmpRec emp_list[MAX_EMPLOYEES];
    int size;
public:
    void insert();
    void print();
    void clear();
};
```

Now the following is legal

```
DataBase base;
base.clear();
```

The term *class* will be used interchangeably with ADT, and `class` [in program font] will refer to the C++ reserved word.

Actually, `structs` and `classes` are identical except for their default access. The reserved word `private` indicates private access. The following two ADTs have elements with equivalent access privileges:

```
class X {               struct Y {
    int   a;                int  c;
    float b;                double d;
public:                  private:
    int   c;                int  a;
    double  d;                  float  b;
};                       };
```

The labels `public` and `private` can be used in any order throughout `structs` and `classes`:

```
class X {
public:
        int    a;
private:
        float b;
        int    c;
public:
        char   d;
};
```

The a and d fields of `class X` are freely accessible; fields b and c are generally inaccessible. A concern might be "Of what use are `private` data fields if they can't be accessed?" The answer is that `private` elements cannot be accessed from *outside* the class, but they can be accessed from *inside* the class. The next question naturally follows: "How does one access a field from within a class?" Private fields can be accessed through member functions.

Prior to this chapter, our discussion of functions has dealt with globally visible functions. Functions may be called as long as they have been properly declared and their definitions appear somewhere. Somewhere can mean in the same file, in a different file, or compiled in a library. Just as the visibility of variables can be limited through the use of local variables, the visibility of functions can also be limited. Class membership restricts the visiblity of functions to objects of that particular class.

Recall the concept of complex numbers from algebra. Complex numbers can be written in the form a + bi, where i is the square root of –1. a is the real component, and b is the imaginary component. The following class `Complex` represents complex numbers:

```
class Complex {
    double real;
    double imag;
public:
    void print();
    void assign(double, double);
    double real();
    double imaginary();
};

void Complex::print() {
    cout << real << " + " << imag << 'i';
}

void Complex::assign(double r, double i) {
    real = r;
    imag = i;
}

double Complex::real() {
    return real;
}

double Complex::imaginary() {
    return imag;
}
```

`print()`, `assign()`, `real()`, and `imaginary()` are the member functions of class `Complex`. The operator `::` associates a function definition with a particular class (just as it does with `struct`s).

Given the above definitions, the following section of code could interact with a `Complex` class "variable":

```
Complex comp;              //  Declares comp to be a Complex
comp.assign(3.0, 4.5);     //  Assigns comp to 3.0 + 4.5i
cout << comp.real();       //  Looks at real field of comp
comp.print();              //  Displays 3.000 + 4.500i
```

A "variable" of a particular class is called an *object*. Variables are objects of a built-in type. True objects are instances of a user constructed class (or `struct`); thus, an object is an instance of a class, just as a variable is an instance of a built-in type.

The statement `comp.print()` calls the `print()` member function of the class `Complex` for the object `comp`. All objects of class `Complex` would use the same `print()` function; however, the function would use the data of the particular object. Another class could have its own `print()` member function, which would be distinct from `Complex`'s. Consider program 8.2:

```
#include <iostream.h>
class Complex {
    double real;
    double imag;
public:
    void print();
    //  Other member functions follow
};

class Vector {
    double x;
    double y;
    double z;
public:
    void print();
    //  Other member functions follow...
};

void Complex::print() {
    cout << real << " + " << imag << 'i';
}

void Vector::print() {
    cout << '(' << x << ',' << y << ',' << z << ')';
}

void main() {
    Complex c1, c2;
    Vector  v1, v2;
    //  Some code to initialize the objects goes here...
    c1.print();  //  Calls Complex::print() with c1's data
    c2.print();  //  Calls Complex::print() with c2's data
    v1.print();  //  Calls Vector::print() with v1's data
    v2.print();  //  Calls Vector::print() with v2's data
    //  Remainder of main() would follow...
}
```

Program 8.2

In order to distinguish member functions in our discussion, the scope resolution operator and class name will be used to qualify the function name (e.g., Complex::print() versus Vector::print()).

Notice that member functions have free access to private elements of a class. The user of a class can only have access to private data items as the public member functions allow. This interface can be used to prevent direct tampering with the data structure preventing possible errors as mentioned above.

Member functions can be private. Member functions are often made private when they are used by other public member functions but are not meant to be called directly by client code.

In general, all data in a class should be made private. Its accessibility should be as restricted as possible. The private data of a class and the body of the member functions (member function definitions) that act upon the private data are called the *implementation* of the class. The public access to the class, whether it is through public member functions (member function declarations) or public data, is called the *interface* to the class. A class's implementation and interface should be kept distinct. Client code that uses the class sees the interface but not the implementation. When classes are designed properly, the class author should be free to change the implementation of the class without the possibility of damaging client code that is already written. The client code depends on the interface, not the implementation.

The database program from earlier in the chapter can be rewritten to take advantage of these OOP features. It will resemble a "real world" effort more closely than any other program considered thus far because it is distributed over three different files. One of the files is the header file db-oop.h (program 8.3a) that is #included by the other two cpp source files.

```
//  File db-oop.h

const int MAX_STR_LEN  =  25,
          MAX_EMPLOYEES = 100;

typedef char String[MAX_STR_LEN];

class EmpRec {
     unsigned  ID_number;
     String    last_name;
     String    first_name;
     unsigned  age;
     float     salary;
     int       seniority;
public:
     void get();
     void print() const;
};

class DataBase {
     EmpRec emp_list[MAX_EMPLOYEES];
     int  size;
public:
     void insert();
     void print() const;
     void clear();
     char do_menu() const;
};
```

Program 8.3a

None of the member functions is defined, but all are declared within their respective classes. Nothing needs to be #included by this file, since it uses no library functions or classes. Notice that DataBase::print(), DataBase::do_menu(), and EmpRec::print() have the reserved word const following their parameter lists but before the semicolon. In this context, const instructs the compiler (or anyone viewing this header file) that these member functions will not modify any data within the class. Said more formally, applying any of these member functions to an object will not change its state.

The implementation of the DataBase's member functions is found in the file db-oop.cpp (program 8.3b):

```
#include <iostream.h>
#include <ctype.h>
#include "db-oop.h"

//  The static specifier means this function is not accessible outside
//   of this file
static int more_records() {
     char in_ch;
     int done = 1, response;
     do {
          cout << "Enter another record <Y>es or <N>o?";
          cin >> in_ch;
          switch ( toupper(in_ch) ) {
               case 'N':  response = 0;
                          done = 1;
                          break;
               case 'Y':  response = 1;
                          done = 1;
                          break;
               default :  done = 0;
          }
```

```
        } while ( !done );
        return response;
}

void EmpRec::get() {
        cout << "Enter Employee ID number: ";
        cin  >> ID_number;
        cout << "Enter last name: ";
        cin  >> last_name;
        cout << "Enter first name: ";
        cin  >> first_name;
        cout << "Enter age: ";
        cin  >> age;
        cout << "Enter salary: ";
        cin  >> salary;
        cout << "Enter seniority:";
        cin  >> seniority;
}

void EmpRec::print() const {
        cout << "ID: " << ID_number << "\nLast: " << last_name
             << "\nFirst: " << first_name << "\nAge: " << age
             << " Salary: " << salary << " Seniority: "
             << seniority << '\n';
}

void DataBase::insert() {
        int more = 1;
        while ( size < MAX_EMPLOYEES  &&  more ) {
                emp_list[size].get();
                size++;
                more = more_records();
        }
}

void DataBase::clear() {
        size = 0;
}

char DataBase::do_menu() const {
        cout << "************************************************\n"
             "*                  Database Menu               *\n"
             "************************************************\n"
             "*         I          Insert                    *\n"
             "*         P          Print                     *\n"
             "*         C          Clear                     *\n"
             "*         Q          Quit                      *\n"
             "************************************************\n";
        char ch;
        cin >> ch;
        return toupper(ch);
}

void DataBase::print() const {
        int i;
        cin.get();   // Remove "enter" character from menu selection
        for ( i = 0;  i < size;  i++ ) {
                emp_list[i].print();
                cout << "[Enter] continues...\n";
                cin.get();
        }
        cout << "No more records.\n";
}
```

Program 8.3b

Some parts of db-oop.cpp warrant comment. Starting at the top, it #includes several standard header files because it makes use of a library character function (toupper()) and some stream objects (cin and cout). The header file we created is also #included since it contains the declarations for the EmpRec and DataBase classes. Without the inclusion of this header file, the compiler would report that these classes were undeclared identifiers. The file name is enclosed within double quotes because it is located in the same directory as the file being compiled. The angle brackets are used to denote files found in the standard header file subdirectory, whatever that might be for a particular system.

As in the header, the implementations of some of the member functions use the const specifier. Omitting it in the implementation when it appears in the interface is an error. An attempt to use the following statement within DataBase::print() would also generate a compiler error:

```
size++;
```

since size is a member of a DataBase object and changing it would alter the object's state.

The function more_records() has the static specifier before its return type. The static specifier indicates that this function cannot be called from functions outside of this file. more_records() is, in essence, local to the file db-oop.cpp. This feature is extremely useful in large multifile projects. A function written for private use in one module (cpp source file) will not have a name clash with another function in another file with the exact same name and signature (parameter list). By default, all functions are global to the program even if the program is made up of separately compiled source files linked together. As another option, more_records() could have been made a private member function of the DataBase class. This, too, would limit its use to other DataBase member functions and render it inaccessible outside of the class. This was not done here, since more_records() does not directly interact with a DataBase object and does not access any private data.

Notice also that this source file lacks a main() function. When the source code is distributed over multiple files, only one file may contain the function main(). db-oop.cpp cannot be compiled as a stand-alone program.

Finally, the client file, stored in db-main.cpp is presented (Program 8.3c):

```
#include "db-oop.h"

DataBase base;   //  External to save stack space

void main() {
    int done = 0;
    base.clear();
    while ( !done )
        switch ( base.do_menu() ) {
            case 'I': base.insert();  break;
            case 'C': base.clear();   break;
            case 'P': base.print();   break;
            case 'Q': done = 1;
        }
}
```

Program 8.3c

This file is so small because most of the work is hidden away in the db-oop.cpp file. This file does not even directly use streams, so the normally ubiquitous <iostream.h> header file is missing. It merely manages a loop by interacting with a DataBase object's menu member function. The object itself "knows" what menu options to display based on the methods available through its member functions. (The object only "knows" what to do due to skillful crafting by the DataBase class programmer, of course.) When the choice is made, the object is directed to take the appropriate action.

Exercises

1. How is a C++ `class` different from a C++ `struct`?

2. What does the reserved word `public` indicate within a class?

3. What is a member function?

4. What is an object?

5. What does the reserved word `private` indicate within a class?

6. Distinguish between a class's *interface* and *implementation*.

7. Define *abstract data type*.

8. What is meant by the term *encapsulation*?

Questions 9–23 refer to the following definitions:

```
struct X {
      int a, b;
      void f() { cout << a << ' ' << c; }
private:
      int c, d;
      void g() { cout << b << ' ' << d; }
};

class Y {
      int a, b;
      void f() { cout << a << ' ' << c; }
public:
      int c, d;
      void g() { cout << b << ' ' << d; }
};

X x1, x2;
Y y1, y2;
```

Indicate whether or not each of the following statements is syntactically legal or illegal. If the statement is illegal, indicate why it is illegal. If it is legal, interpret the statement.

9. `x1.a = x2.a;`

10. `y1.a = y2.a;`

11. `x1.a = y1.a;`

12. `x1 = x2;`

13. `y1 = y2;`

14. `x1 = y1;`

15. `y1 = x1;`

16. `x1.f();`

17. `y1.f();`

18. `x1.g();`

19. `y1.g();`

20. `y1.a = y1.b;`

21. `y1.a = y2.c;`

22. `x1.a = y1.c;`

23. `cout << y1.d;`

8.6   IMPROVED ANIMATION

The bouncing ball program from chapter 7 can now be made much more useful. Recall a ball was animated within a two-dimensional array that could be displayed on the screen on a frame-by-frame basis. (It was suggested that the animation could be made to display in real time on systems equipped with the appropriate hardware and graphics libraries. The same improvement can be just as easily added to this updated program.) Like the database program above, it is distributed over several files.

The file bncball.h (program 8.4a) contains the declarations for the Ball class:

```
//   File Ball-OOP.H

const char BLOCK   = 'O',
           EMPTY   = ' ';

const int  XHI     = 60,
           XLO     = 20,
           YHI     = 18,
           YLO     = 5,
           MAXROWS = 24,
           MAXCOLS = 79;

typedef char ScreenArray[MAXCOLS][MAXROWS];

class Ball {
      int   x, y;    //  Ball's (x,y) position
      char shape;    //  Character used to display the ball
      int dx, dy;    //  Ball's change in x and y
public:
      int set(int, int, char = 'o');  //  Sets x, y, and shape
      int move(ScreenArray);   //  Updates the ball's position
      int x_pos();   //  Returns x value, thus x is a read-only member
      int y_pos();   //  Returns y value, thus y is a read-only member
};
```

Program 8.4a

The file bncball.cpp (program 8.4b) contains the Ball class implementation:

```
#include "ball-oop.h"

int Ball::set(int _x, int _y, char shp) {
      x   = _x;
      y   = _y;
      dx = 1;
      dy = 1;
      shape = shp;
      //  Returns 1 if in the box, 0 if outside or on border
      return x > XLO  &&   x < XHI  &&  y > YLO  && y < YHI;
}

int Ball::move(ScreenArray screen) {
      int collision = 0;  // no collision
      //  Check for collision...
      if ( x + dx >= XHI   ||  x + dx <= XLO ) {
            dx = -dx;          //  Collision with left or right wall
            collision = 1;   //  Note the collision
      }
      if ( y + dy >= YHI   ||  y + dy <= YLO ) {
            dy = -dy;          //  Collision with ceiling or floor
            collision = 1;
      }
```

```
        //  Erase ball in old position
        screen[x][y] = EMPTY;
        //  Update ball's position
        x = x + dx;  y = y + dy;
        //  Draw ball in new position
        screen[x][y] = shape;
        return collision;
}
int Ball::x_pos() {
        return x;
}

int Ball::y_pos() {
        return y;
}
```

Program 8.4b

Observe that `Ball::set()` and `Ball::move()` return integer results that client code can check, if necessary. `Ball::set()` returns zero if the object is placed outside of the box and one otherwise. `Ball::move()` returns one if the ball collided with a wall and zero otherwise.

The `ballmain.cpp` file is shown in program 8.4c.

```
#include <iostream.h>
#include "ball-oop.h"

/*
 *      initialize()
 *          Clears the screen array, frequency array.
 */
void initialize(ScreenArray screen, ScreenArray freq) {
        int row, col;
        //  Initialize the screen array...
        for ( row = 0;  row < MAXROWS;  row++ )
            for ( col = 0;  col < MAXCOLS;  col++ )
                if ( ((row == YLO || row == YHI) && col >= XLO && col <= XHI)
                     || ((col == XHI  || col == XLO)  && row >= YLO &&  row
                        <= YHI)  )
                    screen[col][row] = BLOCK;
                else
                    screen[col][row] = EMPTY;

        //  Clear frequency array...
        for ( row = 0;  row < MAXROWS; row++ )
            for ( col = 0;  col < MAXCOLS;  col++ )
                freq[col][row] = 0;
}

/*
 *      update_frequency()
 *          Increments the table at the ball's current position.
 */
void update_frequency(ScreenArray f, int x, int y) {
        f[x][y]++;
}

/*
 *      scroll_up()
 *          Clears the screen by scrolling it up one frame.
 */
void scroll_up() {
        //  "Clear" screen by scrolling it up one frame
        for ( int row = 0;  row < MAXROWS;  row++ )
            cout << '\n';
}
```

```
/*      report_frequency()
 *            Displays a map of the ball's travels.
 */
void report_frequency(ScreenArray f) {
    int i, j;
    scroll_up();
    for ( j = 0;  j < MAXROWS;  j++ ) {
        for ( i = 0;  i < MAXCOLS;  i++ )
            if ( f[i][j] > 3 )
                cout << '@';
            else if ( f[i][j] > 2 )
                cout << 'O';
            else if ( f[i][j] > 1 )
                cout << 'o';
            else if ( f[i][j] > 0 )
                cout << '.';
            else
                cout << ' ';
        cout << '\n';
    }
}


/*
 *        draw_screen()
 *              Draws the current configuration—the walls and the ball.
 */
int draw_screen(ScreenArray screen) {
    int row, col;
    scroll_up();
    //  Draw the borders or ball
    for ( row = 0;  row < MAXROWS;  row++ ) {
        for ( col = 0;  col < MAXCOLS;  col++ )
            cout << screen[col][row];
        cout << '\n';
    }
    // Wait for enter key
    return  cin.get() == '\n';
}

ScreenArray scrn, freq;    // Declared extern to save stack space

void main() {
    initialize(scrn, freq);
    Ball b;
    b.set(XLO + 5, YLO + 5, '+');
    do {
        b.move(scrn);
        update_frequency(freq, b.x_pos(), b.y_pos());
    } while ( draw_screen(scrn) );
    report_frequency(freq);
}
```

Program 8.4c

Does this object-oriented approach offer any advantages over the first version? This second version more closely represents the problem conceptually. Instead of four disjoint variables (x, y, dx, and dy) needed to animate a nameless ball, the Ball structure essentially "animates itself." A Ball object keeps track of its own coordinates and direction. This version is much more extensible as well. Without touching any of the other functions, main() can be easily modified to animate any number of balls simultaneously. (See program 8.5.)

```
void main() {
    initialize(scrn, freq);
    Ball b1, b2, b3, b4;
    b1.set(XLO +  5, YLO +  5, '+');
    b2.set(XLO + 10, YLO + 10, 'o');
    b3.set(XLO + 15, YLO + 10, '@');
    b4.set(XLO + 20, YLO + 10, '*');
    do {
        b1.move(scrn);
        b2.move(scrn);
        b3.move(scrn);
        b4.move(scrn);
        //  Here frequency only updated for b1
        update_frequency(freq, b1.x_pos(), b1.y_pos());
    } while ( draw_screen(scrn) );
    report_frequency(freq);
}
```

Program 8.5

Imagine the horrors of modifying the nonobject-oriented version for multiple balls. Separate x and y position variables would need to be created as well as separate static dxs and dys within the old update_position() function for each new ball. Each time an extra ball would need to be added to the old program, critical functions would need to be modified substantially. Any time working code needs to be changed, the possibility of introducing logical errors exists. Since errors don't always become immediately apparent, the programmer has to question his or her trust in the modified code, even though it has yet to exhibit any errors. Consider the other situation; namely, a working code that is not touched continues to perform as reliably as always. The judicious use of OOP can reduce the amount of old code that needs to be rewritten when increased functionality must be added to a system. We will eventually see the ultimate C++ language tool for code reuse and extension—inheritance.

Assignments

1. Extend this chapter's database program example to allow the database to be stored and retrieved from disk. Allow the database to be sorted by last name and ID number.

2. Create a statistics database class that has all the functionality of the statistics package assignment described in chapter 7. Write a client module that makes use of it (tests it thoroughly).

3. Create an ExtendedInt class based on the information from the assignment described in chapter 7. A client programmer should not have access to the inner details of an ExtendedInt object. Write some client code to test your class.

4. Write the *Life* program (described in the chapter 7 assignments) so that a class is used to encapsulate the two-dimensional array of cells. Member functions should be provided to clear the board, allow entry of initial populations, generate the next board configuration, and, of course, display the board.

5. Modify the ball animation example so that the wall positions are encapsulated within a Wall object. Allow the dimensions (length and width) of the box to be altered (by pressing appropriate keys) as the ball is moving.

CHAPTER 9

POINTERS AND DYNAMIC MEMORY MANAGEMENT

9.1 INTRODUCTION TO POINTERS

In C++, variables have a name, a type, a value, and a location in memory. This location in memory, or address, is where the variable's value is stored. The compiler associates the name of the variable with its address. The programmer does not need to worry about a variable's actual address to store a value; he or she need only use the variable's name to store a value. The variable's type determines how much space is reserved at the variable's address for the value it must hold.

Sometimes it is convenient to access a variable by its actual memory address, instead of by its name. The following code illustrates:

```
int i;
int *p;    /*  p is a pointer to an int        */

 i = 10;   /*  i is assigned the value 10      */
 p = &i;   /*  p is assigned the address of i  */
*p = 20;   /*  actually changes i's value      */
cout << "i = " << i << '\n';
```

The variable p is called a *pointer* variable. It holds an *address*. p can point to an address that stores an int. The statement

```
int *p;
```

is best read right to left. The asterisk indicates that p is a pointer variable; thus, p is declared to be a pointer to an int.

The & is the *address-of* operator. The statement

```
p = &i;
```

sets p to point to i's address in memory. p is said to "point to" i or "refer to" i or "reference" i.

The statement

```
*p = 20;
```

does not change p. *p refers to the *value* at the address pointed to by p. Changing *p   changes what p is pointing to, in this case i. So, changing *p to 20 changes i from 10 to 20.

Figure 9.1 illustrates each of the above statements.

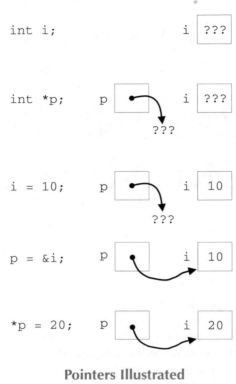

Pointers Illustrated
Figure 9.1

The code could be compressed to

```
int  i = 10,  *p = &i;
*p = 20;
cout << "i = " << i << '\n';
```

Here, i is initialized with the value 10, and p is initialized to point to i. The expression

```
*p = &i
```

is valid only in a declaration. If it were a statement all by itself following the declaration

```
*p = &i;     /*   Wrong   */
```

 it would be an error since

p is a pointer to an int,
*p is an int (the int that p points to),
&i is an address of an int (not an int), and so
*p = &i attempts to assign an address to an int

which is a type mismatch. (The assignment operator can't assign an address to an int directly; it can be done with a cast, but we will have no need to do this.)

Notice that the value of the variable i can be changed in two ways. The variable itself can be reassigned

```
i = 50;
```

and its value can be modified through the pointer

```
*p = 50;
```

So *p is an *alias* for i; that is, p and i refer to the same location in memory. Consider

```
int i = 10, j = 20, *p = &i, *q = &j;
cout << "i = " << i << " j = " << j
     << " *p = " << *p << " *q = " << *q << '\n';

*p = *q;
cout << "i = " << i << " j = " << j
     << " *p = " << *p << " *q = " << *q << '\n';

i = 100;
cout << "i = " << i << " j = " << j
     << " *p = " << *p << " *q = " << *q << '\n';

p = q;
cout << "i = " << i << " j = " << j
     << " *p = " << *p << " *q = " << *q << '\n';
```

The statement

```
*p = *q;
```

says "change the value to which p points into the value to which q points." Figure 9.2 illustrates this operation.

The statement

```
p = q;
```

says "change p so that it points to the same place q is pointing." Figure 9.3 shows the pointer redirection.

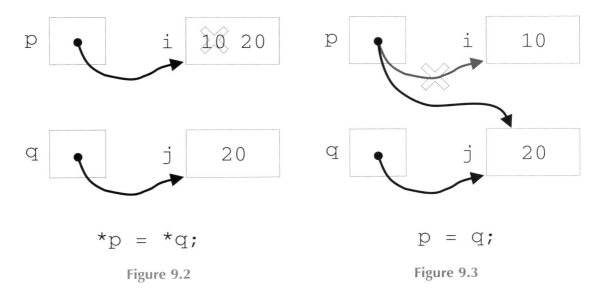

$$*p = *q;$$

$$p = q;$$

Figure 9.2   Figure 9.3

The unary * is called the *pointer indirection* operator or *pointer dereferencing* operator. It is essentially the inverse of &. & returns the address of a variable; * returns the value stored at a particular address. Neither can work with constants:

```
p = &25;    /*    Wrong    */
i = *25;    /*    Wrong    */
```

The indirection operator works with a pointer variable returning a value of the type to which the pointer is declared to point. The address-of operator returns a pointer to (the address-of) a variable.

Exercises

1. What is a pointer?

2. How would one declare the variable `arrow` to be a pointer to a `long double`?

3. How are the unary * and unary & operators related?

   For questions 4–9, assume the following definitions:
   ```
   int i, j, *p, *q;
   ```

4. What is printed by the following code? `p = &i; i = 5;  cout << i << ' ' << *p;`

5. Is the following statement legal? `p = i;`

6. Is the following statement legal? `p = q;`

7. Is the following statement legal? `*p = *q;`

8. What is printed by the following code?

   `p = &i;  q = &j;  i = 10;  j = 20; *p = *q;  cout << i << ' ' << j;`

9. What is printed by the following code?

   `p = &i;  q = &j;  i = 10;  j = 20;  p = q;  cout << i << ' ' << j;`

9.2 CALL-BY-REFERENCE USING POINTERS

The previous examples illustrate pointer syntax, but they are rarely used in practice. Typically, there is no need to provide such an alias to get access to a simple variable; in fact, such use can easily lead to bugs that are difficult to locate. Pointers are most useful in providing an alternate way for functions to modify the parameters they are sent. Pointers can be used instead of reference parameters to achieve call-by-reference. Consider program 9.1:

```
#include <iostream.h>
const double PI = 3.1416, RHO = 45.2377;

void initialize(int *a, int *b) {
        double diam;
        int temp;

        cout << "Please enter diameter: ";
        diam << diam;
        temp = PI*diam*(RHO/2 - 1);
        *a = temp;
        *b = temp + PI;
}

void main()
{
        int val1, val2;

        initialize(&val1, &val2);
        cout << "val1 = " << val1 << ", val2 = " <<  val2 << '\n';
}
```

Program 9.1

Here, `initialize()` is a call-by-reference function. The values of `val1` and `val2` are not copied to a new location when they are passed to a function. Their *addresses* are copied to a new location, and the values of the actual variables in `main()` are modified in `initialize()` through those addresses.

The statement

```
*a = temp;
```

means "copy the value of `temp` into the memory location pointed to by `a` (which is literally `val1's` memory location)."

To use function call-by-reference, three steps must be followed:

1. Declare the function to accept pointers as parameters
2. Use the dereferenced pointers within the body of the function
3. When calling the function, pass the addresses of the variables to be modified

How would one write a function to interchange the values of two variables using pointer call-by-reference? The `swap()` function presented in chapter 6 can be written:

```
void swap(int *x, int *y) {
        int temp;
        temp = *x;
        *x = *y;
        *y = temp;
}
```

The correct call to `swap()` would be

```
swap(&val1, &val2);
```

The following function reduces a rational number (fraction) to simplest form, like the reduce function in chapter 6:

```
/*  Returns greatest common factor of x and y  */
int GCF(int x, int y)
{
        /*  Body of GCF...  */
}

void reduce(int *numerator, int *denominator)
{
```

```
int common_factor = GCF(*numerator, *denominator);
*numerator   /= common_factor;
*denominator /= common_factor;
}
```

(Remember that when `reduce()` is called, the *addresses* of the actual parameters must be passed.)

Why does C++ use two different methods for call-by-reference? Why use the pointer style of call-by-reference at all, since it uses syntax that is more complicated? Old C does not have reference parameters; it must use pointers for call-by-reference. Many standard C library functions called from C++ use pointer parameters. Pointer parameters still have their place in C++. Some contend that pointer parameters are preferred to reference parameters, especially for the built-in types. Their reasoning is compelling: programmers using a pointer call-by-reference function are forced to be aware that the function can modify their actual parameters because the *address-of* operator must be used during the call. The call of a reference parameter call-by-reference function looks just like the call of a call-by-value function. If the programmer thinks that a pointer call-by-reference function is actually call-by-value, the compiler generates an error since the *address-of* operator is omitted. If the programmer thinks that a reference parameter call-by-reference function is actually call-by-value, the compiler uses call-by-reference anyway with no notice given to the programmer. Forcing the programmer to pass the address of an argument reinforces the fact that the function intends to modify the variable sent to it. Using references, the function call cannot be distinguished from a call-by-value situation, and the programmer may be lulled into thinking the variable's current value is safe. Also, it is not syntactically illegal to pass a constant to a function using reference parameters. The attempt to pass the address of a constant to a pointer parameter function will cause a compile error, since it is illegal to use & with a constant.

Exercises

1. How does the pointer call-by-reference protocol differ from call-by-value discussed in chapter 6?

2. How does the pointer call-by-reference protocol differ from the *reference* call-by-reference discussed in chapter 6?

3. What three steps must be taken to accomplish call-by-reference with pointers?

4. What advantages does pointer call-by-reference have over call-by-reference using references?

9.3   POINTERS AS ARRAYS AND ARRAYS AS POINTERS

In C++, pointers and arrays have a unique relationship that is unlike most other higher-level programming languages. In many instances, pointers and arrays can be used interchangeably, with a pointer being used as an array or vice-versa. While they are closely related, they are distinct entities. Their subtle differences can be confusing for beginning programmers. When mastered, the judicious use of pointers with arrays leads to elegant, efficient programs.

The following section of code illustrates C++'s ability to treat a pointer as if it were an array:

```
int a[100], *p;
/*  a is an int array, p is an int pointer  */

p = a;
a[0] =  2;
*p   = 10;     /*  Changes a[0]  */
p[3] = 12;     /*  Changes a[3]  */
*a   = 45;     /*  Changes a[0]  */
```

The pointer p is set to point to the array a. Recall that a pointer is a variable that holds an address. An array name is the address of the starting point of that array in memory. After the assignment p = a, p and a refer to the same location in memory. *p refers to a[0] because *p means the int at address p, and a[0] means the int at position zero in array a, at address a, which is the same as address p. The reference to p[3] actually refers to the same location as a[3]; thus, pointer p becomes an alias for array a and can be treated exactly the same.

Array a is treated as if it were a pointer in the statement

```
        *a = 45;
```

*a is the value found at address a, which is equivalent to a[0], and, in this case, also equivalent to *p and p[0].

When p is assigned to a, some logically identical expressions include

```
*p      is equivalent to   a[0]

p[i]    is equivalent to   a[i]

p       is equivalent to   &a[0]

p       is equivalent to   a
```

It is always the case that

```
*p      is equivalent to   p[0]

*a      is equivalent to   a[0]

p       is equivalent to   &p[0]

a       is equivalent to   &a[0]
```

With all of their similarities, pointers and arrays are not identical. A pointer is a variable; hence, it can be reassigned. An array is like a *constant* pointer because its value cannot be changed; thus,

```
p = a; //  Ok
```

is ok, but

```
a = p; //  Error, can't reassign an array
```

is an illegal statement. An array cannot be reassigned; that is, an array name cannot appear all by itself on the left side of an assignment operator (=, +=, -=, ++, --). Its elements can be reassigned, of course, if they are simple types. (Arrays of *arrays* make things more complicated.)

Being able to reassign an array would mean its address would be changed to somewhere else in memory. (This is what happens in pointer assignment.) As an alternative, a block of memory beginning at a certain address just large enough to fit into the declared size of the array would be copied into the array. In the first situation, the initial work that the compiler went through to allocate memory properly for the array would be discarded. Attempts to allocate and deallocate memory properly to accommodate the changes would make the code generated by the compiler quite complex and inefficient. In the second case, many items in memory might have to be copied, again a slow process.

What advantage is there to the interchangeability in notations? Pointers can be used to access arrays more efficiently as will be seen after a discussion of pointer arithmetic.

9.4 POINTER ARITHMETIC

Pointer variables can take part in certain arithmetic expressions. The following arithmetic operators can be applied to pointer variables:

$$+ \quad - \quad ++ \quad -- \quad += \quad -=$$

Integral types can be added or subtracted from pointer variables, and pointer variables can be incremented or decremented. Pointer arithmetic is interesting in that the compiler adjusts the amount increased or decreased according to the type to which the pointer refers. Consider the code:

```
int    i = 10,   *ip = &i;
double d = 10.0, *dp = &d;
char   c = 'A',  *cp = &c;

ip++;   dp += 3;   cp = cp + 5;
```

If `i` is located at address 210 in memory, `ip` is initialized to the address of `i`, so it has the value 210. Let's say `d` is stored at address 350, so `dp` has the value 350, and `c` is stored at 382, so `cp` holds 382. The size of an `int` is system dependent, but for the sake of discussion we'll assume it is two bytes. The `double` is likely the eight byte IEEE floating point standard, and the `char` requires one byte of storage. Incrementing `ip` (by `ip++`) changes the value of `ip` to 212. The statement `dp += 3` changes `dp` to 374, and `cp = cp + 5` changes `cp` to 387. When a pointer to an `int` is incremented by one, it is changed to point to the next `int` position in memory, which would be two bytes higher. When a `double` pointer is incremented by one, it points to the next `double` position in memory which would be eight bytes higher.

Since the compiler adjusts the pointer calculations automatically for the particular type involved, the programmer need not worry about how many actual bytes are added to the address. The programmer can think in terms of "adding three to an `int` pointer moves the pointer three `int`s up in memory." This ability to ignore the size of the data type when calculating pointer movements and offsets lessens some of the work required to produce portable code.

The following formula can be used to find the pointer's new address:

```
p′ = p + si
```

where p' is the new pointer value, `p` is the current pointer value, `s` is the size (in bytes) of the type that is pointed to, and `i` is the value added to the pointer.

If the pointer arithmetic formula looks familiar, it's because it is essentially identical to the array subscript formula found in chapter 7. Recall that the compiler adjusts automatically to the size of the types that an array holds when calculating an array subscript offset. The compiler performs the same adjustment when calculating pointer offsets. This uniform treatment makes pointers and arrays so interchangeable. Consider the following equivalent expressions:

```
p[0]  is equivalent to  *(p + 0)   which is just *p
p[5]  is equivalent to  *(p + 5)
a[5]  is equivalent to  *(a + 5)
```

The parentheses are required in each case because without them the precedence rules dictate

```
*a + 5  is equivalent to  (*a) + 5
```

which is the same as a[0] + 5. a[0] + 5 means the element at position zero with five added to it. The expression a[5] refers to the element at position five.

Pointers and pointer arithmetic can be used to optimize array access. Consider the following function that exchanges two values within an array:

```
void array_swap(int a[], int pos1, int pos2)
{
        int temp;

        temp = a[pos1];
        a[pos1] = a[pos2];
        a[pos2] = temp;
}
```

An array element is accessed through a subscript four times in this function. Each time the compiler must calculate an offset based on the formula in chapter 7. If this function is called within a loop that executes 10,000 times and time is critical, the overhead of calculating these offsets could become intolerable. Consider an alternative approach using pointers:

```
void array_swap(int a[], int pos1, int pos2) {
        int temp, *p1, *p2;

        p1    = &a[pos1];
        p2    = &a[pos2];

        temp = *p1;
        *p1  = *p2;
        *p2  = temp;
}
```

Here, the subscript offsets are calculated only twice, to assign p1 and p2; thus, the number of offset calculations that the compiler must generate is reduced by 50 percent. The five simple assignments, two additions, and two multiplications will be more efficient than the original three assignments, four additions, and four multiplications.

A formula from physics states:

$$d = v_0 t - \tfrac{1}{2} g t^2$$

where d is the vertical distance an object falls, given: v_0 its initial vertical velocity; g, the acceleration due to gravity (9.8 m/sec^2); and t, the amount of time it has been falling. Assume a function is to be written that calculates d for a particular v_0 given a list of times. The list of times is found in an array of double called time. The function is to display the results for each time. The straightforward approach would be:

```
void print_distances(double init_vel, double time[], int size)
{
        int i;

        for ( i = 0;  i < size;  i++ )
                cout << "Object #" << i << " distance = "
                     << init_vel*time[i] - 0.5*G*time[i]*time[i] << '\n';
}
```

If the array holds 10,000 items, the array offset would need to be calculated 30,000 times in the above function. The work for calculating the offsets requires 30,000 multiplications and 30,000 additions. It could be optimized by calculating the offset only once per iteration:

```
void print_distances(double init_vel, double time[], int size)
{
```

```
        int i;
        double t;
        for ( i = 0;  i < size;  i++ ) {
                t = time[i];
                cout << "Object #" << i << " distance = "
                        << init_vel*t - 0.5*G*t*t << '\n';
        }
}
```

This version requires 10,000 multiplications and 10,000 additions to calculate the array offset. Everything else is the same, except for the 10,000 assignments to the temporary variable. Even though assignments, additions, and multiplications all have different actual execution times (in particular, multiplications are much more expensive than either assignments or additions), we see a swap of 60,000 operations for 30,000, a reduction of 50 percent.

A pointer version might look as follows:

```
void print_distances(double init_vel, double *time, int size)
{
        int i;

        for ( i = 0;  i < size;  i++ ) {
                cout << "Object #" << " distance = "
                        << init_vel* *time - 0.5*G* *time * *time << '\n';
                time++;
        }
}
```

This version does a single additon to the pointer each time through the loop. The offset is not calculated. It also does not require the temporary `double` variable.

In a function's *parameter list* the declarations

```
int time[]
```

and

```
int *time
```

mean the same thing; namely, the address of an array in memory. It is safe to modify the value of the formal parameter `time` within the body of the function even though the actual parameter is a true array because only a copy of the array's address is sent to the function. In actuality, C++ is quite consistent because the array's address *is* passed by value. We say arrays are passed by reference because the address of the array allows access to the actual array elements; the elements are actually passed by reference.

To further illustrate the syntactical differences in array and pointer notation, consider a function that shifts all the elements of an array of size `size` forward one position to make room for a new element in position `pos`. The new size of the array (one bigger) is returned.

```
/*  Using array notation  */
int shift_up(int a[], int size, int pos) {
        int i;
        for ( i = size; i > pos;  i-- )
                a[i] = a[i - 1];
        return size + 1;
}
```

A version strictly using pointers could be written:

```
/*  Using pointer notation  */
int shift_up(int *a, int size, int pos) {
        int *p;
        int *stop = a + pos;
```

```
        for ( p = a + size;  p > stop;  p-- )
            *p = *(p - 1);
        return size + 1;
}
```

For most people, the array notation is clearer. Since both offer about the same efficiency, the array version is likely the better choice.

Many times the increment and decrement operators (++ and − −) are used in the same expression with the dereferencing operator (*). Consulting the operator chart, ++ and * have equal precedence and the same associativity. Consider ++ by itself for a moment and the following declarations:

```
int i = 0, j = 100;
```

The statements

```
i++;
```

and

```
++i;
```

would accomplish the same result; namely, assigning to i the value 1. The following two statements, however, do subtly different things:

```
i = j++;
```

and

```
i = ++j;
```

When the ++ precedes the variable, it is the *preincrement* version. When it follows the variable, it is the *postincrement* version. The preincrement version, when part of a complicated expression, increments the variable first, then uses the new value. In the postincrement form, the value of the variable is used first, then it is incremented; thus, i = j++; assigns 100 to i then changes j to 101. i = ++j; changes j to 101 then assigns 101 to i.

Given the declarations

```
int a[100], *p = a;
```

what does

```
*p++ = 10;
```

do? Consider

```
(*p)++;
```

This means dereference p and increment it (or, in effect, increment a[0]). By contrast

```
*(p++);
```

means increment p and then dereference it; that is, access the value at a[1]. In reality, *(p++) is the correct interpretation of *p++. For obvious reasons, there is no confusion in the absence of parentheses about what is meant by

```
++*p;
```

and

```
*++p;
```

The − − operator has similar pre- and postfix properties.

The following routine copies the elements from one array into another using pointer notation.

```
void array_copy(int *dest, int *source, int size)
{
    int count = 0;
    while ( count++ < size )
      *dest++ = *source++;
}
```

In the `while` condition, `count` is compared to `size` *before* it is incremented. In the body, `*dest` is assigned the value of `*source`, before either of the pointers are incremented. In English pseudocode, the copy could be described:

while you've done this loop less than `size` times:

1. assign to what `dest` is pointing to the same value that `source` is pointing to
2. change `dest` and `source` so they both point to the next position within their respective arrays.

The standard string functions (inherited from C) use pointer notation to do their jobs. The prototype for `strcpy()` found in `<string.h>` usually has the form:

```
char *strcpy(char *, const char *);
```

Indeed, the `str_cpy()` function in chapter 7 could be rewritten:

```
int str_cpy(char *dest, char *source) {
    while ( (*dest++ = *source++) != '\0')
      ; /* Body of loop empty */
}
```

Here, the assignment `*dest++ = *source++` is made, and if the null character is assigned (signalling the end of the `source` string), the value of the assignment will cause the loop to stop. Since the null byte (`'\0'`) has value zero (false), the function could be written very compactly, albeit somewhat obscurely as

```
int str_cpy(char *dest, char *source) {
    while ( *dest++ = *source++ )
      ; /* Again, empty loop body */
}
```

Here, if the null byte is assigned, the value of the assignment is '\0', which is `int` zero, which is false, and the loop is terminated. It is code like this that has perpetuated the legend (born of C) that C++ is a programmer-friendly language. (Actually, reliance on too much tricky code like this can make C++ a very programmer-unfriendly language!)

When members of `classes` or `structs` are accessed through a pointer, an alternative to the `*` syntax improves the code readability. If the following structure is defined:

```
struct Block {
    float height, width;
    int color;
    void show();
    float calc(float);
};
```

and the pointer `p` and object `blk` are declared:

```
Block blk, *p = &blk;
```

then the color field of the `Block` referenced through `p` could be accessed as follows:

```
(*p).color = 5;
```

The parentheses are required. Consulting the rules for operator precedence, we see that . has higher precedence than *; therefore, without parentheses, the statement would be interpreted as

```
*(p.color) = 5;
```

which is an attempt to treat p as if it were a struct (it is not, it's a pointer to a struct) and an attempt to dereference the color field as if it were a pointer (which is a syntax error). Since the correct syntax with the parentheses is somewhat clumsy looking, and since accessing a struct or class member through a pointer is done so often, a more convenient syntax is available. The -> operator, called the *structure pointer operator*, can be used:

```
p->color = 5;
```

Just as the structure member operator (.) requires that its left operand be a structure (struct or class) and its right operand be the name of a field within a structure of that type, the structure pointer operator (->) requires that its left operand be a pointer to a structure (struct or class) and its right operand be the name of a field within a structure of that type.

The following function, modified from chapter 8, illustrates the structure pointer operator's use in a pointer call-by-reference function:

```
//  DataBase is the struct version, not the class version
void insert_database(DataBase *d) {
    int more = 1;
    while ( d->size < MAX_EMPLOYEES  &&  more ) {
        get_record(d->emp_list[d.size]);
        d->size++;
        more = more_records();
    }
}
```

Exercises

1. How can a pointer be treated as if it were an array?

2. How can an array be treated as if it were a pointer?

3. How is pointer arithmetic different from normal arithmetic on ints?

4. Why does the statement *a involve fewer hidden calculations than the equivalent a[0]?

   For questions 5–36, assume the following declarations:

   ```
   int n, a[1000], *p;
   ```

   Classify each of the following assignment statements as syntactically legal or illegal. For this exercise don't worry about staying within the bounds of array a or whether or not pointer p has been initialized properly. Simply examine the statement and see if the compiler would accept it as a valid C++ statement. If it is an illegal statement, indicate why it is syntactically improper. If the statement is correct, interpret its meaning.

5. `*p = 45;` 6. `a[4] = n;` 7. `p[2] = 45;` 8. `a[n] = 4;`

9. `a[n] = a[n + 1];` 10. `p = a;` 11. `a = p;` 12. `p = &a[12];`

13. `p = &n;`	14. `p = n;`	15. `n = p;`	16. `&n = p;`
17. `*n = 4;`	18. `*(p + 2) = 10;`	19. `*a = 1;`	20. `*a + 2 = 10;`
21. `*(a + 2) = 10;`	22. `n = (*p)++;`	23. `n = *p++;`	24. `p = &125;`
25. `p = 125;`	26. `p = *125;`	27. `p = (int *) 125;`	28. `n = *++p;`
29. `n = ++(*p);`	30. `n = ++*p;`	31. `n = *++p;`	32. `a[a[3]] = n;`
33. `a[a[3]]=a[a[n]];`	34. `p[a[n]] = 5;`	35. `n = *p-----*p;`	36. `p = &*a;`

For questions 37–48, assume the following declarations. Indicate whether the following expressions are syntactically legal or illegal. If an expression is illegal, indicate why it is illegal. If it is legal, interpret its meaning.

```
enum Gender { female, male };
enum Status { probationary, standard, elite, retired, deceased };
struct Date {
     int year, month, day;
};
struct EmpRec {
     char lastname[20];
     char firstname[20];
     char middleinitial;
     int  ID_number;
     Date DOB;
     Gender sex;
     float salary;
     Status stat;
};
EmpRec r[100], *p, record;
Date d;
char word[20], ch;
int i;
Gender g;
Status s;
```

37. `p = &record;`	38. `p = r;`	39. `r[4] = record;`
40. `p->salary = 20000.00;`	41. `*p.stat = elite;`	42. `(*p).stat = retired;`
43. `p[5].ID_number = 8;`	44. `d->day = d->year;`	45. `strcpy(p->lastname, word);`
46. `p.ID_number = 75;`	47. `*p = record;`	48. `r[4] = p;`

49. What determines when the structure pointer operator should be used instead of the structure member operator?

9.5 UNINITIALIZED POINTERS

In all of the examples above, each pointer has been assigned either to the address of a variable or to an array. When a pointer variable is declared within a function, it (like all other `auto` variables) has an undefined value. Its value consists of whatever random sequence of bits exist on the stack in the space reserved for that pointer. It is the programmer's responsibility to give that pointer a valid value. Consider program 9.2:

```
#include <iostream.h>
void main()
{
    int a[] = { 1, 2, 3, 4, 5, 6, 7, 8 };
    int *p;

    for ( i = 0;  i < 8;  i++ )
        cin >> p[i];
    for ( i = 0;  i < 8;  i++ )
        cout << p[i] << ' ';
    cout << '\n';
}
```

Program 9.2

From the use of p, it appears as if array a is intended to be reassigned through the input statement in the loop; however, the crucial

```
p = a;
```

assignment statement is missing that should appear before the first for loop. When p is created, it contains a random address in memory. Reading data into random addresses in memory is very hazardous. The degree of danger depends on the sophistication of the operating system. At one extreme, the operating system may not allow an executing program to access memory that has not been specially reserved for it. Attempting to do so will cause the program to be terminated. Multitasking operating systems like Unix and Microsoft Windows have this capability to some extent. At the other extreme, many microcomputers run a single-user operating system like DOS. Such operating systems are responsible for getting the program running. Once running, the program has complete control, and the operating system can only get control back when the program allows, often only when it is finished executing. On such systems, memory is not protected and the program has access to any part of memory.

Memory must hold the current program being run and its associated data, the operating system and its associated buffers, data tables, interrupt vectors (to respond to keyboard or mouse input, for example), etc. Changing "any old" memory location is never good to do. Under the best circumstances, the program could cripple itself (by writing over its own machine language instructions stored in memory) or corrupt its own data. In an unprotected environment, a misbehaving program could corrupt the OS and cause the computer to lock up or display unusual characters on the screen. The colloquial term for such an event is a *crash*. It is possible to corrupt memory that is not currently in use, and the above program would appear to work fine. The next day, it might crash, or it may cause unusual things to happen on a different machine. A program that works fine most of the time but crashes occasionally is probably the worst situation. The intermittent nature of the problem when the program is run with identical inputs confounds most debugging strategies that are used for finding errors in program logic.

p above is called an *uninitialized pointer* or *wild pointer*. Wild pointers are dangerous because on many systems (such as PCs) they allow open access to all of memory. Fortunately, most sophisticated operating systems have facilities for dealing with wild pointers in a more graceful fashion (e.g., terminating the program before any damage can be done to memory outside the program's domain). Some development environments provide tools known as *debuggers* that can be used to help find and correct problems arising from uninitialized pointers.

9.6 STRING PROBLEMS

Beginning C++ programmers often confuse the array and pointer notation of strings. When observing most published C++/C code and the library routine prototypes, it is clear that string parameters to functions are most often declared as char *. Novice programmers sometimes associate the char * in parameter lists with strings they want to use in a program. Consider the following code:

```
void main() {
        char *str;  //  str is a string
        cin  >> str;
        cout << str;
        .
        .  //  Rest of program follows...
        .
}
```

Here str is declared to be a pointer to a char. It is not initialized to point to anywhere safe before the characters are extracted from the input stream. str is a wild pointer. The >> operator copies keyboard input into memory beginning at the address stored in str. Something will be overwritten, perhaps another variable in the program. On some systems, the machine language code of the program itself, part of the C++ development environment or part of the operating system can also be overwritten. As mentioned before, since programs are loaded differently on different machines with different memory configurations, the program may usually work fine on one machine but rarely work on another. The program may work fine most of the time on all machines but occasionally fail. Such is the life of a program containing references to wild pointers.

The following code is perfectly legal:

```
char *str;
str = "This is a string";
```

since str is a pointer. The string literal "This is a string" is stored somewhere in memory and str is set to point to it. The following pair of statements are not legal:

```
char str[20];
str = "This is a string";
```

Since str is declared to be an *array* of char, str itself cannot be reassigned (see chapter 9). The following is incorrect because of the aforementioned wild pointer problem:

```
char *str;
cin >> str;
```

but the following is safe as long as the user doesn't attempt to enter more than 19 characters:

```
char str[20];
cin >> str;
```

Recall that the better approach is

```
char str[20];
cin.getline(str, 20);
```

Since str is an array, space has been set aside by the compiler, and characters typed into the keyboard buffer can be safely copied into str.

Another problem involves local strings and local arrays in general. Read carefully the following function:

```
char *process_str(char *s) {
        char *result;
```

```
                char working_str[MAXSTR] = "";
                if ( strlen(s) < MAXSTR ) {
                        strcpy(working_str, s);
                        for ( i = 0;  working_str[i] != '\0';  i++ )
                                if ( working_str[i] == 'A' )
                                        working_str[i] = '*';
                }
                result = working_str;
                return result;
        }
```

A typical call to `process_str()` could be

```
char *str, word[MAXSTR];
cin.getline(word, MAXSTR);   //  Get word from user
str = process_str(word);     //  Filter out 'A's
cout << str << '\n';
```

The insidious thing about `process_str()` is that it appears to work perfectly most of the time. It is not guaranteed to work on all platforms, however, since `working_str` is an `auto` variable most likely allocated on the stack. Its official existence is over when the function is finished handling the call. The values it contains might still reside on the stack until they are overwritten by other function calls. The function should be written

```
void process_str(char *working_str, char *s) {
        strcpy(working_str, "");
        if ( strlen(s) < MAXSTR ) {
                strcpy(working_str, s);
                for ( i = 0;  working_str[i] != '\0';  i++ )
                        if ( working_str[i] == 'A' )
                                working_str[i] = '*';
        }
}

char str[MAXSTR], word[MAXSTR];
cin.getline(word, MAXSTR);
process_str(str, word);
cout << str << '\n';
```

If a string is going to be analyzed by stepping through it one or more characters at a time, and this traversal is to be done by a function that must be called repeatedly throughout the process, and the position of the scan within the string must be remembered between calls to the function, then the string will need to be passed by reference. Consider the following very simple string scanning function:

```
//  Bad string_scan()
void string_scan(char *s) {
        if ( *s == 'A' )
                cout << "Capital A found in string!\n";
        s++;
}
//  Corresponding bad main()
void main() {
        char in_string[100], *cursor;
        cin.getline(in_string, 100);
        cursor = in_string;
        while ( cursor[0] != '\0' )
                string_scan(cursor);
}
```

The intention is to use the pointer `cursor` to move through the `in_string` array and print out the message whenever an *A* character is located in `in_string`. However, the loop will be infinite; that is, `cursor` never gets changed by `string_scan()`. It shouldn't be changed because it is being passed *by value*. The following version uses the call-by-reference protocol to achieve the desired effect:

```
//  Better string_scan()
void string_scan(char **s) {    //  Pointer to pointer
    if ( **s == 'A' )
        cout << "Capital A found in string!\n";
    (*s)++;
}

//  Corresponding better main()
void main() {
    char in_string[100], *cursor;
    cin.getline(in_string, 100);
    cursor = in_string;
    while ( cursor[0] != '\0' )
        //  Pass address of pointer
        string_scan(&cursor);
}
```

Here, `cursor` is passed *by reference*, and its value can be changed. Passing a pointer by reference implies passing a pointer to a pointer, hence the double indirection, **. Two asterisks have to be used to get at the single `char` that the parameter is referencing. The pointer parameter can be modified within the function by accessing it with one asterisk.

The new version of the program will scan through any string until the null character is encountered. Each time an *A* is found, the message will be printed. At the end of the program, `cursor` is at the end of the string, but no characters within the string to which it was pointing will have been modified. None of the characters are changed because the function was written carefully to avoid the possibility. A careless programmer may write `string_scan()` incorrectly so that the contents of the string get corrupted. The chance of incorrectly modifying the contents of a string can be eliminated by using the `const` specifier as described below.

A particular program requires that a programmer store strings in an array, as done in chapter 7. Consider the consequences of the following declarations:

```
#define MAXSTRINGS 10
typedef char *String;
typedef String StrArray[MAXSTRINGS];

StrArray wordlist;
```

The following code is obviously faulty:

```
int i;
for ( i = 0;  i < MAXSTRINGS;  i++ )
    cin >> wordlist[i];
for ( i = 0;  i < MAXSTRINGS;  i++ )
    cout << wordlist[i] << '\n';;
```

since user input will be copied into memory referenced by uninitialized pointers. The second approach avoids the wild pointer problem:

```
int i;
char temp[80];
for ( i = 0;  i < MAXSTRINGS;  i++ ) {
    cin.getline(temp, 80);
    wordlist[i] = temp;
}
for ( i = 0;  i < MAXSTRINGS;  i++ )
    cout << wordlist[i] << '\n';
```

Since `temp` reserves memory for the user-entered characters, and each position in `wordlist` simply stores the address of `temp`, memory is safe with this new section of code. The results, however, are somewhat unexpected; namely, every position in the `wordlist` array contains the same string—the last string entered by the user. Each time through the loop the variable `temp` is being used as a *buffer* to hold the string captured by the stream extractor. The address of this string is then copied into the current position within `wordlist`. The buffer `temp` is being reused each time through the loop, and since it is an array, its address is constant; thus, all the pointers in `wordlist` point to the same address, and all the strings printed will be identical to the value entered. (See figure 9.4.) A solution will be presented in the next section.

Any discussion about strings and pointer notation would be incomplete without mention of command line arguments. The function `main()` can receive parameters just like any other function. Arguments can be passed to `main()` in an array of strings declared using pointer notation as in program 9.3:

```
int main(int argc, char *argv[]) {
    for ( int i = 0;  i < argc;  i++ )
        cout << argv[i];
    return 0;
}
```

Program 9.3

If this program is called `arg.cpp` and compiled to `arg.exe` and executed from the command line as follows:

```
arg hello there world
```

the following is printed:

```
c:\arg.exe
hello
there
world
```

In this way strings can be passed to programs. The parameters `argc` and `argv` can be renamed to any legal identifier, but these names (*for argument count* and *argument vector*) are traditionally used. `argv` is an array of strings that contains the parameters to be passed to `main()`, and `argc` is the number of parameters passed. No sizes need to be specified for the `argv` array, since it is passed in as an array of pointers to characters instead of a two-dimensional array of characters. The program is not responsible for allocating space for any characters; the operating system takes care of that. Notice that the compiled program's literal name (`c:\arg.exe`) is considered the first (0th) parameter. `argc`, in this case, has the value four.

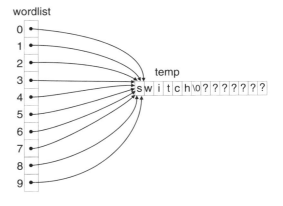

Faulty Array of Strings
Figure 9.4

Recall program 5.9, which, when executed using redirection, read in a textfile and substituted every occurrence of the letter 'A' with an asterisk. It will be modified to produce program 9.4. If program 9.4 is complied into the executable program named `charconv.exe` (or just `charconv` on some systems), one could type

```
charconv E $ < file1.dat > file1.new
```

The file `file1.dat` would be copied to the `file1.new`, but every occurrence of the letter 'E' would be replaced by the symbol '$'. Program 9.4 accepts two parameters from the command line. The first is the target character and the second is the replacement character. `charconv` can replace any single character with any other.

```
#include <iostream.h>
#include <ctype.h>
void main(int argc, char *argv[]) {
      char ch;
      if ( argc < 3 )
          cout << "Invalid number of parameters\n";
      else
          while ( (cin.get(ch) != EOF )
              if ( toupper(ch) == toupper(argv[1][0] )
                  cout << argv[2][0];
              else
                  cout << ch;
}
```

Program 9.4

9.7 DYNAMICALLY ALLOCATED MEMORY

Sometimes pointers need to be created that do not reference any other existing variable or array. Recall that space for arrays is determined at compile-time; thus, true dynamically sized arrays are not possible using the standard array declaration described in chapter 7. If the declaration says

```
int a[100];
```

space for 100 integers is reserved for the array for the lifetime of the variable a. The value in the square brackets must be an integral constant. To emphasize, one cannot say

```
int arrsize;
cin >> arrsize;
int a[arrsize];    //  Error!
```

@%#&!

since here the array's size cannot be determined until runtime, when the user enters the array's size.

Fortunately, C++ provides a way to create dynamically sized arrays. The operator `new` returns a pointer to memory that is guaranteed to be unoccupied and large enough to hold the amount of data requested. (This area of memory reserved for dynamic allocation and deallocation is known as the *heap*.) For example:

```
int arrsize;
int *a;
cin >> arrsize;
a = new int[arrsize];
```

Even though a is technically a pointer, it can, for all practical purposes, be treated exactly like an array after the memory allocation by `new`. Its size is `arrsize`, and the space for the "array" was determined at runtime, not compile-time. It is almost as if the illegal declaration `int a[arrsize];` was used. The exception: a is a pointer and can be reassigned. Arrays cannot be reassigned. The operator `new` must be provided a type name and an optional size within square brackets. If the size is omitted, space for only one item of a particular type is allocated. The statement

```
float *x = new float;
```

declares x to be a pointer to a `float` and assigns it to point to a location in memory that is guaranteed to be safe.

The code from the previous section can now be fixed by dynamically allocating space for each pointer in the array:

```
int i;
char temp[80];
for ( i = 0;  i < MAXSTRINGS;  i++ ) {
      cin.getline(temp, 80);
      wordlist[i] = new char[strlen(temp) + 1];
      strcpy(wordlist[i], temp);
}
for ( i = 0;  i < MAXSTRINGS;  i++ )
      cout << wordlist[i] << '\n';
```

Figure 9.5 illustrates a possible allocation. If the original declarations were changed to

```
#define MAXSTRINGS 10
typedef char String[80];
typedef String StrArray[MAXSTRINGS];

StrArray wordlist;
```

then the code could be simplified to

```
int i;
for ( i = 0;  i < MAXSTRINGS;  i++ )
      cin.getline(wordlist[i], 80);
for ( i = 0;  i < MAXSTRINGS;  i++ )
      cout << wordlist[i] << '\n';
```

since `wordlist` is now an array of arrays instead of an array of pointers. The disadvantage to this approach is that the array (now actually a two-dimensional array of characters) always requires $10 \times 80 = 800$ bytes of storage. The array of strings in figure 9.5 only uses 68 bytes plus 10 pointers. (The pointers are likely to be four bytes each, so the total is around 108 bytes.)

`delete` deallocates memory that was previously reserved by `new`. In the above dynamic array example, when "array" `a` is no longer needed, the statement

```
delete [] a;
```

will release the space it occupies so that it may be used elsewhere. Notice that the empty brackets precede the pointer in `delete`. A size does not need to be given to the `delete` operator; the heap manager keeps track of the memory and frees up the appropriate amount. In the case of the `float` pointer x above, the square brackets would not be used at all because space for only one `float` was allocated.

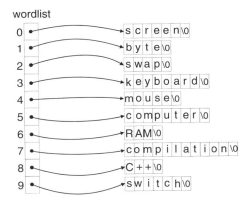

**Dynamically Allocated
Array of Strings
Figure 9.5**

A good rule to follow is "Every successful call to `new` eventually should have a corresponding call to `delete` sometime before the program terminates." What constitutes a successful call? There is one constant value that legally can be assigned to any pointer—0. It sometimes goes under the name of NULL. The constant NULL is defined in the header file `<iostream.h>`, among others. Some programmers prefer to use NULL instead of 0, since it immediately distinguishes a pointer from a normal numeric type. If the `new` operator cannot successfully allocate the memory requested (because not enough memory is available), then it returns a null pointer; therefore, the call to `new` above is better written

```
a = new int [arrsize];
if ( a == NULL )
        exit(0);
```

or, more compactly:

```
a = new int [arrsize];
if ( !a )
        exit(0);
```

The library function `exit()` is declared in `<stdlib.h>`. It immediately exits the program passing an `int` value back to the operating system. What the operating system does with this value is system dependent, but it usually corresponds to some status code. Many programmers would collapse the two statements into one:

```
if ( !(a = new int[arrsize]) )
        exit(0);
```

The return value of the `new` operator should always be checked. Attempting to use a null pointer can be disastrous (see the previous case against wild pointers).

Once memory is allocated, it should eventually be freed for reuse later. Programs that use dynamic memory (i.e., pointers to memory allocated with `new`), when run for a while, will sometimes use up all of the available memory on the heap. If error checking as described above is done on all calls to `new`, then the program will exit gracefully when memory runs out. The following example illustrates:

```
#include <iostream.h>

void main()
{
        int *p, done = 0;
        unsigned long count = 0;
        while ( !done ) {
                if ( !(p = new int) ) {
                        cout << "Memory exhausted!\n";
                        done = 1;
                }
                else
                        cout << "Allocating int #" << count << '\n';
                count++;
        }
}
```

Memory is constantly allocated and never freed. A program that never frees memory when it could and eventually runs out of memory (sometimes called *blowing up*) is said to have a *memory leak*.

The `delete` operator should not be used to free space that was not allocated by `new`. If such an attempt is made, the heap management routines will be disrupted and the program will eventually crash. It is safe, however, to `delete` a null pointer (nothing will happen). Undefined things also happen when an attempt is made to use a `deleted` pointer as a valid pointer. While this recommendation seems obvious, previously `deleted` pointers are sometimes accidentally accessed with favorable results. In fact, on many systems, since `delete` does not modify the pointer that it is passed nor the memory to which it points (it only marks the memory to which it points as being available for reuse), that pointer can be used for a short time as if it were not `deleted`. Eventually, a call to `new` might reuse that space, and the pointer that was seemingly "valid" will get trashed. The program will work sometimes, and sometimes it will not work, and there will be no obvious reasons for its strange behavior.

```
int *p;

if ( !(p = new int) )
     exit(0);
*p = 19;
cout << *p << '\n';
delete p;
cout << *p << '\n';      /*  Oops, but apparently no problem...  */
```

To recap, the following "pointers" are presented to troubleshoot pointer problems:

1. Before any pointer is accessed it should be initialized in one of the following ways:
    a. Set to the address of an existing object
    b. Set to memory allocated with the new operator
    c. Set to 0.
2. Always verify that new allocated the space requested.
3. Pointers assigned to memory allocated by new should eventually be deleted before the program is finished.
4. Never reassign a pointer allocated by new until that space is either assigned to another pointer or deleted. (Otherwise, there will be no way to get to the memory that it used to reference to free it up.)
5. Never delete a pointer that wasn't allocated by new.
6. Never delete a pointer that has already been deleted (and has not subsequently been reallocated with new).
7. Never attempt to access a pointer that has been deleted.

Pointers have a much more significant role to play than simply serving as array aliases, allowing dynamically sized arrays to be created, or providing an alternative way to do call-by-reference. They are crucial for the construction of complex data structures that can be used to build truly powerful applications. The next two chapters show how pointers make this possible.

Exercises

1. What is a wild pointer?

2. What predefined constant value can any pointer be assigned, regardless of the pointer's type?

3. How can programmers allow arrays to be created dynamically during the program's execution so that the array's size is not fixed at compile-time?

4. What is a memory leak?

5. What does the operator new do?

6. When should the operator delete be used?

7. What is the heap?

    For questions 8–19, indicate whether each statement is syntactically legal or illegal. If it is legal but contains a logic error, indicate why it is wrong. If it is completely correct, interpret its effects. Assume the statement immediately follows the declarations with no intervening code.

```
char word[5] = "ABC", name[10], *str, *textpattern = "XYZ";
```

8. `str = word;`   9. `word = str;`   10. `strcpy(str, word);`

11. `strcpy(word,"ABC");` 12. `strcpy(name, "ABC");` 13. `strcpy(word, "ABCDE");`

14. `word = "ABC";`   15. `str = "ABC";`   16. `str = textpattern;`

17. `name = word;`   18. `strcpy(word, textpattern);` 19. `name[3] = word[2];`

9.8   THE const SPECIFIER

We've seen the reserved word `const` used in several contexts. It is used in C++ to indicate that an object's value will not, should not, and cannot be changed. The value of a `const` object must be given at the point of definition:

```
const int maxavail = 1000;
```

Here, `maxavail` is an `int` object that permanently has the value of 1000. It is not called a variable, since its value does not vary. Unlike a variable, no memory is reserved for a constant. A constant can also be used in certain situations where variables are prohibited:

```
const int size = 100;
double array[size];
```

We've seen how symbolic constants are useful for replacing literal constants. A single point of definition makes program modification easier because literal constants may be spread throughout a large program and have multiple meanings that would thwart a simple global *search-and-replace* action with the text editor. Constants are also very valuable in certain situations in which it would be helpful to define a *read-only* pointer; that is, the value to which the pointer points can be accessed, but its value cannot be modified through the pointer. In C++ this can be specified in the declaration

```
int i = 10, j;
const int *p = &i;

j = *p;     //  ok, j is assigned value to which p points
*p = 20;    //  illegal, trying to change the value to which p points
p = &j;     //  ok, changing p, not changing what it points to
```

Best read right to left, the declaration of `p` says "`p` is a pointer to a constant `int`." The pointer `p` can be changed to point anywhere, but it cannot change the value to which it points.

An alternate situation might be: How does one specify that a value to which a pointer points can be modified through that pointer, but the pointer cannot be changed to point anywhere else? In C++, it can be done as follows:

```
int i = 10, j;
int *const p = &i;

j = *p;     //  ok, j is assigned value to which p points
*p = 20;    //  ok, changing the value to which p points
p = &j;     //  illegal, trying to change where p points
```

The ultimate in pointer security is combining both situations; that is, `p` is a pointer that cannot be changed to point anywhere else, and the value to which `p` points cannot be changed:

```
int i = 10, j;
const int *const p = &i;
```

```
j = *p     //  ok, j is assigned value to which p points
*p = 20;   //  illegal, changing value to which p points
p = &j;    //  illegal, trying to change where p points
```

The `const` specifier is most useful when used with function parameters. The prototype for the library function `strcpy()` is actually

```
char *strcpy(char *destination, const char *source);
```

This indicates that `strcpy()` will not modify the string to which the parameter `source` points. Memory where `destination` points will, however, be modified because it will contain a copy of `source`'s string.

When pointers or references are used to pass large structures to functions for the sake of efficiency, `const` is often used to guarantee that their contents will be unchanged:

```
//  EmpRec as defined above in chapter 8
void print_rec(const EmpRec &r) {
cout << r last_name << ", " << r first_name << " (" << r ID_number << ")\n";
//  r.ID_number = 4;  statement would be illegal since r is a const EmpRec &
}

void print_rec_bad(EmpRec &r) {
    cout << r.last_name << ", " << r.first_name << " (" << r.ID_number <<
        ")\n";
    r.ID_name = 4;   //  Oops, this is legal but shouldn't be done!
                     //  It will affect r outside the function!
}
```

Using `const` pointer or `const` reference parameters allows the efficiency of the call-by-reference protocol for large objects with the safety of call-by-value.

Exercises

1. What does the `const` specifier indicate?

    For questions 2–33, assume the following declarations:

    ```
    int i = 10;
    const int ci = 10;
    int *ip = &i;
    const int *cip = &i;
    int *const icp = &i;
    const int *const cicp = &i;
    ```

    Indicate whether the following statements are syntactically legal or illegal. If the statement is illegal, indicate why it is illegal. If the statement is legal, interpret its meaning.

    2. `i = 55;`   3. `i = ci;`   4. `ci = 55;`   5. `ci = i;`

    6. `*ip = i;`   7. `ip = cip;`   8. `ip = icp;`   9. `cip = ip;`

    10. `*cip = i;`   11. `*icp = i;`   12. `icp = ip;`   13. `i = *ip;`

    14. `i = *cip;`   15. `i = *icp;`   16. `i = *cicp;`   17. `ci = *cip;`

    18. `*cip = ci;`   19. `*icp = ci;`   20. `*cicp = i;`   21. `*cip = *cicp;`

    22. `cip = cicp;` 23. `icp = cicp;` 24. `ip = &i;`   25. `cip = &i;`

26. `icp = &i;`   27. `ip = &ci;`   28. `cip = &ci;`   29. `icp = &ci;`

30. `cicp = &i;`   31. `cicp = &ci;`   32. `cip++;`   33. `icp++;`

Assignments

1. Modify the statistics package class from the previous chapter's assignments so that the array of floating point numbers is dynamically allocated from the heap. Remember to deallocate the memory when the program is finished executing.

2. Further modify the statistics package in assignment 1 so that pointer notation exclusively is used throughout the program. The only place `[ ]` should appear is when `new` is used to allocate the memory for the array.

3. Modify the database program from chapter 8 so that all the arrays (even the name strings within the individual records) are dynamically allocated. Be sure memory is freed up properly before the program finishes executing.

CHAPTER 10

LINKED LISTS, ABSTRACT DATA TYPES, AND RECURSION

10.1 INTRODUCTION

Procedural programming is a style of programming in which programs are decomposed into functions in a top-down manner as covered in chapter 6. In procedural programming, functional decomposition is only half of the work necessary to create good programs. Algorithms, as implemented with functions, must act on data. Just as functions are best developed in an organized fashion, data too must be organized in some way. We've seen how data can be collected into arrays and structures. These are forms of *data structures*. An array holds a collection of similar objects (types), but it is not the best data structure for all situations in which a collection of similar types must be stored. Object-oriented programming encapsulates the data structures and algorithms that act on those data structures into self-contained units called objects.

We've seen how the efficiency of a program is dictated by the quality of the algorithm used. We shall see how program efficiency is also dramatically affected by the choice of a data structure. Fortunately, the study of computer science is not that new, and some data structures have become well established to work in conjunction with common algorithms. We will examine several data structures that are pervasive throughout all areas of computer science including compiler construction, operating systems, database systems, simulation and modeling, computer graphics, and artificial intelligence.

Data structures can be viewed on two levels. At one level, they are abstract concepts that have their own unique characteristics apart from any computer implementation. On another level, data structures in a particular program are closely tied to the particular computer system and programming language used in development. Fortunately, the C++ language has a rich complement of features supporting data structure creation, and more importantly, abstract data types. Some languages are not so generous. This chapter focuses on how to integrate the data structures at the implementation level with the abstract data types at the conceptual level. As mentioned in chapter 8, the availability of abstract data types (ADTs) in a language facilitates the construction of large programs. Modules built by other programmers are easier to understand and use.

This chapter focuses on linear structures, the simplest of the programmer-defined linked structures. It introduces the concept of *self-referential structures*, which are crucial to the construction of advanced ADTs. Some C++ features, such as constructors, destructors, and class operators, all of which facilitate ADT implementation and use, are also examined.

10.2 LINEAR STRUCTURES—LINKED LISTS

One of the simplest data structures is the *linear* data structure. An entity is said to have linear structure if:

1. There is a unique element called *first*
2. There is a unique element called *last*
3. Every element except the first has a unique predecessor
4. Every element except the last has a unique successor.

Thus, an element chosen at random from a linear structure has only one element that immediately comes before it (unless the element chosen is the first element), and it also has only one element immediately following it (unless the element chosen is the last element).

The simple array is an example of a linear structure. Given the declaration

```
int list[SIZE];
```

`list[0]` is the first element, `list[SIZE-1]` is the last element, and for any n, 0 < n < SIZE-1, `list[n-1]` is the predecessor of `list[n]`, and `list[n+1]` is the successor of `list[n]`.

An array is not the best linear structure in all situations. Consider a linear list of `int`s that is to be kept in order by inserting new elements into their proper places within the array; thus, the array is not to be sorted after each addition—the element is to be placed in its correct position to start. If the `list` array contains

```
10   14   20   21   34   67   80
```

and element 19 is to be added, 19 is placed in `list[2]`, and the elements in `list[2]` through `list[6]` must be shifted one position forward within the array (actually the shifting must be done first). The result is

```
10   14   19   20   21   34   67   80
```

The C++ code to perform this task is provided in program 10.1, which is spread out over three files. An array list class is created and a `main()` is used to test it. (Notice that no checking is done during insertion to see if the array will exceed its allocated size. `AList::size` here indicates current size of the array, not its maximum allowable size):

```
/////////////////////////////////////////////////////////////////////
//   File alist.h
/////////////////////////////////////////////////////////////////////
const int list_size = 100;

class AList {
    int list[list_size];
    int size;
```

```
public:
      void initialize();
      int insert(int);
      int remove(int);
      void dispose();
      void print() const;
};

////////////////////////////////////////////////////////////////
//   File alist.cpp
////////////////////////////////////////////////////////////////

#include <iostream.h>
#include "alist.h"

void AList::initialize() {
      size = 0;
}

//   Returns 1 if insertion successful, 0 otherwise

int AList::insert(int new_val) {
      int i = 0;
      while ( i < size  &&  list[i] < new_val )
            i++;    //  Find position to place new item
      if ( i <= size ) {  //  Shift elements up to make room
            for ( int cursor = size;  cursor > i;  cursor--)
                  list[cursor] = list[cursor - 1];
            list[i] = new_val;  //  Add new item
            size++;    //  Adjust size
            return 1;  //  Inserted successfully
      }
      return 0;
}

int AList::remove(int /*del_val*/) {
      int status = 0;    //  Return status, failure unless proven otherwise

      //  Actual code goes here...

      return status;
}

void AList::dispose() {
      //  Do nothing here...
}

//  Print contents of list

void AList::print() const {
      for ( int i = 0;  i < size;  i++ )
            cout << '[' << list[i] << "] -> ";
      cout << "\b\b\b\n";  //  Backspace to erase last arrow
}


////////////////////////////////////////////////////////////
//   File almain.cpp
////////////////////////////////////////////////////////////

#include <iostream.h>
#include <ctype.h>
#include "alist.h"
```

```
void main() {
    AList list;
    list.initialize();
    int value, done = 0;
    char ch;
    do {
        cout << "Enter command: ";
        cin  >> ch;
        switch ( toupper(ch) ) {
            case 'I':
                cin >> value;
                if ( list.insert(value) )
                    cout << value << " inserted\n";
                break;
            case 'D':
                cin >> value;
                if ( list.remove(value) )
                    cout << value << " deleted\n";
                break;
            case 'P':
                list.print();
                break;
            case 'Q':
                done = 1;
                break;
            default:
                //   Clear input stream of bad command
                cin.clear();
                while ( cin.get() != '\n' )
                    ;
                cin.clear();
        }
    } while ( !done );
    list.dispose();
}
```

Program 10.1

(The purpose for the nonfunctional `AList::dispose()` function will be explained shortly.)

For large arrays, the process within `AList::insert()` of shifting all the elements greater than the element to be inserted becomes expensive. It would be helpful if a data structure could be devised that avoids this time-consuming process. A *linked list* is such a data structure.

To build a linked list ADT, a *self-referential* structure must be used. Recall that a field within a `struct` may be of any type—built-in, programmer-defined, or even another `struct`—but it is illegal for a `struct` to contain a field of the same type as itself. Consider the compiler's dilemma when determining how much space should be reserved for a `Block` object:

```
struct Block {
    float  height, width;
    char   name[25];
    Block  extra;
};
```

Even though an object of the same type cannot be used, a *pointer* to an object of the same is permissible and very useful:

```
struct Block {
    float  height, width;
    char   name[25];
    Block  *extra;
};
```

The compiler can easily calculate the size of a `Block` object, since pointers to any type are all the same size (a pointer is simply an address). This self-referencing ability is necessary for building a dynamic linked list.

In a linked list, each data element contains a pointer that is directed towards the succeeding data element. The following C++ `struct` defines the raw materials to build a linked list:

```
struct LinkedListNode {
    int data;
    LinkedListNode *next;
};

typedef LinkedListNode *ListPtr;
/*  ListPtr is a pointer to a linked list node */
```

Notice that each `LinkedListNode` object contains the important `int` data field as well as a pointer to another `LinkedListNode` object. (A *node* is another name for an element in the structure.) There is no array to be found in the definition. In fact, the "linearity" is achieved through the use of pointers, not an array. Program 10.2 illustrates how a linked list might be built by hand:

```
#include <iostream.h>

struct LinkedListNode {
    int data;
    LinkedListNode *next;
};
typedef LinkedListNode *ListPtr;
/*  ListPtr is a pointer to a linked list node  */
void printlist(ListPtr head) {
    ListPtr cursor;  //  Used to step through the list
    cursor = head;
    while ( cursor != NULL ) {
        cout << cursor->data << '\n';  //  Print current element
        cursor = cursor->next;       //  Move to next element
    }
}

void main() {
    //  Declare the list elements
    LinkedListNode node1, node2, node3;
    node1.data = 5;   //  Give the elements their values
    node2.data = 2;
    node3.data = 4;
    //  "String" the elements together in ascending order
    ListPtr list = &node2;   //  list is pointer to our list
    node2.next = &node3;
    node3.next = &node1;
    node1.next = NULL;  //  NULL pointer indicates end of list
    printlist(list);    //  Print out newly constructed list
}
```

Program 10.2

Figure 10.1 is a picture of what program 10.2 constructs. The NULL pointer indicates the end of the list.

In practice, building linked lists by hand *á là* program 10.2 is rarely done. It would be too tedious for large lists, and usually the individual elements and their ordering are not known ahead of time. The class described in program 10.3a defines a general linked list package:

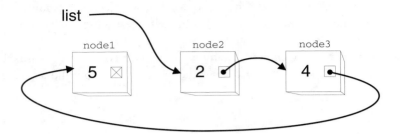

Hand-built Linked List
Figure 10.1

```
///////////////////////////////////////////////////////////
//   File llist.h
///////////////////////////////////////////////////////////
struct LinkedListNode {
     int data;
     LinkedListNode *next;
};

typedef LinkedListNode *ListPtr;
/*   ListPtr is a pointer to a linked list node   */

class LList {
     ListPtr head;
     ListPtr new_node(int);
public:
     void initialize();
     int insert(int);
     int remove(int);
     void dispose();
     void print() const;
};
```

Program 10.3a

Each node in the linked list is the same `struct` as used in the hand-built example above. The pointer to the beginning of the list is encapsulated within the `LList` class member `head`. Client code cannot manipulate the list directly since the `head` field is private.

```
///////////////////////////////////////////////////////////
//   File llist.cpp
///////////////////////////////////////////////////////////
#include <iostream.h>
#include "llist.h"

void LList::initialize() {
     head = NULL;
}

ListPtr LList::new_node(int new_val) {
     ListPtr link = new LinkedListNode;
     if ( link ) {
          link->data = new_val;
          link->next = NULL;
     }
     return link;
}
```

```cpp
//   Returns 1 if insertion successful, 0 otherwise
int LList::insert(int new_val) {
    ListPtr cursor = head, temp = new_node(new_val);
    if ( temp != NULL ) {      //   Node allocated ok
        if ( head == NULL  ||  head->data > new_val ) {
            //   new_val should go on front of list
            temp->next = head;
            head = temp;
        }
        else {
            while ( cursor->next != NULL && cursor->next->data < new_val )
                //   Step through list until proper place is found
                cursor = cursor->next;
            temp->next = cursor->next;
            cursor->next = temp;
        }
        return 1;   //   Success
    }
    return 0;   //   Unable to insert
}

int LList::remove(int del_val) {
    ListPtr cursor, previous;
    int status = 0;    //   Return status, failure unless proven otherwise
    if ( head != NULL ) {   //   Do nothing with empty list
        if ( head->data == del_val ) {    //   First item to be deleted
            cursor = head;  // Remember old head
            head = head->next;   //   Skip old head
            delete cursor;    //   Free up space of old first item
            status = 1;   //   Successful removal
        }
        else {    //   Check rest of list
            previous = head;   //   Remember first position
            cursor = head->next;   //   Start at second position
            while ( cursor != NULL  &&  cursor->data != del_val ) {
                //   Find item to remove
                previous = cursor;   //   Remember previous position
                cursor = cursor->next;   //   Step to next node
            }
            //   At this point either
            //      1.   cursor is null (item not found), or
            //      2.   cursor points to item to remove and
            //           previous points to node before node to remove

            if ( cursor != NULL ) { // Found item to remove
                previous->next = cursor->next; // Bypass
                delete cursor;   // Free up node's space for reuse
                status = 1;   //   Successful removal
            }
        }
    }
    return status;
}

//   Step through list deleting all nodes

void LList::dispose() {
    ListPtr holder;
    while ( head != NULL ) {
        holder = head;
        head = head->next;
        delete holder;
    }
}
```

```
//  Print contents of list
void LList::print() const {
    if ( head != NULL ) {
        ListPtr cursor;  //  Used to step through the list
        cursor = head;
        while ( cursor != NULL ) {
            //  Print current element
            cout << '[' << cursor->data << "] -> ";
            //  Move to next element
            cursor = cursor->next;
        }
        cout << "\b\b\b\n";  //  Erase last arrow drawn
    }
}
```

Program 10.3b

Nodes used in the linked list are allocated dynamically as needed using new. The private member function LList::new_node() allocates and initializes the contents of a node to be added to the list. Before considering the details of the linked list implementation, consider how it might be used in the following client module llmain.cpp (program 10.3c):

```
//////////////////////////////////////////////////////////////////
//  llmain.cpp
//////////////////////////////////////////////////////////////////

#include <iostream.h>
#include <ctype.h>
#include "llist.h"

void main() {
    LList list;
    list.initialize();
    int value, done = 0;
    char ch;
    do {
        cout << "Enter command: ";
        cin  >> ch;

        switch ( toupper(ch) ) {
            case 'I':
                cin >> value;
                if ( list.insert(value) )
                    cout << value << " inserted\n";
                break;
            case 'D':
                cin >> value;
                if ( list.remove(value) )
                    cout << value << " deleted\n";
                break;
            case 'P':
                list.print();
                break;
            case 'Q':
                done = 1;
                break;
            default:
                //  Clear input stream of bad command
                cin.clear();
                while ( cin.get() != '\n' )
                    ;  // Grab characters from stream until newline is
                       //  found
```

```
                        cin.clear();
            }
    }  while ( !done );
    list.dispose();
}
```

Program 10.3c

As far as the client module `llmain.cpp` is concerned, an `LList` object is a true ADT. There is no code in `main()` that implies that a `LList` object is built with pointers. In fact, substitute the class name `AList` for `LList`, and `main()` is identical to the array list above. This is why the dummy function `AList::dispose()` was provided. The `Alist` interface is identical to the `LList` interface; the positive consequences of this interface uniformity are discussed below.

Examining the `LList` implementation more closely, `LList::insert()` works as follows:

1. Create a new node for the new value to add to the list.
2. If the list is empty (`NULL` pointer), or if the new item is less than the first list element, let the new node's successor be the first item on the current list, then let the list point to the new node (new node goes on the front).
3. Otherwise, step through the list until the successor of the node currently viewed is greater than the new item, then make the new node's successor the same as the successor of the node currently being viewed, then make the new node the successor of the node currently being viewed.

Figure 10.2 is a step-by-step account of how an item would be added in the middle of an occupied list after its proper position has been found:

When the `LList::insert()` function is done, the local pointer variables `cursor` and `temp` go out of scope and cease to exist. The space allocated from the heap remains, however, until `delete` is used to deallocate it; thus, even though the new node can no longer be reached through the local pointers, an existing pointer (within the node that was being accessed through `cursor`) has been redirected to point to the new node. The final view of the list, after `cursor` and `temp` disappear, follows in figure 10.3.

Conceptually, it might be better to split up the `LList::insert()` function into two different functions since it is actually doing two different activities. It must *find* the proper place in the list to insert the new item, then it must string the pointers among the nodes to actually insert the new item.

Several new private member functions could be used:

```
/*  Returns 1 if item is at front of list or list is empty; returns
    0 otherwise  */
inline int LList::atfront(int item) {
    return head == NULL  ||  head->data > item;
}

/*  Returns pointer to the item immediately preceding the item
    sought; returns NULL if item is not found  */
inline ListPtr LList::findpreceding(int find_item) {
    ListPtr list = head; previous = NULL;
    while ( list != NULL  &&  list->data < find_item ) {
        previous = list;  //  Remember last node seen
        list = list->next;
    }
    return previous;
}
```

Item 110 is to be inserted after 105

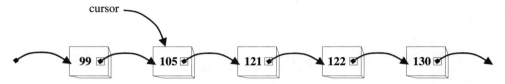

Space allocated for temp pointer

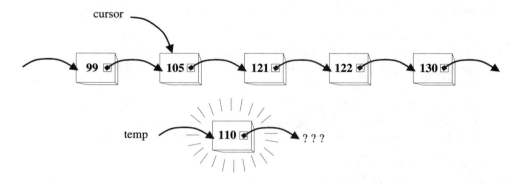

temp→next = cursor → next

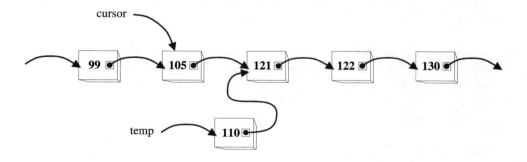

cursor → next = temp

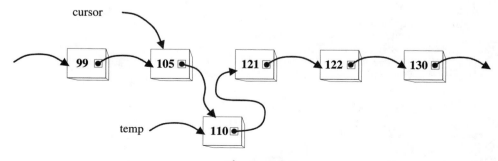

Figure 10.2

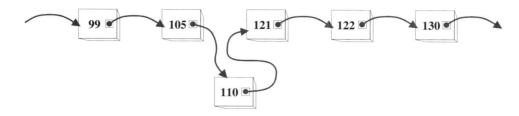

Figure 10.3

```
/*  Adds new node after node pointed to by ptr.  */
inline void LList::insertafter(LinkedListPtr ptr, ListPtr new_item) {
    new_item->next = ptr->next;
    ptr->next = new_item;
}

/*  This would replace the previous version  */
int LList::insert(int new_val) {
    ListPtr temp = newnode(new_item), cursor;
    int inserted = 0;
    if ( temp != NULL ) {
        if ( atfront(list, new_val) ) {
            temp->next = head;
            head = temp;
            inserted = 1;
        }
        else if ( (cursor = findpreceding(list, temp->data)) != NULL )
{
            insertafter(cursor, temp);
            inserted = 1;
        }

    }
    return inserted;
}
```

Notice that each function is small and focused on a single task (checking for insertion on the front, finding the insertion point, inserting at the insertion point, creating a new node, and using the four other functions to accomplish the insertion). This functional decomposition not only makes each function easier to read, but it also makes it easier to develop. Each function can be tested separately for correctness. Also, because the functions are made inline, there may not be the run-time penalty that is usually associated with function call overhead.

The routine LList::remove() is used to delete an element from a list. If the element is not present, the list is unchanged and zero is returned.

Figure 10.4 illustrates the removal of a node from the middle of a linked list.

LList::dispose() steps through the list and deallocates each node so that the space used by the list is returned to the heap. For the given main(), the call to LList::dispose() is likely superfluous. Most systems will reclaim memory allocated from the heap when a program finishes executing. The member function is necessary, however, since a function other than main() may need to use a local, temporary LList object for some processing it must perform. When the function returns, and the local LList object goes out of scope, the memory that it tying up in the linked list will be inaccessible, and the program will contain a memory leak. The fact that the programmer must remember to explicitly call LList::dispose() for the object is troubling, but the perfect solution is provided in the next section below.

Even though the linked list version is a bit more complicated than the array version, it avoids the inefficient process of shifting array elements forward to make room for the new element. Both versions must find the correct position within the list. If a linear search is performed on the array

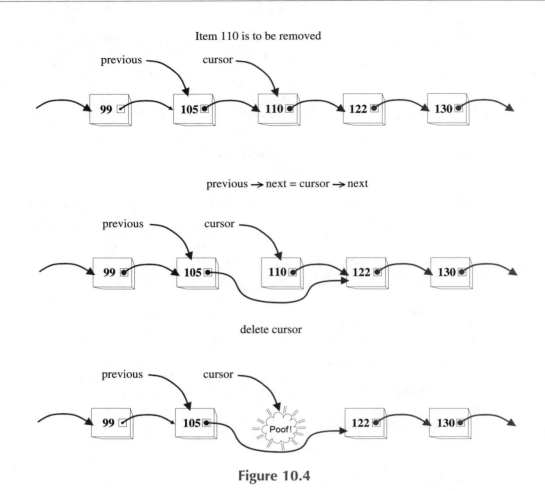

Item 110 is to be removed

previous → next = cursor → next

delete cursor

Figure 10.4

(as is done in this implementation of `AList::insert()`), then the amount of work to find the position is about the same as searching in the linked list. If a binary search is performed on the array, the array has a definite advantage when it comes to searching for the position for insertion or deletion, since binary searching cannot be done on a linear linked list. (The linked data structure answer to this weakness is the *binary search tree* found in chapter 13.) The amount of time required to slide all the remaining elements forward or backward as necessary in the array is no shorter, on average, than traversing the linked list to find the insertion point; thus, the linked list version is more efficient for insertion or deletion on large lists. The linked list version does not specify a maximum size. One does not need to worry about overrunning the bounds of an array because space for new nodes is being allocated dynamically from the heap. Compared to an array's size limitation, heap space is practically unlimited (`new`'s return value is checked to make sure the heap isn't exhausted). Linked lists have the advantage of not requiring the programmer to specify a maximum size for the list. An array's size has to be specified up front at compile-time. The programmer can declare the array to be the largest size most likely to be encountered, but this approach unnecessarily ties up memory. For example, if in most instances only 10 percent of the allocated space is going to be used at any one time, 90 percent of the memory allocated for the array is wasted most of the time.

The linked list implementation does not come without cost. An array of 100 `ints`, assuming a conservative two bytes per integer, requires 200 bytes of storage. A linked list containing 100 `ints` requires 200 bytes of storage for the `ints` plus at least 200 bytes (400 bytes on most systems) for the pointers that link the list together; thus, the linked list version requires 400 bytes of storage. The key here is that each node in the linked list version contains extra information that aids in its construction. This extra information requires storage. Our list here is simple; the only data field is a simple `int`. The linked list version requires at least 100 percent more memory (but more likely 200 percent more) than does the array version, if an equal number of nodes are being stored. If each node contained more information (e.g., a record in a database that stored first and last names, ID number, social security number, date of birth, pay rate, sick days, etc.), the space for the pointer would be insignificant compared to the size of the rest of the node and memory penalty would be relatively slight. Consider:

```
struct EmpListNode {
      char lastname[25];   //   25 bytes
      char firstname[20];  //   20 bytes
      unsigned  ID;        //    2 bytes
      unsigned  long SSN;  //    2 bytes
      unsigned DOB;        //    2 bytes
      float     payrate;   //    4 bytes
      int       sickdays;  //    2 bytes
      EmpListNode *next;   //    2 bytes
  };                       //   61 bytes total per node
```

The actual size of each member is system specific, but in this example, a list with 100 `EmpListNodes` would consume 6,100 bytes of memory, while an array (without the `next` field in each node) would use 5,900 bytes. Here the linked version would be bigger by about 3 percent (about 7 percent if the larger, four-byte pointer were used). While there is still more memory used by the linked version, the relative difference is slight compared to the 100 percent and 200 percent increases noted above!

The penalty to pay for faster insertion is more memory consumption. This tradeoff of time versus space occurs all too frequently when programming. Often a programmer has to make a choice between a fast program that requires a lot of data storage or a slow program that requires little memory to hold its data. The decision should be guided by the particular application.

A linked list is not a random access structure like an array. One cannot immediately access a middle item in a linked list without following a chain of pointers to find it; thus, a binary search cannot be performed on an ordered linked list.

Linked lists need not be ordered as in the example above. If items can always be added to the front of the list, the `insert()` routine is as simple as:

```
int LList::insert(int new_val) {
    ListPtr temp = newnode(new_val);
    if ( temp != NULL ) {
        temp->next = head;
        head = temp;
        return 1;
    }
    return 0;
}
```

Exercises

1. What is a *data structure*?

2. What is the definition of a *linear structure*?

3. What is a self-referential structure?

4. What is a linked list and how is one implemented?

5. What advantages does a linked list have over an array?

6. What advantages does an array have over a linked list?

10.3   CLASS CONSTRUCTORS AND DESTRUCTORS

The LList class above has two weaknesses. The head member is private—this is a strength, not a weakness—so the programmer must use LList::initialize() to be sure that a LList object points to an empty list before any processing is done with it. An auto LList object will have garbage for its head member until the initialization member is called. None of the other member functions will work correctly if head is not set to NULL to start with. If the programmer forgets to call LList::initialize(), the program will not work sometimes (when the random value in head is zero, which it is more likely to be than anything else, then the program will luckily work in spite of the error). Similarly, if LList::dispose() is not called for a LList object that is no longer used (e.g., goes out of scope), a memory leak develops. The AList code requires the array's size to be set to zero just as in the DataBase example from chapter 8. DataBase::set() had to be called to set the array size to zero. Failure to do so would doom a client database program just as quickly as a program with an uninitialized linked list.

It would be beneficial to be able to automatically initialize objects when they are created. Automatic initialization of objects upon their creation would prevent the frequent errors mentioned above. C++ provides a means to initialize objects automatically through the use of a *constructor*. A constructor is a special member function. It is always called when a class object is created. An object can be created within a block (local, or auto, object), globally (extern object), or with new (dynamically from the heap). A constructor has no return value (not even void). Its name is the same name as the class. Otherwise, it can be overloaded, take default arguments, etc. just as any other C++ function. The above LList class can be rewritten:

```
class LList {
    ListPtr head;
    ListPtr new_node(int);
public:
    LList();
    int insert(int);
    int remove(int);
    void dispose();
    void print() const;
};

LList::LList() {
    head = NULL;
}
//  Other member functions the same...
```

With the addition of the constructor, a programmer no longer needs to initialize a LList object before it is used, it will be done automatically. For an auto object, its constructor is called when the block in which the object is declared is entered. For a pointer to an object, the object's constructor is called when `new` is used to allocate space for it. For an `extern` or `static` object, its constructor is called when the program begins executing.

For the `AList` array list class, the constructor is written simply:

```
AList::AList() {
    size = 0;
}
```

Let us return to the class `Complex` to look at an overloaded constructor:

```
class Complex {
    double real, imag;
public:
    Complex();
    Complex(double);
    Complex(double, double);
};

Complex::Complex() {
    real = 0.0;   imag = 0.0;
}

Complex::Complex(double r) {
    real = r;   imag = 0.0;
}

Complex::Complex(double r, double i) {
    real = r;   imag = i;
}
```

The `Complex` constructor is overloaded; it can accept zero, one, or two parameters. If a constructor is called secretly, how are parameters passed to it? The following declarations illustrate:

```
Complex c1;           //   Complex::Complex() called
Complex c2(5);        //   Complex::Complex(double) called
Complex c3 = 5;       //   Complex::Complex(double) called
Complex c4(5, 7.34);  //   Complex::Complex(double, double) called
```

(Note the special syntax reserved for constructors that take one argument.) A constructor without parameters is known as a *default constructor*.

Constructors can use default arguments as well:

```
class Complex {
    double real, imag;
public:
    Complex();
    Complex(double, double = 0.0);
};
```

The constructor `Complex::Complex(double)` is no longer possible because of the ambiguity with `Complex::Complex(double, double = 0.0)`.

Even though the constructors presented above for the `AList`, `LList`, and `Complex` classes work fine, usually constructors that must initialize members use an *initialization list*, instead of initializing the member in the constructor's body (that is, between the curly braces). The `AList`, `LList`, and `Complex` constructors are better written:

```
AList::AList(): size(0) { }

LList::LList(): head(NULL) { }

Complex::Complex(): real(0.0), imag(0.0) { }

Complex::Complex(double r): real(r), imag(0.0)  { }

Complex::Complex(double r, double i): real(r), imag(i) { }
```

The initializations are made before the bodies, which in all of these cases are empty. The reason for this special syntax is because when objects are created, the constructors for any member objects must be called *before* the statements within the body of the constructor are executed. None of these three classes have member objects that have constructors, but consider:

```
class ComplexPoint {  //  A complex ordered pair
    Complex x, y;
public:
    ComplexPoint();
    ComplexPoint(double, double, double, double);
    //  other member functions follow...
};
```

Without the initialization list, the constructor with arguments must be written as follows:

```
ComplexPoint::ComplexPoint(double ar, double ai, double br, double bi) {
    Complex a(ar, ai), b(br, bi);
    x = a;
    y = b;
}
```

Before the body of the constructor for an object is executed, all of its members must have been already created. Without this guarantee, operations may be performed within the constructor body on the object that has not yet been completely initialized. Manipulating an object that is not well defined is likely to cause problems. In this `ComplexPoint` constructor, the members `x` and `y` will be created and initialized by the default constructor, and then the initialization will be undone by the assignments within the body. The initialization list eliminates the extra work by initializing `x` and `y` only once, instead of twice. If the `Complex` class did not have a default constructor, an initialization list would be required for the `ComplexPoint` class.

A *destructor* is a function that is called automatically when an object's lifetime is over. An `auto` object is destroyed when it goes out of scope. An `extern` object is destroyed when the program is finished executing. A dynamically allocated object is destroyed when `delete` is called.

A destructor should be written for the linked implementation of the `LList` class above. `LList::insert()` uses `new` (via a call to `LList::new_node()`) to allocate space for inserting an item into the list. A destructor can be written so that the programmer is freed from remembering to call `dispose()` explicitly:

```
LList::~LList() {
    dispose();
}
```

Here, the destructor simply calls `LList::dispose()` to do its job. Like a constructor, a destructor has the same name as the class (except for the tilda ~ prefix) and has no return value (not even `void`). Unlike a constructor, a destructor may not have any arguments; therefore, only one destructor may be defined for a class. The destructor frees up the programmer from remembering to do any cleanup that an object may require when its lifetime is finished; the implementer of the class takes care of the job once and for all.

If the programmer does provide a constructor and/or destructor for a class, the compiler provides default versions of each. The default versions essentially do nothing but the minimal memory allocation and deallocation required for any object. Specifically, the default destructor provided by the compiler will not release any memory that the object allocated with `new`. If an `auto` object is declared, space is allocated on the stack for it, but nothing is done to change the raw memory it holds. Notice that the `AList` array list class needs no destructor. The memory held by its array is not allocated from the heap and is therefore automatically freed up when the object goes out of scope. Now that `LList` objects have destructors that call `LList::dispose()` automatically, the call to `LList::dispose()` can be eliminated from `main()`. The dummy `AList::dispose()` can be removed from the `AList` class, and the interface to the two classes can remain identical.

Why is the uniform interface beneficial? Forget for a moment that there are two separate classes `AList` and `LList`. Assume there is only one class, and it is called `List`. The easiest implementation of the `List` class is using the array approach, as `AList` does. If a linear list class needs to be used in an application, and it needs to be made available quickly, the array version might be implemented and used within client functions. Later when the advantages of the linked list version become apparent (efficient insertion and deletion, dynamic memory, etc.), a decision might be made to rewrite the `List` class in a fashion similar to `LList`. If a list is a true ADT (as both `AList` and `LList` are), then the details of its implementation are concealed from client code. Client code must interact with a `List` object through the public member functions, which make up the class's interface; therefore, the programmer of the list class is free to change the internals of the class implementation at any time as long as the interface remains unchanged. When a new `List` class is developed, the `List` developer needs only provide the updated header (.h) file and compiled implementation code (the .cpp source code for the class is not even required). The client code would need to be recompiled and relinked but *not modified*. The ramifications of this are immense. Programs can make use of ADTs based solely on their defined, high-level behavior, independent of their low-level implementation details. This means that the entire client code can be written before the details of the data structures that its ADTs use are finalized. In fact, since the decision about how exactly to implement the details of the ADT can be postponed until after all the client code is written, both ADT and client code can be developed independently, simultaneously. Large programs require the ability to partition the work out to multiple-programming teams for development in parallel. This type of parallel development was done in the past, but the integration step, putting all the parts together, was often difficult. Here, the integration of ADTs to client code is seamless.

The decision may not be to change from the `AList` style of a list to a `LList` style. It may be that the header file will remain untouched, and only the implementation of the member functions within the .cpp file would need to be changed. Perhaps the insertion could be done more efficiently (use binary search instead of linear search), or maybe the member function to remove an item contained a subtle error that was discovered later. If the header file is unchanged, then the client code does not even need to be recompiled—it only needs to be relinked.

Exercises

1. What is a *constructor*, and how is one written?

2. What does a *destructor* do, and when is it executed?

3. Under what circumstances should destructors be written for a class?

4. What is a constructor's initialization list? How is one written?

5. What does a class's default constructor look like?

10.4   DOUBLY LINKED LISTS

The above linked list implementation can be expanded to allow traversal in both directions:

```
struct DoubleListNode {
    int data;
    DoubleListNode *prev, *next;
};
typedef DoubleListNode *Link;
```

Thus, a `DoubleListNode` contains two pointers. One points to the next node, and the other points to the preceding node. This type of list is called a *doubly linked list*. There are two distinguished pointers called *front* and *rear*. One can traverse the list forward from the front pointer or backward from the rear pointer. The following routine inserts a node into a doubly linked list following a given node:

```
/* Inserts an item into list after item pointed to by ptr  */

void insertafter(Link ptr, int new_val) {
    Link temp = newnode(new_val); // Similar to the singly linked version
    temp->next = ptr->next;
    temp->prev = ptr;
    ptr->next = temp;
    if ( temp->next )  //  If not last in list
        temp->next->prev = temp;
}
```

This process is illustrated in figure 10.5.

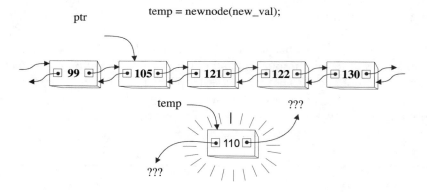

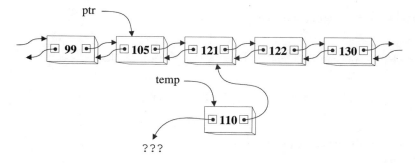

Figure 10.5

temp →prev = ptr;

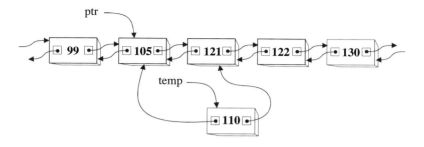

ptr → next = temp ;

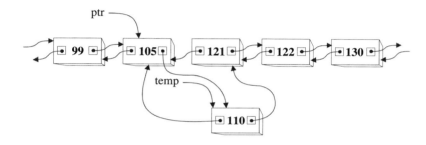

temp → next → prev = temp ;

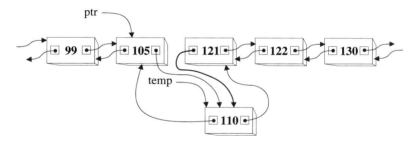

Figure 10.5 (continued)

Removal of a node in the middle of a doubly linked list (*not at the front or the rear*) can easily be accomplished:

```
void remove(Link ptr) {
    if ( ptr->next &&  ptr->prev ) {
        ptr->prev->next = ptr->next;
        ptr->next->prev = ptr->prev;
        delete ptr;
    }
}
```

Removing a node from the front of a doubly linked list must be handled as a special case as it was with the singly linked lists above. Since the list has bidirectional links, removal of the rear node also requires a special case. Care must be taken when using an expression such as

```
ptr->next->prev
```

Since the -> operator associates left to right, the expression is equivalent to

```
(ptr->next)->prev
```

If `ptr` is pointing to the last node in the list, then `ptr->next` is `NULL` and attempting to access the field of a `struct` referenced by a `NULL` pointer is always an error. Unfortunately, since `ptr` is a variable, the compiler has no way of knowing its value at compile-time; thus, this bug is sometimes difficult to identify. The `NULL` pointer is likely address 0 (but does not have to be; see chapter 8), and "NULL->prev" would be garbage stored at an offset from address 0. Some experts insist that the multiple pointer expressions like `ptr->next->prev` be avoided altogether. At the very least, the check for `NULL` pointers should be performed as is done in `remove()` above.

10.5   MULTIWAY LISTS

Consider the situation in which a list must be kept in order by more than one ordering scheme. For example, a list of employees may need to be kept simultaneously in alphabetical order by last name and numerical order by employee ID number. If all the data is kept in one array, then it would need to be sorted in the proper way each time a particular ordering is needed. For a large collection of employee records, this might be time consuming. The situation is no better with either a singly or doubly linked list. The list could be ordered lexicographically or numerically but not both ways at once. A numerically ordered list would have to be completely reconstructed to arrange the records alphabetically.

The concept of multiway lists solves the problem of simultaneously ordering a linked list in many different ways. Instead of using simply `next` and/or `previous` pointers to link the nodes together, multiple `next` and/or `previous` pointers are used. The following definitions illustrate:

```
struct MultiListNode {
    char name[20];
    unsigned  ID;
    MultiListNode *nextname, *nextID, *prevname, *prevID;
};

typedef MultiListNode *Link;

class MultiList {
    Link firstname, lastname, firstID, lastID;
};
```

Each list node contains pointers to the next node in name order and the next node in ID number order. This particular example is a two-way doubly linked list because it also has multiple pointers correctly linking the previous nodes. Notice that even though there are two distinct, independent orderings of the list, each list node appears only once. Figure 10.6 shows a small `MultiList`. The diagram looks complex and messy, but the routines that manage the pointers are fairly straightforward to write. Fortunately, the programmer, user, and even the computer itself do not see the "tangled mess" of pointers. The arrows in the diagram only illustrate the mental concept of a pointer. Remember that pointers are simply memory addresses through which the program can access a data object. The actual code that creates and manipulates two-way doubly linked lists is left as an exercise for the student.

When the two-way, doubly linked lists are mastered, three-way and higher multiway lists are no more difficult to program. A four-way list would be needed for the situation where records are to be stored simultaneously in last name order, social security number order, employee ID number order, and seniority order.

As with most linked structures, the penalty to pay for the convenience of having the list ordered both ways at once is the space taken up by the four pointers in each node. If space (memory) is at

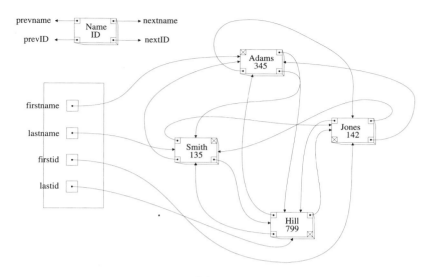

A Two-way Doubly Linked List
Figure 10.6

a premium, then store the data in an array and tolerate the extra time required to sort the array when it needs to be traversed in an order different from its present configuration.

Exercises

1. How does a doubly linked list differ from a singly linked list?

2. What is a multiway list?

3. What advantages does a multiway list provide over a one-way linked list? What penalty must be paid for these advantages?

10.6　Introduction to Recursion

A function is *recursive* when it calls itself, either directly or indirectly.

```
void blow_up() {
    blow_up();
}
```

`blow_up()` is a recursive function. The function's only statement is a call to itself. When a function calls itself within its body, *direct recursion* occurs.

```
void blow_up2_helper();

void blow_up2() {
    blow_up2_helper();
}

void blow_up2_helper() {
    blow_up2();
}
```

`blow_up2()` uses *indirect recursion*, since it does not call itself directly in its body but calls `blow_up2_helper()` which calls `blow_up2()` within *its* body. Notice that in this situation `blow_up2_helper()` must be declared apart from its definition, since it is called before its definition.

The name `blow_up()` is appropriate because a call to `blow_up()` will use up all available stack space. Recall that the part of memory known as the stack is used to communicate parameters, return values, and return locations between called functions and client functions (see chapter 6). The stack is cleaned up when the function is exited. Notice that `blow_up()` is never exited. Before it gets to the end of the function, the function is called again. Since `blow_up()` is a `void` function with no parameters, only the return address is placed on the stack. After so many calls to the function, the stack becomes full, and the program will be abnormally terminated.

In order to work properly, a recursive function must do two things: (1) it must call itself, and (2) it must use a conditional statement that provides a way not to call itself and terminate the recursion. `blow_up()` is not a properly written recursive function because it always calls itself and has no way to stop.

The following `factorial()` function illustrates the proper use of recursion. The mathematical definition of the factorial function is usually given as:

$$n! = \begin{cases} n(n-1)\,!, \; if\, n > 0 \\ 1, \; if\, n = 0 \end{cases}$$

The factorial of negative integers is undefined. The C++ recursive version is almost a direct translation of the mathematical definition:

```
/*  Works only for nonnegative ints   */
int factorial(int n) {
    if ( n > 0 )
            return n * factorial(n - 1);
    else
            return 1;
}
```

Properly written recursive functions always contain some kind of conditional statement. Here, if n is zero, the function is not called. If n is greater than zero, the function is called with a reduced value. Since n must be nonnegative, zero will eventually be passed to `factorial()` terminating the recursion. For obvious reasons, an `inline` function cannot be recursive.

It is important to understand that each call to the function creates new parameters and local variables on the stack; in this way, when a call is made inside the function, the current values of all parameters and local variables are remembered when the function returns. Consider a call of `factorial(5)`:

```
factorial(5):
      Since 5 > 0, factorial(5) = 5 * factorial(4)
      So factorial(4) needs to be found and multiplied by 5.
factorial(4):
      Since 4 > 0, factorial(4) = 4 * factorial(3)
      So factorial(5) is actually 5 * (4 * factorial(3))
factorial(3):
      Since 3 > 0, factorial(3) = 3 * factorial(2)
      So factorial(5) is actually 5 * (4 * (3 * factorial(2)))
factorial(2):
      Since 2 > 0, factorial(2) = 2 * factorial(1)
```

```
        So factorial(5) is actually 5 * (4 * (3 * (2 * factorial(1))))
factorial(1):
        Since 1 > 0, factorial(1) = 1 * factorial(0)
        So factorial(5) is actually
        5 * (4 * (3 * (2 * (1 * factorial(0)))))
factorial(0):
        Since 0 is not greater than 0, factorial(0) = 1
        So factorial(5) is finally 5 * (4 * (3 * (2 * (1 * 1)))) = 120
```

By contrast, the equivalent iterative version looks very different from the mathematical definition:

```
int iter_factorial(int n) {
    int product = 1;
    while ( n > 0 ) {
        product *= n;
        n--;
    }
    return product;
}
```

Which is better? Iterative functions are generally more efficient than recursive functions. Each function call takes time and requires stack space (function call overhead). Recursive functions can be easily written that are impossible to run due to inadequate stack space. A nonrecursive, iterative function requires only one call because the work is done within the loop. Once mastered, recursive functions tend to be conceptually simpler to understand and write. Recursive functions are used quite often to construct and traverse sophisticated data structures. An equivalent iterative function to construct and traverse the same data structure might take more code and, almost certainly, much more time to write. Some problems are more naturally solved by recursion than iteration. For these types of problems, recursive functions should be written and, perhaps, later transformed into iterative functions if their performance is unacceptable.

The following str_len() function is an alternative to the one found in chapter 7:

```
int str_len(char *s) {
    if ( *s == '\0' )
        return 0;
    else
        return 1 + str_len(s + 1);
}
```

This version uses recursion in conjunction with pointer arithmetic. The expression s + 1 passes the "rest of the string" (all but the first character) to the recursive call. The call of str_len("Hello") could be traced as

```
str_len("Hello") = 1 + str_len("ello")
                 = 1 + 1 + str_len("llo")
                 = 1 + 1 + 1 +str_len("lo")
                 = 1 + 1 + 1 + 1 + str_len("o")
                 = 1 + 1 + 1 + 1 + 1 + str_len("")
                 = 1 + 1 + 1 + 1 + 1 + 0
                 = 5
```

Sometimes it is convenient to write a function whose sole purpose is to call a recursive function with certain initial parameters. For example, the str_len() function could be rewritten recursively and avoid using pointer arithmetic:

```
int str_len_helper(char *s, int pos) {
    if ( s[pos] == '\0' )
        return 0;
    else
```

```
                return 1 + str_len_helper(s, pos + 1);
}
int str_len(char *s) {
        return str_len_helper(s, 0);
}
```

Here, an increasing index, initially zero, is passed to each recursive call. Eventually, the recursion will end when the index coincides with the position of the null character within the string.

The greatest common factor (or greatest common divisor) function was part of the assignments in chapter 6, where an iterative solution was expected. The GCF function can be tersely written recursively as:

```
int gcf(int a, int b) {
        if ( b != 0 )
                return gcf(b, a % b);
        else
                return a;
}
```

10.7 THINKING RECURSIVELY

The ability to solve problems recursively is a skill, like many, that takes time to develop. Many beginning programmers that have mastered iterative structures have a difficult time understanding and appreciating the use of recursion. In some ways, writing a recursive function can seem like "cheating." There are inevitably fewer details to keep track of in a recursive function. The equivalent iterative form may have need of several accessory temporary variables to do its job that the recursive version can do without. Notice that *not one* of the recursive functions presented thus far has used any local variables. *All* of the nonrecursive versions could not work without at least one local variable to track the progress through the iteration.

How does one attack the problem of writing a recursive function? Several examples may help to answer this question that proves difficult to answer in a simple sentence. Our task will be to rewrite the following three functions, based on the interface provided above, recursively: LList::insert(), LList::remove(), and LList::dispose(). For each of these functions, our approach will be strikingly uniform. The overall philosophy of our algorithm is summarized in the following outline:

To solve a problem with a list, only one of two steps is necessary:

1. If the list is empty, there is no problem to solve (thus, the problem *is* solved).
2. If the list is not empty,
    2.1–If the problem is solved by processing the first element in the list, then process the first element.
    2.2–Otherwise, solve the problem considering the *rest* of the list.

Of course, step 2 involves solving the problem all over again but with a smaller list. This notion of solving (applying the function to) the rest of the list is what makes the solution seem too easy. The programmer does not need to keep track of progress through the list with counters or pointers or even a loop.

The class interface has three new public and three new private member functions:

```
class LList {
        ListPtr head;
        ListPtr new_node(int);
        ListPtr insert_recursive_helper(ListPtr, int);
        ListPtr remove_recursive_helper(ListPtr, int);
        void    print_recursive_helper(ListPtr) const;
```

```
public:
        LList();
        ~LList();
        int insert(int);
        int remove(int);
        int insert_recursive(int);
        int remove_recursive(int);
        void dispose();
        void print() const;
        void print_recursive() const;
};
```

Considering the `LList::insert()` from above, the following pairs of functions look too easy:

```
ListPtr LList::insert_recursive_helper(ListPtr hd, int val) {
  // Base case:  new item goes on the front of the list
  if ( hd == NULL  ||  val < hd->data ) {
       ListPtr temp = new_node(val);
       temp->next = hd;
       hd = temp;
  }
  else // Recursive case: add new item to the rest of the list
       hd->next = insert_recursive_helper(hd->next, val);
  return hd;
}

int LList::insert_recursive(int val) {
  head = insert_recursive_helper(head, val);
  return 0;
}
```

The removal operation is just as simple:

```
ListPtr LList::remove_recursive_helper(ListPtr hd, int val) {
  if ( hd != NULL ) {
       // Base case:  Remove item at the front of the list
       if ( hd->data == val ) {
            ListPtr temp = hd;
            hd = hd->next;
            delete temp;
       }
       else  // Recursive step:  Remove item from the rest of the list
            hd->next = remove_recursive_helper(hd->next, val);
  }
  return hd;
}
int LList::remove_recursive(int val) {
  head = remove_recursive_helper(head, val);
  return 0;
}
```

The print routines are only slightly complicated by the need to erase the final arrow (the backspacing must be done outside of the recursion):

```
void LList::print_recursive_helper(ListPtr h) const {
  if ( h != NULL ) {
       cout << "[" << h->data << "] -> ";
       print_recursive_helper(h->next);
  }
}
```

```
void LList::print_recursive() const {
  if ( head != NULL ) {
        print_recursive_helper(head);
        cout << "\b\b\b    \n";
  }
}
```

Notice that in the recursive functions the programmer does not need to keep track of extra local pointers to navigate through the list.

This concept of recursion is a powerful programming technique. The idea that a problem can be solved by repeatedly applying a simple, straighforward definition to an ever diminishing problem until the solution trivially appears is unsettling for most novice programmers well versed in iterative techniques. This ability to shift the burden of keeping track of the details from the programmer to the program (as it recurses) allows routines to process more complex data structures like trees (see chapter 13) to be written in a simple and elegant fashion.

Exercises

1. When is a function said to be recursive?

2. What is the difference between direct and indirect recursion?

3. What two features are always found in a properly working recursive function?

4. Which technique generally produces more efficient code, recursion or iteration?

5. Why can't `inline` functions be recursive?

Assignments

1. Rewrite `LList::dispose()` so that it makes use of a call to a recursive function.

2. Construct a program that stores employee information in a two-way doubly linked list. The information stored is simply last name and ID number. The records (nodes) should be linked together with forward and backward name links and forward and backward ID number links. If one starts at the beginning name link and travels forward throughout the name links, the nodes will be visited in lexicographical (alphabetical) order by name. Traveling backward beginning with the ending name link traverses the nodes in reverse lexicographical order. Simultaneously, the records are kept in ID number order by using ID number links threaded appropriately. Similar traversals are possible using the ID number links (see figure 10.7).

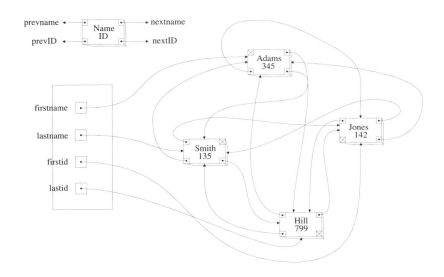

Figure 10.7

The following definitions should be used:

```
struct Node {
        char name[SIZE];
        unsigned ID;
        Node *nextname, *prevname;
        Node *nextID, *prevID;
};

typedef Node *Link;

class TWDLList {
        Link firstname, lastname;
        Link firstID, lastID;
public:
        TWDLList();
        ~TWDLList();
        int insert(char *newname, int newID);
        int remove(char *delname, int delID);
        void printtnamefrwd() const;
        void printnamebkwd() const;
        void printIDfrwd() const;
        void printIDbkwd() const;
};
```

Write a `main()` function that conveniently tests your class. `TWDLList::insert()` returns 0 if memory cannot be allocated to insert the new node; otherwise, it returns 1. It inserts a new record properly arranging the pointers so that the name and ID number orders in the list are preserved. `TWDLList::remove()` returns 0 if a node with the given name and ID number cannot be found in the list; otherwise, 1 is returned. It removes the node from the list properly reattaching the pointers on the remaining nodes to preserve the orderings. (Obviously, nothing should be done to modify the list if either of these functions returns a 0.) `TWDLList::printnamefrwd()`, etc. print out the nodes in the list in the appropriate order. Provide an appropriate constructor and destructor.

3. Build a doubly linked list class called `DLList` with all the functionality found in the `LList` class presented in this chapter. The class's interface is:

```
struct DLinkedListNode {
    int data;
    DLinkedListNode *next, *prev;
};

typedef DLinkedListNode *DListPtr;
/*  DListPtr is a pointer to a doubly linked list node  */

class DLList {
    DListPtr head;
    DListPtr new_node(int);
public:
    DLList();
    ~DLList();
    int insert(int);
    int remove(int);
    void dispose();
    void print() const;
};
```

CHAPTER 11

LEGITIMIZING ADTS IN C++: CLASS OPERATORS, COPY SEMANTICS, AND GENERIC TYPES

11.1 INTRODUCTION

Several popular languages have the ability to create abstract data types. Modula-2 (and 3), Ada, and the new object-oriented Pascals, in addition to C++, provide language support for ADTs. It takes more than language features to build good ADTs and to do good OOP. Using a language that supports these styles of programming is convenient but not essential. OOP can be done in plain C with a disciplined approach and the willingness to do a little more work than would be required in C++. The big advantage of using an OOP language that supports ADTs like C++, over doing OOP in a non-OOP language like C, is the compiler is built to enforce certain rules required for proper OOP. The programmer receives better feedback when errors are made. A C compiler translates C code; thus, it can do no checking to prevent, for example, access to private data. A C programmer must build the C program itself in such a way so that this checking is performed by the logic of the program itself. Obviously, this is not impossible, since the early C++ systems translated C++ code into C code and then passed it on to a normal C compiler for compilation into machine language. To build such a C program from scratch, however, would be a formidable task.

Programmers are more efficient when the tools they use more closely match the problem they must solve. One of the design goals of C++ was to allow the language to be adapted easily to the problems that it would be asked to solve. A mathematician, engineer, or scientist requiring a library of classes and functions to do matrix calculations would prefer to use the same symbols, or as close to the same symbols as possible, that they naturally use when they write the problems on paper.

C++ provides the means to redefine the meaning of operators when they are applied to programmer-defined types. The programmer who designs a class and redefines the operators for that class has total control (within the restrictions listed below) over what that operator means and does. In this way, programmer-defined classes approach the same status of the built-in types. They are convenient to use because they can be easily combined and intermingled with other programmer-defined objects and built-in types using operators that are terse but intuitive. The goal is to make programmer-defined types as natural to use as the built-in types. Details that make the programmer-defined types difficult to use (e.g., memory allocation/deallocation or internal restructuring) should be invisible to the user of the class.

11.2 CLASS OPERATORS

C++ provides a means for the programmer to *overload* operators to be used in conjunction with programmer-defined types (classes). Consider the following String class:

```
// File str.h   (so as not to confuse it with the standard header
<string.h>)

#include <iostream.h>

class String {
    char *word;
    void duplicate(const char *);
public:
    String();             //   default constructor
    String(const char *);   //   make from an "old C" string
    String(const String &);  //   make from another String (a.k.a. copy
                                       constructor)
    String(char);         //   make from a character
    ~String();
    operator const char *() const; //  Cast to an "old C" string
    int length() const;
    String &operator=(const String &);
    char &operator[](int) const;
    friend String operator+(const String &, const String &);
    friend int operator==(const String &, const String &);
    friend int operator!=(const String &, const String &);
    friend int operator<(const String &, const String &);
    friend int operator<=(const String &, const String &);
    friend int operator>(const String &, const String &);
    friend int operator>=(const String &, const String &);
    friend ostream &operator<<(ostream &, const String &);
    friend istream &operator>>(istream &, String &);
};
```

Program 11.1a

Notice that the class constructor String() is overloaded (see chapters 6 and 10). It may be passed no arguments, a "standard C string" argument, another String argument, or a single char as an argument. There is a destructor declared, as well as eleven functions, that have a radically new format. The reserved word operator is used to indicate that one of C++'s operators is being redefined in the context of this class. Nine of these operator functions are not member functions but friend functions. friend functions are not members of the class, but they have access to all of the class's private data as if they were actually members. The reason for doing this is given below. Other classes can be granted friend status, if necessary.

Consider the member function definitions:

```
#include <string.h>
#include <iostream.h>
#include "str.h"
void String::duplicate(const char *s) {      //  Private duplication function
     if ( (word = new char[strlen(s) + 1]) != NULL )
          strcpy(word, s);
     else
          word = NULL;
}
String::String() {        //  No initialization for String
     word = NULL;
}

String::String(const char *s) {    //  Initialize new String with char *
     duplicate(s);
}

String::String(const String &s) {    //  Initialize String with another
     String duplicate(s.word);
}

String::~String() {
     delete [] word;
}

String::operator const char *() const{    //  Cast String to const char *
     return word;
}

int String::length() const {
     return strlen(word);
}

String &String::operator=(const String &s) {
     if ( this != &s ) {      //  this explained below...
          delete [] word;
          duplicate(s.word);
     }
     return *this;
}

char &String::operator[](int pos) const {
   if ( pos < 0  || pos >= strlen(word) )
        cout << "Error: accessing position outside of string\n";
   return word[pos];
}


//  Friend functions of class String

String operator+(const String &s1, const String &s2) {
     char buffer[100];
     strcpy(buffer, s1.word);
     strcat(buffer, s2.word);
     return buffer;  //  Casts char * to String to return
}

int operator==(const String &s1, const String &s2) {
     return !strcmp(s1.word, s2.word);    //  Return 1 if 0 and 0 if nonzero
}

int operator!=(const String &s1, const String &s2) {
     return strcmp(s1.word, s2.word);
}
```

```
int operator<(const String &s1, const String &s2) {
    return strcmp(s1.word, s2.word) < 0;
}

int operator<=(const String &s1, const String &s2) {
    return strcmp(s1.word, s2.word) < 0  ||  s1 == s2;
}
int operator>(const String &s1, const String &s2) {
    return strcmp(s1.word, s2.word) > 0;
}

int operator>=(const String &s1, const String &s2) {
    return strcmp(s1.word, s2.word) > 0  ||  s1 == s2;
}

ostream &operator<<(ostream &os, const String &str) {
    os << str.word;
    return os;
}


istream &operator>>(istream &is, String &str) {
    char buffer[100];      //  Temporary buffer for string entry
    is >> buffer;          //  Extract string
    str = buffer;          //  Assign to str
    return is;
}
```

Program 11.1b

The `String` class can be treated more like a built-in data type:

```
String s;                            // Line #1

s = "Hello";                         // Line #2
if ( s == "Hello" )                  // Line #3
    cout << "Same string\n";
String w = " there";                 // Line #4
w = s + w;                           // Line #5
cout << s << ' ' << w << '\n';       // Line #6
cin >> w;                            // Line #7
s[1] = '*';                          // Line #8
```

The declaration at Line #1 calls the class constructor with no parameter; thus, no space is allocated for `String` object s, and s.word is set to NULL. In Line #2, the C-style string (i.e., a char *) is assigned to s. This assignment is accomplished by calling the member function `String::operator=()`. The argument of `String::operator=()` should be a `String`, not a char *, and so a temporary `String` is created with the `String::String(const char *)` constructor and then passed to the assignment operator. In fact, Line #2 could be rewritten

```
s.operator=("Hello");
```

although no one would write such a horrendous statement because the other way looks so elegant. Redefined member binary operators use the object itself as the left operand and the argument to the function as the right operand.

The reserved word `this` within the body of a member function (the only place it can legally appear) refers to the address of the particular object at hand. The assignment operator function illustrates the use of `this`:

```
String &String::operator=(const String &s) {
    if ( this != &s ) {
        delete [] word;
        duplicate(s.word);
```

```
        }
        return *this;
    }
```

`this` is the address of the particular object for which the assignment member function is being called:

```
String s1, s2;
s1 = s2;  //  same as s1.operator=(s2);  "this" is address of s1.
```

The assignment function first checks to see if an object is being assigned to itself:

```
String s1 = "One"
s1 = s1;  //  Assigning a String object to itself
```

If the condition were not checked first, the pointer to the string would be deallocated by `delete` and then that same pointer would be used to copy the contents of the previously deallocated string into itself. In most cases no problem would show up, but it is always a logical error to use a pointer that has been `deleted`. The program might work during development but not run correctly on other computer systems. The return of `*this` indicates that the value returned is what was assigned, just like the standard = operator does. This permits chained assignment:

```
s1 = s2 = s3 = s4;
```

The use of `this` is only possible within class (or `struct`) member functions.

The comparison in the `if` in Line #3 invokes the `operator==()` function, which is a `friend` function to the class `String`. In a nonmember operator function, the first parameter is the left operand and the second parameter is the right operand. This `operator==()` function compares two `String`s for equality. Since the second argument is not a `String` (as specified by `operator==()`) but a `char *` literal, a conversion must take place to generate a temporary `String` value from the `char *` to allow the comparison to take place. The same thing happens in the following situation:

```
int   i = 10;
float f = 2.0;
if ( i == f )
    cout << i << "is exactly the same as " << f << '\n';
```

Here `i == f` is a mixed expression, and since `float`s dominate `int`s, `i` is converted into a `float` for the purpose of the comparison (remember to be careful about using == with two floating point types). The compiler is instructed how to cast by explicitly writing a cast operator (like `operator const char*()` which converts a `String` into a `const char *`) or by writing an appropriate constructor. Here, `String::String(const char *)` indicates how `char *` can be copied to a `String` during declaration and initialization; this same function can be used behind the scenes to do implicit casting. The statement

```
if ( s == "Hello" )
    cout << "Same string\n";
```

is actually accomplished by the compiler producing code something like

```
String temp = "Hello";
if ( operator==(s, temp) )
    cout << "Same string\n";
```

Fortunately, the programmer does not need to worry about the details of this implicit conversion except to provide the constructor that the compiler will have to use.

Line #4 declares a `String` w and initializes it to " there," and so the constructor is called with a `char *` argument. Line #5 makes use of the programmer-defined concatenation operator and assignment operator. The statement at Line #5 makes using `Strings` as natural as using `int`s or any other built-in data type. Line #6 inserts a `String` into the output stream, even though this process is unknown to the routines and classes in `<iostream.h>`. This is possible because the stream insertion and extraction operators are also overloaded for this class. Line #8 uses the overloaded array subscript operator `[]` for the `String` class. It allows `String` objects to be treated more like "old C strings," with the added benefit that it performs range checking on the subscript. Such errors normally are difficult to find. Since the function returns a `char &` instead of a simple `char`, its return value can be used as an *lvalue*. An lvalue can appear on the left-hand side of the assignment operator. This allows a character position within the array to be both read from and written to.

A `friend` function should be used when a function needs access to the private members of two or more different classes, or, as in this case, operators are being defined that are *symmetric*. Symmetric operators include +, -, ==, etc. Consider the alternative:

```
class Int {
        int data;
public:
        Int(int i = 0) { data = i; }
        Int operator+(Int &i) {
                return Int(data + i.data);
        }
};
```

(Here, the `Int::operator+()` member function's body is given inside the class definition. When this is done, the function is `inline`.)

Given the declarations

```
Int x = 3, z;
int y = 5;
```

the code

```
z = x + y;
```

is equivalent to

```
z = x.operator+(y);
```

Since `y` is a plain `int` instead of an `Int` and `Int::operator+()` expects an `Int` argument, `y` will be cast to an `Int` using the constructor `Int::Int()`. The resulting temporary `Int` value will be sent to `Int::operator+()` and everything works as planned. The following is not possible, however:

```
z = y + x;
```

Since `y` is a plain `int`, the normal + operator must be applied. (There is no special `int::operator+()` that can be developed since `int` is an atomic type, not a class.) `x` is an object of a class that contains a + operator, but it is not the left-hand operand. The solution is to use a `friend` function:

```
friend Int &operator+(Int &x, Int &y) {
        return Int(x.data + y.data);
}
```

Now, either the left or right operand of the + can be converted as necessary.

When operators are overloaded for classes, the following restrictions apply:

1. The *arity* of the operators cannot be changed—a unary operator must remain unary; a binary operator must remain binary.

2. The precedence and associativity of the operators may not be changed.
3. Only the available operators can be overloaded (cannot make # an operator).
4. A few operators cannot be overloaded: . .* :: ? :
5. Some operators must be member functions (= () [] ->).

Although not required by the language, the following suggestions promote better programs:

1. The relative meaning between operators should stay the same. For example, consider the relationship among the following statements:

```
x = x + 1;
x += 1;
x++;
```

The `String` class above would be more consistent and more comfortable for other programmers to use if the += operator were adapted to it so the statement

```
s1 = s1 + s2;
```

which is currently possible can be replaced with

```
s1 += s2;
```

if desired.

2. For reasons given above, symmetric operators should be made friends, so the programmer is not forced to always use the class as the left-hand operand if a conversion is available.

A discussion of how the inserter and extractor stream operators were overloaded will be postponed until a more thorough discussion of streams is possible after introducing the concept of inheritance.

The `String` class is as natural to use now as an `int` (especially if a few more features are added like `operator+=()`). The normal string problems such as attempting to `strcpy()` into a buffer that is too small is eliminated. C strings and `String`s are interchangeable, with the restriction that a C string can't be assigned to a `String` to gain access to its private character array. Strings are much more pleasant and natural to use with these overloaded operators; no longer must critically named functions with obscure return values be endured. The details of the obscure functions and the code that makes these functions safe to use must be managed by the implementor of the class, of course. The client programmer, however, can enjoy the benefits of a well-designed class by producing client code faster and with fewer errors.

The output streams class `ostream` redefines the << operator. The statement

```
cout << x;
```

can be written

```
cout.operator<<(x):
```

Not only is the operator redefined specially for the class, but it is also overloaded to accept all the displayable built-in data types. One of its versions is quite interesting:

```
ostream& ostream::operator<<( ostream & (*f)(ostream &) );
```

This member operator function accepts a parameter which is a pointer to a function (`f`) that accepts an `ostream &` parameter and returns an `ostream &`. Just like an array name (when used all by itself) represents the address of the array, a function name (when not used in the function definition or call) represents the address of the function in memory. The compiled machine language code that makes the function work is stored in memory; therefore, it has an address. A similar extractor operator is defined for `istream`s. It is this version of the extractor operator that allows the `inflush()` function presented in chapter 6 to be used as a stream manipulator. Remember the call

```
inflush(cin);
```

can also be written

```
cin >> inflush;
```

Here, `inflush` is not used as a call since the parentheses are omitted. The call can be rewritten as

```
cin.operator>>(inflush);
```

which, recalling the definition for `inflush()`, is exactly the form needed to match the overloaded insertion operator expecting a pointer to a function as specified above.

Any function of the form

```
ostream &func(ostream &)
```

can be used as an output stream manipulator, and any function of the form

```
istream &func(istream &)
```

can be used as an input stream manipulator. Manipulators are handy because they work so naturally with the insertion and extraction operators. Compare

```
cin >> x;
inflush(cin);
cin >> y;
inflush(cin);
```

to

```
cin >> x >> inflush >> y >> inflush;
```

The following manipulator scrolls the screen up:

```
ostream &scrollup(ostream &os) {
    //  The number of newlines should equal the number of rows of the
          display screen
    os << "\n\n\n\n\n\n\n\n\n\n\n\n\n\n\n\n\n\n\n\n";
    return os;
}
```

It can be used as follows:

```
cout << "Read me quick\n" << scrollup << "Did you read it?\n";
```

Exercises

1. Why does C++ allow operators to be redefined?

2. Can operators be overloaded for the built-in data types?

3. What restrictions are imposed on programmers wishing to redefine operators?

4. List three operators that cannot be overloaded.

5. Write a manipulator called `bell()` that causes the computer to beep. (The ASCII character 7 causes most terminals and PCs to beep.)

6. Write an input manipulator to ignore all input entered until the string "SECRET" is entered. The stream should then behave as normal. Call your manipulator `password()`. The `istream::getline()` will prove useful.

11.3 COPY SEMANTICS AND THE SECRET LIFE OF C++ OBJECTS

C++ is a far more sophisticated language than its predecessor, C. In C, whenever an object of a particular type is created, memory large enough to hold that object is reserved for its use. If the object is an `auto` (local) object, it is allocated on the stack when the function that defines it is called. If the object is an `extern` variable or `static` variable local to a function, it is allocated in static memory when the program begins executing. If the variable is a pointer to an object, space for that object is allocated when the operator `new` is invoked. (In C, the `malloc()` library function actually would have to be used because `new` doesn't exist. `malloc()` should not be used in C++ because `new` invokes a constructor if necessary and `malloc()` does not.) If the object is given an initial value when declared, that value is copied into the newly allocated memory, and the new object is an exact bit for bit duplicate of the initializer. If no initializer is provided, the memory contains whatever it did before it was reserved for the object—undefined bit patterns (except for `extern` objects whose memory is filled with zeroes). In C++, the process is conceptually similar. Memory is reserved in the manner described above, and the initializer (if any) is copied into that space; however, classes in C++ can have constructors defined that are invoked whenever an object of that class is created. These constructors are particularly useful when a bit for bit copy (usually just called a *bit copy*) during initialization is not what is intended. Consider the following code in program 11.2 which implements a faulty `String` class:

```
#include <iostream.h>
#include <string.h>
#include <ctype.h>

class String_f {
    char *str;
public:
    String_f(char *);
    ~String_f();
    void print() const;
    void uppercase();
};

String_f::String_f(char *s) {
    str = new char[strlen(s) + 1];
    strcpy(str, s);
};

String_f::~String_f() {
    delete [] str;
}

void String_f::print() {
    cout << str;
}

void String_f::uppercase() {
    for ( int i = 0;  i < strlen(str);  i++ )
        str[i] = toupper(str[i]);
}
```

```
void main() {
    String_f s1 = "Hello, I'm a string";
    String_f s2 = s1;
    s1.uppercase();
    s1.print();
    cout << '\n';
    s2.print();
}
```

Program 11.2

In both cases "HELLO, I'M A STRING" is printed but not expected. The declaration and initialization of s2 filled s2 with the bit patterns that make up s1, including its pointer to str. In other words, a bit copy (sometimes called a *shallow copy*) from s1 to s2 was performed. The str fields of both objects are identical and, thus, reference the same memory. (A more serious problem arises when the objects go out of scope; this problem is described below.) The constructor String_f::String_f(char *) allocates space for a new character string when it is used. The statement String_f s2 = s1 cannot use this constructor because s1 is not a char * and the compiler cannot automatically convert a String_f to a char * to use this constructor. The programmer could define such a conversion as done in the example at the beginning of the chapter, but none is provided here. What is needed is a constructor of the form String_f::String_f(String_f &), or better yet, String_f::String_f(const String_f &). If X stands for a class then X::X(const X &) is called the *copy constructor* for that class. The const specifier is used so that both const and non-const objects can be used as initializers. The reference parameter is used because, as indicated below, call-by-value is impossible in copy construction. In this case, the proper copy constructor to add is:

```
String_f::String_f(const String_f &s) {
    str = new char[strlen(s.str) + 1];
    strcpy(str, s.str);
}
```

This code will perform a *deep copy* instead of the shallow bit copy. Figure 11.1 illustrates. The char * constructor is retained for when String_fs must be initialized with "C strings." After this addition, the program prints

HELLO, I'M A STRING

Hello, I'm a string

because s1 and s2 now have distinct storage for their str fields. The programmer is not required to provide a copy constructor; the compiler will provide one by default; namely, the simple bit copy. In this case, the default copy constructor does not adequately meet the program's needs. The following code could be fixed by adding the copy constructor:

```
//  Note: no copy constructor defined for this code--default bit copy is used
String_f s1 = "Hello", *sptr;
sptr = new String_f(s1);  //  Allocate dynamically and initialize with s1
//  Unfortunately, only s1's pointer to the char array is duplicated, not the
//     array itself
s1.print();
sptr->print();
delete sptr;   //  Destructor called here freeing up char array pointed to by
                 //  sptr.str
//  Which is the same char array that s1 is pointing to!
s1.print();  // Logical error, attempting to access array that has been deleted
//  When s1 goes out of scope, s1.str will be deleted by the destructor--but it
//       was already deleted two statements ago!
```

Prior to definition of S2

After the definition and initialization: String s2 = 21;

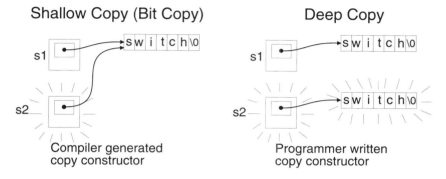

Shallow vs. Deep Copy Construction
Figure 11.1

If a programmer passes an object to a function by value, it must be copied to the stack to be used by the function. In the process, its copy constructor is called, and any initialization is performed as dictated by the constructor. When the function is finished and returns, the parameters are destroyed with the appropriate destructors called. If a function is to return an object by value (as opposed to returning a pointer to an object or a reference to an object), a temporary memory location (usually just called a *temporary*) is reserved for the value, and the object is copied into that location via the copy constructor for that class. Since parameters passed by value must be created using the copy constructor for the class, a constructor of the form X(X) or X(const X) is impossible. The compiler must use the compiled machine code to do copy construction in order to compile the source code that defines how to do copy construction. This irreconcilable recursion is similar to attempting to define a struct as a field inside of itself (as opposed to a pointer to a struct identical to itself) and is just as illegal.

It is only natural to have assignment work the same way as initialization. Assignment is a different activity than initialization. Initialization makes space for the object and copies data into it; assignment uses space that was already allocated and copies new data into the same storage. With built-in types the difference is minor, and programmers can be oblivious to the differences and not have any problems. Programmer-defined types likely have constructors; however, and constructors are called during initialization and *not* called during assignment. Consider a different main() replacing that from above:

```
void main() {
        String_f s1 = "switch";
        String_f s2 = "swap";
        s2 = s1;
        s1.print();
        s2.print();
}
```

As with the copy constructor, the programmer is not required to define an assignment operator. Also, as with the copy constructor, if the programmer omits an assignment operator definition,

Prior to the assignment

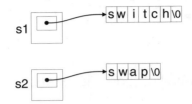

After the assignment: s2 = 21;

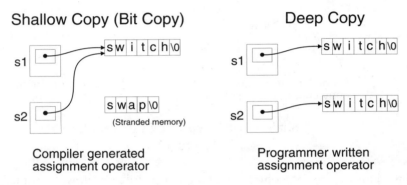

Shallow vs. Deep Copy in Assignment
Figure 11.2

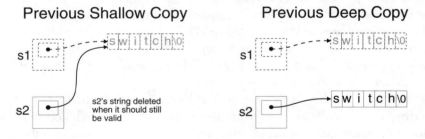

Referencing `deleted` **Memory**
Figure 11.3

the compiler will generate a bit copy assignment operator automatically. The bit copy performed for the statement `s2 = s1` obliterates `s2`'s old `str` value. The array containing "swap," allocated by `s2`'s constructor, can no longer be accessed (see figure 11.2). When `s2` goes out of scope, its destructor does not deallocate the correct memory referenced by its `str` element (see figure 11.3). Worse yet, the `delete` operator will be applied twice to the same memory location—once for `str` in `s1` and again for `str` in `s2`. Since this activity is occurring in `main()`, and since `s1` and `s2` go out of scope only when the program is finished executing, the effects are likely to be harmless here. Do the same thing within a function other than `main()` and the effects will be devastating. Not being able to access allocated memory is a memory leak, and deallocating the same memory more than once will likely cripple the memory management routines that service `new` and `delete`. The insidious part of these problems is that the programmer can be content with the `main()` that he or she has written, even though it contains serious errors that would cause the program to fail if its design were used in other functions.

The solution is to write an assignment operator that works in a similar fashion to the copy constructor:

```cpp
String_f &String_f::operator=(const String_f &s) {
        if ( this != &s ) {
                delete [] str;  //  Deallocate old str
                str = new char[strlen(s.str) + 1];
                strcpy(str, s.str);
        }
        return *this;
}
```

The `if` statement avoids the problem of assigning a string to itself (`s1 = s1`). If the test for self-assignment is not done, the `str` field will first be deallocated and then referenced as if it is still a legitimate value (since within the function body defined above `this->str` is the same as `s.str`). The `this` reserved word is used to indicate the address of the particular object upon which the member function is currently acting. `*this` is returned so that chained assignment can be performed as naturally as with the built-in types:

```cpp
s1 = s2 = s3 = s4;
```

Since = associates right-to-left, the expression is interpreted as `s1 = (s2 = (s3 = s4))`. The statement `s3 = s4` (which, recall, is a nicer way of writing `s3.operator=(s4)`) returns a reference to `s3`, so the expression simplifies during evaluation to `s1 = (s2 = s3)`. `s2 = s3`, in turn, returns a reference to `s2`, so as the evaluation continues, the expression reduces to simply `s1 = s2`. `s1 = s2` returns a reference to `s1`. The value of the complete expression, therefore, is `s1`. During the course of the evaluation, `s1`, `s2`, and `s3` all acquired `s4`'s value. The effect is the same as the following sequence of separate statements:

```cpp
s3 = s4;
s2 = s3;
s1 = s2;
```

Why return a `String_f &` instead of a plain `String_f`? As mentioned, when a value (not a pointer or reference) is returned by a function, a temporary is created (with the requisite copy constructor called). In the previous chained expression, the assignment operator is called three times, and so three different temporaries would need to be created to process this statement. The execution would proceed as follows:

```
s1 = s2 = (s3 = 4)   //  temp1  ←  (s3 = s4)
s1 = (s2 = temp1)    //  temp2  ←  (s2 = temp1)
s1 = temp2           //  temp3  ←  temp2
```

A temporary is a transient, intermediate value that the program creates while it is evaluating an expression or statement. The lifetime of a temporary is not guaranteed beyond the expression in which it is created and used. Normally, the programmer is oblivious to the creation of these temporaries. The program creates them secretly as often as is necessary to adhere to the call-by-value or return-by-value protocol. The proliferation of unnecessary temporaries (as is done in the return-by-value version of `String_f::operator=()`) is wasteful but, in this case, not harmful. This "secret" activity sometimes leads to inefficiencies that are invisible to the programmer not aware of the principles of temporary creation and destruction.

A programmer that defines a copy constructor and assignment operator for a class is said to be taking control of the *copy semantics* of that class. That is, the programmer is dictating how the copy (initialization) is to be performed. The words *syntax* and *semantics* have identical usage in programming languages as they do in natural languages (like English). Syntax refers to the structure or form of a language; that is, the rules for constructing grammatically correct sentences. Semantics refers to the meaning of the sentence and depends on the choice and arrangement of words within a sentence. The programmer has no control over the syntax of the assignment operator. Its arity (number of operands), precedence, and associativity are dictated by the language. The programmer, as we have seen, has considerable freedom over what the operator does (its meaning). In general, a copy constructor and assignment operator should be defined for most classes, especially those that deal with dynamically allocated memory as String does above. It is almost always wrong to define one without the other. If the copy constructor has to do something special to perform a correct initialization, it is most likely that the assignment operator will also have to do something special and vice-versa. The inconsistency of defining one and having the compiler specify a bit copy for the other will probably introduce errors that are difficult to find. After all, since initialization and assignment look and act so similar for the built-in types, it is often easy for programmers to believe that they are identical.

Now that copy construction and assignment have been examined, a more practical example showing the need for initialization lists for constructors can be given. Data members of classes can themselves be classes and may need to be constructed. Since the object has to be created before the body of the constructor is called, work done by the default constructors of data elements might have to be undone. Consider:

```
//  String class is as defined above (not String_f)...
class X {
        String str;
        int size;
public:
        X(String s) { str = s;  size = strlen(s); }
        //  Other member functions follow...
};
```

The following declaration of word and strclass:

```
String word = "ABCDEF";
X strclass = word;
```

causes the following to occur:

1. word is created and word.word points to "ABCDEF":
    1.1 space is allocated for word.word
    1.2 "ABCDEF" is copied into word.word
2. strclass is created:
    2.1 strclass.str is created and is initialized to NULL (by String's default constructor)
    2.2 strclass.str is reassigned to point to "ABCDEF":
        2.2.1 strclass.str.word is deallocated
        2.2.2 strclass.str.word is reallocated
        2.2.3 word.word is copied into strclass.str.word
    2.3 strclass.size is assigned the length of "ABCDEF"

The alternate (preferred) approach is:

```
class X {
      String str;
      int size;
public:
      X(String s): str(s) { size = strlen(s); }
      //  Other member functions follow...
};
```

Now when `word` and `strclass` are declared, the following occurs:

1. `word` is created and `word.word` points to "ABCDEF":
   1.1 space is allocated for `word.word`
   1.2 "ABCDEF" is copied into `word.word`
2. `strclass` is created:
   2.1 `strclass.str` is created and is initialized to point to "ABCDEF" (by `String`'s `String(String &)` constructor):
      2.1.1 `strclass.str.word` is allocated
      2.1.2 `word.word` is copied into `strclass.str.word`
   2.2 `strclass.size` is assigned the length of "ABCDEF"

The creation of an `X` object does not cause the unnecessary default construction of possibly complex (time-consuming to construct and memory-consuming) component classes.

Exercises

1. Why should programmers write copy constructors and assignment operators when the compiler can provide them for free?

2. Assuming the `String` class definitions from above, how many constructor calls will be made in the following two lines of code?

   ```
   String s1 = "Hello", s2 = s1;
   s1 = "Bye";
   ```

11.4 GENERIC ADTS: TEMPLATES

The linked list ADTs developed in chapter 10 worked very well for integers. Given the tools at our disposal at this point, the only way to make a linked list ADT for `String`s (as defined above) is to rewrite the code. The code for the insert operation is monotonously similar for a linked list of `int`s, a linked list of `float`s, or a linked list of `String`s (as defined above).

The integer version:

```
struct IntLinkedListNode {
      int data;
      IntLinkedListNode *next;
};

typedef IntLinkedListNode *ListPtr;
/*  ListPtr is a pointer to a linked list node  */
```

```
class IntLList {
        ListPtr head;
        ListPtr new_node(int);
public:
        IntLList();
        ~IntLList();
        int insert(int);
        int remove(int);
        void dispose();
        void print() const;
};
```

The floating point version:

```
struct FloatLinkedListNode {
        float data;
        FloatLinkedListNode *next;
};

typedef FloatLinkedListNode *ListPtr;
/*  ListPtr is a pointer to a linked list node  */

class FloatLList {
        ListPtr head;
        ListPtr new_node(float);
public:
        FloatLList();
        ~FloatLList();
        int insert(float);
        int remove(float);
        void dispose();
        void print() const;
};
```

The `String` version:

```
struct StringLinkedListNode {
        String data;
        StringLinkedListNode *next;
};

typedef StringLinkedListNode *ListPtr;
/*  ListPtr is a pointer to a linked list node  */

class StringLList {
        ListPtr head;
        ListPtr new_node(String);    //  new_node(const String &) is better
public:
        StringLList();
        ~StringLList();
        int insert(String);          //   insert(const String &);
        int remove(String);          //   remove(const ElementType &);
        void dispose();
        void print() const;
};
```

Computers are famous for automating repetitive tasks, and the above code cries out for automation. It would be convenient to design the ADT once, then use it to hold whatever type is necessary for a particular application. What is needed is *generic* ADT. Reconsider the `LList` class. It contains a private pointer to the head of a dynamically allocated linked list of integers. One option to introduce genericity is to use a `typedef`:

```
//////////////////////////////////////////////////////////////////////
//   File Element.h
//////////////////////////////////////////////////////////////////////
typedef int ElementType;
```

Program 11.3a

The new linked list header file would be:

```
//////////////////////////////////////////////////////////////////////
//   File llist.h
//////////////////////////////////////////////////////////////////////

#include "element.h"
struct LinkedListNode {
        ElementType data;
        LinkedListNode *next;
};

typedef LinkedListNode *ListPtr;
/*  ListPtr is a pointer to a linked list node  */

class LList {
       ListPtr head;
       ListPtr new_node(const ElementType &);
public:
       LList();
       ~LList();
       int insert(const ElementType &);
       int remove(const ElementType &);
       void dispose();
       void print() const;
};
```

Program 11.3b

The linked list implementation file is updated accordingly:

```
//////////////////////////////////////////////////////////////////////
//     llist.cpp
//////////////////////////////////////////////////////////////////////

#include <iostream.h>
#include "llist.h"

LList::LList() {
     head = NULL;
}

LList::~LList() {
     dispose();
}

ListPtr LList::new_node(const ElementType &new_val) {
     ListPtr link = new LinkedListNode;
     if ( link ) {
            link->data = new_val;
            link->next = NULL;
     }
     return link;
}

//  Returns 1 if insertion successful, 0 otherwise

int LList::insert(const ElementType &new_val) {
     ListPtr cursor = head, temp = new_node(new_val);
     if ( temp != NULL ) {     //   Node allocated ok
```

```
        if ( head == NULL  ||  head->data > new_val ) {
            //  new_val should go on front of list
            temp->next = head;
            head = temp;
        }
        else {
            while ( cursor->next != NULL  && cursor->next->data <
                                                   new_val )
                // Step through list until proper place is found
                cursor = cursor->next;
            temp->next = cursor->next;
            cursor->next = temp;
        }
        return 1;   //  Success
    }
    return 0;   //  Unable to insert
}

int LList::remove(const ElementType &del_val) {
    ListPtr cursor, previous;
    int status = 0;     //  Return status, failure unless proven otherwise
    if ( head != NULL ) {  //  Do nothing with empty list
        if ( head->data == del_val ) {    //  First item to be deleted
            cursor = head; // Remember old head
            head = head->next;   //  Skip old head
            delete cursor;    //  Free up space of old first item
            status = 1;   //  Successful removal
        }
        else {    //  Check rest of list
            previous = head;  //  Remember first position
            cursor = head->next;  //  Start at second position
            while ( cursor != NULL  &&  cursor->data != del_val ) {
                //  Find item to remove
                previous = cursor;  //  Remember previous position
                cursor = cursor->next;  //  Step to next node
            }

            //  At this point either
            //    1.  cursor is null (item not found), or
            //    2.  cursor points to item to remove and
            //         previous points to node before node to remove
            if ( cursor != NULL ) { // Found item to remove
                previous->next = cursor->next; // Bypass
                delete cursor;  // Free up node's space for reuse
                status = 1;  //  Successful removal
            }
        }
    }
    return status;
}

//  Step through list deleting all nodes

void LList::dispose() {
    ListPtr holder;
    while ( head != NULL ) {
        holder = head;
        head = head->next;
        delete holder;
    }
}
```

```
//  Print contents of list
void LList::print() const {
    if ( head != NULL ) {
        ListPtr cursor;  //  Used to step through the list
        cursor = head;
        while ( cursor != NULL ) {
            //  Print current element
            cout << '[' << cursor->data << "] -> ";
            //  Move to next element
            cursor = cursor->next;
        }
        cout << "\b\b\b\n";
    }
}
```

Program 11.3c

Finally, the client code (updated to take advantage of the constructor and destructor):

```
//////////////////////////////////////////////////////////////////////
//  llmain.cpp
//////////////////////////////////////////////////////////////////////

#include <iostream.h>
#include <ctype.h>
#include "llist.h"

void main() {
    LList list;
    int done = 0;
    ElementType value;
    char ch;
    do {
        cout << "Enter command: ";
        cin >> ch;
        switch ( toupper(ch) ) {
            case 'I':
                cin >> value;
                if ( list.insert(value) )
                    cout << value << " inserted\n";
                break;
            case 'D':
                cin >> value;
                if ( list.remove(value) )
                    cout << value << " deleted\n";
                break;
            case 'P':
                list.print();
                break;
            case 'Q':
                done = 1;
                break;
            default:
                //  Clear input stream of bad command
                cin.clear();
                while ( cin.get() != '\n' )
                    ;
                cin.clear();
        }
    } while ( !done );
}
```

Program 11.3d

This program works identically to the original version. Notice that nowhere is the type `int` explicitly mentioned as the data member of a linked list node. The identifier `ElementType` is `typedef`ed in the file `element.h`. `ElementType` is the type name used by all the other files when referring to the data member type. How powerful is this `typedef` approach? The file `element.h` could instead contain:

```
///////////////////////////////////////////////////////////////////
//   File Element.h
///////////////////////////////////////////////////////////////////
#include "str.h"

typedef String ElementType;
```

Program 11.3e

Not one of the other source files would need to be touched, and the linked list stores `String`s (as defined above) just as easily as integers! The compiled `str.cpp` file would have to be linked in, and all of the other source files would need to be recompiled and linked, but the important thing is that no source code needs to be modified for the program to work (except the minor changes to `element.h` just mentioned).

Here `LList` serves as a *container* class. The role of a container class is to hold other types in an organized way.

Examining the code found in `llist.cpp` and `llmain.cpp` reveals that this `typedef` technique above requires that any type substituted for `ElementType` must be able to handle `operator=()`, `operator==()`, and `operator<()` in a reasonable way. Integers do it naturally. Our programmer-defined string class has the capability programmed into it. The following change would have undesirable consequences:

```
typedef char *ElementType;
```

If the type to be stored is a standard C string, then all the `.cpp` files would need to be changed (except `str.cpp`, which wouldn't be used anymore) to use `strcpy()` instead of `operator=()`, and `strcmp()` instead of `operator<()` and `operator ==()`. If this change is not made, then pointers themselves will be reassigned and compared instead of the strings to which they are pointing. The moral to the story is: make ADTs act as much as possible like the simple built-in types. In this way, their use with a container class like this linked list will be seamless.

The `typedef` process to create a generic ADT container class, then, is straightforward. In a separate file, define the actual type to be contained. Verify that the type to be contained responds as expected to the operators that the ADT implementation code requires. Everything else takes care of itself. With such a simple process (compared to rewriting the ADT every time a new type is to be used), it is difficult to imagine why a better approach is required. There are two problems with this technique. One lies in modifying the `element.h` file. Any time source code must be touched, the opportunity for introducing errors arises. In the conversion from integers to programmer-defined strings not only is the actual type name changed, but an `#include` also had to be added. In large, complex programs, the type definition changes to make may not be so clear or simple. The other problem is much more serious. The disadvantage of using `typedef`s to create generic classes in this manner is that the class's interpretation is fixed for that particular program. One cannot have a linked list of integers and another linked list of strings *simultaneously*. The `ElementType` type can only be interpreted one way at a time. The better approach, using *templates*, provides a clearer, more self-documenting way of building generic classes and allows multiple interpretations of the ADT within the same program.

The `template` feature, one of the later additions to C++, provides the mechanism for automating repetitive code. The reserved word `template` is used to define a pattern that the compiler can use to generate code. Two types of templates can be generated: class templates and function templates. A class template is what is needed here.

Template syntax is somewhat obscure because it is unlike other C++ syntactical structures. It appears overly complex but is necessary so that the compiler can properly analyze the source code without the compiler being overly complex itself. The following example illustrates the class template syntax:

```
/////////////////////////////////////////////////////////////
//   File llist.h
/////////////////////////////////////////////////////////////

#include <iostream.h>

template <class T> struct LinkedListNode {
     T data;
     LinkedListNode<T> *next;
};
template <class T> class LList {
     LinkedListNode<T> *head;
     LinkedListNode<T> *new_node(const T &);
public:
     LList();
     ~LList();
     int insert(const T &);
     int remove(const T &);
     void dispose();
     void print() const;
};

template <class T> LList<T>::LList() {
     head = NULL;
}

template <class T> LList<T>::~LList() {
     dispose();
}


template <class T> LinkedListNode<T> *LList<T>::new_node(const T &new_val) {
     LinkedListNode<T> *link = new LinkedListNode<T>;
     if ( link ) {
          link->data = new_val;
          link->next = NULL;
     }
     return link;
}

//   Returns 1 if insertion successful, 0 otherwise

template <class T> int LList<T>::insert(const T &new_val) {
     LinkedListNode<T> *cursor = head, *temp = new_node(new_val);
     if ( temp != NULL ) {      //   Node allocated ok
          if ( head == NULL  ||  head->data > new_val ) {
               //   new_val should go on front of list
               temp->next = head;
               head = temp;
          }
          else {
               while ( cursor->next != NULL  && cursor->next->data < new_val )
                    //   Step through list until proper place is found
                    cursor = cursor->next;
               temp->next = cursor->next;
               cursor->next = temp;
          }
```

```
                    return 1;   //  Success
            }
        return 0;   //  Unable to insert
}

template <class T> int LList<T>::remove(const T &del_val) {
        LinkedListNode<T> *cursor, *previous;
        int status = 0;    //  Return status, failure unless proven otherwise
        if ( head != NULL ) {   //  Do nothing with empty list
            if ( head->data == del_val ) {     //  First item to be deleted
                cursor = head; // Remember old head
                head = head->next;   //  Skip old head
                delete cursor;    //  Free up space of old first item
                status = 1;   //  Successful removal
            }
            else {    //  Check rest of list
                previous = head;   //  Remember first position
                cursor = head->next;   //  Start at second position
                while ( cursor != NULL &&  cursor->data != del_val ) {
                    //  Find item to remove
                    previous = cursor;   //  Remember previous position
                    cursor = cursor->next;   //  Step to next node
                }
                //  At this point either
                //    1.  cursor is null (item not found), or
                //    2.  cursor points to item to remove and
                //         previous points to node before node to remove
                if ( cursor != NULL ) { // Found item to remove
                    previous->next = cursor->next; // Bypass
                    delete cursor;  // Free up node's space for reuse
                    status = 1;   //  Successful removal
                }
            }
        }
        return status;
}


//  Step through list deleting all nodes

template <class T> void LList<T>::dispose() {
        LinkedListNode<T> *holder;
        while ( head != NULL ) {
            holder = head;
            head = head->next;
            delete holder;
        }
}


//  Print contents of list

template <class T> void LList<T>::print() const {
        if ( head != NULL ) {
            LinkedListNode<T> *cursor;  //  Used to step through the list
            cursor = head;
            while ( cursor != NULL ) {
                //  Print current element
                cout << '[' << cursor->data << "] -> ";
                //  Move to next element
                cursor = cursor->next;
            }
            cout << "\b\b\b\n";
        }
}.
```

Program 11.4a

Notice that all of the above code appears in the header file. The implementation is not a separate `CPP` file. This is because it cannot be separately compiled. In fact, the code in the header file cannot be compiled until code that *instantiates*, or uses, the template is compiled. The above definition simply serves as a pattern that the compiler will use to substitute the appropriate types when those types are made known.

`template` is a reserved word, and `T` is an identifier that can be replaced with some other name if preferred. `T` serves as a place holder into which the actual type will be placed. In comparison to defining a `LList template`, using one is easy. In order to use a linked list of `int`s, one need only do the following:

```
LList<int> i_list;
```

This definition of the actual `LList` object with a given type is called the template *instantiation*. If `Complex` values must be used, simply instantiate it as:

```
LList<Complex> cmplx_list;
```

The access to linked list objects is identical to other classes:

```
i_list.insert(45);
if ( !i_list.remove(66) )
    cout << 66 << " not found is list << '\n';
```

The linked list client program is adapted as follows:

```
//   llmain.cpp

#include <iostream.h>
#include <ctype.h>
#include "llist.h"
#include "str.h"

void main() {
    LList<int>    i_list;
    LList<String> s_list;
    int done = 0;
    int    i_value;
    String s_value;
    char ch;
    do {
        cout << "Enter command: ";
        cin  >> ch;
        switch ( toupper(ch) ) {
            case 'I':
                cin >> i_value;
                if ( i_list.insert(i_value) )
                    cout << i_value << " inserted\n";
                break;
            case 'D':
                cin >> i_value;
                if ( i_list.remove(i_value) )
                    cout << i_value << " deleted\n";
                break;
            case 'P':
                i_list.print();
                s_list.print();
                break;
            case 'S':
                cin >> s_value;
                if ( s_list.insert(s_value) )
                    cout << s_value << " inserted\n";
                break;
```

```
                case 'Q':
                        done = 1;
                        break;

                default:
                        //   Clear input stream of bad command
                        cin.clear();
                        while ( cin.get() != '\n' )
                                ;
                        cin.clear();
                }
        } while ( !done );
}
```

Program 11.4b

Notice how two different types of linked lists based on the same template can be managed at the same time.

The following example (program 11.6) implements a generic dynamic array that includes range checking, which is a valuable tool when developing large applications because running outside the bounds of arrays is a frequent error that is very difficult to find. It employs several new preprocessor directives: #ifndef, #define, and #endif. These directives allow certain parts of the source code to be ignored by the compiler based on certain conditions. It is common practice to "wrap" header files between these two directives if there is any chance that they might be #included more than once by the same file. Program 11.5 illustrates:

```
/////////////////////////////////////
//  File block.h
/////////////////////////////////////

class Block {
   //  Whatever...
};

/////////////////////////////////////
//  File brick.h
/////////////////////////////////////

#include "block.h"  //  Uses the Block class

class Brick {
        Block blk;
        //  Other stuff...
};

/////////////////////////////////////
//  main.cpp
/////////////////////////////////////

#include "block.h"  //  Uses Block objects
#include "brick.h"  //  and Brick objects

void main() {
        Block b1;
        Brick brk;
        //  Other code follows...
};
```

Program 11.5

The programmer habitually includes block.h when Block objects are to be used and includes brick.h when Brick objects are to be used. Since main.cpp uses both kinds of objects, it makes sense to include both files; however, since brick.h itself includes block.h, `block.h` is included more than once in `main.cpp`. The `#ifndef...#endif` wrapper prevents the multiple inclusion by only including the code if a certain symbol is not defined. The `#define` registers an identifier with the preprocessor. The existence of the identifier can subsequently be checked with the `#ifdef` or `#ifndef` directives. In this case, the solution is to wrap the headers as follows:

```
///////////////////////////////////////
//  File block.h
///////////////////////////////////////

#ifndef _BLOCK_H_
#define _BLOCK_H_

class Block {
     //  Whatever...
};

#endif

///////////////////////////////////////
//  File brick.h
///////////////////////////////////////

#ifndef _BRICK_H_
#define _BRICK_H_

#include "block.h"  //  Uses the Block class

class Brick {
     Block blk;
     //  Other stuff...
};

#endif
```

The symbols defined in both of these cases (`_BLOCK_H_` and `_BRICK_H_`) were derived from the header file name, which is a common practice. The naming rules are the same as for standard C++ identifiers. The file `str.h`, the header for the general purpose `String` class presented above, would best be wrapped as:

```
#ifndef _STR_H_
#define _STR_H_

//  Rest of str.h goes here...

#endif
```

Of course, if the programmer is careful only to include a header if it is not included in another header to be included, the `#ifndef...#endif` wrapper is not needed. For projects of reasonable size, however, this approach is not practical; twenty header files may be included with circular references to other header files. The inclusion sequence can get complicated, and the programmer has enough to worry about besides sorting out whether a header file should or should not be included.

Finally, the array template follows:

```
#ifndef _ARRAY_H
#define _ARRAY_H

#include "error.h"

template <class T> class Array {
     T *vector;
     int size;
public:
     Array(int = 0);
     Array(const Array &);
     ~Array();
```

```
        Array &operator=(const Array &);
        Array &operator=(const T &);
        T &operator[](int) const;
        int operator==(const Array &) const;
        int operator!=(const Array &) const;
};

template <class T> class Matrix {
        Array<T> *row;
        int rows, cols;
public:
        Matrix(int, int, const T &);
        Matrix(const Matrix &);
        ~Matrix();
        Matrix &operator=(const Matrix &);
        Matrix &operator=(const T &);
        Array<T> &operator[](int) const;
        int rows_val() const { return rows; }
        int cols_val() const { return cols;   }
        int operator==(const Matrix &) const;
        int operator!=(const Matrix &) const;
};

template <class T> Array<T>::Array(int x): size(x) {
        if ( size > 0 )
            vector = new T[x];
        else
            vector = NULL;
}

template <class T> Array<T>::Array(const Array<T> &ca): size(ca.size) {
        vector = new T[ca.size];
        for ( int i = 0;  i < size;  i++ )
            vector[i] = ca.vector[i];
}

template <class T> Array<T> &Array<T>::operator=(const Array<T> &ca) {
        if ( this != &ca ) {
                delete [] vector;
                vector = new T[ca.size];
                size = ca.size;
                for ( int i = 0;  i < size;  i++ )
                    vector[i] = ca.vector[i];
        }
        return *this;
}

template <class T> Array<T> &Array<T>::operator=(const T &t) {
        for ( int i = 0;  i < size;  i++ )
            vector[i] = t;
        return *this;
}

template <class T> int Array<T>::operator==(const Array<T> &ca) const {
        if ( size != ca.size )
                return 0;
        for ( int i = 0;  i < size;  i++ )
            if ( vector[i] != ca.vector[i] )
                return 0;
        return 1;
}

template <class T> int Array<T>::operator!=(const Array<T> &ca) const {
        if ( size != ca.size )
          return 1;
        for ( int i = 0;  i < size;  i++ )
```

```
                    if ( vector[i] != ca.vector[i] )
                        return 1;
        return 0;
}

template <class T> Array<T>::~Array() {
        delete [] vector;
}

template <class T> T &Array<T>::operator[](int pos) const {
                if ( pos < 0  ||  pos >= size )
                    exit_error("Error: Array subscript out of range");
 return vector[pos];
}

template <class T> Matrix<T>::Matrix(int _rows, int _cols, const T &x):
        rows(_rows), cols(_cols) {
        row = new Array<T>[rows];
        Array<T> temp(cols);
        for ( int i = 0;  i < cols;  i++ )
                temp[i] = x;
        for ( i = 0;  i < rows;  i++ )
                row[i] = temp;
}

template <class T> Matrix<T>::Matrix(const Matrix<T> &m):
        rows(m.rows), cols(m.cols) {
        row = new Array<T>[rows];
        for ( int i = 0;  i < rows;  i++ )
                row[i] = m[i];
}

template <class T> Matrix<T>::~Matrix() {
        delete [] row;
}

template <class T> Matrix<T> &Matrix<T>::operator=(const Matrix<T> &m) {
        if ( this != &m ) {
                delete [] row;
                rows = m.rows;
                cols = m.cols;
                row = new Array<T>[rows];
                for ( int i = 0;  i < rows;  i++ )
                        row[i] = m[i];
        }
        return *this;
}


template <class T> Matrix<T> &Matrix<T>::operator=(const T &t) {
        for ( int i = 0;  i < rows;  i++ )
                row[i] = t;
        return *this;
}

template <class T> int Matrix<T>::operator==(const Matrix<T> &m) const {
        if ( rows != m.rows  ||  cols != m.cols )
                return 0;
        for ( int i = 0;  i < rows;  i++ )
                if ( row[i] != m[i] )
                        return 0;
        return 1;
}
```

```
template <class T> int Matrix<T>::operator!=(const Matrix<T> &m) const {
    if ( rows != m.rows  ||  cols != m.cols )
        return 1;
    for ( int i = 0;  i < rows;   i++ )
        if ( row[i] != m[i] )
            return 1;
    return 0;
}

template <class T> Array<T> &Matrix<T>::operator[](int r) const {
    if ( r < 0  ||  r >= rows )
        exit_error("Error: Matrix subscript out of range");
    return row[r];
}

#endif
```

The `Array` template allows one-dimensional array creation, and the `Matrix` template can be used to create a two-dimensional array. Arrays and matrices can be created as easily as:

```
Array<float> list(10);          //  list is a 1-D array of ten floats
Matrix<String> words(12,20);    //  words is a 12x20 2-D array of Strings
```

The above `Array` and `Matrix` templates create space dynamically. An alternate approach is to specify the size at compile time. This can be accomplished by using nontype parameters with templates as briefly shown here:

```
template <class T, int S>
class Array {
    T vector[S];
public:
        //  member functions here...
};
```

`T` represents the generic type and `S` is a nontype (in this case integer) parameter that is used to determine the size of the array. It is called a nontype parameter since the type will not vary, but its value will. Type information will not be established at the template instantiation for nontype parameters. An array of 100 `floats` would then be instantiated as:

```
Array<float, 100> my_list;
```

Observe that the size of the array is determined at compile time, not runtime. The original version would allow runtime size determination. The virtual array example in the next section makes use of nontype parameters to templates in this manner.

These templates offer several big advantages over the built-in array feature of C++:

1. An array made this way is created dynamically from the heap; therefore, creating a local array does not consume stack space. The space is released automatically when the array goes out of scope (when the destructor is called). The local array acts like an `auto` array.
2. Direct array assignment is made possible through the overloaded assignment operator. Separate array copy functions do not need to be written, and the danger of overflowing an array is eliminated. Dynamic memory is allocated and deallocated as necessary.
3. Two arrays can be compared for equality with the `==` and `!=` operators.
4. The arrays can be accessed as naturally as the built-in arrays using the subscript operator. Bounds checking is performed, however, unlike built-in arrays that do no range checking. The operator[] returns a reference to a type instead of the type itself; this allows the operator function to be used as an *lvalue*. It can appear on the left side of the assignment operator. Both of the following assignments are permissible:

```
Array<int> list(25);
int x;
//  Intervening code...
x = list[8];
list[3] = x;
```

The statement `list [3] = x;` would be impossible if the reference weren't returned.

Notice that a `Matrix<T>` object contains an array of `Array<T>`. Recall that a two-dimensional array (or table) is simply an array of one-dimensional arrays; thus, each row in a `Matrix<T>` object is itself an `Array<T>` object and can be acted upon with any member function available to `Array<T>`. A significant portion of the work in building the `Matrix` class template has been done already in the construction of the `Array` class template. The operator `[]` is defined for a `Matrix<T>` object, and it returns an `Array<T>` reference. Using the double subscript with a `Matrix<T>` object refers to a single object of type `T` just as expected. Both subscript operators do range checking to prevent out-of-bounds array accesses. Bugs due to accessing out of bounds "elements" of an array are often difficult to detect and track down.

The class template `Array` has been *reused* in the construction of the `Matrix` class template. An array of `Array<T>` objects is merely a component of every `Matrix<T>` object. Building a two-dimensional `T` array class from scratch would require longer, more detailed member functions. Wisely incorporating the `Array<T>` class into `Matrix<T>` reduces the labor involved.

Function templates can be used to make functions more generic. Recall the `select_sort()` function from chapter 7:

```
void select_sort(double list[], int size) {
    int i, j;
    double temp;
    for ( i = 0;  i < size - 1;  i++ )
        for ( j = i + 1;  j < size;  j++ )
            if ( list[i] > list[j] ) {
                temp = list[i];
                list[i] = list[j];
                list[j] = temp;
            }
}
```

This `select_sort()` function works specifically for arrays of `double` values. This function could be made more generic:

```
typedef float ElementType;
//  or #define ElementType float

void select_sort(ElementType list[], int size) {
    int i, j;
    ElementType temp;
    for ( i = 0;  i < size - 1;  i++ )
        for ( j = i + 1;  j < size;  j++ )
            if ( list[i] > list[j] ) {
                temp = list[i];
                list[i] = list[j];
                list[j] = temp;
            }
}
```

The programmer would have to be sure that `operator>()` is defined for the type (or class) that substitutes for `ElementType`. `operator=()` may need to be defined if a simple compiler-defined bit copy is not sufficient. These operators come for free with the built-in numeric types, but database records may be developed so that `operator>` orders by ID number, social security number, or some other key field. The disadvantage of using `typedefs` to create generic functions in this manner is exactly the same as with generic classes—the function's interpretation is fixed for that particular program. One cannot have a `select_sort()` that works on both `floats` and database records within a single program without providing two different `select_sort()` functions and, thus, rewriting the code. A similar sort could be written for `ints`, `floats`, etc. Since C++ allows function names to be overloaded, each function could be called `select_sort()` and would not need to be given some possibly obscure name to distinguish it (`int_select_sort()`, for example).

Again, the programmer is forced to produce repetitive code. A job done correctly should not need to be redone. Errors may be introduced into the new code if the duplication is not done with care. Maintenance of the software becomes a much more formidable task. If a minor enhancement is made to any one of the `select_sort()` functions, all should be changed so they work in a consistent manner. Making the changes is not the difficult part; it is remembering all the places that should be changed that is hard, especially when the functions may be spread out over many source files.

Function `templates` let the programmer rest easier. In this case, the solution is simple:

```
template <class T> void select_sort(T list[], int size) {
    int i, j;
    T temp;
    for ( i = 0;  i < size - 1;  i++ )
        for ( j = i + 1;  j < size;  j++ )
            if ( list[i] > list[j] ) {
                temp = list[i];
                list[i] = list[j];
                list[j] = temp;
            }
}
```

This function uses the template feature to create what is commonly known as a *parameterized* type. Functions use parameters to communicate information (values to operate on) to functions. In this case, not only are the values sent, but the types of the parameters are also communicated as well; thus, the type itself is a parameter.

A generic `swap()` routine could be written:

```
template <class T> void swap(T *x, T *y) {
    T temp = *x;
    *x = *y;
    *y = temp;
}
```

It will interchange any two values, regardless of their type. Programmer-defined types (like `String` from above) may require the assignment operator to be defined to work in an expected manner. Other structured types should be handled carefully also. For example, consider what happens if two common, null-terminated C strings are `swap()`ed, as in the following program:

```
#include "exiterr.h"
#include <string.h>
#include <iostream..h>

void main() {
    char *str1, *str2;
    str1 = new char[10];
    str2 = new char[10];
    if ( str1 == NULL  ||  str2 == NULL )
        exit_error("Out of memory");
    strcpy(str1, "Hello");
    strcpy(str2, "there");
    swap(&str1, &str2);
    cout << str1 << " " << str2 << "\n";
    delete str1;
    delete str2;
}
```

Program 11.6

Original strings:

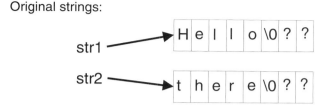

Strings after call to swap(&str1, &str2):

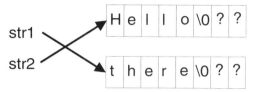

What the programmer might prefer to accomplish:

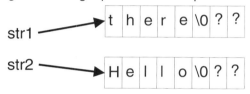

Possibly Faulty Copy
Figure 11.4

The values of the pointers are swapped, not the contents of where they are pointing. The practical effect is the same, but the programmer should be wary, because this may or may not be what he or she actually intended to do (see figure 11.4). To avoid such surprises, a `String` class should be developed as above that specifically defines how the assignment operator and copy constructor work.

The template feature is strictly a programmer convenience. Less code for the programmer to develop does *not* lead to less code for the compiler to compile and less compiled code for the computer to execute. The compiler must generate separate code for each `template` instance declared; thus, `matrix.h` from above cannot be precompiled to work with all possible data types. It is included as a header file, and it is not until a particular `Matrix` object type is declared that the compiler can generate and compile the member functions required to process it. Just as the name indicates, a template is a pattern that can be used to generate the needed classes or functions. With class inheritance (chapter 14), the actual compiled code of the member functions from the base class is shared by the derived classes; thus, code is not duplicated as it is with `templates`.

Prior to C++, generic behavior was generally accomplished through `void` pointers and complicated code and macros. The process was not *type-safe*; if the programmer passed values of incorrect types to functions, the compiler was usually unable to either "do the right thing" or generate an error message. The use of `void` pointers rendered all types equivalent. The limitations of the C language tended to work against the benefits that can be obtained by generalizing and abstracting the data and functions. C++ templates provide a type-safe means of implementing generic functions and generic objects that can save the programmer time and produce more reliable code.

Exercises

1. What is a C++ `template`?

2. Why can't template classes be compiled into object code files?

3. How are template functions and overloaded functions different?

4. Define a linked list template class that could be used to implement a linked list of any kind of objects that have the assignment and equality operators defined for them in a reasonable way. Provide the interface only.

5. Provide the implementation for the linked list class in question 4. Allow for insertion (always on front), deletion, and search (find). Provide a suitable constructor, destructor, `operator=()` and friend `operator==()`.

11.5 BINARY FILES AND RANDOM ACCESS—TOOLS FOR BUILDING A VIRTUAL ARRAY CLASS TEMPLATE

Disk files were introduced in chapter 7. `ofstream` and `ifstream` objects were used to store data to disk almost as easily as using the common `cout` and `cin` streams. The actual, physical file is a sequence of magnetic images stored on a diskette or fixed disk. It is stored on a particular *track* (tracks are concentric bands) and *sector* (sectors are equal length portions of each track) of the disk. The programmer using C++'s high-level file routines does not need to worry about the physical details of the file; the library classes and operating system attend to these low-level matters. File stream objects have constructors that accept a string and an integer. The string represents the name of the file to be accessed or created; the integer specifies the access mode, which includes an indication of whether the file is to be opened for reading or writing or both reading and writing. The constructor, with copious help from the operating system, associates the file streams object with a physical file on the disk.

Many of the streams classes have overloaded constructors:

```
ofstream f("myfile.dat", ios::nocreate);  //  Filename and access mode
ofstream f("myfile.dat");       //  Filename (default access for ofstream is
                                //  ios::out)
ofstream f;                     //  No arguments, file must be opened elswhere
```

Chapter 15 lists the `ios` file modes that can be used when opening a file. When the default constructor is used, the file is not opened, since no filename is specified. The `ofstream::open()` member function must be used:

```
f.open("myfile.dat", ios::noreplace);
```

Here, the output file stream `f` is associated with `myfile.dat`, which currently must not exist (hence the "no replace" mode).

The destructor closes the file. A file may be closed explicitly:

```
f.close();
```

This `ofstream::close()` member function is handy when a file must be closed and reopened before the stream object goes out of scope. The file must be properly closed to assure that the data is written out completely to the file. Data transfer normally goes through a special area of memory known as a *buffer*. A buffer is a section of memory (RAM) that is used as a temporary holding place for data being transferred to or from a disk file. Data transfer to or from the disk is much slower than transfer from one part of memory to another (such as when the value of one variable is assigned (copied) to another variable). Assume the contents of an array are going to be stored on disk. Instead of copying each element directly one at a time from the array to disk, each element will be copied to the buffer, and in turn, when the buffer is filled, transferred from the buffer to the file. This buffer method allows faster, more consistent data transfer to disk. Several buffers may be used simultaneously for interaction with several different files. A file that is not closed properly may leave some or all of its data in the buffer to be lost when the program finishes or the buffer goes out of scope.

The example in chapter 7 created a *textfile*. Textfiles are composed of ASCII text and can be viewed and edited with a standard text editor or wordprocessor. Textfiles are terminated with a special character, the end-of-file character. (The actual character that is used for the end-of-file character is system dependent; `<iostream.h>` defines the constant EOF that is the ASCII value of the system's end-of-file character.) Textfiles are convenient. When an array is stored with `array_save()` from chapter 7, the file can be examined and modified with a text editor. The contents of the file are exactly what would have printed on the screen if `cout.operator<<()` had been used instead of `out_file.operator<<()`. For example,

```
ofstream f("mydata.dat");
float a[size];
f.precision(2);
f.setf(ios::showpoint);
for ( int i = 0;  i < size;  i++ )
    outfile << a[i] <<  ' ';
```

would produce a file that contains something like

```
89.34   9.00   12.00   12.50   4.03
```

whereas

```
f.precision(5);
f.setf(ios::showpoint);
for ( int i = 0;  i < size;  i++ )
    f << a[i] << '\n';
```

would produce

```
89.34521
9.00000
12.00000
12.50000
4.03560
```

One could load the file into an editor, modify the second value (9.00000) to be 8.00000, and then use `array_load()` to load an array with the values including the updated second value.

Consider the penalty for this convenience. Assume that a file is to hold the following 10 `int`s:

```
34 12098 10000 5 9912 16 32275 234 24560 400
```

Notice that each `int` is separated by a space in the textfile. In order to use `ifstream::operator>>()` to read the numbers back in, white space (a space, tab, or newline) is used to delimit the values.

In our generic, but conservative, two-byte-per-integer machine, an array of these 10 `ints` would require 20 bytes of storage. Notice that the textfile requires two bytes for 34 (two characters: '3' and '4'), five bytes for 12098 (five characters: '1', '2', '0', '9', and '8'), five bytes for 10000, etc. for a total of 35 bytes for the values. The spaces between (delimiters) take up nine bytes, and the end-of-file character (invisible here but nonetheless present) uses one byte. The file requires a minimum of 45 bytes of valuable disk space, over twice as much space as the array consumes. Internally, the `int` 5 and the `int` -32,768 both use two bytes of memory, even though the displayed character '5' uses only one byte, and the characters '-', '3', '2', '7', '6', and '8' use six bytes collectively. In general, unless a file of `ints` is known to contain only one digit positive integers, a textfile is an expensive way to store `ints`. On a 32-bit machine, the space discrepancy is still an issue. The smallest space possible to store a 32-bit integer in a textfile is two bytes: the values 0–9, plus a delimiter to separate adjacent values. Since 32-bit integers range from –2147483648 to 2147483647, these values represent a small percentage of the possible values. –2147473648 would require twelve bytes of storage, three times more than is needed to store it internally in two's complement binary form. On the average, 32-bit integer textfiles will be larger than the arrays that are used to store their values in memory. The storage penalty for textfiles can be severe.

In the examples above that dealt with `floats`, the number of decimal places was restricted in both files. In terms of saving space, this approach is good. If `floats` are stored in four bytes on a particular system, then restricting the number of decimal places will allow the textfile to store fewer characters, unless the values stored are significantly larger than or smaller than zero. Even then, the storage required for decimal point, delimiter, and digits will usually exceed the four-byte internal storage space per `float`.

Limiting the decimal places stored can save space, but precision is sacrificed. Storing the floating point types in a textfile leads to errors in rounding in the conversion to and from text form. The less significant digits that were not recorded when the array was saved would not be recoverable when the array is loaded back into memory. If 2.25512345 is stored as 2.255 in a textfile and then read back in, only the value 2.255 will be recovered because the less significant digits were not stored. Even if all the decimal places were saved, there might be a slight discrepancy between the base ten text version and the internal base two version.

Fortunately, there is a solution to the above textfile problems. In a *binary file*, values are stored on disk exactly as they are stored internally in RAM. In most situations, the size of a binary file will be dramatically smaller than a textfile containing the same values. However, binary files are sometimes not as convenient to work with as textfiles, since they cannot be easily manipulated with a text editor or otherwise viewed as text (like with the DOS `TYPE` or Unix `more` command). Opening a file in binary mode is easy:

```
ofstream f("mydata.dat", ios::binary);
```

Sending a value to a binary file stream results in its internal binary representation being stored to disk instead of its textual base ten representation. This has two positive effects: (1) storage is saved, since the internal representation is, in general, smaller than the displayed form, and delimiters are not needed to separate individual values and (2) no precision is lost when floating point numbers are saved and reloaded from files, since the bit patterns that make the internal representations are literally copied bit-by-bit to the file.

When arrays are to be stored on disk, which is a frequent activity, the following approach can be used. The `ofstream::write()` and `ifstream::read()` functions are useful for storing and retrieving large chunks of contiguous data (like arrays). Their prototypes are

```
ofstream &ofstream::write(char *, int);
ifstream &ifstream::read(char *, int);
```

The first parameter is a pointer to a buffer. In `ofstream::write()`, this buffer holds the data to be stored on disk; in `ifstream::read()`, this buffer is where the data read in will be stored. The second parameter indicates how many characters (bytes) are to be either placed in the buffer or copied out of the buffer. Arrays of any type can be stored in binary form, but they first must be cast to type `char *` and then their size must be calculated in number of bytes. For example, to store an array of double-precision floating point values, called `a`, that contains n elements, the statement to use is

```
out_file.write((char *)(a), n*sizeof(a[0]));
```

assuming `outfile` is an `ofstream` object opened in binary mode. No delimiters are inserted to separate entries in the file; all entries are `sizeof(a[0])` (that is, `sizeof(double)`) bytes big and can easily be read back into an array (assuming the file is opened for a binary read). The total size of the file will be n × `sizeof(a[0])` bytes, which is the same size as the internal array itself. To read values into an array

```
in_file.read((char *)(a), n*sizeof(a[0]));
```

can be used. In this case, `in_file` is an `ifstream` object opened in binary mode.

Program 11.7 illustrates binary file processing. Since the binary load function does not use a loop that reads individual elements until the end-of-file character is encountered, the save function stores the size (number of items) in the data file as the first item. When the binary load function is used to load the array back into memory, the first item is read in (the size), and then all the items to be retrieved are loaded at once with the `ifstream::read()` function. No loop is necessary.

```cpp
#include <fstream.h>
const int MAXGRADES = 100;
typedef int GradeList[MAXGRADES];
/*
 *      Get_grades
 *      Allows user to enter up to max_size grades into array g.  Returns the
 *      actual number of grades entered.
 */
int get_grades(GradeList g, int max_size) {
    int count = 0;

    //  Loop until maximum size is attained or user types a
    //  nonnumber
    while ( count < max_size  &&  cin.good() ) {
        cin >> g[count];
        if ( cin.good() )  //  Increment count unless nonnumber entered
            count++;
    }
    return count;
}
/*
 *    Print_grades
 *    Displays the array of grades.
 */
void print_grades(GradeList g, int size) {
    for ( int count = 0;  count < size;  count++ )
        cout << g[count] << '\n';
}
/*
 *    tsave
 *    Saves the array to a textfile.
 */
```

```
void tsave(GradeList g, int size, char *filename) {
      ofstream out(filename);
      for ( int count = 0;  count < size;  count++ )
            out << g[count] << '\n';
}


/*
 *    tload
 *    Loads the array from a textfile.
 */

void tload(GradeList g, int &size, int maxsize, char *filename) {
      ifstream in(filename);
            size = 0;
      while ( size < maxsize  &&  !in.eof() ) {
            in >> g[size];
            if ( !in.eof() )
                  size++;
      }
}


/*
 *    bsave
 *    Saves the array to a binary file.
 */

void bsave(GradeList g, int size, char *filename)  {
      ofstream out(filename, ios::binary);
      out.write((char *) (&size), sizeof(size));  //  Save size info
      out.write((char *)(g), sizeof(int)*size);  //  Save array
}


/*
 *    bload
 *    Loads the array from a binary file.
 */

void bload(GradeList g, int &size, int maxsize, char *filename) {
      ifstream in(filename, ios::binary);
      in.read((char *)(&size), sizeof(size));  //  Get size
      if ( size > maxsize )
            size = maxsize;  //  Adjust size to no more than max
      in.read((char *)(g), sizeof(int)*size);  //  Get Array
      if ( in.gcount() < sizeof(int)*size )
            cout << "Error: file truncated\n";
}


/*
 *    Avg_grades
 *    Returns the arithmetic mean of the grades
 *    stored in array g.
 */

double avg_grades(GradeList g, int size) {
      double sum = 0.0;
      for ( int count = 0;  count < size;  count++ )
            sum += g[count];
      return sum/count;  /*  Division by zero unchecked  */
}

void main() {
      GradeList grades;
      int numgrades;
```

```
        cout << "Enter the grades to average [Q] quits:\n";
        numgrades = get_grades(grades, MAXGRADES);
        cout << "The average of the grades\n";
        print_grades(grades, numgrades);
        cout << "is " << avg_grades(grades, numgrades) << '\n';
        tsave(grades, numgrades, "data.txt");
        tload(grades, numgrades, MAXGRADES, "data.bin");
        print_grades(grades, numgrades);
        bsave(grades, numgrades, "data.bin");
        bload(grades, numgrades, MAXGRADES, "data.bin");
        print_grades(grades, numgrades);
}
```

Program 11.7

When large amounts of data are going to be stored, binary files should be used to save storage space. Storage and retrieval is also faster than with textfiles. (Notice that no loop is required with binary reads and writes.) Binary files also assume a uniform file format; that is, they contain no whitespace, and the precision of floating types is the same as their internal representation (no need to worry about rounded off text versions being saved).

An array is a *random access* structure; that is, any element in an array can be retrieved immediately given its subscript. The files examined so far have been *sequential access* structures. The first item in a file must be read in, then the second, third, and so forth. If the 60th item in a file is to be retrieved, items 1 to 59 would have to be read in until the 60th position was found. A file pointer maintained by the file stream object moves to the next position within the file each time an item is read (or written). Sequential binary files are a bit better than textfiles because items 1 to 59 could be read in at once (using `ofstream::read()`), and then the next item could be read in and used.

File transfers are time consuming and should be minimized as much as possible. Suppose an array is needed that is larger than memory will hold. The decision is made to store the contents of the array on disk in a binary file. The C++ streams classes provide functions that allow the internal file pointer of a file stream object to be positioned anywhere within the file; thus, random access of file data is possible. Four functions are useful:

`ofstream::seekp(long x);`	Positions the file pointer x bytes from the beginning of an output file
`ifstream::seekg(long x);`	Positions the file pointer x bytes from the beginning of an input file
`ofstream::tellp();`	Returns the current position (bytes from beginning) of an output file
`ifstream::tellg();`	Returns the current position (bytes from beginning) of an input file

To illustrate their use, program 11.8 builds a *virtual array* class. The programmer can use a virtual array as if it were in memory like an actual array, but, in fact, most of the elements in the array are not in memory at all but are stored on disk. When the client code attempts to access an element of the array that is not currently in memory, the part of the array stored on disk containing the desired position must be loaded into memory to be accessed. This file activity is invisible to the programmer and user of the program, except for the longer delay required to access the disk as opposed to RAM.

In program 11.8, an `fstream` object is defined that can be read from and written to as needed. The statement

```
        fstream fstrm(filename, ios::binary | ios::in  | ios::out | ios::trunc);
```

associates the file named `filename` with the stream `fstrm`. The file can be written to and read from, it will store the data in binary form, and it will overwrite the file if it currently exists. The use of the | operator is discussed in chapter 15; for now, it is sufficient to use it with the understanding that it combines the characteristics of the mode specifiers. Since `fstrm` is an object of class `fstream` (instead of `ofstream` or `ifstream`), it can be used to both read and write data. The virtual array template class in program 11.8 makes use of a read/write binary file. It also uses both type and nontype template arguments. The nontype arguments are useful for allowing the size of arrays within objects to be determined when an object is defined. In the virtual array template, the type of element to be stored in the array is a type argument, the array size limit is a nontype argument (a `long` value), and the buffer size is a nontype argument (an `int` value).

```
#include <fstream.h>
#include <iomanip.h>
#include <stdlib.h>

template <class TYPE, long maxsize, int buffsize>
class VirtualArray {
      fstream fstrm;    //  Total array is stored on disk, not in memory
      TYPE *buffer;     // RAM buffer, dynamically allocated
      long current_start;       //  Current buffer start on disk
      void swap_out_buffer(long);
public:
      VirtualArray(const char *, const TYPE &);
      ~VirtualArray();
      TYPE &operator[](long);
      TYPE read(long);
      void write(long, const TYPE &);
};

void exit_error(char *msg) {
      cout << msg << '\n';
      exit(0);
}


istream &flush(istream &istrm) {
      istrm.clear();  // Reset stream status to good
      int ch;
      do
            ch = istrm.get();    //  flush out remaining characters
      while ( ch != '\n'  &&  ch != EOF );
      istrm.clear();  //  Reset status back to good
      return istrm;
}


template <class TYPE, long maxsize, int buffsize>
VirtualArray<TYPE, maxsize, buffsize>::VirtualArray
                        (const char *filename, const TYPE &fill):
                              fstrm(filename, ios::binary | ios::in |
                                  ios::out | ios::trunc),
                                  current_start(0L) {
      if ( !fstrm )
            exit_error("Cannot create file");
      fstrm.seekp(0L);  //    Begin at beginning
      buffer = new TYPE[buffsize];
      if ( !buffer )
            exit_error("No memory for virtual array");
      //  Clear "array"
      long pos = 0L;
      while ( pos < maxsize ) {
            fstrm.write((char *) &fill, sizeof(TYPE));
            if ( pos < buffsize )
                  buffer[int(pos)] = fill;  //  Store first 1000 in buffer
            if ( pos % 1000 == 0 )
                  cout << "Clearing position " << pos << '\n';
            pos++;
      }
}
```

```cpp
template <class TYPE, long maxsize, int buffsize>
VirtualArray<TYPE, maxsize, buffsize>::~VirtualArray() {
    delete [] buffer;
}

template <class TYPE, long maxsize, int buffsize>
void VirtualArray<TYPE, maxsize, buffsize>::swap_out_buffer(long position) {
    //   Position file pointer to write buffer back in correct place
    fstrm.seekp(current_start*sizeof(TYPE));

    //   Write buffer data to disk, updating virtual array
    fstrm.write((char *)(buffer), sizeof(TYPE)*buffsize);

    //   Move file pointer to position sought in virtual array
    if ( position + buffsize > maxsize )    //   Don't attempt to read
        position = maxsize - buffsize; //   past the end of the file
    fstrm.seekg(position*sizeof(TYPE));

    //   Fill buffer, beginning with position sought
    fstrm.read((char *)(buffer), sizeof(TYPE)*buffsize);
    if ( fstrm.gcount() != sizeof(TYPE)*buffsize )   //   Check for error
        exit_error("Error reading virtual array file");

    //   Update position of buffer relative to the virtual array
    current_start = position;
}

template <class TYPE, long maxsize, int buffsize>
TYPE &VirtualArray<TYPE, maxsize, buffsize>::operator[](long position) {
    if ( position < 0  ||  position >= maxsize )
        exit_error("Array subscript out of range");
    //   Is position in buffer?
    if ( position < current_start  ||
         position >= current_start + buffsize )
        swap_out_buffer(position);   //   Replace contents of buffer
    return buffer[int(position - current_start)];
}


//   Instantiate a Virtual array type of 200,000 floats with a
//   RAM buffer size of 1000 floats
typedef VirtualArray<float, 200000L, 1000> fVirtualArray;

int insertatVirtualArray(fVirtualArray &a) {
    float value;
    long position;
    cout << "Enter position and value:";
    cin >> position >> value;
    if ( !cin.good() ) {
        cin >> flush;
        return 0;
    }
    a[position] = value;
    return 1;
}

void printVirtualArray(fVirtualArray &b, long start, long stop) {
    cout.precision(2);
    cout.setf(ios::showpoint);
    for ( long i = start;  i < stop;  i++ ) {
        cout << setw(10) << i << setw(10) << b[i] << '\n';
    }
}
```

```
void viewpartVirtualArray(fVirtualArray &a) {
    long position;
    for ( ; ; ) {   //  No definite termination
        cout << "Enter first position to view:";
        cin >> position;
        if ( !cin.good() )
            return;
        cout << '\n';
        cout << "Positions " << position << " to " << (position + 9) << '\n';
        printVirtualArray(a, position, position + 10);
        cout << '\n';
    }
}

void interactVirtualArray(fVirtualArray &a) {
    cout << "[Q] quits\n";
    while ( insertatVirtualArray(a) )
        ;   //  Empty loop, all work done in insertatVirtualArray()
    if ( !cin.good() )
        cin >> flush;
    viewpartVirtualArray(a);
}

fVirtualArray array("c:\\virtarr.dat", 0.0);   //  Extern VirtualArray

void main() {
    interactVirtualArray(array);
}
```

Program 11.8

The virtual array class could be designed so that it reads and writes data directly to the disk using the seek member functions of the file streams objects. The buffer implementation shown in program 11.8 is a much better approach because data has to be transferred to or from disk only when an item sought is not currently in the buffer. For example, when the `printVirtualArray()` function is executed to display the entire array, the buffer will be swapped out to disk 20 times. Initially, positions 0 to 999 will be in the buffer. When position 1,000 is to be printed, the buffer is copied to the virtual array, and virtual array items 1,000 to 1,999 are loaded into the buffer. The items in the buffer can be used as is until position 2,000 is needed, then another swap occurs. This process continues until the entire virtual array has been accessed. It is faster to read in (or write out) 1,000 items each a total of 20 times than it is to read in (or write out) 1 item each a total of 20,000 times.

To get an idea of the time savings, accessing a position within an actual array in memory is about 100 times faster than accessing an item from disk. (The factor is approximate because fixed disks have faster access times than floppy disks.) The memory access is strictly electronic; electrical impulses move from one part of the computer system to another at almost the speed of light. Disk access involves an electromechanical process. The read-write head of the drive must be positioned over the surface of the disk on the proper track (*seek* time) and the disk must be rotated to the proper sector (*rotational latency*) so the data can be transferred. The speed of RAM is measured in *nanoseconds* (10^9 seconds), and a typical DRAM (dynamic RAM) chip is rated at about 100 ns, while fixed disk access times are rated in *milliseconds* (10^3 seconds), and a 10 ms rating is good. Thus, an access time of 0.0000001 sec for RAM is 100,000 times faster than the 0.01 access time for the disk. Moving as much of the array into memory as possible, and then accessing the elements directly from RAM can greatly speed up the process.

Operating systems use a process similar to this one to implement *virtual memory*. With virtual memory, a processor thinks it has more RAM available than it actually has. A computer system may have only one megabyte of actual memory with ten megabytes of disk space reserved for virtual memory use. When the processor accesses a memory location, the operating system maps that address to the virtual memory. At any given time, one of the ten megabytes is present in actual memory. If the address requested is found in a part of virtual memory that is already in actual memory, the access is performed as normal. If the address requested is not found in the current actual memory, the one megabyte segment containing the desired address is copied off disk into RAM. This process of swapping data between memory and disk to implement virtual memory is called *paging*. Think of virtual memory as a book; the computer can store only one page of the book in actual memory at any one time. The data are the words that make up each page. If RAM currently contains page 30, and the processor needs to see the fiftieth word on page 78, the operating system would need to copy page 30 to disk (its contents may have been modified), and then copy page 78 from disk into RAM. The fiftieth word would then be accessed normally.

As you might imagine, the process of swapping pages from memory to disk (called a *page fault*) is time consuming. Fortunately, memory is most often accessed sequentially, and data for a particular program tends to be localized to a single page. Finding ways to avoid page faults is important for large programs running on large computer systems. Sometimes two logically equivalent programs may have vastly different performance on a system using virtual memory. Consider the following code (meant to be executed on a large system):

```
typedef int Array[1000][1000];   /*  1,000,000 ints  */
void zero1(Array a) {
    for ( int i = 0;  i < 1000;  i++ )
        for ( int j = 0;  j < 1000;  j++ )
            a[i][j] = 0;
}

void zero2(Array a) {
    for ( int j = 0;  j < 1000;  j++ )
        for ( int i = 0;  i < 1000;  i++ )
            a[i][j] = 0;
}
```

On a particular system using virtual memory, only half of an `Array` will fit in memory at any given time. What are the performance consequences of the two functions? In `zero1()`, the column subscript is the faster changing subscript, since it is varied within the inner loop. In `zero2()`, the opposite is true; the row subscript is modified faster compared to the column subscript. Recall that two-dimensional arrays are stored in row major order. Thus, elements `a[0][0]` through `a[499][499]` would be stored on one page, and elements `a[500][0]` through `a[999][999]` would be stored on another page. `zero2()` would require two page faults each time through the inner loop (only one the first time through and two each of the 999 times thereafter); and, since the outer loop is performed 1,000 times, it would require 1,999 page faults to access each element within an `Array` object. On the other hand, `zero1()` only performs a page fault when the row changes from 499 to 500, once in the whole function call. If a page fault requires a delay of 0.01 sec in the program's execution, then the delay for `zero1()` would be 0.01 sec, and the delay for `zero2()` would be 0.01 sec per fault × 1,999 faults = 19.99 sec, or about 20 sec.

11.6 SMART POINTERS

As a final example of the power that overloaded operators provide, consider the unfortunate situation caused by the following code that is based on the linked list template `LList` presented earlier in this chapter:

```
template <class T>
  LinkedListNode<T> *LList<T>::find(const T &sought) {
      LinkedListNode<T> *cursor = head;
      while ( cursor->data != sought )
          cursor = cursor->next;
      return cursor;
  }
```

This code works fine as long as the link is not empty and the item `sought` is somewhere in the list. If it is not, `cursor` eventually becomes null. Accessing `cursor->next` or `cursor->data` at this point may cause the operating system to terminate the program and issue some kind of error about accessing memory illegally. On nonprotected operating systems, the program may exhibit all kinds of strange behavior before eventually dying. The cure of course is to check to see if `cursor` is null before attempting to access an object through it. This kind of error frequently occurs when programming self-referential structures like linked lists and, as will be seen in chapter 13, trees and graphs. Constructors would not be needed if programmers always remembered to properly initialize objects before they are used. It would be nice if a similar facility existed to provide the check for null when the `->` operator is used to access a member of a class.

The solution is to overload the structure pointer (`->`) operator in a special way. Special rules apply to the overloading of the structure pointer operator. As previously mentioned, it must be a member operator (it cannot be a `friend` operator). It must return an object to which the `->` operator can be applied—either an object of a class or structure that defines `->` or a pointer to a class or structure with which the built-in `->` operator can be used. The following class illustrates:

```
//   spointer.tpl
//   Smart pointer template
template <class T>
class SPointer {
protected:
    T *ptr;
public:
    SPointer(): ptr(0) {}
    SPointer(T *t): ptr(t) {}
    SPointer(const SPointer<T> &cptr): ptr(cptr.ptr) {}
    SPointer<T> &operator=(const SPointer<T> &cptr) {
        if ( this != &cptr ) {
            ptr = cptr.ptr;
        }
        return *this;
    }
    void dispose() {
        if ( !ptr )
            cout << "Deleting a NULL pointer";
        delete ptr;
        ptr = 0;
    }
    T *operator->() const {
        if ( ptr )
            return ptr;
        else
            cout << "Accessing a NULL pointer.\n";
        return 0;
    }
    int operator!() const { return !ptr; }
    int operator==(const T *t) const {  return ptr == t;  }
    int operator!=(const T *t) const {  return ptr != t;  }
};
```

The `SPointer` template class only has meaning when used with another class. It cannot be used for a built-in type like an `int`, since the structure pointer operator cannot be used with an `int`. It can be incorporated nicely into the `LList` class template:

```
//   File llist.h

#include <iostream.h>
#include "spointer.tpl"
```

```
template <class T>
struct LinkedListNode {
    T data;
    SPointer<LinkedListNode<T> > next;
};

template <class T>
class LList {
    SPointer<LinkedListNode<T> >head;
    SPointer<LinkedListNode<T> >new_node(const T &);
public:
    LList();
    ~LList();
    int insert(const T &);
    int remove(const T &);
    void dispose();
    void print() const;
};


template <class T>
LList<T>::LList() {
    head = 0;
}

template <class T>
LList<T>::~LList() {
    dispose();
}

template <class T>
SPointer<LinkedListNode<T> >LList<T>::new_node(const T &new_val) {
    LinkedListNode<T> *link = new LinkedListNode<T>;
    if ( link ) {
        link->data = new_val;
        link->next = NULL;
    }
    return link;
}


//  Returns 1 if insertion successful, 0 otherwise

template <class T>
int LList<T>::insert(const T &new_val) {
    SPointer<LinkedListNode<T> > cursor = head, temp = new_node(new_val);
    if ( temp != NULL ) {      //  Node allocated ok
        if (  !head  ||  head->data > new_val ) {
            //  new_val should go on front of list
            temp->next = head;
            head = temp;
        }
        else {
            while ( cursor->next != NULL  && cursor->next->data < new_val )
                //  Step through list until proper place is found
                cursor = cursor->next;
            temp->next = cursor->next;
            cursor->next = temp;
        }
        return 1;  //  Success
    }
    return 0;  //  Unable to insert
}
```

```
template <class T>
int LList<T>::remove(const T &del_val) {
      SPointer<LinkedListNode<T> > cursor, previous;
      int status = 0;    //  Return status, failure unless proven otherwise
      if ( head != NULL ) {   //  Do nothing with empty list
            if ( head->data == del_val ) {     //  First item to be deleted
                  cursor = head; // Remember old head
                  head = head->next;   //  Skip old head
                  cursor.dispose();    //  Free up space of old first item
                  status = 1;   //  Successful removal
            }
            else {    //  Check rest of list
                  previous = head;   //  Remember first position
                  cursor = head->next;   //  Start at second position
                  while ( cursor != NULL  &&  cursor->data != del_val ) {
                        //  Find item to remove
                        previous = cursor;   //  Remember previous position
                        cursor = cursor->next;   //  Step to next node
                  }
                  //  At this point either
                  //    1.  cursor is null (item not found), or
                  //    2.  cursor points to item to remove and
                  //          previous points to node before node to remove
                  if ( cursor != NULL ) { // Found item to remove
                        previous->next = cursor->next; // Bypass
                        cursor.dispose();   // Free up node's space for reuse
                        status = 1;   //  Successful removal
                  }
            }
      }
      return status;
}
//  Step through list deleting all nodes
template <class T>
void LList<T>::dispose() {
      SPointer<LinkedListNode<T> > holder;
      while ( head != NULL ) {
            holder = head;
            head = head->next;
            holder.dispose();
      }
}

//  Print contents of list

template <class T>
void LList<T>::print() const {
      if ( ! !head ) {
            SPointer<LinkedListNode<T> > cursor; // Used to step through the list
            cursor = head;
            while ( cursor != NULL ) {
                  //  Print current element
                  cout << '[' << cursor->data << "] -> ";
                  //  Move to next element
                  cursor = cursor->next;
            }
            cout << "\b\b\b\n";
      }
}
```

This code is almost identical to the `LList` template code appearing earlier in this chapter. Here, however, the type `LinkedListNode<T> *` is not used except in `LList:new_node()`. No longer is the pointer to a `LinkedListNode` used directly. A `LinkedListNode` object is now only accessed through the "smart" pointer, `SPointer<LinkedListNode<T> >`. (Note that the space is required between the two right angle brackets. The compiler will treat them as operator `>>` if the space is not placed between them.) If `cursor` is an `SPointer<LinkedListNode<T> >`, then `cursor->data` actually evaluates to `cursor.ptr->data`. This access of `cursor` also automatically checks `cursor` to see if it is null.

The client code in `llmain.cpp` does not need to be touched at all! It still works as is, needing only to be recompiled. Such is the beauty of properly constructed ADTs. The null access protection could have been added after the client code had been up and running for a while. The only observable effect is that the code may run a little slower. This slow down will probably be imperceptible in this particular program. The price to pay for security is the slight runtime penalty of always checking for null before applying operator `->` in the context of this `LList` class.

Exercises

1. What is a file buffer?

2. When speaking of diskettes and fixed disks, what do the terms track and sector mean?

3. What is the difference between a textfile and a binary file?

4. What advantages do textfiles have over binary files?

5. What advantages do binary files have over textfiles?

6. What constant is used to indicate the end-of-file character?

7. What limitation is introduced when a `float` is stored in a textfile with the insertion operator?

8. Why must the size (number of entries) in a binary file be saved to disk when it is not necessary to save the size in a textfile?

9. Assume `floats` require four bytes of storage on a particular system. Consider the following `float` values:

    23.44, 100.0, 16.0, 88.418, 19.022, 0.023, 1.72, 65.04

    If these values are stored in a textfile, what is the minimum size of the file (in bytes)?
    If these values are stored in a binary file, what is the minimum size of the file (in bytes)?

9. How is random access performed on a binary file?

10. What is virtual memory?

Assignments

1. Add the following overloaded operators to the linked list class template presented in this chapter:

    Member operators:

    +=   inserts an item into the list
    -=   removes an item from the list
    =   duplicates a list, properly deallocating any nodes the left-hand list may contain
    !   unary operator to remove all the nodes in a list
    []   to access the nth node in a list (as used with arrays)
    Friend operators:

    ==   checks to see if two linked lists contain exactly the same nodes in exactly the same sequence
    !=   checks to see if two linked lists are not exactly the same

    Test your new class template by using it to store integers, floats, and Strings (as defined in this chapter).

2. Modify the String class constructors and destructor so a message is displayed when each is called. Write a client program that uses String objects—assigns them, initializes them, passes them to functions by value and by reference, dynamically allocates arrays of them, declares auto arrays of them, etc. Based on the activities observed, report on the behind-the-scenes complexity that String processing entails.

3. Build a complete rational number (fraction) class. Fractions should be able to be treated as much like built-in types as possible. Provide a member function to reduce a fraction, and use it within all the arithmetic operator functions to reduce the return value automatically. Allow I/O to be performed with the standard stream operators (as with the String example).

4. Make up a doubly linked list template with the functionality of the linked list template provided in this chapter.

5. Extend assignment 4 by adding the functionality described in assignment 1.

6. Modify assignment 4 so that smart pointers are used throughout.

CHAPTER 12

STACKS AND QUEUES

12.1 MOTIVATION

The concepts of data structures and abstract data types, as introduced in chapter 10, are critical to the development of sophisticated programs. A good programmer has a thorough knowledge of the principles of good data structure construction. A good programmer is well grounded in the fundamental data structures such as linked lists. The proper marriage of data structures and their associated algorithms yields programs with substantial power. ADTs prevent programmers from writing custom code that accesses the internals of these data structures. The unlimited ability to access the details of a data structure often leads to problems in large programs, especially if multiple programmers are involved. ADTs hide the internal details of a data structure so that access to the data structure is limited to a fixed number of specific operations. This process of restricting access to data structures is called *encapsulation*. The internal details of the data structure are encapsulated by an interface that provides a set of legal operations on that data structure. This description defines an ADT.

The idea of tying a programmer's hands may seem to be contrary to the goal of learning programming principles; however, good programmers know what not to do, as well as how to do what needs to be done. `ints` are built-in data types. Access to the `int` type is normally restricted to assignment, addition, and so forth. Many of C++'s operators can use `ints` as operands. Normally, an `int` consists of sixteen or more bits. In addition, a programmer does not go in and try to change the individual bits that make up an `int`, although the programmer could. (See chapter 15.) Most applications work quite well with access to `ints` being restricted to normal assignment, addition, etc.

Consider any of the linked list ADTs mentioned in chapter 10. Specifically, consider the `LList` class. If a programmer wrote a routine to modify a linked list (e.g., to attempt to sort it if it were not already in order), he or she would need to redirect pointers to restructure the list. Pointers, as you know by now, can be tricky. The programmer may not have considered all cases when writing the code. A subtle error could be introduced that does not become apparent for some time. When a list of a particularly rare configuration of values is sorted, and the programmer's code handles a pointer improperly, part of the list could be lost. Worse yet, the programmer may not completely understand the inner workings of the linked list code; thus, error-laced code will result.

In general, it is best for the author of a module that defines a data structure to be able to limit the access to a client programmer. This encapsulation ability limits errors that can be introduced by client code. The ADT becomes a black box that *must* be used as intended. Any misuse could (and should) be handled gracefully by the black box.

This chapter examines two of the most pervasive ADTs in computer science—the stack and the queue.

12.2   THE STACK ADT

The *stack* ADT is pervasive throughout computer science. A stack is used to pass parameters to functions, to allocate space for `auto` variables and objects, to translate and compile programming languages, to nonrecursively traverse complex data structures, and to evaluate arithmetic expressions. The list of applications goes on and on. It is remarkable that such a useful structure is, in fact, quite simple.

A stack is simply a linear collection of items that has restricted access. Insertions, deletions, and general access of items in the stack is limited to one end of the stack, usually called the *top*. (Stacks are often pictured as vertical structures growing from the bottom up.) Items are placed on the top of the stack, and items must be removed from the top of the stack. Item A placed on the stack before another item B cannot be accessed or removed until after item B is removed. Typical stack operations include:

```
push():  places a new item onto the top of the stack
pop():   removes the top item of a stack
full():  indicates whether or not a stack is full
empty(): indicates whether or not a stack is empty
top():   returns the value of the top item without removing it
```

Given an initially empty stack, the following sequence of operations

```
push(10)   push(3)   pop()   push(7)   push(2)   pop()
```

is pictured in figure 12.1.

A generic stack ADT is easily implemented in C++:

```
const int maxstack = 100;

template <class T> class Stack {
    T list[maxstack];
    int top;
public:
    Stack() { top = -1; }  // Create empty stack
    void push(const T &x)  { list[++top] = x; }
    T pop()  { return list[top--]; }
    int full()  { return top >= maxstack - 1; }
    int empty() { return top < 0; }
    T top() { return list[top]; }
};
```

Recall that the bodies of member functions, when included in the body of the class definition as above, are `inline` member functions. They offer the same advantages as the normal `inline` functions mentioned above. In general, member functions that are three lines or fewer and involve no loops or recursion are often written as `inline` member functions. The bodies of `inline` member functions can appear outside of the definitions if the `inline` reserved word is used:

```
inline void Stack::pop() {
    return list[top--];
}
```

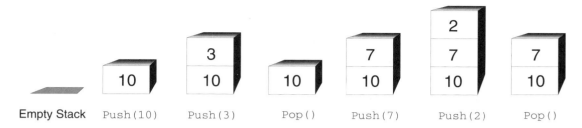

Stack Manipulations
Figure 12.1

This approach is better for hiding more implementation details from the client. A better implementation might check for stack *overflow* and *underflow*, as in program 12.2a, which is a stack template:

```
///////////////////////////////////////////////////////////////
//   File STACK.TPL
///////////////////////////////////////////////////////////////

#ifndef _STACK_TPL_   //  Prevent multiple inclusion
#define _STACK_TPL_

const int MAXSTACK  = 100;

template <class T> class Stack {
    T list[MAXSTACK];
    int top;
public:
    Stack() { top = -1; }
    void reset() { top = -1; }
    int push(const T &);
    int pop(T &);
    int topofstack(T &);
};

template <class T> int Stack<T>::push(const T &s) {
    if ( top < MAXSTACK -1 )
        list[++top] = s;
    else
        return 0;
    return 1;
}
template <class T> int Stack<T>::pop(T &s) {
    if ( top >= 0 )
        s = list[top--];
    else
        return 0;
    return 1;
}
template <class T> int Stack<T>::topofstack(T &s) {
    if ( top >= 0 )
        s = list[top];
    else
        return 0;
    return 1;
}

#endif
```

Program 12.2a

In this template version, push and pop return an integer that indicates success or failure.

Program 12.1 makes use of a `Stack` ADT. In this program, adapted from Smith [Smith 1987], an input string representing an arithmetic expression in *infix* form is translated into its equivalent *postfix* form. An infix expression is an arithmetic expression in normal, algebraic form, including parentheses, if necessary. A typical infix string is:

```
(4 + 12 * 3)/(33 + 56)
```

In an infix string, the operator is placed between its two operands. A postfix string is an alternate way of expressing an arithmetic expression. Many of the Hewlett-Packard scientific calculators use infix notation, also called Reverse Polish Notation (RPN). (The name is due to the fact that a Polish mathematician devised it.) The advantage of RPN is that parentheses are not necessary for correctly evaluating an expression. In a postfix expression, the operator comes after its two operands.

This translation program uses a table to determine what action to perform. The following actions are possible:

- A character in the input (infix) string could be copied directly into the output (postfix) string (an operand).
- A character from the input string could be pushed onto the stack for future use (an operator).
- A character from the input string could be discarded altogether (a right parenthesis).
- A character could be popped off the stack and copied into the output string (an operator).
- A character could be popped off the stack and discarded (a left parenthesis).

The action table is shown in table 12.1.

Table 12.1   Stack-based Action Table

		Input	String	Symbol			
		endofstr	operand	add_sub	mult_div	left_par	right_par
Top	endofstr	done	copy	push	push	push	error
of	operand	error	error	error	error	error	error
Stack	add_sub	pop	copy	pop	push	push	pop
Symbol	mult_div	pop	copy	pop	pop	push	pop
	left_par	error	copy	push	push	push	dump
	right_par	error	error	error	error	error	error

The program is distributed over five files: `gettoken.h`, `stack.tpl`, `str.h`, `str.cpp`, and `i_to_p.cpp`. The template file (`stack.tpl`) and the string header and implementation files (`str.h` and `str.cpp`) have been seen in chapter 11.

The function `gettoken()` is used not only in this program, but also in several programs that follow:

```
////////////////////////////////////////////////////////////////////////////
//   File gettoken.h
////////////////////////////////////////////////////////////////////////////
#ifndef _GET_TOKEN_H   // Avoid multiple inclusion
#define _GET_TOKEN_H

inline int isoperator(int c) {
    return  c == '+'  ||  c == '-'  ||  c == '*'  ||  c == '/';
}
```

```
inline int isparenthesis(int c) {
    return c == '('  ||  c == ')';
}

int gettoken(const char **instring, char *token) {
    while ( isspace(**instring) )
        *(*instring)++;  //  Skip over leading whitespace
    if ( **instring == '\0' ) {
        *token = '\0';
        return 1;  //  End of string
    }
    if ( isdigit(**instring) ) {
        while ( isdigit(**instring) )
            *token++ = *(*instring)++;
        *token = '\0';  //  Properly terminate token
        return 0;
    }
    if ( isoperator(**instring)  || isparenthesis(**instring) ) {
        *token++ = *(*instring)++;
        *token   = '\0';
        return 0;
    }
    return -1;  //  Error condition
}
#endif
```

Program 12.2b

Notice that `isoperator()` and `isparenthesis()` are `inline` functions so that the relatively high overhead associated with such small functions can be avoided. To review pointer notation, the parameter declaration `char **instring` means that `instring` is a pointer to a pointer to a `char` or, in essence, a pointer to a C string. The effect is that the pointer is called by reference allowing it to be changed by the function. Since `gettoken()` scans through the string by moving a pointer along each character stopping at a delimiter (space, operator, parenthesis, or number), the pointer's latest position within the string must be remembered between function invocations. Since an integer result is also returned to indicate a possible error condition (which is ignored here), the call-by-reference protocol is necessary. The double indirection can be confusing at first: `**instring` refers to a particular character, `*instring` refers to the whole string, and `instring` is the address of the string (a pointer to the string). Consider the different applications of the ++ operator:

```
instring++;        // instring now points to another string (could be an
                       array of strings)
*(*instring)++     // instring now points to the next position within the
                       current string
(**instring)++     // the first char in the string is incremented
```

`gettoken()` is limited to strings of arithmetic expressions of positive integers. The operators +, - , *, and / can be used, as well as parentheses. White space is required to separate two operands, but it is not needed to separate operators from operands or other operators.

```
//////////////////////////////////////////////////////////////////////
//  File i_to_p.cpp
//////////////////////////////////////////////////////////////////////

/*
 *      Program: Infix to Postfix
 *          Programmer:  Richard L. Halterman
 *          Adapted from Smith, Data Structures: Form and Function
 *          Date Completed: May 1994
 */
```

```
#include <iostream.h>
#include <ctype.h>
#include "string.h"
#include "stack.tpl"
#include "gettoken.h"

//  Tokens that comprise input string
enum Token { endofstring, operand, add_sub,
             mult_div, leftparen, rightparen };

//  Stack actions
enum Action { copy, push, pop, dump, done, error };

//  Precedence table to determine action to perform
const Action precedence[6][6] =
        { { done,   copy,  push,  push,  push,  error },
          { error,        error, error, error, error,   error },
          { pop,  copy,  pop,   push,  push,  pop  },
          { pop,  copy,  pop,   pop,   push,  pop  },
          { error,      copy,  push,  push,  push, dump },
          { error,        error, error, error, error,   error } };

//  Tokenize() classifies a String and returns its associated token
Token tokenize(const char *s) {
    switch ( s[0] ) {
        case '\0':  return endofstring;
        case '+' :
        case '-' :  return add_sub;
        case '*' :
        case '/' :  return mult_div;
        case '(' :  return leftparen;
        case ')' :  return rightparen;
        default  :  return operand;
    }
}

/*  In_to_post() translates an infix string expression into its
    equivalent postfix form   */

Stack<String> stk;   //  Extern since big

void in_to_post(const String &infix, String &postfix) {
    int finished = 0, did_pop = 0;
    String top_item;
    char current_token[20];  //  Current piece to add to postfix string
    const char *cursor = infix;  //  Used to move through infix string
    Token cndx, rndx;
    stk.reset();
    stk.push("");
    postfix = "";
    while ( !finished ) {
        if ( !did_pop ) {
            gettoken(&cursor, current_token);
            cndx = tokenize(current_token);
        }
        did_pop = 0;
        stk.topofstack(top_item);
        rndx = tokenize(top_item);
        switch ( precedence[rndx][cndx] ) {
        case copy:  //  Copy character from input string to output string
            postfix = postfix + String(current_token);
            postfix = postfix + String(" ");
            break;
        case push:  //  Push input character onto stack
            stk.push(current_token);
            break;
```

```
                    case pop:  //  Pop off top stack item and copy to output string
                        stk.pop(top_item);
                        postfix = postfix + top_item;
                        postfix = postfix + String(" ");
                        did_pop = 1;
                        break;

                    case dump:  //  Pop off and lose top stack item (don't output left
                                //  parenthesis)
                        stk.pop(top_item);
                        break;

                    case done:
                        finished = 1;
                        break;
                    default:
                        cout << "Erroneous situation!\n";
                        finished = 1;
                        break;
                }
            }
    }
}
void main() {
        char buffer[80];
        String line_in, line_out;
        do {
            cout << "Enter infix line: ";
            cin.getline(buffer, 80);
            if ( buffer[0] != '\0' ) {
                line_in = buffer;
                in_to_post(line_in, line_out);
                cout << '\n' << line_in << " ==> " << line_out << '\n';
            }
        } while ( buffer[0] != '\0' );
}
```

Program 12.2c

Table 12.2 shows a trace of the program when the string

```
(4 + 12 * 3)/(33 + 56)
```

is translated.

Program 12.2 is an example of using a stack for program translation. Compilers and interpreters use stacks in various forms to assist their translations from higher-level languages to machine code. The resulting postfix expression can be evaluated with a stack also. A stack is a convenient postfix expression evaluator. Calculators with RPN entry use an internal stack to perform their calculations. Program 12.3 reads in a postfix expression one token at a time. Operands are pushed onto the stack; operators cause the top two values to be popped off the stack. Those arguments are then combined with the operator to yield a result which is pushed back onto the stack for further calculations, if necessary. Consider the expression

```
23 12 + 7 / 10 4 + +
```

Table 12.2   Sample Run of Infix-to-postfix Program

Infix String	Stack			Action	Postfix String									
(4 + 12*3)/(33 + 5)				push										
4 + 12*3)/(33 + 5)	(			copy	4									
+ 12*3)/(33 + 5)	(			push	4									
12*3)/(33 + 5)	(	+		copy	4	12								
*3)/(33 + 5)	(	+		push	4	12								
3)/(33 + 5)	(	+	*	copy	4	12	3							
)/(33 + 5)	(	+	*	pop	4	12	3	*						
)/(33 + 5)	(	+		pop	4	12	3	*	+					
)/(33 + 5)	(			dump	4	12	3	*	+					
/(33 + 5)				push	4	12	3	*	+					
(33 + 5)	/			push	4	12	3	*	+					
33 + 5)	/	(		copy	4	12	3	*	+	33				
+ 5)	/	(		push	4	12	3	*	+	33				
5)	/	(	+	copy	4	12	3	*	+	33	5			
)	/	(	+	pop	4	12	3	*	+	33	5	+		
)	/	(		dump	4	12	3	*	+	33	5	+		
	/			pop	4	12	3	*	+	33	5	+	/	
				done	4	12	3	*	+	33	5	+	/	

Reading the expression would cause the following sequence of events:

See 23:	Push 23 onto the stack
See 12:	Push 12 onto the stack
See +:	Pop 12 and 23 off the stack; push 23 + 12 (that is 35) onto the stack
See 7:	Push 7 onto the stack
See /:	Pop 7 and 35 off the stack; push 35/7 (that is 5) onto the stack
See 10:	Push 10 onto the stack
See 4:	Push 4 onto the stack
See +:	Pop 4 and 10 off the stack; push 10 + 4 (that is 14) onto the stack
See +:	Pop 14 and 5 off the stack; push 5 + 14 (that is 19) onto the stack
End of string:	Value is found on the top of the stack

```
#include <iostream.h>
#include <ctype.h>
#include "str.h"
#include <stdlib.h>
#include "stack.tpl"
#include "gettoken.h"

Stack<String> stk;  //  Extern since 8K in size

int eval(String exp) {
    String strarg1, strarg2;
    char token[10], strresult[10];
    const char *cursor = exp;
    int  arg1, arg2;
    stk.reset();

    while ( !gettoken(&cursor, token) ) {
        if ( !isoperator(*token) )
            stk.push(token);
```

```
        else {
            stk.pop(strarg1);      stk.pop(strarg2);
            arg1 = atoi(strarg1);  arg2 = atoi(strarg2);
            switch ( token[0] ) {
                case '+': itoa(arg2 + arg1, strresult, 10);
                          stk.push(strresult);    break;
                case '-': itoa(arg2 - arg1, strresult, 10);
                          stk.push(strresult);    break;
                case '*': itoa(arg2 * arg1, strresult, 10);
                          stk.push(strresult);    break;
                case '/': itoa(arg2 / arg1, strresult, 10);
                          stk.push(strresult);    break;
            }
        }
    }
    stk.topofstack(String(strresult));
    return atoi(strresult);
}


void main() {
    char line_in[80];
    do {
        cout << "Enter postfix expression: ";
        cin.getline(line_in, 80);
        if ( line_in[0] != '\0' ) {
            cout << line_in << " evaluates to " << eval(line_in) << '\n';
        }
    } while ( line_in[0] != '\0' );
}
```

Program 12.3

The library function `atoi()` (protyped in `<stdlib.h>`) converts the string representation of integer values into their internal `int` form for the purpose of calculations.

After the discussion of class operators, it might seem odd that `Stack::push()` was not implemented as:

```
template <class T> int Stack<T>::operator+=(const T &s) {
    if ( top < MAXSTACK - 1 )
        list[++top] = s;
    else
        return 0;
    return 1;
}
```

or, if a separate `Stack::push()` function was to be maintained also:

```
template <class T> int Stack<T>::operator+=(const T &s) {
    return push(s);
}
```

To push a five on an integer stack named `stk` would be

```
stk += 5;
```

The code is cute, and the meaning is intuitive. (The stack is being increased by the value five; therefore, it must be pushing five onto the stack.) But how would this operator fit in with a `Stack::operator-=()`? With an `operator+=()` it would seem natural to provide (or expect) the complementary `operator-=()`. What would the following statement do?

```
stk -= x;
```

The matching meaning, using the reasoning above, pops the top item into the variable x. The fact that `operator-=()` modifies its right operand is troubling. That is not the way it works for the built-in types, and it seems awkward. Would `Stack::operator++()` (the unary operator which is normally related to `operator+=()`) mean duplicate the item on the top of the stack and push it back on? If so, its meaning would not be obvious. In computer science, the operations push and pop are the standard terms used; indeed, most processors have assembly language op-codes called `PUSH` and `POP` to interact with the machine stack. It seems unnatural here to use class operators. Of course, `Stack::operator+=()` could be the only operator provided, but the reason for its inclusion is questionable. Operator overloading is meant to make the programming more natural, as with the `String` class above. To force the use of class operators—so using them is less natural than not—is defeating their purpose.

Exercises

1. What is a *stack*?

2. What operations are possible on a stack ADT?

3. Explain how it is possible to construct two fundamentally different implementations of the stack ADT, an array version and a linked list version, in which a client module can use either without any modification to the client source code (only recompilation).

4. List three applications of stacks.

5. What operators would be reasonably overloaded for stacks? Justify your selection.

12.3   THE QUEUE ADT

The *queue* ADT is a linear data structure that allows restricted access to both ends. Items to be placed in the queue must be added to one end and removed from the other. In contrast to the stack which is a last-in, first-out (LIFO) structure, the queue is a "first-in, first-out" (FIFO) or "first-come, first-served" data structure. Anyone that has had to wait in a line for anything understands the complexities of a queue. The end of the queue into which new items are placed is called the *rear*, and the other end, from which items are served, is called the *front*.

Typical queue operations include:

`enqueue():`   inserts a new item into the rear of the queue
`dequeue():`   removes the item at the front of the queue
`empty():`   indicates whether or not the queue is empty
`full():`   indicates whether or not the queue is full
`front():`   returns the item at the front of the queue without removing it

Figure 12.2 illustrates interaction with a queue. The value 5 is placed on the queue followed by 2 and 4. 5 is served from the front, and 12 is placed on the rear. Finally, each of the remaining queue elements are served in turn.

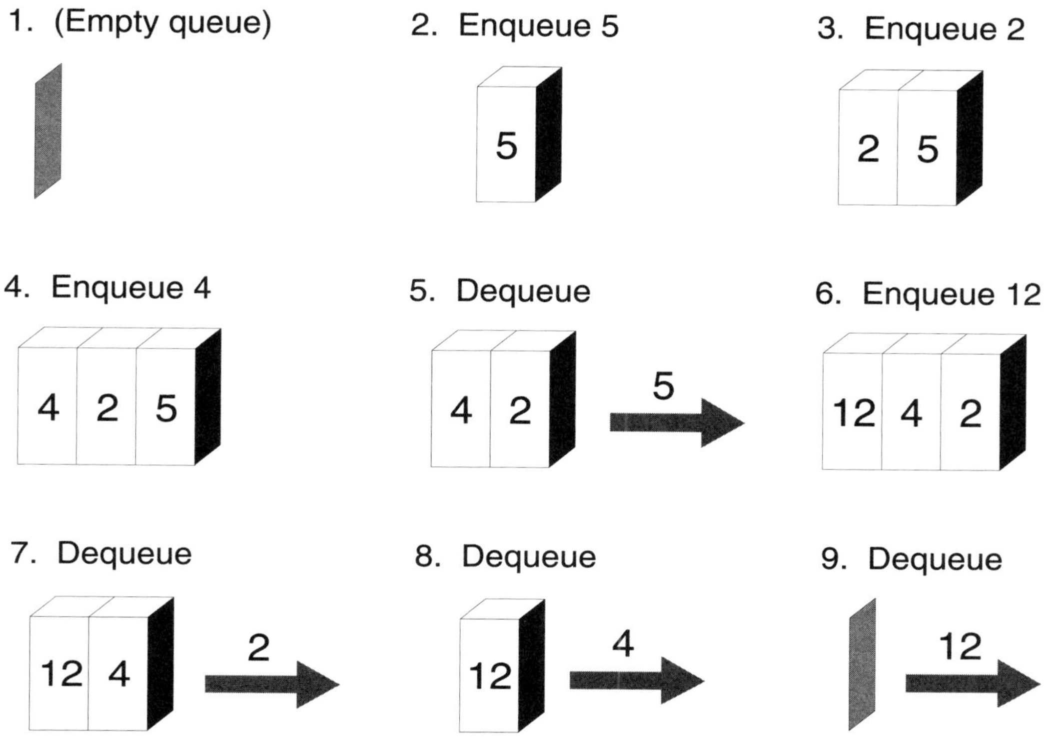

1. (Empty queue)

2. Enqueue 5

3. Enqueue 2

4. Enqueue 4

5. Dequeue

6. Enqueue 12

7. Dequeue

8. Dequeue

9. Dequeue

Queue Operations
Figure 12.2

Queues are most naturally implemented as linked lists. Program 12.4 illustrates:

```
///////////////////////////////////////////////////////////////////////////////
//  Contents of the file QUEUE.TPL
///////////////////////////////////////////////////////////////////////////////
    #ifndef _QUEUE_TPL_
    #define _QUEUE_TPL_

    template <class T> struct ListNode {
        T          data;
        ListNode<T> *next;
    };

    template <class T> class Queue {
        ListNode<T> *front, *rear;
        int full;
        ListNode<T> *newnode(const T &) const;
    public:
        Queue() { front = rear = NULL;  full = 0; }
        int enqueue(const T &);
        int dequeue(T &);
        void clear();
        int empty() const { return front == NULL; }
        T atfront() const { return front->data; }
    };

    template <class T> ListNode<T> *Queue<T>::newnode(const T &x) const {
        ListNode<T> *p = new ListNode<T>;
        if ( p != NULL ) {
```

```
                    p->data = x;
                    p->next = NULL;
            }
            return p;
    }

    template <class T> int Queue<T>::enqueue(const T &e) {
            ListNode<T> *p = newnode(e);
            if ( p == NULL ) {
                    full = 1;   //  No more room in queue
            return 1;
            }
            if ( empty() )
                    front = rear = p;
            else {
                rear->next = p;
                rear = p;
            }
            return 0;   // No error
    }

    template <class T> int Queue<T>::dequeue(T &e) {
            if ( !empty() ) {
                    e = front->data;
                    ListNode<T> *temp = front;
                    front = front->next;
                    delete temp;
                    return 0;   //  No error
            }
            return 1;
    }

    template <class T> void Queue<T>::clear() {
            ListNode<T> *cursor = front, *temp;
            while ( cursor ) {      //  Free up nodes in queue list
                    temp = cursor;
                    cursor = cursor->next;
                    delete temp;
            }
            full = 0;
            front = rear = NULL;
    }

    #endif
```

Program 12.4a

```
/////////////////////////////////////////////////////////////////////////
//   q-main.cpp
/////////////////////////////////////////////////////////////////////////
    #include <iostream.h>
    #include <ctype.h>
    #include "queue.tpl"

    void main() {
            Queue<int>    waiting_line;
            int done = 0, value;
            char ch;
            do {
                    cout << "Enter command: ";
                    cin  >> ch;
                    switch ( toupper(ch) ) {
                            case 'E':
                                    cin >> value;
                                    if ( !waiting_line.enqueue(value) )
```

```
                                cout << value << " enqueued\n";
                            break;
                    case 'D':
                            if ( !waiting_line.dequeue(value) )
                                cout << value << " served\n";
                            break;
                    case 'Q':
                            done = 1;
                            break;
                    default:
                            //   Clear input stream of bad command
                            cin.clear();
                            while ( cin.get() != '\n' )
                                ;
                            cin.clear();
                }
        } while ( !done );
}
```

Program 12.4b

Figure 12.3 shows a sample queue built from the linked list implementation from chapter 10. Items are placed on the `rear` of the queue and served from the `front`.

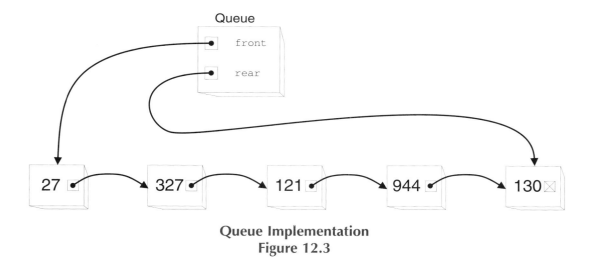

Queue Implementation
Figure 12.3

Queues can also be implemented as arrays. The scheme, however, is more complicated than for a stack that inserts and deletes from the same end of the structure. For a queue, two array indices must be maintained: the `front` and `rear` indices. The indices move in the same direction—`front` moves to the right upon an `enqueue()` operation and `rear` moves to the right upon a `dequeue()` operation; thus, the whole body of the queue drifts to the right as interaction with the queue proceeds. If the queue is implemented as a linear array in the normal sense, it will become useless after a period of time because space used at the beginning of the array will no longer be used as the body of the queue shifts to the right. Consult figure 12.4. The value 5 is placed in the queue. Since it is the only element in the queue, it is both the first (front) and last (rear) item. The `rear` index would be incremented when 6 is added and again when 2 is enqueued. Serving 5 increments `front` so that the next item to be served would be 6. Notice as items are placed into and removed from the queue that the queue drifts to the right. Eventually, there is no more room to enqueue new items even though this array of size six has never had more than three items in it at any one time.

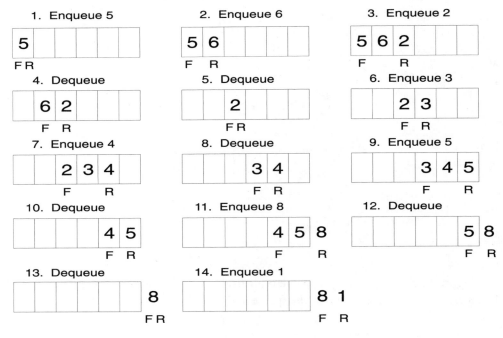

Linear Array Queue "Drift"
Figure 12.4

The solution to the problem is to reuse space at the beginning of the array by causing the array to "wrap around" into itself. This *circular array* of size N could hold no more than N items at one time. When `front` (or `rear`) is located at position N – 1, `front` (or `rear`) would become 0 as an item is enqueued (or dequeued). Figure 12.5 shows such a circular queue

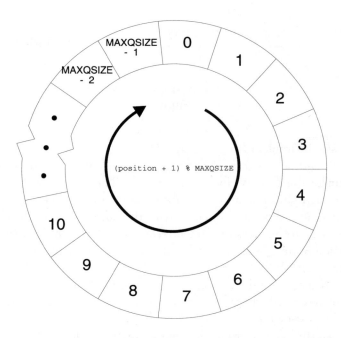

Circular Array Queue
Figure 12.5

Program 12.5 implements the circular array version of a queue.

```
//////////////////////////////////////////////////////////////////////
//   Contents of file ARQUEUE.H
//////////////////////////////////////////////////////////////////////
      #ifndef _ARQUEUE_TPL_
      #define _ARQUEUE_TPL_

      const int MAXQSIZE = 100;

      template <class T> class Queue {
          T data[MAXQSIZE];
          int front, rear;
          int count;
      public:
          Queue() { front = count = 0;   rear = MAXQSIZE - 1; }
          int enqueue(const T&);
          int dequeue(T &);
          int empty() {   return count == 0; }
          void clear();
          };

      template <class T> int Queue<T>::enqueue(const T &e) {
          if ( count == MAXQSIZE )
               return 1;   //   Full queue
          rear = (rear + 1) % MAXQSIZE;
          data[rear] = e;
          count++;
          return 0;   // No error
      }

      template <class T> int Queue<T>::dequeue(T &e) {
          if ( !empty() ) {
               e = data[front];
               front = (front + 1) % MAXQSIZE;
               count--;
               return 0;   // No error
          }
          return 1;   // Error
      }

      #endif
```

(Contents of the main file to test the queue remain the same as before, except #include "queue.h" is changed to #include "arqueue.h")

Program 12.5

The modular arithmetic front = (front + 1) % MAXQSIZE allows the front index to wrap around back to the beginning of the array when it reaches the end. The exciting thing to note is that the main() function remains untouched from before. *Either* queue implementation could be used and the implementation details (linked list or array) are transparent to the client function— in this case main(). As we have seen before, this implementation transparency is the key to ADTs. Client code only needs to know the proper interface to the ADT (legal operations, etc.). The client code does not need to know how the ADT is constructed. The stack module above could easily be redone with a linked list instead of an array. As long as the interface remained the same (the same member functions with the same parameters and return values), the in_to_post() function in program 12.2 could remain exactly the same if stack.h and stack.cpp were rewritten with a linked list as the primary data structure.

The beauty of ADTs is that a programmer can work on part of a large program using a stack or a queue module written by another programmer without being concerned about how the internals of the stack or queue ADTs work. If the developer of the stack ADT finds a bug and corrects it or optimizes some part of his or her code to make the stack more efficient, no other programmers need to change any of their code already written that makes use of the stack. (It may need to be recompiled in some situations, but the source code is untouched.)

Queues are useful in scheduling programs and simulations. Multitasking operating systems contain queues that hold tasks that await execution. Print jobs over a network are held in a queue until the printer becomes available. Any program that simulates events over time would likely use a queue to hold the events until they are scheduled to occur. Consider a program that is to simulate traffic at an intersection. The intersection is shown in figure 12.6.

Vehicles approach the intersection from four possible directions: north, south, east, and west. The light will be green for two of the oncoming lanes and red for the other two oncoming lanes. Cars may pass through the interesection one at a time if the light is green and they are making a right-hand turn or going straight. A left-hand turn requires that the oncoming lane is free from traffic as no left-hand turn arrow is provided at this intersection. One car can pass through the intersection in one second. Cars wait in a queue until it is their turn to go through. Four queues, one for each direction, must be used to simulate the traffic flow. Each queue can only be served if the conditions for safe intersection entry are met (e.g., green light, no oncoming traffic if turning left, etc.).

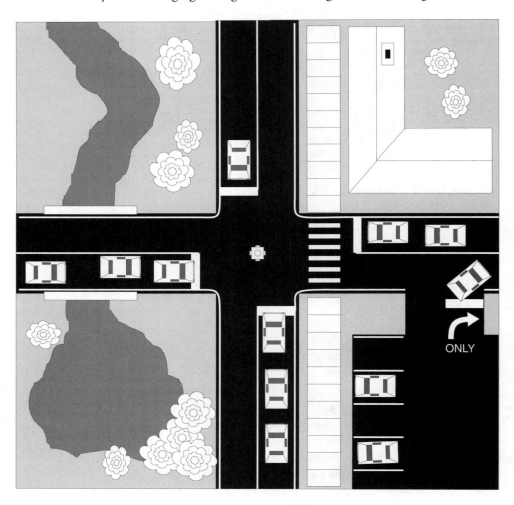

Intersection Queues
Figure 12.6

Time is the ultimate manager of the situation. (The traffic light cycles every so many seconds, automobiles enter the intersection at certain times, etc.). The data for the simulation is stored in a file with the following format:

```
TIME LANE DIRECTION
```

Where `TIME` is the time of the vehicle's arrival at the intersection (starting time for simulation is 0 seconds), `LANE` is the particular lane queue that the vehicle is to enter (north, south, east, or west), and `DIRECTION` is the vehicle's direction to travel through the intersection (left, straight, or right).

Exercises

1. What is a *queue*?

2. What operations are possible on a queue?

3. How does modular arithmetic help implement a circular array version of a queue?

4. List three applications of queues.

5. What operators would be reasonably overloaded for queues? Justify your selection.

Assignments

1. Rewrite the `Stack` ADT so that its underlying data structure is a linked list, instead of an array. Its interface (except for private data descriptions) should remain identical so that any client code that currently uses the array `Stack` would not need to be modified to use the linked list `Stack`. (The linked list routines here are simple to write since insertion and deletion are always performed on one end of the list.)

2. Consider a simple math processor that has a single register, a small memory, and six instructions (see figure 12.7):

```
LOD X   X is loaded into the register
STR X   copies the value of the register into X
ADD X   adds X to the register and stores the result in the register
SUB X   subtracts X from the register and stores the result in the register
MUL X   multiplies X by the register value and stores the result in the
        register
DIV X   divides the register by X and stores the result in the register
```

X is a variable that represents a memory location. Write a program that transforms a postfix expression into assembly language code for this math processor. The postfix expression should consist of single-letter alphabetic operands and the operators +, -, *, and /. The assembly code produced is simply the sequence of processor instructions that evaluates the postfix expression (leaving its result in the register). To accomplish the task in a simple, regular fashion, use variables of the form `Tn` as temporary variables that hold intermediate results. For example, the postfix expression

ABC+*DE-/

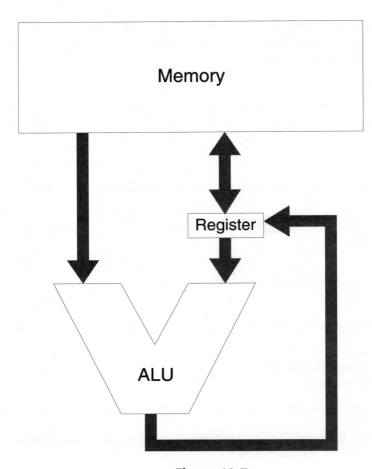

Figure 12.7

should produce the following assembly code:

```
LOD B
ADD C
STR T1
LOD A
MUL T1
STR T2
LOD D
SUB E
STR T3
LOD T2
DIV T3
STR T4
```

Use a stack that holds strings (since the temporary variables Tx are multicharacter) to assist the assembly and clearly indicate the push and pop operations implemented in your code. The procedure to follow is fairly simple:

1. Scan the input postfix string character by character.
2. If a variable (all variables are one character long) is seen, push it onto the stack.
3. If an operator is seen, pop the top two operands off the stack and generate the code

```
LOD [next to top item]
OP  [top item]
STR Tn
```

where OP is either ADD, SUB, MULT, or DIV, depending on the operator scanned. Tn is either T1, T2, etc. depending upon how many temporary variables are needed.

4. Push the string Tn onto the stack and continue at step 1 until the end of the input string is encountered.

If you wish, you may optimize the preassembler so that it generates fewer lines of assembly code (be sure that the optimized code will result in the same overall effect). (This assignment is adapted from Tenenbaum and Augenstein.)

3. Consider traffic flow at the intersection of two roads controlled by a traffic signal, as diagrammed in figure 12.6. Assume the following:

- A car may encounter a red or green light (to simplify, omit the yellow light)
- If a car encounters a red light, it stops for the light
- If several cars have stopped for the light, they wait in a queue; when the light changes to green, cars waiting in the queue may continue, traffic conditions permitting, passing through the intersection at a rate of one car each second
- If a car encounters a green light, there are two possibilities:
  —if there are cars ahead that are still in the queue from a previous red light, the car stops in the queue
  —if there are no cars ahead, the car proceeds through the intersection
- A car may pass through the intersection by:
  —going straight ahead
  —turning right
  —turning left
  —comments: A right turn is the same as going straight ahead. The turning car need not yield to oncoming traffic and all roads post the sign "NO TURNS ON RED." A left turn requires that either there is no oncoming traffic or that the immediate oncoming car is also making a left turn. Obviously, a car making a left turn may need to wait a while and tie up traffic behind it—that's life!

The intersection is initially empty (4:00 AM? Actually TIME = 0). The east-west light has just turned green. Read in a block of data from the file TRAFFIC.DAT. The format is TIME LOCATION DIRECTION (all integer values, North = 0, East = 1, South = 2, West = 3, Left = 0, Straight = 1, Right = 2), which indicates when a vehicle has arrived at a particular road and in which direction it wishes to go when it gets its chance. (It may be at the back of a long line.) The light cycles every 20 seconds (10 seconds red, 10 seconds green). If the light is green and the car has the right-of-way, it takes only 1 second to traverse the intersection. Have a variable called TIME that is initialized to 0 and continuously incremented to simulate the passage of time. When TIME equals the time field of the current record being read in, place that vehicle in the appropriate queue. (If the queue is empty and the light is green, discard the record since it can immediately pass through the intersection.) All of the records on the file will be in chronological order, but be aware that different locations may have identical times (a car can arrive at the west and south intersections simultaneously). When finished, print out the average waiting times for the cars going in each direction.

CHAPTER 13

TREES AND GRAPHS

13.1 HIERARCHICAL STRUCTURES—TREES

Whereas the C++ `struct` is another example of a data structure in and of itself, `struct`s are most valuable when used as building blocks for other data structures. As we've seen with linked lists, stacks, and queues, `struct`s and pointers can be used to link together linear structures. These linear structures can be encapsulated within generic ADTs so that programmers can use them as needed. Linear structures will now be extended to allow nodes to have multiple successors. These *hierarchical structures* address some of the shortcomings of linked lists.

A hierarchical structure has the following characteristics:

1. There is a unique element called *root*.
2. Every element except root has a unique predecessor.
3. Every element has zero or more successors.

Another name for a hierarchical structure is a *tree*. The structure charts in chapter 6 provide good pictures of trees. When dealing with trees, immediate predecessors are usually called *parents*, and immediate successors are usually called *children*. Each element of a tree is called a *vertex* or *node*. Nodes that have the same parent are called *siblings*. Nodes are connected through *edges* or *arcs*. When drawing a tree, the root is normally placed at the top. If m is a node and n is another node, and n can be reached from m by following an alternating sequence of successive nodes and their connecting edges, a *path* is said to exist between nodes m and n. The *length* of a path is the number of edges contained in the path. Since each node has a unique parent, no paths are possible between two siblings in a tree. Also, no path is possible that begins at a node and leads back to that same node. (Such a path is called a *cycle*; trees are *acyclic*.) Nodes that have no children are called *leaves* of the tree. The *height* of a tree is the length of the longest path from the root to a leaf, plus one; thus, a tree with one node (itself both the root and the only leaf) has height one. An empty tree has height zero. Any node in a tree is found on a particular *level*. A node's level is the length of the path from the root to that node. If any edge in a tree is broken, two new *subtrees* are formed. One of the subtrees will retain the old root, and the root of the other subtree will be the vertex that the severed edge connected. Figure 13.1 will be used to illustrate some properties of trees.

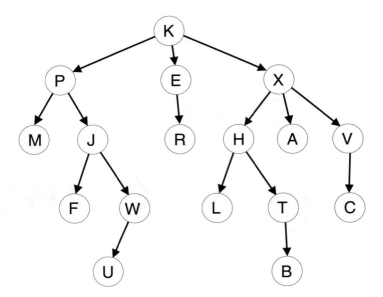

A Typical Tree
Figure 13.1

The tree in figure 13.1 contains 17 nodes. The node containing K is the root node. K has three children: P, E, and X. Node P has two siblings, E and X. Nodes M, F, U, R, L, B, A, and C are all leaves. The sequence of nodes K-X-H represents a path in the tree. The path K-X-H-T-B is a path from the root to a leaf. It is tied for the longest path from the root to a leaf (length 4); therefore, the height of the tree is 5. The nodes F, W, L, T, and C are on level 3.

The trees examined here will follow the standard mathematical and computer science convention that the root appears at the top of the diagram. If arrowheads are not drawn on the arcs, then by default they all point down away from the root.

A *binary* tree is a restricted form of a tree in which every node has zero, one, or two children. The following definitions can be used to implement binary trees in C++:

```
struct TreeNode {
    int data;
    TreeNode *left;    //  Pointer to left child
    TreeNode *right;   //  Pointer to right child
};

typedef TreeNode *TreePtr;  //  A TreePtr is a pointer to a TreeNode
```

(In this section, no class or template features will be used. The data type within the tree node will be an integer. These simplifications will allow us to concentrate on the principles behind the functions that process binary trees without having to wade through the associated template and class "clutter" that can obscure the discussion. A generic, encapsulated binary search tree ADT is presented in the next section.)

A tree node contains two pointers to other tree nodes. These are called `left` and `right` to signify left child and right child. The following code in program 13.1 builds a binary tree "by hand":

```
void main() {
    TreeNode node1, node2, node3, node4, node5;
    TreePtr root = &node1;
    node1.data  = 10;
    node2.data  = 15;
    node3.data  =  3;
```

```
        node4.data  = 12;
        node5.data  = 15;
        node1.left  = &node2;
        node1.right = &node3;
        node2.right = &node4;
        node3.left  = &node5;
        node2.left  = node3.right = node4.left  = node4.right
                    = node5.left  = node5.right = NULL;
        printtree(root);   //  A routine described below
}
```

Program 13.1

The tree constructed by the above code is diagrammed in figure 13.2.

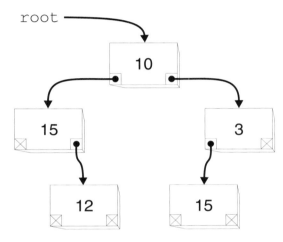

The "Hand-built" Binary Tree
Figure 13.2

As with linked lists, trees are rarely constructed this way. To see a more typical construction, we will examine a special binary tree called a *binary search tree* (BST). A BST is a binary tree in which, for any given node, the node's left child is less than the node, and the node's right child is greater than the node. A BST provides a means to do a binary search on a linked structure. (Recall that a binary search is impossible with a linear linked list.)

Assume a BST is to hold strings. The following strings are to be inserted into the BST:

```
"melon" "banana" "apple" "cherry" "orange" "nectarine" "kiwi" "mango" "grape"
"peach"
```

The strings are to be inserted into the tree in the order they appear above. Their ordering within the tree is lexicographic (i.e., they are ordered alphabetically as in a dictionary). The following sequence of additions illustrates the growth of a BST.

Initially, the tree is empty. Root points to NULL.

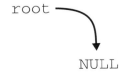

"melon" is the first string added. Root now points to "melon."

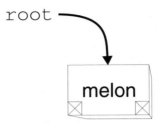

Since "banana" is less than "melon," and "melon" has no left child, "banana" becomes the left child of "melon."

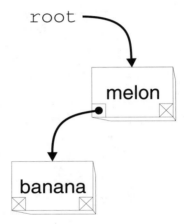

When "apple" is inserted, its proper location within the BST is determined by following pointers from the root, guided by comparing "apple" to each node along the way. "apple" is less than "melon" so the left path from the root is taken. It is also less than "banana," and "banana" has no left child, so "apple" becomes the left child of "banana."

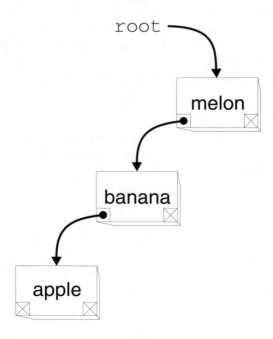

"cherry" is less than "melon" but greater than "banana." Thus, "cherry" becomes the right child of "banana."

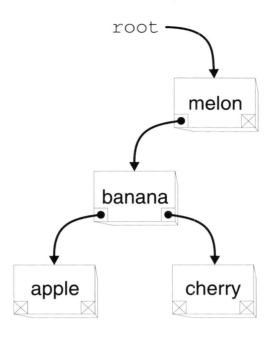

"orange" is greater than "melon," and becomes the right child of "melon."

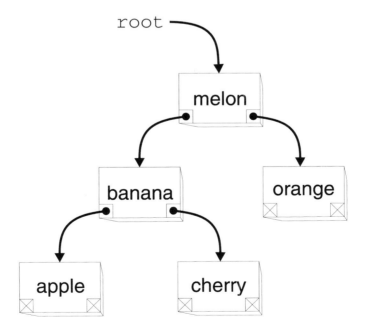

"nectarine" is greater than "melon," and, thus, must be compared to the right child of "melon." It is less than "orange"; therefore, "nectarine" becomes the left child of "orange."

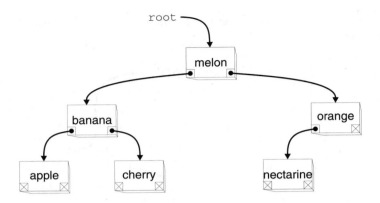

In similar fashion, "kiwi" < "melon," "kiwi" > "banana," and "kiwi" > "cherry."

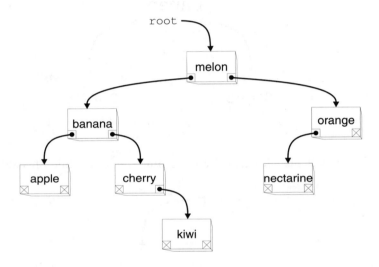

"mango" < "melon," "mango" > "banana," "mango" > "cherry," and "mango" > "kiwi."

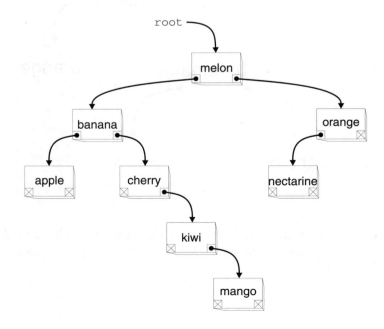

"grape" is added as the left child of "kiwi."

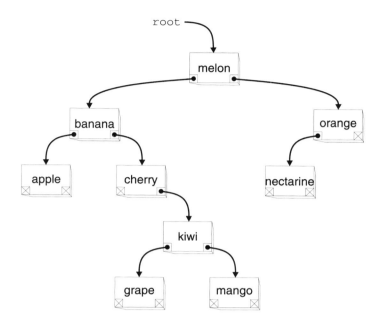

Finally, "peach" is inserted into its proper place.

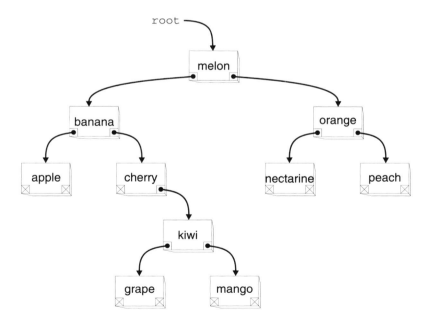

Items can be found in a BST quite rapidly, especially if the tree is close to being *balanced*. Every node in a binary tree has a left and right subtree. The left subtree of a node is the tree that has the node's left child as its root. The right subtree of a node has the node's right child as its root. A binary tree is said to be balanced if, for every node in the tree, the height of the node's left and right subtrees differ by at most one. Balanced trees have each level filled as much as possible. When searching for a particular node in a balanced BST, each decision whether to go left or right cuts the number of nodes remaining to be considered in half; thus, a binary search is conducted as dictated by the tree's structure.

An unbalanced tree will degrade the search efficiency of a BST. Consider the extreme example of inserting the following sequence into an empty BST:

`"apple" "banana" "cherry" "grape" "kiwi" "mango"`

The resulting tree is

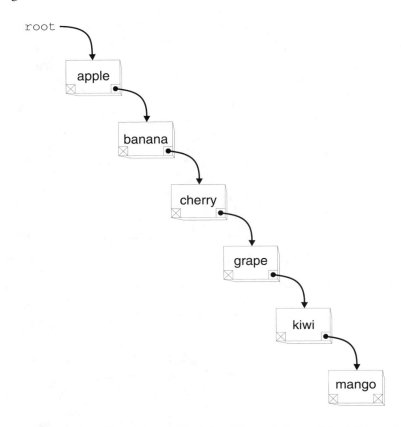

This degenerate tree is actually a linear linked list. No node has a left child, and thus the decision to go right when searching for a node is always made. At each node, the number of remaining nodes to search in the tree is reduced by one, not divided in two.

Algorithms that deal with balanced BST construction (the most famous being the *AVL* trees) are well known but are complicated. We will concentrate on the simpler routines that do no automatic height balancing. These routines will build BSTs that are most often "balanced enough" for our purposes. The discussion of height-balanced trees is left for a more advanced data structures course.

Routines that deal with BSTs are easiest to write with recursion. Returning to the original definition above where each node contains an `int`, the `BSTinsert()` function could be written

```
TreePtr newBSTnode(int x) {
    //  Allocates space for new node and initializes it
    TreePtr temp = new TreeNode;
    if ( !temp ) {
        temp->data = x;
        temp->left = temp->right = NULL;
    }
    return temp;
}
```

```
TreePtr BSTinsert(TreePtr t, int new_item) {  //  Add int to BST
     if ( !t )
          t = newBSTnode(new_item);
     else if ( t->data > new_item )  //  Add to left subtree
          t->left = BSTinsert(t->left, new_item);
     else if ( t->data < new_item )  //  Add to right subtree
          t->right = BSTinsert(t->right, new_item);
     //  Else new_item value already present, so ignore it
     return t;
}
```

Finding a particular node in a BST is equally easy:

```
/*  Returns pointer to node in BST t that contains sought_item; returns NULL
         sought_item is not in t.  */
   TreePtr BSTfind(TreePtr t, int sought_item) {
        if ( !t )
             return NULL;
        else if ( t->data == sought_item )
             return t;
        else if ( t->data > sought_item )
             return BSTfind(t->left, sought_item);
        else    /* t->data < sought_item */
             return BSTfind(t->right, sought_item);
   }
```

Each of the recursive BST routines could be rewritten in a more efficient iterative form. The BSTfind() function could be rewritten as:

```
TreePtr BSTfind(TreePtr t, int sought_item) {
        TreePtr cursor = t;
        while ( cursor )
             if ( cursor->data == sought_item )
                  return cursor;
             else if ( cursor->data > sought_item )
                  cursor = cursor->left;
             else
                  cursor = cursor->right;
        return cursor;
}
```

Deleting a node in a BST is a bit trickier than an insertion. Let the node to be removed be called N. If N is a leaf, then all that needs to be done is to delete N and set to NULL the parent's pointer that is directed to N. If N is not a leaf but has only one subtree attached (either left or right, it doesn't matter), N can merely be bypassed. (The grandchild of N's parent [N's child] becomes the new child of N's parent.) The ordered structure of the BST will remain intact. If N has both a left and right subtree, then merely bypassing N is impossible since the single pointer leading from N's parent to N cannot be split between N's two descendents. One technique that is sometimes used is to find the left most node in the right subtree of N. Let this node be called LMRST (for leftmost in right subtree). Copy the data fields (not the pointer fields) of LMRST into the data fields of N. Then delete and bypass the LMRST node. Two find operations are needed: find N, and find LMRST. A function called delLMRST() will be used to augment the function BSTdelete():

```
void delLMRST(TreePtr delnode) {        //  delnode is node to be removed
   //  delnode must have both left and right subtrees for delLMRST() to work
   //  properly
   TreePtr cursor = delnode->right,  //  cursor points to right subtree
        parent = delnode;              //  parent of cursor
   while ( cursor->left ) {    //  Find left-most node
        parent = cursor;
        cursor = cursor->left;     //  cursor is left-most found so far
   }
```

```
    if ( parent == delnode )    //  delnode's child is left most
        delnode->right = cursor->right;
    else
        parent->left = cursor->right;  //  Bypass left-most node
    delnode->data = cursor->data;    //  Copy left-most's data into delnode
    delete cursor;
}
```

The LMRST node can replace N because it is the node that is greater than N and yet less than every other node in N's right subtree. No other node in the tree is both greater than N and less than LMRST. The tree's BST ordering is preserved. The complete BSTdelete() is left as an exercise for the student.

Exercises

1. What is the definition of a *hierarchical structure*?

   Questions 2–15 refer to the figure on the right.

2. What is the root node in the tree?

3. List all the leaves.

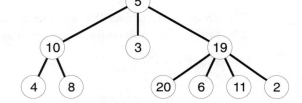

4. What is the height of the tree?

5. List all the children of the node containing 10.

6. List all the siblings of node 11.

7. List all the descendents of node 5.

8. Is the tree a binary tree?

9. Define the term *binary tree*.

10. Define the term *binary search tree*.

11. Draw the BST formed by inserting the following ints in the order given:

    67, 12, 4, 79, 123, 88, 66, 69, 2, 3

12. Explain how a BST allows binary search to be performed on a linked structure.

13. What is the penalty to pay for the ability to perform binary search on a BST (as opposed to an ordered array)?

14.   What is an AVL tree?

15.   Why is a BST's balance critical to its search efficiency?

13.2   BINARY SEARCH TREE CONTAINER CLASS

The following file provides a starting point for a BST container class. A class template is used so that the BST can be seamlessly adapted to store the proper types required by the application. It is an ADT; thus, client code cannot interfere with its internal data structures. Anyone who has access to the source code to this class library (which is presented here) wishing to extend its functionality should not violate its ADT properties.

```cpp
/////////////////////////////////////////////////////////////////////////
//   File bst-adt.tpl
//   Binary Search Tree Template
/////////////////////////////////////////////////////////////////////////

#include <iostream.h>

template <class T> struct BSTNode {
  T data;
  BSTNode<T> *left, *right;
};

template <class T> class BST {
  BSTNode<T> *root;
  BSTNode<T> *new_node(const T &) const;
  void tree_dispose(BSTNode<T> *);
  void inordertrav(BSTNode<T> *) const;
  void preordertrav(BSTNode<T> *) const;
  void BSTDrawHelper(BSTNode<T> *, int, char) const;
  BSTNode<T> *BSTInsert(BSTNode<T> *, const T &);
  BSTNode<T> *BSTInsert_iterative(BSTNode<T> *, const T &);
  BSTNode<T> *BSTFind(BSTNode<T> *, const T &) const;
public:
  BST();
  ~BST();
  void insert(const T &);
  void insert_iterative(const T &);
  void draw() const;
  void print_traversals() const;
  int  find(const T &) const;
};


template <class T>
BST<T>::BST() {
  root = 0;
}

template <class T>
void BST<T>::tree_dispose(BSTNode<T> *p) {
  if ( p != NULL ) {
        tree_dispose(p->left);
        tree_dispose(p->right);
        delete p;
  }
}
```

```
template <class T>
BST<T>::~BST() {
  tree_dispose(root);
}

template <class T>
BSTNode<T> *BST<T>::new_node(const T &new_data) const{
BSTNode<T> *temp = new BSTNode<T>;
  if ( temp != NULL ) {
        temp->data = new_data;
        temp->left = temp->right = NULL;
  }
  else
        cout << '\a';
  return temp;
}


template <class T>
BSTNode<T> *BST<T>::BSTInsert(BSTNode<T> *rt, const T &new_item) {
  if ( rt == NULL )
        rt = new_node(new_item);
  else if ( rt->data > new_item )
        rt->left = BSTInsert(rt->left, new_item);
  else if ( rt->data < new_item )
        rt->right = BSTInsert(rt->right, new_item);
  //  else rt->data == new_item, ignore duplicate entry
  return rt;
}


template <class T>
void BST<T>::insert(const T &new_item) {
  root = BSTInsert(root, new_item);
}

template <class T>
BSTNode<T> *BST<T>::BSTInsert_iterative(BSTNode<T> *rt, const T &new_item) {
  //  Case 1:  Tree is empty
  if ( rt == NULL )
        rt = new_node(new_item);

  //  Case 2:  Tree is not empty
  else {
        BSTNode<T> *cursor = rt, *parent;
        while ( cursor != NULL   &&   cursor->data != new_item ) {
              parent = cursor;
              if ( cursor->data > new_item )
                    cursor = cursor->left;
              else if ( cursor->data < new_item )
                    cursor = cursor->right;
              //  else cursor->data == new_item, ignore duplicate
        }
        if ( cursor == NULL ) {
              if ( parent->data > new_item )
                    parent->left = new_node(new_item);
              else
                    parent->right = new_node(new_item);
        }
  }
  return rt;
}

template <class T>
void BST<T>::insert_iterative(const T &new_item) {
  root = BSTInsert_iterative(root, new_item);
}
```

```
template <class T>
BSTNode<T> *BST<T>::BSTFind(BSTNode<T> *rt, const T &seek) const {
   if ( rt != NULL ) {
         if ( rt->data == seek )
               return rt;
         else if ( rt->data > seek )
               return BSTFind(rt->left, seek);
         else
               return BSTFind(rt->right, seek);
   }
   return rt;
}

template <class T>
int BST<T>::find(const T &seek) const {
   return BSTFind(root, seek) != NULL;
}

template <class T>
void BST<T>::BSTDrawHelper(BSTNode<T> *edge, int depth, char symbol) const {
   if ( edge != NULL ) {
         //  Print right subtree one level down
         BSTDrawHelper(edge->right, depth + 1, '/');

         //  Print the node
         for ( int i = 0;  i < 3*depth;  i++ )
              cout << ' ';
         cout << symbol << edge->data << '\n';

         //  Print left subtree one level down
         BSTDrawHelper(edge->left, depth + 1, '\\');
   }
}

template <class T>
void BST<T>::draw() const {
   BSTDrawHelper(root, 0, '-');
}

template <class T>
void BST<T>::preordertrav(BSTNode<T> *rt) const {
   if ( rt != NULL ) {
         cout << rt->data << ' ';
         preordertrav(rt->left);
         preordertrav(rt->right);
   }
}
template <class T>
void BST<T>::inordertrav(BSTNode<T> *rt) const {
   if ( rt != NULL ) {
         inordertrav(rt->left);
         cout << rt->data << ' ';
         inordertrav(rt->right);
   }
}

template <class T>
void BST<T>::print_traversals() const {
   cout << "Preorder:   ";
   preordertrav(root);
   cout << '\n';
   cout << "Inorder:   ";
   inordertrav(root);
   cout << '\n';
}
```

Program 13.2a

This template class provides both recursive and nonrecursive insert routines to illustrate how each type of member function can be written. The draw function draws the tree sideways, using the symbols '\' and '/' to indicate the branching direction and help orient the viewer.

The following client code can be used to exercise the class:

```
////////////////////////////////////////////////////////////////////////
//  Program to test Binary Search Tree Class
////////////////////////////////////////////////////////////////////////
#include <iostream.h>
#include <stdlib.h>
#include <ctype.h>
#include "bst-adt.tpl"

enum Command { insert, draw, print, find, quit };

void get_command(Command &command, int &newid) {
  char in_string[20];
  int done;
  do {
        done = 1;
        cout << "Please enter command: ";
        cin.getline(in_string, 20);
        if ( toupper(in_string[0]) == 'I' ) {
                newid = atoi(in_string + 1);
                command = insert;
        }
        else if ( toupper(in_string[0]) == 'D' )
                command = draw;
        else if ( toupper(in_string[0]) == 'P' )
                command = print;
        else if ( toupper(in_string[0]) == 'Q' )
                command = quit;
        else if ( toupper(in_string[0]) == 'F' ) {
                newid = atoi(in_string + 1);
                command = find;
        }
        else {
                done = 0;
                cout << '\a';
        }
  } while ( !done );
}


void build_random_tree() {
  BST<int> t;
  int node_number = random(20) + 1,
      new_value;
  cout << "A random tree with " << node_number << " nodes:\n";
  for ( int i = 0;  i < node_number;  i++ ) {
        do {
                new_value = random(100);
        } while ( t.find(new_value) );
        t.insert(new_value);
  }
  t.draw();
}

void main() {
  BST<int> bstree;
  int done = 0, value;
  Command command;
```

```
        do {
                get_command(command, value);
                switch ( command ) {
                        case insert:
                                cout << "Inserting " << value << " into tree.\n";
                                bstree.insert(value);
                                break;
                        case draw:
                                bstree.draw();
                                break;
                        case print:
                                bstree.print_traversals();
                                break;
                        case find:
                                if ( bstree.find(value) )
                                        cout << value << " is in the tree.\n";
                                else
                                        cout << value << " is *NOT* in the tree.\n";
                                break;
                        case quit:
                                done = 1;
                                break;
                }
        } while ( !done );

        /*  Build and display some random trees  */
        randomize();
        do {
                build_random_tree();
        } while ( toupper(cin.get()) != 'Q' );
}
```

Program 13.2b

The first part of the client code allows the user to insert items into the tree and display it. (The meanings of the two traversals will be explained in the next section.) When the user tires of this interaction, the program finishes up by printing randomly generated trees with at most 20 nodes.

13.3 BINARY TREE TRAVERSAL

All binary trees (not just BSTs) can be traversed in three standard ways—*preorder*, *inorder*, and *postorder*. The description of each type of traversal is best described recursively. In a preorder traversal, the root node is "processed" before either its left or right subtrees are traversed. "Processed" can mean simply visited for a search, printed, or being involved in some other computation. An empty tree is traversed by doing nothing. Consider the simple binary tree in figure 13.4 that is to be traversed (each node in the tree is to be printed):

The C++ code for a preorder traversal compactly illustrates the process:

```
        void preorderprint(TreePtr t) {
                if ( t != NULL ) {
                        cout << t->data << ' ';
                        preorderprint(t->left);
                        preorderprint(t->right);
                }
        }
```

The function `preorderprint()` processes the tree above to display:

A B D E C F G

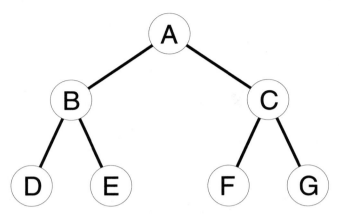

A Simple Binary Tree
Figure 13.4

After the data in the root node is printed, the root's left subtree (which has B as its root) and right subtree (which has C as its root) each must be traversed in a preorder fashion. Conceptually, the situation is:

```
A (Left subtree of A) (Right subtree of A)
```

The next steps must carry out the subtraversals ((Left subtree of A) becomes B (Left subtree of B) (Right subtree of B)):

```
A B (Left subtree of B) (Right subtree of B) C (Left subtree of C) (Right subtree of C)
```

The next step is (LST and RST mean "left subtree of" and "right subtree of", respectively)

```
A B D (LST D) (RST D) E (LST E) (RST E) C F (LST F) (RST F) G (LST G) (RST G)
```

Since all the leaves have no children (left and right subtrees are NULL), the recursion stops:

```
A  B  D  E  C  F  G
```

An inorder traversal traverses the left subtree, then processes the node, then traverses the right subtree:

```
void inorderprint(TreePtr t) {
        if ( t != NULL ) {
            inorderprint(t->left);
            cout << t->data << ' ';
            inorderprint(t->right);
        }
}
```

An inorder print of the tree would reveal

```
D  B  E  A  F  C  G
```

It is important to note that an inorder print of a BST produces an ordered display of its elements; thus, the term "inorder" makes perfectly good sense when dealing with BSTs. (An inorder print on a general binary tree will not necessarily produce an ordered output.)

The postorder traversal processes both the left and right subtrees of a node before processing the node itself. A postorder print would yield

```
D  E  B  F  G  C  A
```

The code for `postorderprint()` is similar to the above two print routines with the recursive calls appropriately rearranged. The concept of postorder traversal is used in calculators that use *Reverse Polish Notation* (RPN) instead of the more widely used *algebraic entry* notation. (Recall the discussion of RPN and stack based evaluation in chapter 12.) Consider the expression tree in figure 13.5:

An inorder traversal of the tree yields

```
2 * 3 + 5
```

which is the sequence of keys that must be pressed (followed by the *equals* key) when evaluating the expression on the typical algebraic entry calculator.

The postorder traversal yields

```
2 3 * 5 +
```

which is the sequence of keys that must be pressed (with the *enter* key pressed between 2 and 3) when evaluating the expression on an RPN calculator like most advanced Hewlett-Packard models.

The postfix form looks strange but it has some advantages over the traditional infix form of representing mathematical expressions. Consider the evaluation of the expression in figure 13.6.

The infix form is

```
(2 + 3) * 5
```

while the postfix form is

```
2 3 + 5 *
```

Parentheses are not needed to override default operator precedences in postfix notation. Omitting the parentheses in the infix form would yield an incorrect result due to multiplication's dominance over addition. Chapter 12 presented a program that converted from infix to postfix form and another that evaluated an expression in postfix form.

Given the traversals of a binary tree, can its structure be deduced and a picture of it be drawn? A binary tree can, in fact, be constructed from its preorder and inorder traversals. Consider the traversals:

```
Preorder:   BQAETCRF

Inorder:    AQTECBRF
```

The first node in the preorder list is used to partition the inorder list into three sections: the nodes in the left subtree, the root node, and the nodes in the right subtree.

```
Preorder:    [ B ]   [ QAETCRF ]

Inorder:     [ AQTEC ]   [ B ]   [ RF ]
```

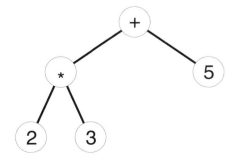

An Arithmetic Expression Tree
Figure 13.5

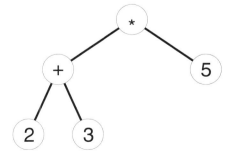

Another Expression Tree
Figure 13.6

The nodes in the left and right subtrees of the inorder arrangement are used to split off the nodes in the preorder group:

```
QAETCRF  -->  [ QAETC ]  [ RF ]
```

Thus, the tree has B for its root, some ordering of the nodes in { Q, A, T, E, C } as its left subtree, and some ordering of the nodes { R, F } for B's right subtree. Each subtree can then be attacked in similar fashion recursively as shown in figure 13.7.

The final picture is formed when all the subtrees consist of single nodes.

In general, two traversals must be used to generate the structure of a tree. Consider the preorder traversal

```
Preorder:   ABCD
```

All of the trees in figure 13.8 would generate the same preorder traversals:

Their inorder traversals would differ, however. All of these trees are formed with just four nodes; consider how many different trees can be formed from preorder traversals of 5, 6, etc. nodes. (The number of possible trees grows enormously.) Can the structure of a tree be deduced given only the pre- and postorder traversals of a binary tree?

If not all nodes are the same, (e.g., the expression trees above have *operator* nodes and *operand* nodes), sometimes the tree's structure can be deduced from only one type of traversal. The following section shows how a tree can be built given only the preorder traversal of an arithmetic expression tree.

The BST drawing function provided in the template class in the previous section performed a backwards inorder traversal to display a sideways picture of the tree. The [right subtree][node][left subtree] recursive sequence, with the depth of each node tied to the depth of the recursion is just the technique needed to draw a binary tree on line-oriented display (text screen, line printer, etc.) that must print output left-to-right, top-to-bottom.

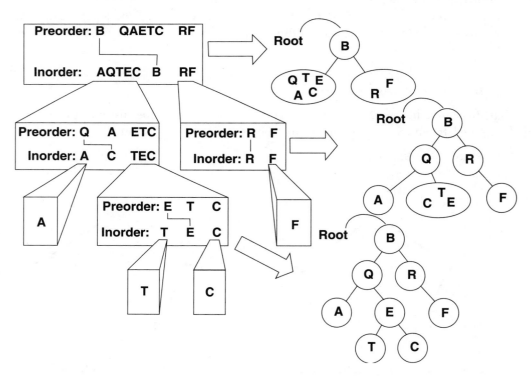

Constructing a Tree from Traversals
Figure 13.7

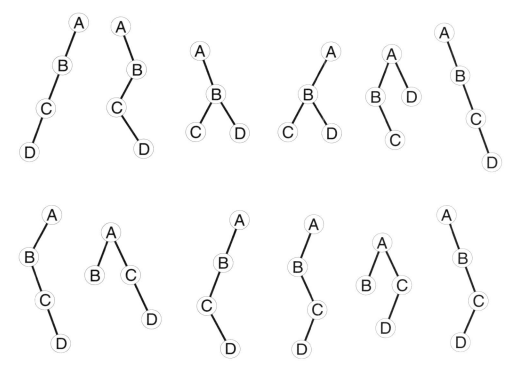

Trees with Identical Preorder Traversals
Figure 13.8

Exercises

1. Provide a preorder traversal of the final "fruit" tree formed in section 13.1.

2. Provide an inorder traversal of the final "fruit" tree formed in section 13.1.

3. Provide a postorder traversal of the final "fruit" tree formed in section 13.1.

4. Can the structure of a tree be deduced from its preorder traversal?

5. Construct an arithmetic expression tree for the following infix expression:

   $((12 + 2)/(2 - 5 * 3)) - (4 *((35 - 2) * 15))$

6. Translate the expression in 5 to prefix form.

7. Construct the binary tree whose traversals are given.

Preorder traversal:	ETCVLRWBP
Inorder traversal:	CTERWLBVP

13.4 BINARY EXPRESSION TREE PROGRAM

Program 13.3 uses a binary tree as an arithmetic expression evaluator. A string is read in and then *parsed*. Parsing a string involves breaking it up into its component parts, classifying each part, and performing various actions depending on the characteristics of each part of the string. In this example, the components of the string are numerical operands and operators. Just as the expression trees examined in the previous section, the tree will have the operands as its leaves, and the internal nodes will consist entirely of operators. The library function `atoi()` converts the string representation of integer values into their internal `int` form for the purpose of calculations. Whitespace is required to separate two operands, but it is not needed to separate operators from operands or other operators. The input string is to be in *postfix* form, like RPN calculators, thereby rendering parentheses unnecessary and simplifying the parsing process. The operands are restricted to integers within C++'s `int` range, and to further simplify the parsing, only positive integers should be entered (unary + and - signs should not be used). The program does not check for illegally formulated postfix expressions. The BST template class is not used here since the expression tree is *not* a BST.

Even though `gettoken()` (introduced in chapter 12) checks for parentheses, expressions for program 13.3 should *not* contain any parentheses since they are in postfix form.

```cpp
#include <iostream.h>
#include <ctype.h>
#include <string.h>
#include <stdlib.h>
#include "gettoken.h"

enum Token { op, arg };

typedef char String[20];        //  A string

struct TreeNode {
    String data;
    TreeNode *left, *right;
};

typedef TreeNode *Link;

void exit_error(char *msg) {
    cout << msg << '\n';
    exit(1);
}

inline Token tokentype(char *tok) {
    if ( isdigit(tok[0]) )
        return arg;
    else
        return op;
}

Link makesubtree(Link t, char **exp) {
    String token;
    t = NULL;
    if ( !gettoken(exp, token) ) {
        if ( (t = new TreeNode) == NULL )
            exit_error("out of memory.");
        strrev(token);  //  "Un-reverse" token
        strcpy(t->data, token);
        if ( tokentype(token) == op ) {
            t->right = makesubtree(t->right, exp);
            t->left  = makesubtree(t->left, exp);
        }
        else //  Operand node has no children
```

```
                t->left = t->right = NULL;
        }
        return t;
}

Link build_exp_tree(Link t, char *exp) {
    Link result;
    char *front = exp;
    strrev(exp);
    result = makesubtree(t, &exp);
    strrev(front);
    return result;
}

void printtree_helper(Link t, char arc, int depth) {
    if ( t ) {
            printtree_helper(t->right, '/', depth + 5);
            for ( int i = 0;  i < depth;  i++ )
                    cout << ' ';
            cout << arc << t->data << '\n';
          printtree_helper(t->left, '\\', depth + 5);
    }
}

inline void printtree(Link t) {
    printtree_helper(t, ' ', 0);
}

int eval_exp_tree(Link t) {
 if ( t ) {
        if ( isoperator(t->data[0]) )
              switch ( t->data[0] ) {
                    case '+':
                            return eval_exp_tree(t->left) + eval_exp_tree(t->right);
                    case '-':
                            return eval_exp_tree(t->left) - eval_exp_tree(t->right);
                    case '*':
                            return eval_exp_tree(t->left) * eval_exp_tree(t->right);
                    case '/':
                            return eval_exp_tree(t->left) / eval_exp_tree(t->right);
              }
        else
              return atoi(t->data);
 }
 return 0;
}


/*
 * Deltree()
 *         Frees up the space occupied by the nodes in tree t
 */

Link deltree(Link t) {
    if ( t ) {
            t->left  = deltree(t->left);
            t->right = deltree(t->right);
            delete t;
    }
    return NULL;
}

void preorderprint(Link t) {
 if ( t ) {
        cout << t->data << ' ';
         preorderprint(t->left);
```

```
            preorderprint(t->right);
        }
    }
void inorderprint(Link t) {
    if ( t ) {
        if ( t->data[0] == '+'  ||  t->data[0] == '-' )
            cout << '(';
        inorderprint(t->left);
        cout << t->data << ' ';
        inorderprint(t->right);
        if ( t->data[0] == '+'  ||  t->data[0] == '-' )
            cout << "\b)";
    }
}
void postorderprint(Link t) {
    if ( t ) {
        postorderprint(t->left);
            postorderprint(t->right);
        cout << t->data << ' ';
    }
}
void printresults(Link t) {
    printtree(t);
    cout << "The preorder expression is:     ";
    preorderprint(t);
    cout << "\nThe inorder expression is:     ";
    inorderprint(t);
    cout << "\nThe postorder expression is: ";
    postorderprint(t);
    cout << "\nThe expression evaluates to " << eval_exp_tree(t) << '\n';
}
void main() {
    Link root = NULL;
    char expression[100];
    while ( cout <<"\nEnter postfix expression: \n",
            cin.getline(expression, 100),
            strcmp(expression, "") != 0 ) {
        root = build_exp_tree(root, expression);
        printresults(root);
        root = deltree(root);   //  Dispose of the tree's nodes
    }
}
```

Program 13.3

13.5   N-ARY TREES

In general, hierarchical structures can have nodes with more than two children. An *n-ary* tree is a tree in which each node may have up to n children. The structure chart found in chapter 6 is an example of an n-ary tree in which the maximum number of branches shown is 3. Consider the tree in figure 13.9:

In attempting to represent this tree in C++, one might provide the following definitions:

```
struct TreeNode {
    int data;
    TreeNode *child1, *child2, *child3,
            *child4, *child5, *child6,
            *child7, *child8, *child9;
};
typedef TreeNode *Link;
```

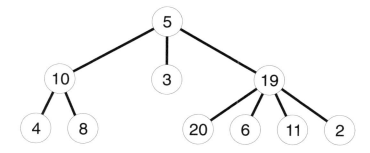

An N-ary Tree
Figure 13.9

These definitions are parallel to the binary tree definitions above. Each binary tree node can have up to two children; hence, a left and right pointer was provided in each node. Here, the maximum number of children is unknown, but nine seems like a generous estimate; therefore, nine child pointers are provided in each n-ary tree node. This approach has two problems. First, there is no guarantee that another instance of this tree might not have a node with ten children. Also, even if every node in the tree is guaranteed to have no more than nine children, most of the nodes have far fewer than nine children. Each pointer takes some space, thus storing nine pointers in each node when on average only about one pointer is needed per node is wasteful. Consider the following alternate definitions:

```
struct TreeNode {
     int data;
     TreeNode *child;
     TreeNode *sibling;
};
typedef TreeNode *Link;
```

Program 13.4a

This structure is physically identical to the binary tree `TreeNode` above. The `left` and `right` fields are merely renamed to `child` and `sibling`. Our n-ary tree will be represented by a binary tree! The code in programs 13.4a and 13.4b "hand builds" the n-ary tree of figure 13.9:

```
void main() {
    Link root;
    TreeNode n1, n2, n3, n4, n5, n6, n7, n8, n9, n10;
    //   Place data fields
    n1->data = 5;  n2->data = 10;  n3->data = 3;  n4->data = 19;  n5->data = 4;
    n6->data = 8;  n7->data = 20;  n8->data = 6;  n9->data = 11;  n10->data = 2;
    // String child pointers
    n1->child = &n2;  n2->child = &n5;  n4->child = &n7;
    n3->child = n5->child = n6->child = n7->child
              = n8->child = n9->child = n10->child = NULL;
    //   String sibling pointers
    n2->sibling = &n3;  n3->sibling = &n4;
    n5->sibling = &n6;  n7->sibling = &n8;
    n8->sibling = &n9;  n9->sibling = &n10;
    n1->sibling = n4->sibling = n6->sibling = n10->sibling = NULL;
    //   Direct root
    root = &n1;
    printtree(root);  //  See printtree() below
}
```

Program 13.4b

The internal structure of the tree is shown in figure 13.10:

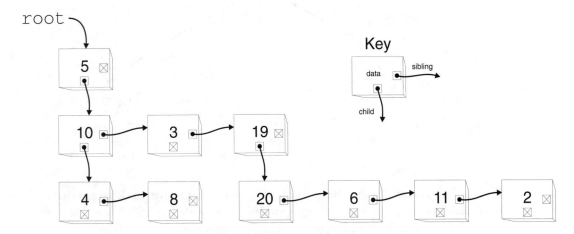

The Internal Structure of the n-ary Tree
Figure 13.10

Notice that the actual structure of the tree is binary; the intended structure is produced by clever interpretation of the two different pointers.

The following `printtree()` function illustrates an n-ary tree traversal:

```
void printtree(Link root) {
     if ( root ) {
          cout << root->data << ' ';
          while ( root->sibling ) {
               printtree(root->sibling);
               root = root->sibling;
          }
          printtree(root->child);
     }
}
```

The order in which the nodes are printed is determined by the particular algorithm that chases the pointers emanating from the root node. Just as binary trees have standard traversals (pre-, in- and postorder), so do n-ary trees. The two predominant traversals are *breadth-first* and *depth-first* traversal. A traversal must be performed when searching a tree for a particular node. Since the tree has no inherent ordering as does a BST, each node must be visited until the sought node is found or all the nodes have been considered. The two techniques for traversal are commonly called *breadth-first* search (BFS) and *depth-first* search (DFS).

Not only can an n-ary tree be represented by an ADT, but the BFS and DFS traversals of the tree will be facilitated by ADTs that we have already constructed: the stack and the queue. The two searches are shown in the following functions:

```
NTree *breadth_first_search(NTree *root, int sought) {
     Queue q;
     NTree *x, *cursor;
     q.enqueue(root);
     while ( !q.empty() ) {
          q.dequeue(x);
          if ( x->data == sought )
               return x;
          else {
```

```
                              cursor = x->child;
                              while ( cursor ) {    //  Enqueue all of x's children
                                    q.enqueue(cursor);
                                    cursor = cursor->sibling;
                              }
                        }
                  }
            return NULL;    //  Not found
      }

      NTree *depth_first_search(NTree *root, ElementType sought) {
            Stack s;
            Ntree *x, *cursor;
            s.push(root);
            while ( !s.empty() ) {
                  s.pop(x);
                  if ( x->data == sought )
                        return x;
                  else {
                        cursor = x->child;
                        while ( cursor ) {    //  Push all of x's children
                              s.push(cursor);
                              cursor = cursor->sibling;
                        }
                  }
            }
            return NULL;    //  Not found
      }
```

The n-ary tree template class that follows in program 13.5a shows how a n-ary tree ADT could be implemented. It is not very general; the insertion routine prompts the user for direction about how to insert values into the tree. In this case, the client `main()` is using the n-ary tree to represent a classification hierarchy. Test it out by entering the following items and observing the resulting tree:

cat dog fish collie poodle spider vertebrate trout amoeba animal siamese black-widow insect goldfish ant monkey butterfly

If you answered the classification questions correctly, the resulting tree (drawn in outline form) would be:

```
-animal
    -vertebrate
        -cat
            -siamese
        -dog
            -collie
            -poodle
        -fish
            -trout
            -goldfish
        -monkey
    -spider
        -black-widow
    -amoeba
    -insect
        -ant
        -butterfly
```

(You did remember that a spider is not an insect, of course.)

```
///////////////////////////////////////////////////////////////////////
//    File nTree.tpl    n-ary tree container class
///////////////////////////////////////////////////////////////////////
///////
template <class T>
struct nTreeNode {
    T data;
    nTreeNode<T> *child,
                 *sibling;
};

template <class T>
class Tree {
    nTreeNode<T> *root;
    void dispose(nTreeNode<T> *);
    void print_rec(nTreeNode<T> *, int) const;
    nTreeNode<T> *insert_rec(nTreeNode<T> *, const T &);
    nTreeNode<T> *new_node(const T &) const;
    int ask(const T &, const T &) const;
public:
    Tree();
    ~Tree();
    void print() const;
    void insert(const T &);
};

#include <iostream.h>
#include <ctype.h>

template <class T>
Tree<T>::Tree(): root(0) {}

template <class T>
Tree<T>::~Tree() { dispose(root); }


template <class T>
void Tree<T>::dispose(nTreeNode<T> *p) {
    nTreeNode<T> *hold;
    while ( p ) {
        dispose(p->child);
        hold = p;
        p = p->sibling;
        delete hold;
    }
}
template <class T>
void Tree<T>::print_rec(nTreeNode<T> *p, int deep) const {
    while ( p ) {
        for ( int i = 0;  i < deep;  i++ )
            cout << "    ";    // Tab over
        cout << '-' << p->data << '\n';
        print_rec(p->child, deep + 1);
        p = p->sibling;
    }
}
template <class T>
void Tree<T>::print() const {
    print_rec(root, 0);
    cout << '\n';
}
```

```
template <class T>
nTreeNode<T> *Tree<T>::new_node(const T &new_item) const {
    nTreeNode<T> *node = new nTreeNode<T>;
    node->data = new_item;
    node->sibling = node->child = 0;
    return node;
}

template <class T>
int Tree<T>::ask(const T &x, const T &y) const {
    char response;
    cout << "Is [" << x << "] a type of [" << y << "] ?\n";
    cin  >> response;
    return response == 'y'  ||  response == 'Y';
}

template <class T>
nTreeNode<T> *Tree<T>::insert_rec(nTreeNode<T> *p, const T &val) {
    nTreeNode<T> *newptr, *lastchild, *t1, *t2;
    //  Case 1:  Subtree is empty
    if ( p == NULL ) {
        p = new_node(val);
        p->child = p->sibling = NULL;
    }
    //  Case 2:  New value is a descendent of the root node
    else if ( ask(val, p->data) )
        p->child = insert_rec(p->child, val);
    //  Case 3:  New value becomes a new root level node
    else if ( ask(p->data, val) ) {
        newptr = new_node(val);
        newptr->child = p;
        t2 = newptr;    t1 = newptr->child->sibling;
        lastchild = newptr->child;
        while ( t1 != NULL ) {
            if ( ask(t1->data, val) ) {
                lastchild = t1;
                t1 = t1->sibling;
            }

            else {
                t2->sibling = t1;
                t1 = t1->sibling;
                lastchild->sibling = t1;
                t2 = t2->sibling;
            }
        }
        t2->sibling = NULL;
        p = newptr;
    }
    //  Case 4:  New value is a sibling of the root node
    else
        p->sibling = insert_rec(p->sibling, val);
    return p;
}

template <class T>
void Tree<T>::insert(const T &new_item) {
    root = insert_rec(root, new_item);
}
```

Program 13.5a

The client code tests the n-ary tree with `String` objects:

```
#include "nTree.tpl"
#include "str.h"

void main() {
    String end_string = "done", str;
    Tree<String> tree;
    while ( cin >> str, str != end_string ) {
        tree.insert(str);
        tree.print();
    }
}
```

Program 13.5b

13.6 Pseudopointer Tree Representation

Not all programming languages have the convenient feature of dynamic memory and pointers. FORTRAN, BASIC, and COBOL are popular languages that are heavily used in certain applications but traditionally provide no support for pointers. They do provide facilities for arrays and possibly `structs` also. Since arrays are inherently linear structures, how can hierarchical structures like trees be represented in languages such as these?

The question will be answered by representing a binary tree in C++ *without* true, dynamic pointers. "Fake" pointers (also called *pseudopointers* or *cursor pointers*) will be employed in a fashion that must be used in a language that provides no dynamic memory support. Consider the following definitions:

```
struct TreeNode {
    int data;
    int left, right;
};

typedef TreeNode Tree[MAXNODES];
```

Program 13.6a

The following code hand builds the same binary tree of figure 13.2:

```
void main() {  //  Note: MAXNODES from above should be at least 5
    Tree t;
    t[0].data  = 10;
    t[1].data  = 15;
    t[2].data  =  3;
    t[3].data  = 12;
    t[4].data  = 15;
    t[0].left  =  1;
    t[0].right =  2;
    t[1].right =  3;
    t[2].left  =  4;
    t[1].left  = t[2].right = t[3].left  = t[3].right
               = t[4].left  = t[4].right = -1;
    printtree(t, 0);
}
```

Program 13.6b

Figure 13.11, a picture of the internal representation of the tree, looks linear, yet it represents a hierarchical structure. The pseudopointers do not refer to memory addresses allocated by `new` as in

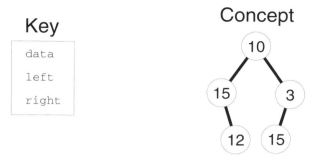

Key

```
data
left
right
```

Concept

A Pseudopointer Binary Tree Representation
Figure 13.11

Internal Representation

10	15	3	12	15
1	-1	4	-1	-1
2	3	-1	-1	-1
0	**1**	**2**	**3**	**4**

the dynamic pointer scheme; they point to a position within the tree array itself. The root node is position 0, by definition. The left subtree can be found by going to the position specified by root's `left` field; thus, `t[0]` is the root node, and `t[t[0].left]` is the root of root's left subtree. The rightmost great grandchild of root (if it exists) is merely `t[t[t[0].right].right]`. A `NULL` pointer is not truly `NULL` (that is, 0) since 0 represents a valid array position. The value -1 is used to signify a `NULL` pointer in this pseudopointer binary tree implementation.
The `printtree()` based upon a preorder traversal could be written as:

```
void printtree(Tree t, int cursor) {
    if ( cursor != -1 ) {
        cout << t[cursor].data) << ' ';
        printtree(t, t[cursor].left);
        printtree(t, t[cursor].right);
    }
}
```

Observe that this pseudopointer version does not save any space over the true linked version. When arrays and linked lists were compared above in chapter 10 in the context of linear structures, arrays were found to save space, since the pointers to the next item in the structure did not need to be stored in each node. Here, each node must store the position of each of its children, just like in the real pointer version. The memory requirements are basically the same.

If the language to be used does not support `structs` (like most BASIC implementations), three separate arrays would have to be used:

```
int node[MAXNODES];
int left[MAXNODES];
int right[MAXNODES];
```

This partitioning of node information makes the coding a bit more obscure, but it does allow the representation of hierarchical structures.

Exercises

1. How can an *n-ary* tree be implemented?

2. Why is it useful to study *pseudopointer* tree representations?

3. Does the pseudopointer tree representation have any advantages over the linked version? What are its disadvantages?

13.7   GRAPHS

A graph can be described mathematically as a structure

$$<V, E, f>$$

where **V** is a set of *vertices*, or nodes, **E** is a set of *edges* or arcs, and *f* is a function associating each edge with a (possibly ordered) pair of vertices. Using terminology developed during the discussion of linked lists and trees, a graph is a structure in which there is no unique first or last element, and every element may have multiple predecessors and successors. Figure 13.12 shows the pictorial representation of a typical graph.

The nodes in a graph are labeled to indicate objects in the problem domain. The arcs may be labeled to indicate cost or time of some transition or activity between two nodes. The arcs (and, therefore, the graphs) may be directed or undirected. The graph in figure 13.12 is a directed graph because the arcs have arrowheads attached to them. In an undirected graph, the activity between any two nodes connected by an arc can flow in both directions. Trees are a generalization of linear linked lists. Instead of nodes being restricted to single successors, trees allow multiple successors. Graphs are generalized trees. Graphs are also called *networks*. A tree would be inadequate to represent a flowchart that involved iteration or branching; a flowchart is a type of graph where each symbol is a node and flowlines are the arcs. Graphs have applications in many diverse fields. (See figure 13.13.) A computer network is a graph, where each workstation is a node and the connections between workstations represent arcs. A complex molecule can be represented as a graph; the atoms are the nodes,

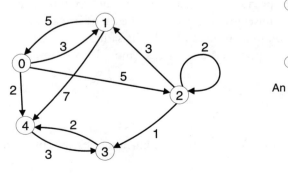

A Picture of a Graph
Figure 13.12

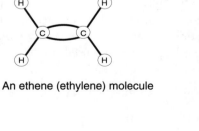

An ethene (ethylene) molecule

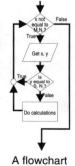

A flowchart

Applications of Graphs
Figure 13.13

and the molecular bonds between each pair of atoms are the arcs. A road map shows how roads (arcs) connect cities (nodes). An electronic circuit can be represented as a graph in which the wires (arcs) interconnect the various components (nodes). The flow of raw materials and partially constructed products from parts of a factory to other parts in the course of assembly can be represented as a graph.

Programs that analyze graphs are very useful. Utility companies can dynamically monitor power usage across a wide area and adjust production from available generating plants to meet demands. How the delivery of that power is distributed among various substations is a problem in network analysis. When a printed circuit board is designed, the length of the traces (wires) between the various components must be minimized for optimum performance. A telephone switching network must determine how to efficiently route long distance calls when various options are available. When one hub becomes overloaded, calls must be rerouted through a different switching hub. A manufacturing firm must deliver goods to suppliers across the country. Based on the goods ordered, the most efficient route for a delivery truck must be determined. The route chosen should visit all the suppliers and yet minimize the time and fuel costs. The path must begin at the warehouse and end at the warehouse (with an empty truck). To further complicate the situation, it must be determined in what order the goods are going to be loaded into the individual trucks so that the order of unloading appropriately matches the schedule of deliveries. These situations are all examples of network analysis problems that are routinely solved by computer software using graphs to model the problem domain.

At some level, each network analysis program must represent the graph in some data structure. The simplest representation is the *adjacency matrix*. The adjacency matrix for the graph in figure 13.14 is

$$\begin{bmatrix} 0 & 3 & 5 & 0 & 2 \\ 5 & 0 & 0 & 0 & 7 \\ 0 & 3 & 2 & 1 & 0 \\ 0 & 0 & 0 & 0 & 2 \\ 0 & 0 & 0 & 3 & 0 \end{bmatrix}$$

An Adjacency Matrix
Figure 13.14

In a C++ program, a graph ADT based on an adjacency matrix can be designed as follows:

```
////////////////////////////////////////////////////////////////////////////
//  graph.h
////////////////////////////////////////////////////////////////////////////
#include "array.tpl"

class Graph {
    Matrix<int> adj_mat;
    int nodes;
public:
    Graph(int n, int fill = 0): adj_mat(n, n, fill), nodes(n) {}
    ~Graph() {}
    void print();
    int &set(int r, int c) {  return adj_mat[r][c];  }
    int shortest_path(int, int);
};
```

Program 13.7a

Notice the inclusion of `set.tpl` in the implementation file below, program 13.7d. Since graphs are mathematical objects, many graph algorithms have been developed by mathematicians and expressed in the language of mathematics. Sets are used in the formal definition of a graph, and sets are used in the descriptions of many graph algorithms. The following set template is a minimal tool for creating and manipulating mathematical sets.

```
///////////////////////////////////////////////////
//  set.tpl
///////////////////////////////////////////////////
//  A mathematical set ADT

#ifndef _SET_TPL_
#define _SET_TPL_

#include <iostream.h>
#include "inflush.h"
#include "array.tpl"

const int MAXSET = 100;

template <class T>
class Set {
    Array<T> set;
    int current_size;
public:
    Set();
    Set(int);
    Set(const Set<T> &);  //  Copy constructor
    ~Set() {}
    Set<T> &operator=(const Set<T> &);  //  assignment
    int operator!();
    int in(const T &);  //  element of
    void operator+=(const T &);  //  insert element
    void operator-=(const T &);  //  remove element
    const T &operator[](int i) const {  return set[i];  }
    friend Set<T> operator+(const Set<T> &, const Set<T> &);// union
    friend Set<T> operator*(const Set<T> &, const Set<T> &);  // intersection
    friend ostream &operator<<(ostream &, const Set<T> &);  // print
    friend istream &operator>>(istream &, Set<T> &);        // input
};

template <class T>
Set<T>::Set(): set(MAXSET), current_size(0) {}

template <class T>
Set<T>::Set(int n): set(n), current_size(0) {}

template <class T>
Set<T>::Set(const Set<T> &s): set(s.set), current_size(s.current_size) {}

template <class T>
Set<T> &Set<T>::operator=(const Set<T> &s) {
    if ( &s != this ) {
        set = s.set;
        current_size = s.current_size;
    }
    return *this;
}

template <class T>
int Set<T>::operator!() {
    return current_size == 0;
}

template <class T>
int Set<T>::in(const T &e) {
    for ( int i = 0;  i < current_size;  i++ )
```

```
                    if ( set[i] == e )
                        return 1;  //  Found it
            return 0;  // Not present
    }

    template <class T>
    void Set<T>::operator+=(const T &e) {
        for ( int i = 0;  i < current_size;  i++ )
            if ( set[i] == e )  //  Don't insert duplicate
                return;
        set[current_size++] = e;
    }

    template <class T>
    void Set<T>::operator-=(const T &e) {
        for ( int i = 0, j;  i < current_size;  i++ )
        if ( set[i] == e ) {
            for ( j = current_size - 2;  j >= i;  j-- )
                set[j] = set[j + 1];    //  Fill in "hole"
        }
    }

    //  Set union
    template <class T>
    Set<T> operator+(const Set<T> &s, const Set<T> &t) {
        Set<T> tempset(MAXSET);
        for ( int i = 0;  i < s.current_size;  i++ )
            tempset += s[i];
        for ( i = 0;  i < t.current_size; i++ )
            tempset += t[i];
        return tempset;
    }

    //  Set intersection
    template <class T>
    Set<T> operator*(const Set<T> &s, const Set<T> &t) {
        Set<T> tempset(MAXSET);
        for ( int i = 0, j;  i < s.current_size;  i++ )
            for ( j = 0;  j < t.current_size;  j++ )
                if ( s[i] == t[j] )
                    tempset += s[i];
        return tempset;
    }

    template <class T>
    ostream &operator<<(ostream &os, const Set<T> &s) {
        os << "{";
        if ( s.current_size > 0 ) {
            for ( int i = 0;  i < s.current_size;  i++ )
                os << s.set[i] << ',';
            os << "\b}";
        }
        else
            os << "}";
        return os;
    }

    template <class T>
    istream &operator>>(istream &is, Set<T> &s) {
        s.current_size = 0;
        T in_val;
        while ( is.good() ) {
            is >> in_val;
            if ( is.good() )
                s.set[s.current_size++] = in_val;
        }
```

```
        is >> flush;
        return is;
}
#endif
```

Program 13.7b

The underlying data structure is simply an array. The implementation could be modified for better performance. A binary search tree could be used to speed up the test for set membership (Set<T>::in()), but the BST container class as presented above does not have the appropriate member functions available to perform the operations necessary for set union and intersection. A copy constructor and assignment operator would need to be provided as well as a way to retrieve individual elements from two separate trees to combine into a new tree. In order to use the BST class, it would have to be opened up and significantly modified; the array template was available and worked as is. The beauty of ADTs is the ability to use a less than ideal underlying implementation that minimally does what is necessary and still develop the main application. When time is found to improve the details of the ADT implementation, nothing should need to be changed in client code if the ADT interface is unchanged.

Once the graph has been represented internally as an adjacency matrix, algorithms implemented as member functions can be used to manipulate the graph. One useful task is to find the shortest path between any two nodes in a graph. The following algorithm from discrete mathematics finds the shortest path between node A and node B:

Definitions:

> Let A be the start node and B be the end node on the shortest path.
>
> Let **Visited** be the empty set.
>
> Let **Distance** be an array where each position within the array represents the length of the shortest path found thus far from node A to that node. For example, **Distance**[0] is the distance between node A and node 0, **Distance**[1] is the distance between node A and node 1, etc.
>
> Let **Previous** be an array where each position within the array holds the node that immediately precedes that node on the shortest path determined thus far. For example, if **Previous**[0] is 3, then considering the shortest path from node A to node 0, node 3 would be the last node on the path before reaching node 0. When the algorithm is finished, the **Previous** array is used to trace back the nodes contained on the actual shortest path.
>
> Let **Adj** be the adjacency matrix for the graph.

1. Add node A to the **Visited** set.   (Mark start node as visited.)
2. Initialize the **Distance** and **Previous** arrays:
   > For all nodes i:
   > > **Distance**[i] = **Adj**[A][i];
   > > **Previous**[i] = A
3. While B ∉ **Visited**
   > Choose node x such that x ∉ **Visited** and **Distance**[x] is the minimum.
   > Add node x to **Visited** set.
   > For all nodes i ∉ **Visited** :
   > > distance = **Distance**[i]
   > > **Distance**[i] = Minimum(**Distance**[i], **Distance**[x] + Adj[x][i])
   > > if **Distance**[i] ≠ distance then **Previous**[i] = x;
4. shortest_path_length = **Distance**[B]

5. While i ≠ A   (Display shortest path backwards.)
         i = B
         display i
         i = **Previous**[i];

Step 1 marks the start node as visited. Step 2 initializes the two arrays keeping track of the minimum distance found thus far to a particular node and the node's current predecessor in the shortest path. The Distance array stores the distance from A to every other vertex in the graph based on information in the adjacency matrix. If there is no edge connecting A to a node, the value infinity is recorded (actually INT_MAX, a constant defined in <limits.h> representing the largest integer possible on the system). The loop in step 3 is the heart of the algorithm. The node nearest to A (shortest path from A) is selected to consider. It is called x in the algorithm. It is marked as visited so it will not be considered again. The value in position x in the **Distance** array represents the shortest possible path from A to x. Going through any other nodes other than those already considered and marked as visited will result in a longer path to that node. Then, all the nonvisited nodes in the **Distance** array are checked to see if they need to be updated. Consider a node called y. If the distance to x from A plus the distance from x to y is smaller than the current entry **Distance**[y], then the **Distance**[y] is updated to reflect the shorter distance. (For example, if y was originally determined to be unreachable directly from A, it might be reachable directly from x; thus, the value of **Distance**[y], now infinity, would be replaced with **Distance**[x] + distance from x to y. The distance from x to y can be found in the adjacency matrix.) If y's distance is updated, then its previous node would also need to be changed to x, since the shortest path to y known so far now passes through x.

The C++ code to implement a graph and find the shortest path between two nodes in the graph follows:

```
/////////////////////////////////////////////////////////////////////
//  graph.h
/////////////////////////////////////////////////////////////////////

#ifndef _GRAPH_H_
#define _GRAPH_H_

#include "array.tpl"



class Graph {
    Matrix<int> adj_mat;
    int nodes;
public:
    Graph(int n, int fill = 0): adj_mat(n, n, fill), nodes(n) {}
    ~Graph() {}
    void print();
    int adjacent(int r, int c) {  return adj_mat[r][c] != 0;  }
    int &set(int r, int c) {  return adj_mat[r][c];  }
    int shortest_path(int, int);
};

#endif
```

Program 13.7c

```
/////////////////////////////////////////////////////////////////////
//  graph.cpp
/////////////////////////////////////////////////////////////////////

#include "graph.h"
#include "set.tpl"
```

```
#include <iostream.h>
#include <iomanip.h>
#include <limits.h>   //  For INT_MAX constant

void Graph::print() {
    cout << "+";
    for ( int i = 0;  i < nodes;  i++ )
        cout << setw(4) << ' ';
    cout << " +\n";
    for ( i = 0;  i < nodes;  i++ ) {
        cout << "|";
        for ( int j = 0;  j < nodes;  j++ )
            cout << setw(4) << adj_mat[i][j];
            cout << "|\n";
    }
    cout << "+";
    for ( i = 0;  i < nodes;  i++ )
        cout << setw(4) << ' ';
    cout << " +\n";
}

static int min(int x, int y) {
    if ( x < y )
        return x;
    else
        return y;
}


void dump(int *a) {
    for ( int i = 0;  i < 5;  i++ )
        cout << a[i] << ' ';
    cout << '\n';
}

static inline int dist(int x) {
    //  Adjusts adjacency matrix entry so 0 is an unreachable distance
    return (x > 0)? x: INT_MAX;
}


static inline int inf_add(int x, int y) {
    //  Infinity + anything else = infinity
    if ( x == INT_MAX  ||  y == INT_MAX )
        return INT_MAX;
    else
        return x + y;
}

int Graph::shortest_path(int begin, int end) {
    //  Initialize Visited set
    Set<int> Visited(nodes);
    Visited += begin;

    //  Initialize Distance and Previous arrays
    int *Distance = new int[nodes], *Previous = new int[nodes];
    if ( !Distance  ||  !Previous )
        exit_error("Out of memory");
    for ( int i = 0;  i < nodes;  i++ ) {
        //  Fill in values from adjacency matrix
        Distance[i] = dist(adj_mat[begin][i]);
        Previous[i] = begin;
    }
```

```
            int x, min_distance, distance, not_found;
            while ( !Visited.in(end) ) {
                    min_distance = INT_MAX;
                    not_found = 1;
                    //  Search for minimum distance within nodes not visited
                    for ( i = 0;  i < nodes;  i++ )
                         if ( !Visited.in(i)  &&  Distance[i] < min_distance ) {
                              min_distance = Distance[i];
                              x = i;
                              not_found = 0;
                    }
                    //  Was no node found?
                    if ( not_found ) {
                            //  Can go no farther; no path exists
                            cout << "No path available between node " << begin
                                 << " and node " << end << ".\n";
                            return INT_MAX;
                    }
                    //  Add node to visited set
                    Visited += x;
                    cout << "Visiting " << x << '\n';
                    dump(Distance);
                    cout << Visited << '\n';
                    cin.get();
                    //  Update Distance and Previous arrays, if necessary
                    for ( i = 0;  i < nodes;  i++ )
                         if ( !Visited.in(i) ) {
                              distance = Distance[i];
                              Distance[i] = min(Distance[i],
                                                    inf_add(Distance[x],
                                                          dist(adj_mat[x][i])));
                              if ( Distance[i] != distance )
                                      Previous[i] = x;
                         }
            }
            //  Print shortest path length
            cout << "The shortest path is length " << Distance[end] << ":   ";

            //  Backtrace along shortest path
            i = end;
            while ( i != begin ) {
                    cout << i << " <- ";
                    i = Previous[i];
            }
            cout << begin << '\n';
            int result = Distance[end];

            //  Clean up temporary arrays
            delete [] Distance;
            delete [] Previous;

            //  Return length of shortest path
            return result;
}
```

Program 13.7d

The following main() tests both the set template and graph class:

```
#include <iostream.h>
#include "set.tpl"
#include "graph.h"
```

```
void main() {
      Set<int> s1(10), s2(10), s3;
      cout << "Enter set 1: ";
      cin  >> s1;
      cout << s1 << '\n';
      cout << "Enter set 2: ";
      cin  >> s2;
      cout << s2 << '\n';
      cout << s1 << "    union      " << s2 << " is " << (s1 + s2) << '\n';
      cout << s1 << " intersection " << s2 << " is " << (s1 * s2) << '\n';
      s3 = s1 * s2;
      if ( !s3 )
            cout << s3 << " is empty. \n";
      Graph grf(5, 0);
      grf.print();
      grf.set(0, 1) = 3;      grf.set(0, 2) = 5;
      grf.set(0, 4) = 2;      grf.set(1, 0) = 5;
      grf.set(1, 4) = 7;      grf.set(2, 1) = 3;
      grf.set(2, 2) = 2;      grf.set(2, 3) = 1;
      grf.set(3, 4) = 2;      grf.set(4, 3) = 3;
      grf.print();
      int node1, node2;
      cout << "Enter two nodes to find shortest path between: ";
      cin >> node1 >> node2;
      grf.shortest_path(node1, node2);
}
```

Program 13.7e

Graph traversal is accomplished by either depth-first or breadth-first means as is done with n-ary trees. The nodes in a graph may contain information in addition to simple labels of 0, 1, 2, . . . As before, a stack is used for depth-first traversal and a queue is used for breadth-first traversal. The following members may be added to the Graph class:

```
void Graph::depth_first_trav(int begin) {
      Stack<int> s;
      Set<int> visited(nodes);
      int x;
      s.push(begin);
      while ( !s.empty() ) {
            s.pop(x);
            if ( !visited.in(x) ) {
                  visited += x;   //  Mark x as visited
                  cout << x << ' ';
                  for ( int i = 0;  i < nodes;  i++ )
                        //  Push all of x's nonvisited adjacent nodes
                        if ( adj_mat[x][i] != 0  &&  !visited.in(i) )
                              s.push(i);
            }
      }
      cout << '\n';
}
void Graph::breadth_first_trav(int begin) {
      Queue<int> q;
      Set<int> visited(nodes);
      int x;
      q.enqueue(begin);
      while ( !q.empty() ) {
            q.dequeue(x);
            if ( !visited.in(x) ) {
                  visited += x;   //  Mark x as visited
                  cout << x << ' ';
                  for ( int i = 0;  i < nodes;  i++ )
```

```
                            //  Enqueue all of x's nonvisited adjacent nodes
                            if ( adj_mat[x][i] != 0  &&  !visited.in(i) )
                                q.enqueue(i);
                }
        }
        cout << '\n';
}
```

The adjacency matrix is easy to process, but it has its drawbacks. In an undirected graph, a graph whose edges have no arrowheads because the edges are bidirectional, the adjacency matrix is symmetrical across the diagonal from the upper-left to lower-right corner. In a two-dimensional array, almost twice as much space is used as is needed, since the entries on one side of the diagonal are duplicated on the other. Also, a graph that contains many nodes but relatively few connections among the nodes uses a lot of space for storing a little information. Figure 13.15 illustrates both of these points. The graph contains ten nodes so a 10×10 matrix is required to represent the connections. The edges are not labeled, so the adjacency matrix is a Boolean matrix; zero indicates no edge and one indicates that an edge connects the vertices. Since the graph is undirected, the upper-right diagonal of the matrix is the mirror image of the lower left; thus, of the 100 entries in matrix, 45 elements are redundant information. To make matters worse, the graph contains only nine edges. Is there a more efficient way to store the information about nine edges than using a matrix with 100 elements? A solution to both of these problems is the *adjacency list*.

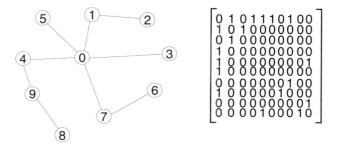

Sparse and Symmetrical Adjacency Matrix
Figure 13.15

An adjacency list can be implemented in several ways, but one popular approach uses a one-dimensional array of pointers to a linked list whose nodes contain pointers to adjacent nodes. A picture does more justice than a verbal description. Figure 13.16 is the corresponding adjacency list for the graph in figure 13.12 (which has weighted edges).

How would the sparse graph fare in an adjacency list structure? To analyze the situation, we'll make several assumptions that will certainly vary from system to system. We'll assume integers (representing the node labels) are stored in two bytes, and pointers are stored in four bytes. Since the matrix above is a Boolean matrix, each list node needs only to contain a node label and a pointer. The additional edge weight shown in figure 13.16 is not required. This makes each list node take up six bytes of memory. Node 0 has five connections, node 1 has two connections, etc. The complete breakdown is shown in table 13.1.

The adjacency matrix would require 200 bytes vs. the 148 bytes for the adjacency list. The savings in this case is significant. Since the pointers take up space (and, in our sample analysis, each pointer required twice as much space as each integer), the adjacency matrix would become the better choice if a few more edges were added.

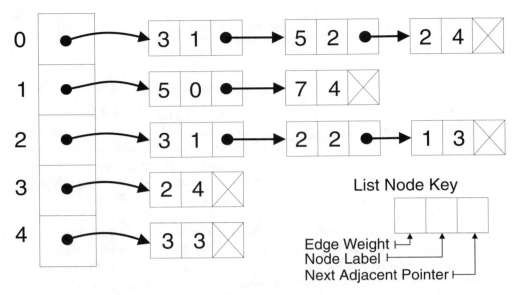

Adjacency List Structure
Figure 13.16

Table 13.1 Analysis of Adjacency List Storage Requirements

Node Number	Number of Edges/ List Nodes	Bytes of Storage
0	5	30
1	2	12
2	1	6
3	1	6
4	2	12
5	1	6
6	1	6
7	2	12
8	1	6
9	2	12
The array itself		40
Total		148

Code that processes adjacency lists tends to be more complex than equivalent adjacency matrix code. The extra space overhead of the pointers is justified when the connection matrix is sparse. Information about the adjacency of two vertices can be determined faster from an adjacency matrix, since a two-dimensional array is a random access structure. The choice of which implementation to use depends upon the nature of the problem. If the graph is dense (many connections among vertices) and adjacency information needs to be determined quickly, the adjacency matrix is the better choice. If the graph is relatively sparse (few connections among the nodes) or nondirected, the adjacency list structure may be the better choice.

The discussion of graphs and their implementation in C++ warrants a final observation. Each of the examples above uses what is called a *coarse-grained* object-oriented design approach. The design process was not performed in a bottom-up manner. The objects are big; a graph is an object, but its component vertices are not real objects. An adjacency matrix or adjacency list structure holds information about connections among vertices, but there are no vertex objects anywhere in the code. A different approach, the so-called *fine-grained* approach attempts to identify all the objects in the problem domain and the relationships that exist among them. In the fine-grained approach, a vertex would be a legitimate object (a `Vertex` class would be defined with member data and functions). Edges could be objects that contain data concerning edge weight. The following definitions illustrate:

```
class Edge;  //  Forward declaration
struct EdgeListNode {
     Edge *edge;
     EdgeNodeList *next;
};


class Vertex {
     int _label;
     EdgeListNode *edgelist;
     //  Plus private member functions
public:
     Vertex(int);
     ~Vertex();  //  Destructor deallocates edges
     void attach(const Vertex &, float);  //  Attach a vertex with a
                                          //  given edge weight
     int label() {  return _label; }  //  _label member is read-only
     //  Plus other public member functions
};
class Edge {
     float _weight;
     Vertex *to;
     //  Plus private member functions
public:
     Edge(const Vertex &, const Vertex &, float);  //  Connects two
             vertices through an edge
     ~Edge();    //  Destructor, if needed
     float weight() {  return _weight;  }  //  _weight member is read-only
     //  Plus other public member functions
};
```

Using these definitions, the internal representation of the graph is closer in structure to the abstract visual representation of a mathematical graph. (Recall that the pure mathematical definitions rely on mathematical set theory which is quite different from this representation.) The advantage of this fine-grained approach is that the computer implementation matches the problem domain more closely. `Vertex` objects can be responsible for displaying themselves on a bitmapped graphical display. They hold information about their size, shape, and (x,y) position within the view window. Some algorithms might be easier to develop using this implementation, but it is important to note that this approach offers some distinct disadvantages as well. Edge information cannot be accessed at random as it can with an adjacency matrix. This fine-grained object-oriented approach can be merged with the course-grained implementation to gain the benefits of both. An implementation that uses an adjacency matrix could store a separate one-dimensional array of `Vertex` objects that are each able to display themselves, keep track of their own position, etc. The internal representation is different from the visual abstract concept (but perhaps not that different from the mathematical set representation). The large `Graph` object has smaller `Vertex` components, and the actual `Edge` objects are abandoned for edge information that can be obtained through a table look up.

Exercises

1. How does an adjacency matrix store edge information about a graph?

2. Explain how a tree is a special type of graph.

3. Translate the adjacency matrix for figure 13.15 into an adjacency list structure.

4. Step through the shortest path algorithm to find the shortest path between nodes 1 and 2 given the adjacency matrix in figure 13.14. (The graph is pictured in figure 13.12.)

Assignments

1. Write a C++ program that reads in a textfile and places the individual words into a BST. The BST is ordered lexicographically. Each word should be inserted as it is read from the file. All punctuation in the file should be ignored. No words will contain embedded punctuation (apostrophes, hyphens, etc.). If the word appears more than once in the file, it should not be inserted again as a new node, but a record of how many times it appears should be kept within the node in the BST (add a frequency data member to the node object). A sample tree node might look like:

```
struct BSTNode {
    String word;    //  A String object
    int  freq;      //  Number of times the word has been seen
    BSTNode *left, *right; //  Pointers to left and right subtrees
};
```

Extend the BST class template provided so that a member function is available for deleting nodes from the tree. Your class should be able to perform pre-, in-, and postorder traversals of the tree, draw the tree sideways, and insert new nodes into the tree. The function to delete a word from the tree should not physically remove the node until the frequency count is zero. Write a reasonable main() function to test your routines.

2. Extend the BST ADT presented here so that each tree node contains a parent pointer in addition to its left and right child pointers. The BST class should also contain a cursor member that can be used to traverse the tree at will. The constructor should set cursor equal to root. Entering the '<' causes the cursor to move to left child, '>' causes the cursor to move to the right child, and '^' (caret) causes the cursor to move to the parent node. If any of these moves is not possible (e.g., the current node has no left child), then the cursor's position should not be changed. After each entry the contents of the current node to which the cursor is pointing should be displayed.

3. Use the extensions suggested in assignment 2 to modify the BST::draw() function. The draw function is inappropriate for very tall trees because the display screen or printer is only so wide. A tree that is too tall produces a chaotic picture. Allow only the portion of the tree that has cursor as its root to be printed. A maximum of five levels of the tree should be printed at any one time; thus, instead of printing the value of the current node each time the cursor movement keys are entered (as in assignment 2), display the tree (up to five levels deep) that has current as its root node.

4. Modify the hierarchical classification tree example to allow deletion of nodes.

5. Build a BST that uses cursor pointers in its implementation instead of real pointers. Its interface (public member functions) should be identical to the BST container class provided in this chapter.

6. Add the ability to remove a node to the cursor pointer BST implementation of assignment 4.

7. Combine the infix-to-postfix program from chapter 12 with the arithmetic evaluation program in this chapter to allow infix expressions to be used to build an expression tree.

8. Construct a graph ADT using an adjacency list as its internal data structure. Provide member functions for depth-first and breadth-first traversal.

9. Reimplement the set template presented in this chapter so that a linked list is used as the underlying data structure.

CHAPTER 14

INHERITANCE AND POLYMORPHISM

14.1 INTRODUCTION

Since the mid-1980s a style of programming known as Object-Oriented Programming (OOP) has been gaining momentum among developers as well as receiving increased attention from the popular computer press. The ideas of OOP are not new; indeed, OOP languages have been around for over 20 years. The recent advent of modern OOP languages (including C++), a better understanding of OOP techniques, as well as a need to address some issues involved in the *software crisis* (i.e., the ever increasing need to produce more complex software, with fewer errors, at a faster rate) have all led to OOP's current popularity.

The history of computer programming is a progression from total obsession with "thinking like the hardware works" to solving the problem "conceptually, in human terms." Higher-level languages have almost completely unshackled programmers from the tyranny of meeting the needs of specific hardware in order to get the job done. Assembly language was dominated by languages like FOR-TRAN, COBOL, and BASIC that allow programmers to think in more symbolic terms as is done in mathematics. Structured languages such as Pascal, Modula-2, Ada, and C arose adding sanity to the organization of the program's component parts. All of these aforementioned languages are known as *procedural* languages. Procedural languages accomplish their tasks by applying algorithms (procedures) to passive data. Data (e.g., the elements in an array) get modified (sorted) because an algorithm (a selection sort routine) is applied to them. The data have no choice but to be manipulated by whatever procedures the programmers wish to impose upon them.

As has been emphasized from chapter 10 on, OOP techniques view the situation from a different perspective. The problem to be solved involves a collection of real world or abstract *objects*. These objects can interact with each other and perform certain tasks. Instead of applying procedures to passive data as in the procedural paradigm, the data themselves contain procedures to modify themselves based on messages that other objects may send them. The methods of program design introduced in chapter 6 are not as useful in OOP. The overall solution to the problem is not envisioned as a hierarchical structure chart of functions and modules where a program is designed top-down through step-wise refinement. The problem is solved by identifying the components (objects) of the problem domain and determining how these components interact and are related. OOP takes a bottom-up approach to development. The correct specification of the details of the objects that make up the system allows the overall structure of the system to evolve into the final solution. Object relationships are emphasized over functional decomposition. The OOP paradigm appears well suited for large projects that must change over time; that is, the prime players cursed by the software crisis.

It is generally accepted that the following concepts are required for OOP: *abstract data types, inheritance,* and *polymorphism.* ADTs have been emphasized since chapter 10. Other non-OOP languages such as Modula-2 and Ada have provisions for ADTs. Inheritance and runtime polymorphism extend ADTs to allow new ADTs to be created from old ones. The method of creation allows old code to be reused in new ways, without modifying the old code itself. Such a development process, when mastered, produces software that is more functional, has fewer errors, and has a faster development cycle.

14.2   INHERITANCE

Recall the stack template from chapter 12. Templates are handy for producing generic ADTs. A program can simultaneously manage a stack of `floats`, a stack of `Strings` (as defined in chapter 10), and a stack of database records, assuming each of these types has operators defined that the stack template class uses. A particular application may have a slightly different need. What if a *single* stack is required that must hold both `ints` and `Strings` at the same time? Fiddling with `typedefs` and templates alone will not solve the problem. Converting an `int` to a `char *` with `itoa()` and then to a `String` and using only a `String` stack would work in this particular situation, but in general this approach is not possible. (Consider a stack holding both `long doubles` and `structs` from an employee database at the same time.) It would be nice to be able to classify `ints` and `Strings` as related types inasmuch as they should be compatible enough to be stored in the same stack without any additional programmer manipulation required to access them.

C++ provides a means by which a class can be extended by means of *inheritance.* A new class can be created that has the characteristics of another class but with additional data or functionality. Two different classes may be treated the same way under certain circumstances if they are derived from a common class. C++ contains many features for building class hierarchies through inheritance that are beyond the scope of this text. What follows in the rest of this chapter serves only as an introduction to inheritance. It shows the most likely way an inheritance tree would be constructed and even contains an example of *multiple* inheritance. The discussion that follows does not scratch the surface as far as the options available to the C++ programmer, there are many options that are very flexible. Refer to *The Annotated C++ Reference Manual* by Margaret Ellis and Bjarne Stroustrup for an exciting journey into the many complex possibilities provided by the C++ language.

The following code declares a class `Block`:

```
class Block {
protected:
    int b1;
    float b2;
public:
    Block();
    int manipulate(int);
};
```

As discussed in chapter 8, `Block` is now a programmer-defined type. As seen in chapter 11, operators can be defined for `Block` so that it looks similar to a primitive data type. The new reserved word `protected` is used in the place of the default `private` specifier. The data elements b1 and b2 are still invisible to entities outside of the class Block (just like being private), but the protected specifier is needed for *class derivation* to work correctly. Another class, Brick, can be created that is based on the existing class Block:

```
class Brick: public Block {
    char b3;
public:
    Brick();
    float rearrange(char x, float y);
        b3 = x;
        b2 = y;   //  member b2 is inherited from Block
    }
};
```

Brick is being derived *publicly* from Block; this means that all of Block's protected and public data are visible to Brick (hence the need to use protected in Block). Class Brick also adds an additional data element, b3, and a new public member function, Brick::rearrange(). The data elements b1 and b2 and member function Block::manipulate() are also a part of Brick because Brick inherits *all* of Block's properties (data and member functions). If the public specifier is missing from the first line of Brick's definition, the default inheritance is private which means none of Block's data and member functions (except the public members) can be accessed by an object of class Brick. For our purposes, public derivation will be the most useful approach. Consider:

```
class Block {
protected:
    int b1;
    float b2;
public:
    Block(int a, float b): b1(a), b2(y) {}
    int manipulate(int);
};
class Brick: Block {  //  Default is private derivation
    char b3;
public:
    Brick(float x, char y): Block(10, x), b3(y) {}
    float rearrange(int x, float y) {
        b3 = x;
        y = b1;  //  Illegal, Block::b1 is not accessible
    }
};
```

The usual process is to make normally private data members protected if there is a chance a class might become a *base* class and to use public inheritance in most situations.

The public inheritance process creates an *is a* relationship between the *derived class* (child class) and the *base class* (parent class). The derived class is a specialization of the base class. In this case a Brick is a Block. The relationship is not reciprocal, however: a Block is *not* a Brick since Brick has added features that do not exist in an object of class Block. Figure 14.1 shows the relationship between the Block class and Brick class in a class hierarchy diagram.

When a derived class declares a member function with the same name as a member function in the base class, the derived class's member function overrides that function from the base class. For example:

```
enum Color { red, green, blue, yellow, orange, purple };

class Fruit {
protected:
    Color color;
```

```
public:
        Fruit(Color c): color(c) {}
        void show_name() { cout << "Fruit"; }
};
class Apple: public Fruit {
public:
        Apple(Color c): Fruit(c) {}
        void show_name() { cout << "Apple"; }
        void extended_show_name() {
                //   Calls Apple's show_name()
                show_name();
                cout << " is a ";
                //   Calls the base class's
                //   show_name() member
                Fruit::show_name();
                cout << '\n';
        }
};
class Banana: public Fruit {
public:
        Banana():
        Fruit(yellow) {}
        //   show_name not redefined here...
};
class Orange: public Fruit {
public:
        Orange():
        Fruit(orange) {}
        void show_name() { cout << "Orange"; }
};
class Macintosh: public Apple {
public:
        Macintosh(): Apple(red) {}
        void show_name() { cout << "Macintosh"; }
};
class Navel: public Orange{
public:
        Navel() {}
        //   show_name() not redefined here
};

class Valencia: public Orange {
public:
        Valencia() {}
        void show_name() {
                cout << "A Valencia is an ";
                Orange::show_name();
        }
};

Fruit  f = 450;
Apple  a = 122;
Macintosh m;
Banana b = 399;
Orange oran(55);
Navel nav = 20;
Valencia v;
```

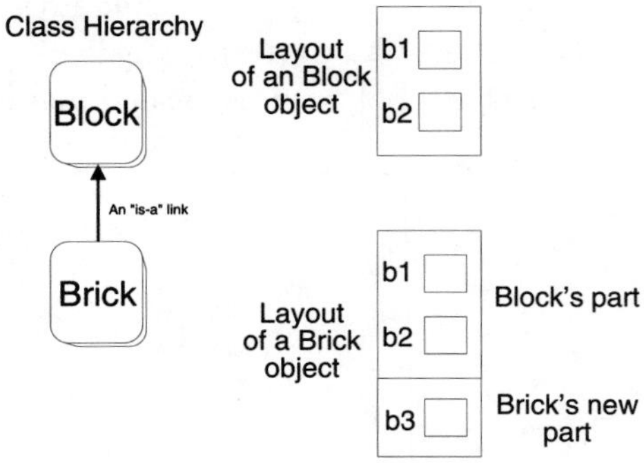

Class Inheritance
Figure 14.1

A call to the base class's constructor is placed *before* the body of the constructor as shown here. The Apple constructor evokes the constructor of Fruit with the color argument of red. In the above `Block` and `Brick` classes, `Brick::Brick()` called `Block::Block()` in its initialization list.

The call `f.show_name()` would print "Fruit," and the call `a.show_name()` would print "Apple." The call `b.show_name()` would print "Fruit," since a `Banana` object just uses the base class's function. `m.show_name()` will print "Macintosh." The call `a.extended_show_name()` would print "Apple is a Fruit." This function calls `Fruit::show_name()` instead of printing the literal string "Fruit." This makes the `Fruit` class responsible for what is displayed in its behalf. If, in the future, the programmer responsible for maintaining the `Fruit` class determines that "Tangy, aromatic, edible vegetation" should be displayed instead of "Fruit," then no other classes need to be touched for this enhancement to propagate through the hierarchy. In a practical problem with hundreds of classes, this ability to localize responsibilities that can have far reaching effects greatly simplifies the task at hand.

Notice that m and v do not need to be initialized since they provide constants to their base class constructors. The inheritance hierarchy is shown in figure 14.2.

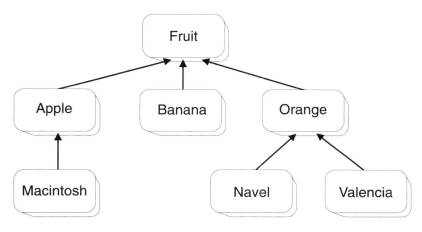

The Fruit Class Hierarchy
Figure 14.2

Exploiting the *is a* relationship can be valuable to programmers. A derived class object is automatically converted into a base class object across assignment. Figure 14.3 shows how the assignment is performed for `Block` and `Brick` objects as defined above. A reference to a derived class is also automatically converted to a reference to its base class. A pointer to a derived class can always be treated as a pointer to a base class. If a function expects a `Fruit` object parameter:

```
void peel(Fruit f);
```

an object of any class derived publicly from `Fruit` can be passed to the function, and it will process the object correctly. The call

```
peel(a);
```

works fine because an `Apple` object is everything a `Fruit` is, plus a little extra. The public members of `Fruit` that `peel()` would access are still present in the `Apple` class.

Recall how constructor initialization lists were used in chapter 10. Constructors are required to have initialization lists if (1) the class being constructed contains a member that has its own constructor, and (2) that member does not have a default constructor (that is, all of its constructors require at least one argument). The initialization list is required because the member object (as well

// Object definitions

Block blk(3, 1.2);
Brick brk(2.5, 'E');

// Reassignment of Block
// object from Brick object

blk = brk;

// Reassignment of Brick
// object from Block object

brk = blk; // Illegal!

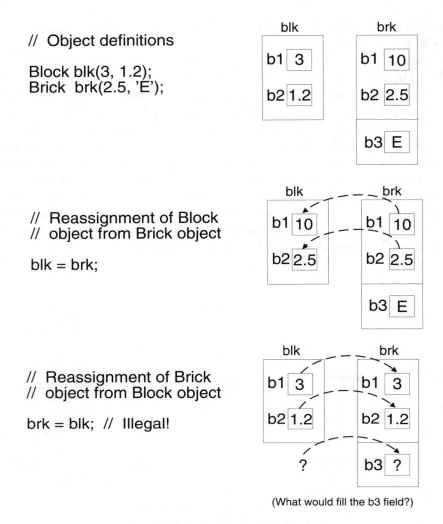

(What would fill the b3 field?)

Derived-base Class Assignment
Figure 14.3

as other data members the class might contain) must be created and initialized properly before the body of the constructor is performed. Similarly, the constructor for a base class must be called in the initialization list of a derived class's constructor if the base class has no default constructor. An object of the derived class must have all of its components constructed properly before the body of its constructor is performed. The body of the derived class's constructor is not executed until the space for the entire object (including the base class parts and the new derived class parts) has been allocated. Since this memory allocation might depend on activities carried out in the creation of the base class's portion of the derived class, the base class's constructor must be called before the constructor for the derived class is defined. A derived class inherits all of its base class's components, and these components must be initialized in the initialization list. Consider the following classes:

```
class W {
     //  Data members here...
public:
     W(int);  //  Constructor requires int arg
     //  Other member functions follow...
};
```

```
class X {
protected:
      W w;    //  Contains a W member
      //  Other data members follow...
public:
      X(int, int);
      //  Other member functions follow...
};
class Y: public X {
protected:
      //  Data members here...
public:
      Y(int);
      //  Other member functions follow...
};

class Z: public Y {
      W t;         //  Contains a W member
      //  Other data members follow...
public:
      Z(int, int);
      //  Other member functions follow...
};
```

Class Z contains a W object as a member. Y is derived from X, and X contains a W member. All of the classes define constructors; therefore, the compiler will not generate a default constructor for any of the classes. Observe the way the constructor implementations are written:

```
//  No members have constructors (other
//  than possibly default constructors)
W::W(int a) {
      /*  Whatever needs to be done  */
}

//  The w member object (of class W)
//  must be initialized
X::X(int a, int b): w(a) {
      /*Whatever needs to be done*/
}
//  Base class constructor must be called
//  so the X part of Y
//  is properly initialized
Y::Y(int a): X(a, 5) {
/*  Whatever needs to be done  */
}
//  Base class and member constructors must be
//  called:
//  the Y part of Z must be initialized and
//  the t member object (of class W) must
//  also be initialized
//  before the body of the constructor
Z::Z(int a, int b): Y(a), t(b) {
      /*  Whatever needs to be done  */
}
```

The member names are used to initialize member objects, and the class names are used to call base class constructors that require arguments.

Figure 14.4 shows a block diagram of the objects involved as well as the class hierarchy.

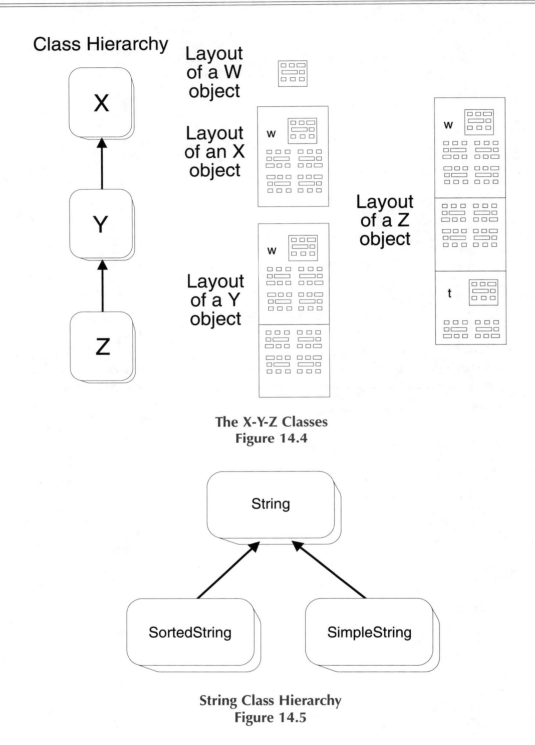

The X-Y-Z Classes
Figure 14.4

String Class Hierarchy
Figure 14.5

14.3   EXTENDING THE STRING CLASS

The `String` class introduced in chapter 11 will be customized to implement some special purpose strings. Figure 14.5 illustrates the desired inheritance hierarchy. For the derivations to work properly, the `String` class interface should be modified to make the previously `private` members `protected`. (The standard approach would have been to use the `protected` specifier from the start; however, such details were omitted intentionally from chapter 11 for the sake of simplicity.) Two new String-like classes will be made. The first, called a SortedString, maintains its contents in ASCII order, no matter how it is initialized or assigned. The second string class, SimpleString, does not allow any characters other than 'A'–'Z', 'a'–'z', and '0'–'9' to be stored. Any special characters that might be included in a string (String or char *) that is assigned to a SimpleString are replaced with the underscore character. For example:

```
SortedString s1, t1 = "bz%cya#x";   //   t1 is initialized to "#%abcxyz"
SimpleString s2, t2 = "bz%cya#x";   //   t2 is initialized to "bz_cya_x"
s1 = "BacCAb";      //   s1 is assigned "ABCabc"  (ASCII order)
s2 = "@#$E*&?";     //   s2 is assigned "___E___"
cin >> t1 >> s2;   // No matter how characters are entered, t1 is sorted
        and t2 is filtered
```

The source code follows:

```
//////////////////////////////////////////////////////////////////////////////
//   File new_str.h
//////////////////////////////////////////////////////////////////////////////

#ifndef _NEW_STR_H_
#define _NEW_STR_H_

#include "str.h"

class SortedString: public String {
protected:
     //   No new data added
     void sort();
public:
     SortedString(): String() {}            //   default constructor
     SortedString(const char *s): String(s) {  sort(); }
     SortedString(const SortedString &s): String(s.word) {  sort(); }
     SortedString(const String &s): String(s) {  sort(); }
     SortedString &operator=(const SortedString &);
     friend istream &operator>>(istream &, SortedString &);
};
class SimpleString: public String {
protected:
     // No new data
     void filter();
public:
     SimpleString(): String() {}
     SimpleString(const char *s): String(s) {  filter(); }
     SimpleString(const SimpleString &s): String(s.word) {  filter(); }
     SimpleString(const String &s): String(s) {  filter(); }
     SimpleString &operator=(const SimpleString &);
     friend istream &operator>>(istream &, SimpleString &);
};

#endif
```

Program 14.1a

Each new class has a protected member function that performs the necessary modification to the word member char * inherited from the String class. SortedString::sort() sorts the string, and SimpleString::filter() replaces all special characters with underscores. Observe that the constructors make use of the corresponding base class constructors to allocate space and copy the string, and then they call their specialized protected member function to modify the string member. The implementation of the other member functions are in new_str.cpp:

```
////////////////////////////////////////////////////////////////////////
//   File new_str.cpp
////////////////////////////////////////////////////////////////////////

#include "new_str.h"
#include <string.h>
#include <ctype.h>

void SortedString::sort() {
        //   Sort contents
        int i, j, length = strlen(word);
        char temp;
        for ( i = 0;   i < length - 1;   i++ )
            for ( j = i + 1;   j < length; j++ )
                if ( word[i] > word[j] ) {
                        temp    = word[i];
                        word[i] = word[j];
                        word[j] = temp;
                }
}

SortedString &SortedString::operator=(const SortedString &s) {
        String::operator=(s);   //   Use base class assignment
        return *this;
}

istream &operator>>(istream &is, SortedString &s) {
        char buffer[100];
        is >> buffer;
        s = buffer;
        return is;
}

void SimpleString::filter() {
        int i = 0;
        while ( word[i] != '\0' ) {   //   Loop until null byte found
            if ( !isalnum(word[i]) )
                    word[i] = '_';
            i++;
        }
}

SimpleString &SimpleString::operator=(const SimpleString &s) {
        String::operator=(s);   //   Use base class assignment
        return *this;
}

istream &operator>>(istream &is, SimpleString &s) {
        char buffer[100];
        is >> buffer;
        s = buffer;
        return is;
}
```

Program 14.1b

Since constructors are not inherited, they had to be rewritten (as is shown inline in the interface). Both derived classes used the appropriate base class constructors as is and then added the call to their protected member function for the final touches of the initializations. The protected members SortedString::sort() and SimpleString::filter() are new (not part of the String class) but do nothing out of the ordinary. Of the other String functions, some were rewritten in the derived classes, and some were left alone. Consider first the functions that were not touched. The member functions that were not redefined will work as expected with the specialized string classes. The `length()` and cast to `const char *` work just as well on ordered and filtered strings. All of the `friend` functions, except the overloaded extractor, were not modified. They are still available for use by `SortedString` and `SimpleString` objects because a `SortedString` object *is a* `String` and so is a `SimpleString` object. None of these `friend` operator functions modify the contents of the strings passed to them; therefore, they are safe to use with the derived classes. The extractor `operator<<()`, however, must read a string from the keyboard and assign it to a `String` (or derived class) object. The specialized strings must be processed properly, either sorted or filtered. Notice, however, how the extractors are written for the derived classes. Both look identical to each other and to the base class extractor. The key difference is the use of the assignment operator within each extractor. The statement

```
s = buffer;
```

appears in all three extractor definitions but means three different things, since each class has defined its own assignment operator. The assignment operator takes care of performing the correct copying action.

Speaking of the assignment operators, the two derived class `operator=()` functions look identical. Both simply call the base class assignment operator to deallocate, reallocate, and fill their `word` member. Neither use their special protected member functions to further process the strings. Why (or better, how) do they work? The secret is the type of the parameter that each expects. The case for the `SortedString` class will be explained; the reasoning is the same for the `SimpleString` class. The `SortedString` assignment operator expects a `const SortedString &` parameter. If a `SortedString` object is passed, nothing special is required, and the base class assignment function works fine. What if a `char *`, `String`, or `SimpleString` object is passed instead? The actual parameter to `SortedString::operator=()` does not match the formal parameter exactly; therefore, a conversion will need to be made. Fortunately, the `SortedString` class contains a constructor that can make a `SortedString` object out of a `char *` and a constructor that can make a `SortedString` object out of a `String` object. The actual parameter passed to `SortedString::operator=()` in either of these two cases will be a temporary `SortedString` object created by the respective constructor. How is a `SimpleString` object handled if it must be assigned to a `SortedString` object? A `SimpleString` *is a* `String`, so the inheritance relationship solves the problem easily.

The following `main()` can be used to test the new string classes:

```
//  Str-test.cpp

#include <iostream.h>
#include "new_str.h"


void main() {
    SortedString s1, t1 = "hello";
    SimpleString s2, t2 = "a@s#d$";

    cout << "Testing initialization " << t1 << ' ' << t2 << '\n';

    cout << "Enter two strings: ";
    cin >> s1 >> s2;
    cout << s1 << ' ' << s2 << '\n';

    cout << "Concatenating (general): " << (s1 + s2) << '\n';

    t1 = s1 + s2;
    cout << "Concatenating (sorted) : " << t1 << '\n';

    t2 = s1 + s2;
    cout << "Concatenating (simple) : " << t2 << '\n';
```

```
        s1 = t2;
        cout << s1 << ' ' << t2;
}
```

Program 14.1c

Notice that the concatenation function (`String::operator+()`) merely concatenates two general strings. If the result is assigned to a specialized string, then the sorting or filtering will occur across the assignment, not before the concatenation is performed.

14.4 PRIVATE INHERITANCE

Why would the *is a* relationship made possible through `public` inheritance ever need to be abandoned, and why might `private` derivation be used instead? Consider a remake of the `Stack<T>` template class:

```
//////////////////////////////////////////////////////////////////////////
//  File stk.tpl
//   A stack ADT template derived from the range checking, dynamically
//   allocated Array template
//////////////////////////////////////////////////////////////////////////
#ifndef _STK_TPL_  // Prevent multiple inclusion
#define _STK_TPL_

#include "array.tpl"  //  Will derive from an Array<T>

const int MAXSTACK = 100;

template <class T>
class Stack: private Array<T> {
    int top;
public:
    Stack(int sz = MAXSTACK): Array<T>(sz), top(-1) {}
    void reset() { top = -1; }
    int push(const T &);
    int pop(T &);
    int topofstack(T &);
};

template <class T>
int Stack<T>::push(const T &s) {
    if ( top < size - 1 )
        vector[++top] = s;  //  vector member inherited from Array<T>
    else
        return 0;
    return 1;
}

template <class T>
int Stack<T>::pop(T &s) {
    if ( top >= 0 )
        s = vector[top--];
    else
        return 0;
    return 1;
}

template <class T>
int Stack<T>::topofstack(T &s) {
    if ( top >= 0 )
        s = vector[top];
    else
```

```
            return 0;
      return 1;
  }
#endif
```

Notice the `private` derivation. (Private derivation is the default, so the reserved word `private` could have been omitted with the same results.) A `Stack` is *not* an `Array`, at least not as far as client modules are concerned. Elements within `Array` objects can be accessed freely with the subscript operator. A `Stack` object, due to the private inheritance, does not grant access to the public members of its base class; therefore, it is impossible to use `operator[]` on a `Stack` object. The member functions of `Stack` objects have access to the subscript operator, of course. The overall effect is the same as the first `Stack<T>` template provided in chapter 12. Assume the `list` element of the original `Stack<T>` is replaced by `Array<T> list;` instead of `T list[maxstack];`. Consider the differences:

- In the original `Stack<T>` template, an `Array<T>` object called `list` is a private data member. The `Stack<T>` member functions access the `list` member through the `Array<T>`'s public interface. Client code cannot access the `list` member because it is private to a `Stack<T>` object.
- In the inheritance example, the `Stack<T>` class is derived from the `Array<T>` class. Since the inheritance is private, the `Stack<T>` member functions have access to the `Array<T>` part of itself only though the public interface of the `Array<T>` class. Client code cannot access the `Array<T>` part at all, not even through the public interface of the `Array<T>` class.

In the first version, an `Array<T>` object is one member of a `Stack<T>` object. In the second version, a `Stack<T>` object is an `Array<T>` object with some components added and all the interface elements of an `Array<T>` object removed. The net effect is the same, so which approach is better? The question is somewhat philosophical. For most programming situations, public inheritance makes the most sense. It creates *is a* relationships between classes and allows sophisticated class hierarchies to be built. The behavior of a particular class in the hierarchy can often be predicted naturally based upon the class's position within the inheritance tree. If the class's base class is well understood, and some knowledge is available about the behavior of classes derived from it, even less than seasoned object-oriented programmers can usually determine its capabilities. Since private class derivation is not as common, many programmers would prefer the first version, thus avoiding the private inheritance.

If the `private` specifier is replaced with `public`, then client code can treat a `Stack<T>` as if it were an `Array<T>`. Stacks could be passed to functions expecting array parameters, and stack objects could be assigned to arrays. The bad news is that the stack template wouldn't be a very good ADT, since the following code is also possible:

```
Stack<int> stk;
stk.push(3); //  O.k.
stk[4] = 11; //  Not good
```

which violates the last-in, first-out restriction. This is only natural, since in the case of public inheritance, a stack is an array, and an array is a random access structure. It follows that a stack would also be a random access structure.

14.5 VIRTUAL FUNCTIONS AND TRUE POLYMORPHISM

Reconsider the `Fruit` class hierarchy described above. The following section of code:

```
Apple apple(green);
Macintosh mac;
apple.extended_show_name();
mac.extended_show_name();
```

prints

```
Apple is a Fruit
Apple is a Fruit
```

Obviously, the `show_name()` function called within the `extended_show_name()` function is always the `Apple` version, even if it is used by a `Macintosh` object. Since `extended_show_name()` is defined as a member of `Apple`, this behavior makes sense. It would be convenient if somehow the `show_name()` function call within `Apple::extended_show_name()` could use `Macintosh::show_name()` when used with a `Macintosh` object and `Apple::show_name()` when used with an `Apple` object. If this could be done, the second line displayed above would be

```
Macintosh is a Fruit
```

which is the desired result.

Consider the following array:

```
Fruit *f[4];
```

Here `f` is an array of pointers to `Fruit`. If an array of `Fruit` were used here instead of an array of pointers to `Fruit`, the following example would not work, since the compiler would merely allocate space for `Fruit` objects which are likely smaller than their derived objects (since derived classes can add data elements and so require more storage space). Pointers are all the same size, no matter what type of object they reference, so the following is possible:

```
Fruit *f[4];
Apple ap = red;
Fruit fr = green;
Banana ba;
Navel nav;
f[0] = &ap;   f[1] = &fr;   f[2] = &ba;   f[3] = &nav;
```

The array `f` is an array of pointers to `Fruit` objects. Since an `Apple` object is a `Fruit`, and a `Banana` object is also a `Fruit`, their pointers can be stored in the `Fruit` pointer array. The following produces undesirable results, however:

```
f[0]->show_name();   //   Prints "Fruit"
f[1]->show_name();   //   Prints "Fruit"
f[2]->show_name();   //   Prints "Fruit"
f[3]->show_name();   //   Prints "Fruit"
```

The middle two effects are expected (remember the `Banana` class did not override `Fruit`'s `show_name()` member function); it would be nice if `f[0]->show_name()` printed "Apple" since it is an `Apple` object. Also, `f[3]->show_name()` should print "Navel." As far as the compiler is concerned, `f` is an array of `Fruit` pointers; thus `Fruit::show_name()` is called in each instance. This choice of which function to use is made by the compiler at compile-time based on the declared type of the object. When this decision is made at compile-time, the process is known as *static binding* (or *early binding*). All the functions presented thus far have used static binding. The following will force the correct result:

```
((Apple *)f[0])->show_name();   // Prints "Apple"
```

since `f[0]` will be treated as an `Apple` pointer instead of the generic `Fruit` pointer, but it requires the programmer to know what type of object is in that position. In general, it is an impossible task. Consider the programmer's dilemma after the following code is executed:

```
i = random(4);   //   i is 0, 1, 2, or 3
j = random(4);   //   j is 0, 1, 2, or 3
```

```
Fruit *temp = f[i];
f[i] = f[j];
f[j] = temp;
f[0]->show_name();   // Good luck!
```

Here the random() function from <stdlib.h> is used to do a random shuffle of the array. Now the programmer has no idea where the Apple pointer went, if it actually moved at all. A similar problem arises with the following code that is perfectly legal:

```
Fruit *p;
int choice;
cin >> choice;
if ( choice == 1 )
    p = new Apple;
else
    p = new Navel;
p->show_name();
delete p;
```

Here, p is a Fruit pointer, but it can point to any instance of a class derived from Fruit—after all an Apple is a Fruit. In both of these cases, the compiler must generate code that checks at runtime what type of object is stored there and then calls the correct function. This process of associating the call of a function with the correct function is called *dynamic binding* (also known as *late binding*). C++ accomplishes dynamic binding through virtual functions. The following redefinition of the Fruit class provides the answer:

```
class Fruit {
protected:
    Color color;
public:
    Fruit(Color c): color(c) {}
    virtual void show_name() { cout << "Fruit"; }
};
```

The code now works:

```
Fruit *f[4];
Apple ap  = red;
Fruit fr  = green;
Banana ba;
Navel nav;
f[0] = &ap;   f[1] = &fr;   f[2] = &ba;   f[3] = &nav;
f[0]->show_name();   //  Prints "Apple"
f[1]->show_name();   //  Prints "Fruit"
f[2]->show_name();   //  Prints "Fruit"
f[3]->show_name();   //  Prints "Navel"
```

The decision about which show_name() function to call is not made by the compiler. The virtual specifier, when used to qualify a member function of a base class, indicates that the function that is called is to be determined at runtime. It may be the function from that base class, or it may be an identically named function with identical parameters from one of its derived classes. The function that is actually called will be a member function from the class of the particular object being considered at the time. This postponement of the decision over which function to call leads to slightly slower execution speed. Instead of the compiler generating a direct call (through the address of the actual function) at compile-time, the executable program must obtain the address of the function from a table accessed through a secret (i.e., not seen by the programmer) pointer stored by the object itself. When the program is executing, the function call will not cause a jump in the program to a new address (the code in the function body) right away; the function call causes the program to look up the address of the proper function to use based on a pointer stored in the object itself. The description of the process is more complicated than the process itself, as merely double indirection is involved instead of the single indirection used in a nonvirtual function call. Attempting the same effects through other means is no more efficient—there is no way around this slight runtime penalty. The actual slow down is usually negligible, and the benefits of runtime binding are immense. Programs of incredible power and flexibility can be built around virtual functions and dynamic binding. This ability to interact with different objects in a uniform manner achieving different results based upon the characteristics of the object is known as *polymorphism*. Polymorphism allows uniform interfaces to be built around diverse classes. All `Fruit` objects know how to show themselves; just tell a `Fruit` object to show itself, and it will perform the right activity regardless of whether it is a `Fruit`, `Apple`, `Banana`, `Navel`, or any object of any class derived ultimately from `Fruit`.

The virtual function mechanism is only applied through pointers to objects, not to objects themselves. The preferred effect with `Apple::extended_show_name()` is now possible, but pointers must be used:

```
Apple *apple = new Apple(green);
Macintosh *mac = new Macintosh;
apple->extended_show_name();
mac->extended_show_name();
delete apple;
delete mac;
```

With this code,

```
Apple is a Fruit
Macintosh is a Fruit
```

is displayed.

The `virtual` specifier may be used again in the derived classes to emphasize that the function is virtual, but its reuse is not required. If a function with an identical *signature* (exactly the same name and types of parameters) to a virtual function in a base class is redefined in a derived class, then the derived class function will automatically be virtual also.

Inheritance and polymorphism can be used to implement the needed integer/string stack module. Program 14.2 implements the generic stack based on the hierarchy shown in figure 14.6.

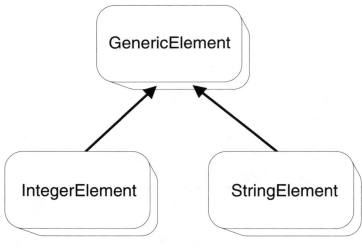

General Types Hierarchy
Figure 14.6.

```
/////////////////////////////////////////////////
//   DualStak.cpp
/////////////////////////////////////////////////
#include <iostream.h>
#include <ctype.h>
#include "str.h"
#include "stack.tpl"
class GenericElement {
     //  No data
public:
     virtual void id() = 0; //  Pure virtual function
     virtual ~GenericElement() { }
};

class IntegerElement: public GenericElement {
     int data;
public:
     IntegerElement(): data(0) {}
     IntegerElement(int x): data(x) {}
     ~IntegerElement() {  cout << "Destroying an integer.\n";  }
     virtual void id() {  cout << data;  }
     operator int()  {  return data;  }
     friend ostream &operator<<(ostream &, const IntegerElement &);
};
class StringElement: public GenericElement {
     String data;
public:
     StringElement(const String &s): data(s) {}
     ~StringElement() {  cout << "Destroying a string.\n";  }
     virtual void id() {  cout << data;  }
     operator String() {  return data;  }
     friend ostream &operator<<(ostream &, const StringElement &);
};

ostream &operator<<(ostream &os, const StringElement &s) {
     os << s.data;
     return os;
}

ostream &operator<<(ostream &os, const IntegerElement &i) {
     os << i.data;
     return os;
}

Stack<GenericElement *> stack;

void main() {
     int done = 0, i_value;
     String s_value;
     GenericElement *gep;
     char ch;
     do {
          cout << "Enter command: ";
          cin  >> ch;
          switch ( toupper(ch) ) {
               case 'I':
                    cin >> ch;
                    switch ( toupper(ch) ) {
                         case 'I':
                              cin >> i_value;
                              gep = new IntegerElement(i_value);
                              break;
```

```
                          case 'S':
                                  cin >> s_value;
                                  gep = new StringElement(s_value);
                                  break;
                          }
                          if ( !stack.push(gep) )
                               cout << "Stack full!\n";
                          break;
                  case 'D':
                          if ( stack.pop(gep) ) {
                               gep->id();
                               cout << '\n';
                               delete gep;
                          }
                          else
                               cout << "Stack empty!\n";
                          break;
                  case 'Q':
                          done = 1;
                          break;
                          default:
                          //   Clear input stream of bad command
                          cin.clear();
                          while ( cin.get() != '\n' )
                                  ;
                          cin.clear();
          }
     } while ( !done );
}
```

Program 14.2

Now the stack can hold both `ints` (Integers) and `Strings` at the same time. Some aspects of the integer/string stack program warrant comment. The base class, `GenericElement`, has a `virtual` function called `GenericElement::id()` that is set equal to zero. This makes `GenericElement::id()` a *pure* virtual function. A class that contains at least one pure virtual function is called an *abstract base class*. No objects of an abstract base class may be declared; its sole purpose is to be used as a base class from which other classes may be derived. The `GenericElement` class has a virtual destructor. The standard rule to follow is every base class that contains a virtual function should declare a virtual destructor. In this program, the statement

```
    delete gep;
```

calls a destructor, if one is available, but which? `gep` is a pointer to a `GenericElement` object; thus, if `GenericElement::~GenericElement()` is nonvirtual, only the base class destructor will be called. If `gep` were allocated as a `StringElement` pointer with `new`, `StringElement`'s destructor would not be invoked. Without `StringElement`'s destructor being called, the `data` member's destructor is not called either. Since `data` is a `String`, the space allocated for its character buffer is not deallocated, and a serious memory leak would be present. Making the base class's constructor virtual solves the problem, since the correct destructor is then selected at runtime. The destructors for `IntegerElement` and `StringElement` do nothing but print messages indicating that the objects are being destroyed. Placing such messages inside constructors and destructors can often be used to understand their behaviors. In this case, remove the `virtual` specifier from the base class destructor and observe the consequences. In the above `Fruit` example where p was directed to point to either an `Apple` object or a `Navel` object (depending on the user's choice) allocated by `new`, the final statement, `delete p;`, would cause problems if destructors were involved that were not `virtual`, and the individual classes within the hierarchy were of different sizes or their destructors carried out significantly different activities.

OOP promotes *software reuse*. Software reuse is the ability to incorporate existing code as is into new programs. Instead of writing new code from scratch, existing code can be extended to do new things. C++'s inheritance feature allows new functionality to be added to existing classes. If a class is designed properly, it can be used as a base class for many other classes. Each of these new derived classes can (and should) add functionality to the original base class. The work done by the existing base class can be left untouched; the derived classes will inherit this functionality of the base class. The programmer does not need to modify existing code to meet the needs of the new derived class as much as simply writing original code to add features above and beyond what the base class provides. The luxury of not having to rewrite the old code to fit the new class also precludes the production of errors that would naturally occur even if the old code were carefully rewritten to fit the new situation. The old code works as is in the new situation; the programmer's task is to write new code that adds the new features and to make sure that the new code works correctly. The next series of examples emphasize code reuse through inheritance.

Exercises

1. What three characteristics must a language possess to be considered object-oriented by most authorities?

2. How does a procedural language differ from an OOP language?

3. What exactly is an *object*?

4. How is inheritance implemented in C++?

5. How can a base class's member function be called from within a derived class, even though the derived class contains an identical member function?

6. What is the purpose of the `protected` specifier within a class definition?

7. What are the consequences of omitting the `public` specifier before the base class name when defining a derived class?

8. What is the difference between static binding and dynamic binding of function calls?

9. What is a `virtual` function, and what does it allow?

10. Why should destructors be specified as `virtual` in classes containing `virtual` functions?

11. What is a pure virtual function? How is one specified, and what is its effect?

12. What is an abstract base class?

14.6   EXAMPLE PROGRAM

The programming example in this section consists of four programs spread over 16 files. A basic class is devised, and then more sophisticated classes are built upon this initial class using class components and inheritance.

Consider the first two files:

```
///////////////////////////////////////////////////////////////
//   cell.h
///////////////////////////////////////////////////////////////

#ifndef _CELL_H_
#define _CELL_H_

enum Status { inactive, active };

class Cell {
protected:
    Status status;
public:
    Cell(Status = inactive);
    virtual ~Cell();
    virtual void draw() = 0;
    void activate(Status);
    virtual int width() = 0;
};

#endif
```

Program 14.3a

```
///////////////////////////////////////////////////////////////////////
//   cell.cpp
///////////////////////////////////////////////////////////////////////

#include "cell.h"

Cell::Cell(Status _stat): status(_stat) { }

Cell::~Cell() {}

void Cell::activate(Status s) {   status = s; }
```

Program 14.3b

The `Cell` class is an abstract base class. It is illegal to define or attempt to use a `Cell` object. The sole purpose for the `Cell` class within the program is to serve as a base class for other classes. In this case, the class `CharCell` is derived from Cell.

```
///////////////////////////////////////////////////////////////////////
//   charcell.h
///////////////////////////////////////////////////////////////////////

#ifndef _CHARCELL_H_
#define _CHARCELL_H_

#include "cell.h"

const char empty = ' ';
class CharCell: public Cell {
    static int wide;
    char ch;
public:
    CharCell(char = empty, Status = inactive);
    CharCell(const CharCell &s): ch(s.ch) {}
    CharCell &operator=(const CharCell &s) { ch = s.ch;   return *this; }
    operator char() { return ch; }
```

```
        virtual void draw();
        virtual int  width() { return wide; }
};

#endif
```

Program 14.3c

```
///////////////////////////////////////////////////////////////////////////
//   charcell.cpp
///////////////////////////////////////////////////////////////////////////

#include "charcell.h"
#include <iostream.h>

CharCell::CharCell(char _ch, Status _stat): Cell(_stat), ch(_ch) {}

void CharCell::draw() {
    if ( status == inactive )
        cout << ' ' << ch << ' ';
    else
        cout << '>' << ch << '<';
}

int CharCell::wide = 1;
```

Program 14.3d

A CharCell object encapsulates a char member. Supposedly, IntCells, FloatCells, etc. could be derived from Cell, if necessary. The examples here use only CharCells. A CharCell object can assume either an active or inactive state, can be displayed, and can be converted to a standard character. The printed width of a CharCell object is one (a single character), and this value is stored in a static data member. When a member of a class is specified as static, all instances of that class share that member; thus, if several CharCells are defined, changing the CharCell::wide member of one of the objects will change the wide field in all of the other CharCell objects also. Since the space that they occupy is not located in any particular object, static members must be initialized differently from normal, non-static members. Allocating space for a CharCell object (auto, extern, or from the heap) does not allocate space for the CharCell::wide member, since this space is shared by all other CharCell objects that might be allocated. The statement

```
    int CharCell::wide = 1;
```

located outside of the body of the class interface definition allows the compiler to properly allocate memory for the static member. This initialization should be located in the implementation code (the .cpp file), not the interface code (the .h file). static members are useful for storing values that are common to all the objects of a class. Memory is not duplicated unnecessarily avoiding two problems: wasting memory and allowing possibly inconsistent values to be stored in two different objects. Since the member is shared by all objects of that class, it can be accessed (restricted by the same access rules of normal, non-static members) through the class name and scope resolution operator:

```
    class X {
    public:
        static int a;
    };
    X x_obj;
    x_obj.a = 10;    // Ok
    X::a = 12;       // Also ok, a is static
```

It is often useful to use a `static` class member as a counter. Initialized to zero at the start of the program, the `static` counter is incremented at each constructor call and decremented in the body of each destructor. When the program is through executing, the counter for each class can be checked to see if each constructor call was matched by exactly one destructor call. When dynamically allocating objects through pointers, this facility can be handy. If `Block::count`, a static counter for the `Block` class, is greater than zero at a point in the program where all the `Block` objects should have already been deallocated, then not all `Block` objects have actually been `deleted`, and a memory leak exists. If `Block::count` is negative, some pointers have been `deleted` more than once which is a serious problem that cannot be ignored. `Block::count` should be exactly zero to indicate that every `new` was eventually followed by a `delete`.

The `CharCell` class will be used in two-dimensional `Grid` objects:

```
///////////////////////////////////////////////////////////////////
//   File grid.h
///////////////////////////////////////////////////////////////////

#ifndef _GRID_H_
#define _GRID_H_

#include "array.tpl"
#include "charcell.h"

class Grid {
protected:
    Matrix<CharCell> grid;
public:
    Grid(int, int, char = empty);
    ~Grid();
    void display();
    void activate(int, int, Status);
};

#endif
```

Program 14.3e

```
///////////////////////////////////////////////////////////////////
//   grid.cpp
///////////////////////////////////////////////////////////////////
#include <iostream.h>
#include <iomanip.h>
#include "grid.h"

static void stars(int cols, int col_width) {
    cout << '+';
    for ( int c = 0;  c < cols;  c++ ) {
        cout << '-';
        for ( int i = 0; i < col_width;  i++ )
            cout << "-";
            cout << '-';
    }
    cout << "+\n";
}

Grid::Grid(int rows, int cols, char fill): grid(rows, cols, fill) {
    cout << "Constructing a grid object\n";
}
Grid::~Grid() {
    cout << "Destroying a grid object\n";
}
```

```
void Grid::display() {
    int r, c, columns = grid.cols_val(),
        column_width = grid[0][0].width();
    stars(columns, column_width);
    for ( r = 0;  r < grid.rows_val();  r++ ) {
        cout << '|'
        for ( c = 0;  c < columns;  c++ )
            grid[r][c].draw();
        cout << "|\n";
    }
    stars(columns, column_width);
}

void Grid::activate(int r, int c, Status s) {  grid[r][c].activate(s); }
```

Program 14.3f

```
//////////////////////////////////////////////////////////////////////////////
//  gridtest.cpp
//////////////////////////////////////////////////////////////////////////////

#include "grid.h"
#include <iostream.h>

//  Simple test of Grid class

void main() {
    Grid testboard(6, 5, '*');
    testboard.display();
    testboard.activate(2, 2, active);
    testboard.display();
}
```

Program 14.3g

The Grid class encapsulates a two-dimensional array of encapsulated characters based on the Matrix template presented in chapter 11. Observe that each cell in the grid is responsible for drawing itself. This allows activated cells to be displayed differently from deactivated cells.

Program 14.4 goes a step farther by defining a PlayingBoard class. This class will form a basis for several board games to be developed in the future.

```
//////////////////////////////////////////////////////////////////////////////
//  Contents of the file playbord.h
//////////////////////////////////////////////////////////////////////////////

#include "grid.h"

const char UP     = 'I',
           RIGHT  = 'K',
           DOWN   = 'M',
           LEFT   = 'J',
           ESCAPE = 'X',
           ACCEPT = 'L',
           ENTER  = '\n';

class PlayingBoard: public Grid {
protected:
    int state;
    int xpos, ypos;
    char prev_entry;
```

```
public:
    PlayingBoard(int, int);
    ~PlayingBoard();
    void load();
    CharCell &set(int, int);
    char get_move();
};
```

Program 14.4a

```
//////////////////////////////////////////////////////////////////////
//   Contents of the file playbord.cpp
//////////////////////////////////////////////////////////////////////

#include "playbord.h"
#include <iostream.h>
#include <ctype.h>
#include "charcell.h"

PlayingBoard::PlayingBoard(int rows, int cols):
                   Grid(rows, cols), state(0), xpos(0), ypos(0) { }

PlayingBoard::~PlayingBoard() {}


void PlayingBoard::load() {
    int r, c, character = 'A';
    for ( r = 0;   r < grid.rows_val();   r++ )
         for ( c = 0;   c < grid.cols_val();   c++ )
              grid[r][c] = character++;
}

char PlayingBoard::get_move() {
    int  done;
    char key_in;
    cout << "IJKM moves, X escapes.\n";
    do {
         cin >> key_in;
         key_in = toupper(key_in);
         done = 0;
         grid[ypos][xpos].activate(inactive);
         switch ( key_in ) {
              case UP:
                   ypos = (ypos > 0) ? ypos - 1 : ypos;
                   break;
              case DOWN:
                   ypos = (ypos < grid.rows_val() - 1) ? ypos + 1 : ypos;
                   break;
              case LEFT:
                   xpos = (xpos > 0) ? xpos - 1 : xpos;
                   break;
              case RIGHT:
                   xpos = (xpos < grid.cols_val() - 1) ? xpos + 1 : xpos;
                   break;
              case ESCAPE:
                   done = 1;
                   break;
              default:
                   prev_entry = set(ypos, xpos);
                   set(ypos, xpos) = key_in;
                   done = 1;
                   break;
         }
         grid[ypos][xpos].activate(active);
```

```
                    display();
            } while ( !done );
            return key_in;
      }


      CharCell &PlayingBoard::set(int r, int c) {
            return grid[r][c];
      }
```

Program 14.4b

```
////////////////////////////////////////////////////////////////////////////
//   Contents of file playmain.cpp:
////////////////////////////////////////////////////////////////////////////
#include "playbord.h"
void main() {
      PlayingBoard p(3, 5);
      p.set(0, 0) = 'A';
      p.set(0, 1) = 'B';
      p.set(0, 2) = 'C';
      p.set(0, 3) = 'D';
      p.set(0, 4) = 'E';
      p.set(1, 0) = 'F';
      p.set(1, 1) = 'W';
      p.set(1, 2) = 'X';
      p.set(1, 3) = 'Y';
      p.set(1, 4) = 'Z';
      p.display();
      while ( p.get_move() != ESCAPE )
            ;  //  Empty Body
}
```

Program 14.4c

The PlayingBoard class is derived from the Grid class; thus, all the features available to a Grid object are also available to a PlayingBoard object. A PlayingBoard object can display itself, since that option is available from the base class. Proper OOP protocol requires that an *is a* relationship exist between the derived and base classes. A derived class should add functionality to the base class, not decrease it. Also, a derived class should not radically modify one of the base class's member functions so as to lose the base function's original meaning or intent. The PlayingBoard::get_move() function allows the user to interact with the board using the keyboard to move around the grid. PlayingBoard's constructor merely passes the number of rows and columns to its base class's constructor. Grid::Grid() does the real work of construction (and much of the work was already accomplished in the template classes). The details of row, column access with range checking is taken care of by the Grid base class and the component template classes, so the author of the PlayingBoard class is free to concentrate on the new features of the derived class.

Two final classes are derived from the PlayingBoard class. The first, TTTBoard, is used in a Tic-Tac-Toe game. Program 14.5 contains all the necessary files.

```
//////////////////////////////////////////////////////
//  File  ttt.h
//////////////////////////////////////////////////////
#ifndef _TTT_H_
#define _TTT_H_
#include "playbord.h"

const int EX  =  1,
          OH  = -1,
          TIE =  2;
```

```
class TTTBoard: public PlayingBoard {
public:
    TTTBoard();
    int win();
    int get_move();
};
#endif
```

Program 14.5a

```
////////////////////////////////////////////////////////////////////////
//  Contents of file ttt.cpp:
////////////////////////////////////////////////////////////////////////
#include "ttt.h"
#include "charcell.h"
#include <iostream.h>

//  This function is local to this file (it's static)

inline static void beep() {
    cout << '\a';   //  Sound the bell
}

TTTBoard::TTTBoard(): PlayingBoard(3, 3) {
    state = EX;   //  X has first move
    xpos  = 1;    //  Position cursor in center square
    ypos  = 1;
    grid[ypos][xpos].activate(active);
}

int TTTBoard::get_move() {
    int move = PlayingBoard::get_move();
    if ( move &&  move != ESCAPE ) {
        if ( prev_entry == empty ) {  //  Move to empty space
            set(ypos,xpos) = (state == EX) ? 'X' : 'O';
            state = !state;   //  Other player's turn
        }
        else {    //  Attempt to overwrite existing move
            beep();   //  Alert player
            set(ypos, xpos) = prev_entry;  //  Restore old value
        }
        display();  //  Redraw board
    }
    return move;
}

int TTTBoard::win() {
    //  Check for win in rows
    for ( int i = 0;  i < grid.cols_val();  i++ ) {
        if ( set(i, 0) == 'X'  &&  set(i, 1) == 'X'
            &&  set(i, 2) == 'X' )
            return EX;
        if ( set(i, 0) == 'O'  &&  set(i, 1) == 'O'
            &&  set(i, 2) == 'O' )
            return OH;
    }
    //  Check for win in columns
    for ( i = 0;  i < grid.rows_val();  i++ ) {
        if ( set(0, i) == 'X'  &&  set(1, i) == 'X'
            &&  set(2, i) == 'X' )
            return EX;
        if ( set(0, i) == 'O'  &&  set(1, i) == 'O'
            &&  set(2, i) == 'O' )
            return OH;
    }
```

```
    //  Check for win in diagonals
    if ( set(0, 0) == 'X'  &&  set(1, 1) == 'X'  &&  set(2, 2) == 'X' )
        return EX;
    if ( set(0, 0) == 'O'  &&  set(1, 1) == 'O'  &&  set(2, 2) == 'O' )
        return OH;
    if ( set(0, 2) == 'X'  &&  set(1, 1) == 'X'  &&  set(2, 0) == 'X' )
        return EX;
    if ( set(0, 2) == 'O'  &&  set(1, 1) == 'O'  &&  set(2, 0) == 'O' )
        return OH;
    int j;
    for ( i = 0;  i < grid.rows_val();  i++ )
        for ( j = 0;  j < grid.cols_val();  j++ )
            if ( set(i, j) == empty )
                return 0;   //  No win or tie, continue game
    return TIE;    //  No more moves, no winner, tie game
}
```

Program 14.5b

```
////////////////////////////////////////////////////////////////////////////////
//  Contents of the file tttmain.cpp:
////////////////////////////////////////////////////////////////////////////////

#include "ttt.h"
#include <iostream.h>

void main() {
    TTTBoard ttt;
    int done = 0;
    ttt.display();
    do {
        done = (ttt.get_move() == ESCAPE);
        switch ( ttt.win() ) {
            case EX:
                cout << "X won!\n";  done = 1;
                break;
            case OH:
                cout << "O won!\n";  done = 1;
                break;
            case TIE:
                cout << "Tie game!\n";  done = 1;
                break;
        }
    } while ( !done );
}
```

Program 14.5c

In this Tic-Tac-Toe program, the TTTBoard class is derived from the PlayingBoard class. Figure 14.7 shows a typical Tic-Tac-Toe game in progress and figure 14.8 shows how it would be displayed by the program.

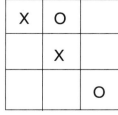

**A Tic-Tac-Toe
Game
Figure 14.7**

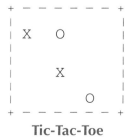

**Tic-Tac-Toe
Program Display
Figure 14.8**

TTTBoard inherits all of PlayingBoard's features and adds a function to check for a winning board configuration. PlayingBoard::get_move() is enhanced to do more, but notice how it is called directly within TTTBoard::get_move(). The code within TTTBoard::get_move() is not responsible for updating the position based upon user input. This repositioning is still done, but since the code to do it has already been written, it is merely *reused* within TTTBoard::get_move(). Overridden functions or virtual functions from base classes (or public functions from any other classes with name conflicts) can be called using the scope resolution operator (::). The programmer of TTTBoard::get_move() only adds code to alternate between player X and player O and to prevent choosing a square that is already occupied (PlayingBoard::get_move() is unconcerned about such activity). TTTBoard's constructor forms a 3 × 3 PlayingBoard and initializes the state and position variables within a TTTBoard object. A TTTBoard object uses the standard Grid::display() exactly as is.

As might be expected, the PlayingBoard class can be used to design many other game boards that can be represented as two-dimensional grids where a row, column position is important. Consider a variation of the 15 Puzzle as provided in program 14.6. The 15 Puzzle consists of 15 tiles arranged within a square wooden or plastic frame. The original game held tiles numbered one through 15. The blank position is to be moved by moving adjacent tiles into its position until the solution is achieved. Figure 14.9 shows the solution to the original game.

One variation of this game places portions of pictures on the tiles; when the tiles are arranged properly the complete picture is then visible in its proper form. Program 14.6 has figure 14.10 for a solution.

```
////////////////////////////////////////////////////////////////////////
//  Contents of the file puz15.h:
////////////////////////////////////////////////////////////////////////

#ifndef PUZ15_H
#define PUZ15_H
const int maxmoves = 500;

#include "playbord.h"

class Puzzle15: public PlayingBoard {
    char movelist[maxmoves];    //  movelist and topmove form a special
    int  topmove;               //  purpose stack to keep track of moves
    void make_solution();
    void scramble_puzzle();
    char do_move(char);
public:
    Puzzle15();
    char get_move();
    int win();
    void unscramble_puzzle();
};

#endif
```

Program 14.6a

```
////////////////////////////////////////////////////////////////////////
//  Contents of the file puz15.cpp:
////////////////////////////////////////////////////////////////////////

#include "puz15.h"
#include <stdlib.h>  //  For random(), randomize()
#include <iostream.h>
#include <ctype.h>

const int NO_MOVE = 0;
```

1	2	3	4
5	6	7	8
9	10	11	12
13	14	15	

A	B	C	D
E	F	G	H
I	J	K	L
M	N	O	

Figure 14.9 **Figure 14.10**

```
inline static void swap(CharCell &x, CharCell &y) {
    CharCell temp = x;
    x = y;
    y = temp;
}

void Puzzle15::make_solution() {
    grid[0][0] = 'A'; grid[0][1] = 'B'; grid[0][2] = 'C'; grid[0][3] = 'D';
    grid[1][0] = 'E'; grid[1][1] = 'F'; grid[1][2] = 'G'; grid[1][3] = 'H';
    grid[2][0] = 'I'; grid[2][1] = 'J'; grid[2][2] = 'K'; grid[2][3] = 'L';
    grid[3][0] = 'M'; grid[3][1] = 'N'; grid[3][2] = 'O'; grid[3][3] = empty;
}

char Puzzle15::do_move(char direction) {
    switch( direction ) {
        case UP   :
            if ( ypos < grid.rows_val() - 1 ) {
                swap(grid[ypos][xpos], grid[ypos + 1][xpos]);
                ypos++;   return UP;
            }
            break;
        case DOWN :
            if ( ypos > 0 ) {
                swap(grid[ypos][xpos], grid[ypos - 1][xpos]);
                ypos-;   return DOWN;
            }
            break;

        case LEFT :
            if ( xpos < grid.cols_val() - 1 ) {
                swap(grid[ypos][xpos], grid[ypos][xpos + 1]);
                xpos++;   return LEFT;
            }
            break;
        case RIGHT:
            if ( xpos > 0 ) {
                swap(grid[ypos][xpos], grid[ypos][xpos - 1]);
                xpos-;   return RIGHT;
            }
            break;
    }
    if ( direction == ESCAPE )
        return ESCAPE;
    else
        return NO_MOVE;
}
```

```
void Puzzle15::scramble_puzzle() {
    int movechoice[] = { UP, DOWN, LEFT, RIGHT }, move;
    for ( int i = 0;  i < maxmoves/10;  i++ ) {
        move = movechoice[random(4)];
        movelist[topmove++] = do_move(move);   //  Push move onto stack
           display();
    }
}

void Puzzle15::unscramble_puzzle() {
    while ( topmove ) {
        switch ( movelist[--topmove] ) {  // Pop previous move off the stack
            case UP:    do_move(DOWN);  break;
            case DOWN:  do_move(UP);    break;
            case LEFT:  do_move(RIGHT); break;
            case RIGHT: do_move(LEFT);  break;
        }
        display();
    }
}

Puzzle15::Puzzle15(): PlayingBoard(4, 4), topmove(0) {
    xpos = 3;  ypos = 3;
    randomize();  //  Seed random number generator
    make_solution();
    scramble_puzzle();
}

char Puzzle15::get_move() {
    char move;
    do {
        move = toupper(cin.get());
    } while ( move != UP  &&  move != RIGHT  &&  move != DOWN
            &&  move != LEFT  &&  move != ESCAPE );
    move = do_move(move);
    if ( move ) {
        movelist[topmove++] = move;
        display();
    }
    return move;
}

int Puzzle15::win() {
    return grid[0][0] == 'A'  &&  grid[0][1] == 'B'  &&  grid[0][2] == 'C'
        &&  grid[0][3] == 'D'  &&  grid[1][0] == 'E'  &&  grid[1][1] == 'F'
        &&  grid[1][2] == 'G'  &&  grid[1][3] == 'H'  &&  grid[2][0] == 'I'
        &&  grid[2][1] == 'J'  &&  grid[2][2] == 'K'  &&  grid[2][3] == 'L'
        &&  grid[3][0] == 'M'  &&  grid[3][1] == 'N'  &&  grid[3][2] == 'O'
        &&  grid[3][3] == empty;
}
```

Program 14.6b

```
///////////////////////////////////////////////////////////////////
//  Contents of the file P15MAIN.CPP:
///////////////////////////////////////////////////////////////////

#include "puz15.h"
#include <iostream.h>

void main() {
    Puzzle15 p;
    p.display();
    char move;
    int done = 0;
    while ( (move = p.get_move()) != ESCAPE  &&  !done )
```

```
            if ( p.win() ) {
                cout << "Winning configuration\n";
                done = 1;
            }
        if ( move == ESCAPE )
            p.unscramble_puzzle();
    }
```

Program 14.6c

Figure 14.11 shows how program 14.6 displays the image of the solution.

```
+ — — — — — — +
| A   B   C   D |
| E   F   G   H |
| I   J   K   L |
| M   N   O     |
+ — — — — — — +
```

The 15 Puzzle
Program Display
Figure 14.11

The `Puzzle15` class introduced in program 14.6 adds even greater functionality to the `PlayingBoard` class than does `TTTBoard`. `Puzzle15::get_move()` does not make use of `PlayingBoard::get_move()` at all. It still maintains the concept of user input with the keyboard, but the movement required is fundamentally different from that allowed by `PlayingBoard::get_move()`. In a `PlayingBoard` object, the cursor could be positioned anywhere on the board within `PlayingBoard::get_move()`. This action was also appropriate for `TTTBoard::get_move()` with the relatively minor restriction that a currently occupied square could not be chosen. `Puzzle15::get_move()`, however, only allows movement one square at a time, either up, down, left, or right. Whereas in Tic-Tac-Toe, if player X chooses the upper left corner, player O may choose the lower right corner, assuming it has not already been chosen. In the 15 Puzzle game, the blank space can only move to an adjacent position; thus, none of the previously written `get_move()` code was reused in `Puzzle15::get_move()`. Several powerful functions were added to create the initial solution, scramble the solution to make a puzzle for someone to play, and finally unscramble the puzzle to return to the solution configuration when the player gives up. A stack is used to remember user moves (plus the moves used when scrambling up the puzzle) so that the solution can be restored.

Even though several new features were added and a critical function from the base class was rewritten completely, the OOP trademark of software reuse is still dominant in the creation of the `Puzzle15` class. `PlayingBoard::display()` is used without modification, and a `Puzzle15` object also still has the same array access protection as class `Grid`.

The complete inheritance diagram is shown in figure 14.12.

14.7 Multiple Inheritance

Single inheritance occurs when a derived class has exactly one base class. All of the examples considered thus far have used single inheritance. Single inheritance is complicated enough for the beginning programmer; therefore, our look at *multiple inheritance* will only be cursory. A derived

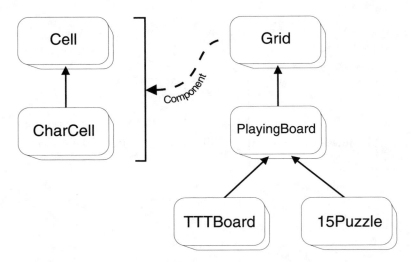

Game Board Inheritance Diagram
Figure 14.12

class can have more than one base class, in which case *multiple inheritance* is involved. The derived class possesses the characteristics of each of its base classes. The following example illustrates:

```
class B1 {
protected:
      int b1a;
};
class B2 {
protected:
      int b2a
};
class B3 {
protected:
      int b3a;
};
class D: public B1, public B2, public B3 {
protected:
      int da;
};
```

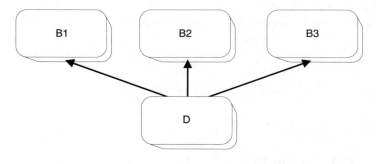

Multiple Inheritance
Figure 14.13

When an object of class D is defined, it will possess b1a, b2a, b3a, and da members. When derived publicly as specified above, it will also have access to B1's, B2's, and B3's `public` and `protected` members. Multiple inheritance is useful when the characteristics of two or more different classes must be blended into one class. In the example above, a D object *is a* B1, and a D object *is a* B2, and a D object *is a* B3. A D object could be passed to a function that expects a B2 object and that function should work correctly.

Consider a practical example. A graphical user interface (GUI) environment supports bit-mapped graphics windows on the screen. The Macintosh interface, Microsoft Windows/ Windows NT, Unix Motif/X Windows, and OS/2 Presentation Manager represent GUIs of this genre. A window is a rectangular portion of the screen in which graphics or text can be drawn. Several overlapping or tiled windows may be displayed simultaneously. A particular window has an (x,y) location (the location of the upper left corner of the window relative to the upper left corner of the screen itself in most cases) and a height and width. It also is drawn with a particular border style and background color. This information and more can be defined as data within a `Window` class. Calls to the operating system that manipulate windows on the screen can be called from member functions of this `Window` class. Thus, a physical window on the screen can be mapped to a `Window` object in a C++ program. Object-oriented programming is ideal for developing applications that must make use of a GUI.

A `Window` object all by itself is not very useful. Figure 14.14 shows a window that might be displayed by an application that manipulates mathematical graphs (see chapter 13). A programmer may have a `Graph` class that has no member functions that perform input or output. It would contain an adjacency matrix or adjacency list as data and have member functions that would allow node insertion and deletion, search for nodes, find shortest paths among nodes, etc. The programmer might create a new class:

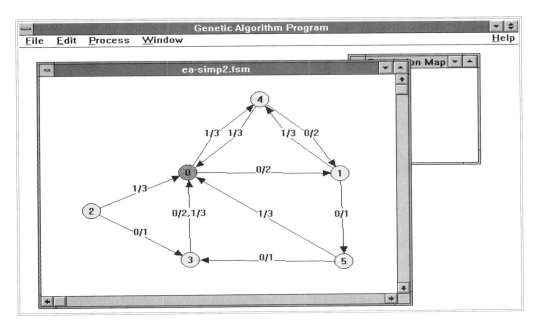

A Graph Window
Figure 14.14

```
class Window {
protected:
     int x, y, height, width;
     //   Other data
public:
     void resize(int new_h, int new_w);
     //   Lots of other member functions
};
class Graph {
protected:
     Matrix<int> adj_mat;
     //   Other data
public:
     void shortest_path(int start, int stop);
     //   Other member functions
};
class GraphWindow: public Window, public Graph {
     //   Details omitted
};

GraphWindow  wnd;
```

An object of this class could be manipulated as if it were a Graph—the shortest path between two nodes in a GraphWindow object could be found:

```
wnd.shortest_path(4, 13);
```

because these methods would have been inherited from the Graph base class. Since a GraphWindow object is also a Window, it can be moved, resized, iconized, etc. as if it were a normal window within that GUI:

```
wnd.resize(10, 24);
```

Notice that wnd, a GraphWindow object, can be treated as either a Window object or a Graph object as desired.

An alternate approach could accomplish the same effect without using multiple inheritance. GraphWindow could have been defined as

```
class GraphWindow: public Window {
     Graph grf;
     //   Other details omitted
};
```

In the former design, a GraphWindow object is a Window and it is also a Graph. Here, a GraphWindow object is a Window, but it has a Graph object embedded within it. The following is still acceptable:

```
wnd.resize(10, 24);
```

but the shortest path determination must be coded as:

```
wnd.grf.shortest_path(4, 13);
```

The design choice should be based on the application at hand. If it is more natural to treat a GraphWindow as if it were a Graph, then the first approach should be used. Many programmers would find the second approach to be better—a GraphWindow is a Window that contains a Graph object. They assert that multiple inheritance should be limited to programs in which its absence would lead to code that is obscure or otherwise unnatural looking. The first approach allows GraphWindow member code to access the protected members of its Graph component parts. The second approach renders protected members of the grf member invisible to Graph-Window's member functions. The following statement

```
adj_mat[2][3] = 0;
```

is legal within a member function of GraphWindow with the multiple inheritance version, but

```
grf.adj_mat[2][3] = 0;
```

cannot be used in a member function in the single inheritance version. In fact, if multiple inheritance is not used, and protected members of grf must be accessed by GraphWindow member functions, then the following declarations would need to be used:

```
class GraphWindow;  //  Forward declaration

class Graph {
protected:
      Matrix<int> adj_mat;
      //  Other data
public:
      void shortest_path(int start, int stop);
      //  Other member functions
      friend class GraphWindow;
      //  Now the private and protected members are accessible by GraphWindow
objects
   };
```

Now

```
grf.adj_mat[2][3] = 0;
```

can be used within a GraphWindow member function of the second version. Excessive use of friend classes leads to a design that undermines the ADT properties of individual classes. Since ADTs are used to reduce program complexity, and therefore reduce the number of programming errors, friend classes should be used sparingly.

Why avoid multiple inheritance unless it is necessary? It is more difficult to use multiple inheritance than single inheritance. Single inheritance is used much more frequently because it more often represents the relationships between types of objects within a problem domain. Common traits are more easily "factored out" using single inheritance. Consider figure 14.15 which diagrams the situation for which multiple inheritance seems perfect. In the natural, biological world, a child inherits characteristics from both parents when sexual reproduction occurs. It might seem "natural" under some circumstances for a Child class to be derived from both a Mother class and a Father class. Consider the ramifications under C++: this means that a Child object *is a* Mother and also *is a* Father object— at the same time! This is most likely not the modeling that the programmer desired! Multiple inheritance should not be forced, even when it seems "natural" to use it.

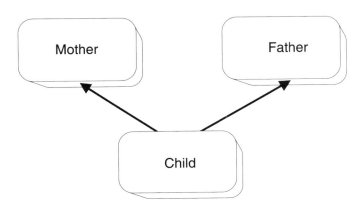

Natural Inheritance
Figure 14.15

Problems with *ambiguities* often occur when multiple inheritance is used. Consider:

```
class A {
protected:
     int a;
};
class B {
protected:
     int a;
};

class C: public A, public B {
public:
     void f(int x) {  a = x;  }    //  Which a? A::a or B::a?
};
```

Here, the actual `a` member must be fully qualified with the class name and scope resolution operator to resolve the ambiguity. `A::a` or `B::a` must be used within `C::f()`.

Consider the case of shared indirect base classes:

```
class A {
     /*  Whatever... */
};
class B: public A {
     /*  Whatever... */
};
class C: public A {
     /*  Whatever... */
};
class D: public B, public C {
     /*  Whatever...*/
}
```

Figure 14.16 illustrates the dilemma. The class `A` parts are duplicated in a `D` object where it would make more sense to have only one copy. The solution is to use a `virtual` base class:

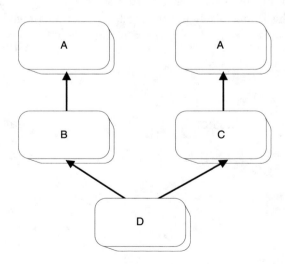

Shared Indirect Base Classes
Figure 14.16

```
class A {
    /*  Whatever... */
};

class B: virtual public A {
    /*  Whatever... */
};

class C: virtual public A {
    /*  Whatever... */
};

class D: public B, public C {
    /*  Whatever...*/
}
```

Figure 14.17 shows the resulting hierarchy. Virtual base classes and the hierarchies they build have certain restrictions placed upon them that complicate their usage even further. Consult the bibliography for sources that explore multiple inheritance and all its nuances more fully.

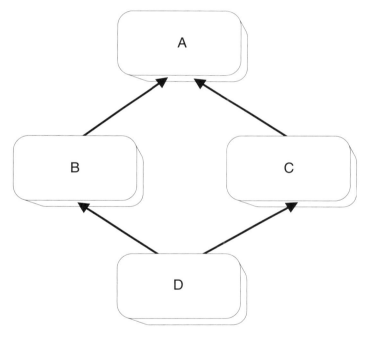

Virtual Base Classes
Figure 14.17

14.8 THE STREAMS CLASSES

One of the first practical uses of C++'s inheritance capabilities was in the design and implementation of I/O *streams*. Stream classes may appear to be part of the C++ language definition itself, since almost every program we've seen makes use of them. In fact, stream classes are programmer-defined standard classes that have been placed in a class library for wide use.

Before streams, the I/O routines available in C and C++ were often frustrating to use. Consult any C book and many C++ books and the following function is ubiquitous: `printf()`. It has been available since the beginning of C, and it is a powerful, useful function. Its prototype is found in `<stdio.h>` along with its often used output relatives `putchar()` and `puts()`, as well as its input cousins `scanf()`, `getchar()`, and `gets()`. These functions listed represent only a small percentage of the functions and constants prototyped in `<stdio.h>`. They essentially perform the same duties as streams functions and operators but with much more opportunities for accidental misuse. Consider the following `printf()` call:

```
int x = 34;
float y = 2.5;
char *s = "This is a string";
char ch = 'X';
long big_int;
double big_float;
long double bigger_big_float;
printf("x = %d, y = %f, s = %s, ch = %c, big_int = %ld, big_float = %lf, "
        "and bigger_big_float = %Lf.\n", x, y, s, ch, big_int, big_float,
        bigger_big_float);
```

The name *printf* stands for *formatted print*. A format string must be provided as the first parameter. An unspecified number of additional parameters is possible, depending on the contents of the format string. Within the format string, the `%` symbol indicates that the printable text representation of a particular variable or constant should be printed in this position of the output string. The order of the `%d`, `%f`, etc. within the format string should match the order of the corresponding variables and/or constants in the additional arguments that follow the format string. The keyword in the previous sentence is *should*. Because of the special nature of the `printf()` function (the number of parameters are not fixed), the compiler can only check to see if the first parameter is a string (`char *`). The `%d` code in the format string indicates that an `int` will follow as an additional parameter. The `%f` code corresponds to the `float` type. The following statement would compile fine but not work:

```
printf("%d, %f\n", 2.5, 4);
```

Normally, when a function expects an integer, and a floating point type is passed instead, the compiler casts the actual parameter to the type specified by the formal parameter of the function. The effect is usually close to what is expected. Here, the compiler is powerless to do any type casting because the string is the only parameter specified in the `<stdio.h>` prototype. Essentially, the control codes within the format string are promises to the `printf()` function that the indicated types will be passed in the order specified. In the example above, the address of the format string will be pushed onto the parameter stack, followed by the `double` (since no f specifier follows the constant) value 2.5 and finally the `int` value 4. (Some systems may reverse the order of the parameters, but the point to be made will still be valid.) For the sake of discussion, assume an integer requires two bytes and the double-precision floating point value requires eight bytes of storage. The `printf()` function reads the format string, character by character, printing each character on the display until a control character (the % symbol) is encountered. Based on the character or group of characters following the percent sign, the function reads a certain number of bytes off the parameter stack. If an integer is to be printed, the internal two's complement binary form must be translated into a displayable decimal form using the proper characters. In this example, the `%d` code means that two bytes must be read in from the parameter stack and interpreted as an integer. Unfortunately, since the actual parameters are reversed, the two bytes used are actually the first one-fourth of the `double` value 2.5. Since all bit patterns are used to represent integers (there is no illegal combination of bits for integers), an integer will be displayed; it is, unfortunately, a meaningless value. The `printf()` function will then grab the next eight bytes off the stack and attempt to interpret them as the mantissa and exponent of a floating point value. Due to the transposition of the parameters, three-fourths of the `double` (in the wrong position to be interpreted correctly, no less) and the two bytes of the integer parameter are incorrectly processed as a `double`. Needless to say, the behavior is unsatisfactory. Mistakes like those above are made quite often.

Consider the code

```
printf("The calculated value is %d (truncated)\n", tan(theta));
```

Here, the intention is to use the truncated value of what the `tan()` function returns. (It returns a `double` value.) At the point the `printf()` function is called, the compiler passes a double value which, as in the example above, will not be interpreted correctly. The programmer must make the control code and parameter types match one way or another:

```
printf("The calculated value is %lf \n", tan(theta));
```

or

```
printf("The calculated value is %d (truncated)\n", int(tan(theta)));
```

Another common error is forgetting to list the arguments completely:

```
printf("x = %f and y = %f\n");
```

Here, imaginary values (i.e., whatever values are left over in the appropriate positions on the stack) are used by `printf()` with corresponding fanciful results.

Another limitation of the standard C I/O functions is their lack of extensibility. Recall the `Complex` class created in chapter 10:

```
class Complex {
        double real;
        double imag;
public:
        //  Member functions follow...
};
```

`printf()` works well (assuming it is used correctly) for built-in types, but there is no control code for `Complex` values. Indeed, there should not be, since `Complex` is a programmer-defined type. One programmer might implement the class differently from another, and the author of the library function `printf()` would have no way of knowing how to display a `Complex` object without knowing its implementation details. The author of `printf()` may not even be familiar with mathematical complex numbers at all! Since programmers can contrive an infinite number of programmer-defined types, `printf()` cannot anticipate all possible data types, neither can it begin to supply the number of different control codes that would be required.

Programmers easily solve the problem by providing their own printing routines that are likely based on `printf()`:

```
void Complex::print() {
        printf("%lf + %lfi", real, imag);
}
```

or even the `cout` stream:

```
void Complex::print() {
        cout <<  real << " + " << imag << 'i';
}
```

The disadvantage of this approach is that `Complex` objects must be treated differently from built-in numerical data types:

```
Complex c;
float f;

printf("%f", f);    //  Print "real" numbers this way
c.print();          //  and complex numbers this way
```

or

```
cout << f;          //  Print "real" numbers this way
c.print();          //  and complex numbers this way
```

This lack of uniformity is not devastating, but it is a bit annoying. One of the design goals of C++ was to allow the language to adapt to better solve the problem. Through the use of overloaded operators, mathematicians can design a complex number program or a matrix manipulation package that appears to be using the standard C++ operators on their programmer-defined data types:

```
//  Declared as a friend function within class Complex
//  Adds two complex numbers together without side effects
Complex operator+(const Complex &a, const Complex &b) {
     Complex result;
     result.real = a.real + b.real;
     result.imag = a.imag + b.imag;
     return result;
}

Complex x(23, 12), y(-2, 0), z;
z = x + y;  //  Looks better than z = ComplexAdd(x, y);  !
```

Certainly I/O, so crucial to almost any useful program, could be handled in such a graceful way.

The solution is a collection of classes known as *streams*. The operators << and >> (respectively the left shift and right shift operators, whose built-in meaning is examined in chapter 15) are used to provide uniform, type-independent access to the screen, keyboard, and files. Observe how the responsibility of type identification in the printf() function has been transferred from the programmer to the stream itself. When integer x is sent to cout, the stream operator << determines its type and processes it accordingly. No control code (%d) is necessary. The programmer that uses streams instead of the standard C library I/O routines eliminates a large class of potential errors that have been plaguing C program development since the 1970s.

The benefits of streams go even deeper than their robustness in handling built-in types. The streams classes ostream (the class of cout) and istream (the class of cin) are only two of sixteen classes that comprise the sophisticated inheritance hierarchy shown in figure 14.18. Observe the many instances of multiple inheritance. The details of all the classes are beyond the scope of this book, but the interested reader can consult the manuals for more information.

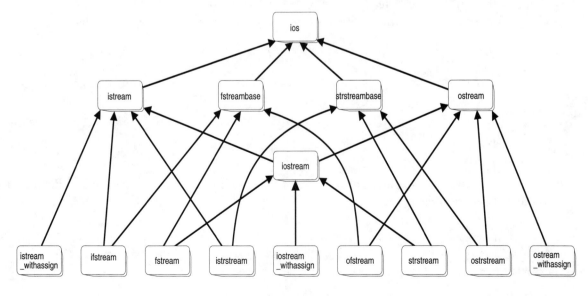

The C++ Streams Class Hierarchy
Figure 14.18

To better understand how streams work, consider the following program which models, in a simplified form, the `ostream` class:

```cpp
#include <stdio.h>

class my_ostream {
public:
    my_ostream(const my_ostream &);   //  Don't define a body
    my_ostream &operator<<(int i) {
        printf("%d", i);
        return *this;
    }
    my_ostream &operator<<(float f) {
        printf("%f", f);
        return *this;
    }
    my_ostream &operator<<(char *s) {
        printf("%s", s);
        return *this;
    }
    my_ostream &operator<<(char c) {
        printf("%c", c);
        return *this;
    }
    //  Etc...  Define << for all printable built-in types
};

my_ostream my_cout;   //  Define a my_ostream object
void main() {
    int i = 10;
    float f = 5.0;
    char *str = "Hello there";
    my_cout << "i = " << i << "  f = " << f << " " << str << '\n';
}
```

When using streams, the above code does not need to be written because a complete implementation is already available in a library module; all a programmer needs to do is to include `<iostream.h>` and use the predefined `cout` object.

Notice that the copy constructor, `my_ostream::my_ostream(const my_ostream &)`, is declared, but no body is defined. This will compile with no problem but will generate a linker error if the copy constructor is called within the program. The declaration indicates to the compiler how a function should be called; its actual body may or may not appear in another file. The linker's job is to associate the call of a function to its compiled body that will be stored somewhere in memory when the program is loaded and executed. If the function is called and its definition (its body) cannot be found anywhere in the list of files to be linked together, then the linker indicates an error. If the function is never called, the linker does not need to find the body; therefore, no error is generated, and no harm is done. Why do such a thing? The fact that it is declared prevents the compiler from creating a default copy constructor, but it does not provide the code for a programmer-defined copy constructor. It is a trick used to guarantee that a `my_ostream` object will not be created and initialized by another `my_ostream` object (which is what copy construction does). In this way, the temporaries that might proliferate with the chained use of << would not be created. The chained use of << is made possible by the fact that << returns a `my_ostream&` instead of a plain `my_ostream`. Since a reference is returned, a temporary is not created for the return value (this is good, since there is no copy constructor to make the temporary anyway). The return value in this case is the actual `my_cout` object itself. Unlike the assignment example in chapter 11, << associates left-to-right; thus, the example above could have parentheses added that illustrate its execution:

```cpp
((((my_cout << x) << ' ') << a) << '\n');
```

Remember that `my_cout << x` is another way of expressing `my_cout.operator<<(x)`. It follows that `(my_cout << x) << ' '` is equivalent to `(my_cout << x).operator<<(' ')`; thus, the expression `my_cout << x` is itself the same as `my_cout` by itself to which the operator<< member function can be applied. The innermost expression `my_cout << x` returns `my_cout` to which the << operator can be reapplied with `' '`, and so on. The net effect is

```
my_cout << x;
my_cout << ' ';
my_cout << a;
my_cout << '\n';
```

which is backwards from the assignment example in chapter 11 but is just what is needed here. Try the above `my_ostream` class with the `my_ostream::operator<<()` defined to return a `my_ostream` instead of a `my_ostream&`. It won't link. For `my_ostream::operator<<()` to return a `my_ostream` object by value, it must create a temporary `my_ostream` object to return. This new, temporary object must be created from `*this`; therefore, a copy constructor is required. The copy constructor is declared in the interface, and this prevents the compiler from creating the default copy constructor (the bit copy). Since no body for the copy constructor is provided, an attempt to call the copy constructor either directly (in an object definition) or indirectly (in call-by-value or value return) will result in an error reported by the linker. The compiler does report the error because C++ code is compiled separately on a file-by-file basis. As far as the compiler is concerned, the body for the `my_ostream` copy constructor may exist in another file; all the compiler needs is the declaration (as it appears in the class interface). There is no need to construct new `my_ostream` objects at each use of the << operator within the chained expression. This takes more time (to call the constructors) and more space (to allocate the temporaries). Let each << return a `my_ostream` (instead of a `my_ostream&`) and give the copy constructor the following body:

```
//  To be defined inline within the class definition above
my_ostream(const my_ostream &m_ostrm) {
        static int count = 0;
        //  Indicates when a my_ostream object is created and how many
        //  have been created (by copy construction) so far
        printf("\n<**Building ostream object #%d.**>\n", ++count);
}
```

Rerun the program and see how many temporaries are made, and then put the references back into the return values of << and count the temporaries produced. During program development, it is often useful to place output statements and counters inside of constructors and destructors to monitor their activity.

Reconsider the problem of displaying a complex number in a manner similar to the built-in types using the standard `<iostream.h>` classes. The following `friend` function can be added to the `complex` class:

```
class Complex {
        double real;
        double imag;
public:
        friend ostream &operator<<(ostream &, const Complex &);
        //  Other member functions follow...
};

ostream &operator<<(ostream &ostrm, const Complex &comp) {
        ostrm << comp.real << " + " << comp.imag << "i";
        return ostrm;
}
```

Now the << operator can be used as follows:

```
int i = 10;
Complex c(12, 3);
cout << " i = " << i << " and  c = " << c << '\n';
```

As the compiler parses the expression, it has complete information about the types involved. The programmer does not need to worry about sending the correct control code, as with printf(). For cout << i, the compiler invokes ostream::operator<<(int), and for cout << c, operator<<(ostream &, const Complex &) is used.

The library routines declared in <iostream.h> are thus extensible. Streams can be made to work with any programmer-defined type, no matter how complicated it might be. The routines in <stdio.h> are fixed and immutable. If the source code is available for the <stdio.h> routines, and it might be obtainable from the compiler vendor for the right price, it may be argued that printf() is also extensible. Yes, with some work the printf() function can be adapted to, for instance, print complex numbers with a %cx control code. This way of extending a library is fundamentally different from the overloading of <<, however. Consider the differences:

1. Extending the << operator in the ostream class as described above cannot "break" it. It may not work correctly for the new type upon which it is defined to operate, but the error would be limited solely to the new, overloaded friend function. It would work as before with all the other types it was designed to handle. When modifying printf(), the programmer may introduce errors that change the way it handles the built-in types; thus, printf() becomes a less trustworthy function even when processing types it was originally designed to handle.

2. The programmer does not need to understand the details of how the << operator works on ostream objects to extend its function; he or she need only understand what it does. In the case of the printf() modification, the programmer must understand completely how it works. Any shortfall in complete comprehension can introduce errors into the function. The source code may include assembly language code or other special features that are beyond the programmer's expertise.

3. In C++, good class design expects that the functionality of the class will be extended in some way. This extension can be accomplished as with << above or more likely through inheritance. Functional extension is encouraged by the features of the language. In contrast, modifying printf() so that it behaves differently from its documentation runs contrary to the idea that standard library functions should act in a consistent, well-defined fashion independent of computer system/architecture (PC, Mac, Sun, etc.), or application.

Of course, one non-C++ solution is to abandon the idea of rewriting printf() and write a similar display function from scratch that may or may not make use of the services of the actual printf() function. The function could be called xprintf() for "extended printf()." This approach addresses point 1 and 2 above, but it is merely a short-term solution. Assume xprintf() has been written so that it performs flawlessly with all the built-in types and all the programmer-defined types currently in use. It is thoroughly tested and completely documented so that it can be used in other applications with as much respect and trust as the venerable printf(). When the time comes to invent a new programmer-defined type, the situation will be identical to the original problem with the nonextensible standard printf() function. The same three issues will arise, and the programmer will quite possibly have a lot of work to do to bring xprintf() back up to speed.

This chapter is about inheritance, and the best thing about streams is the flexibility and functionality that they possess from being part of a class hierarchy. The overloaded operator<<()

has been adapted to display `Strings`, `Complex` numbers, and can be adopted to display any programmer-defined type imaginable. How much work must be done to write a `<<` operator for an `ofstream` object? It would be handy to be able to save `Strings` to textfiles as naturally as the built-in types. An `operator<<()` of the form

```
//  Must be declared a friend operator function within the String class
ofstream &operator<<(ofstream &ofs, const String &s) {
     ofs << s.str;
     return ofs;
}
```

would be handy.

This function is easy enough to write, but even it can be simplified. How could it be simplified any more? The answer may be quite surprising. *Don't write it at all.* The function is already written in the function `ostream& operator<<(ostream &, const String &)`. Consulting the streams class hierarchy, it is seen that an `ofstream` *is a* `ostream`. The consequences of this relationship are significant. Since `operator<<()` has already been written for `ostreams` and `Strings`, and `ofstreams` are `ostreams`, it works just as well for `ofstreams` as it does for simple `ostreams`.

14.9   OBJECT-ORIENTED PROGRAMMING WITHOUT C++

C++ is a *hybrid* OOP language because it is a straightforward extension of C, a procedural language. C++ allows the programmer to use the procedural paradigm and apply OOP techniques when appropriate. *Pure* OOP languages follow the OOP paradigm more closely. SmallTalk is a pure OOP language; in SmallTalk everything is treated as an object including the development environment (editor, compiler, etc.). This uniformity of reference greatly facilitates OOP but often intimidates the traditional procedural programmer. Some people have said that it is easier for a nonprogrammer to learn OOP than for a traditionally trained programmer to adapt to OOP. The ability to think in objects and relationships is foreign to many who are accustomed to simply devising algorithms and building data structures.

OOP programming can be done in non-OOP languages. OOP is more of a mindset than a bag of tricks supplied by a programming language. Chapter 15 provides an example of an OOP program that could be written in standard C using `unions`. People have written books on object-oriented assembly language programming. The idea of ADTs and of objects being in control of their own destiny is OOP. Inheritance is a useful feature that can also be implemented in non-OOP languages but it takes some more effort. It is important to note that the first working versions of the C++ language were translated by a program called *cfront*. The C++ was not compiled into machine language but was translated into normal C, which was then compiled by an available C compiler. The C code itself modeled the ADTs and inheritance; it was not pretty, but it did the job.

OOP is not a programmer's panacea. Arguably more work must be done to create good object-oriented programs. A well-written, object-oriented program can be modified and extended much easier than a traditional nonobject-oriented program. The price to pay for this convenience relatively late in the software life cycle is more work during the design phase. In fact, the majority of the work in OOP comes during the design phase. The objects of the problem domain must be carefully identified and their relationships and interactions well understood. The generalities that OOP can exploit must be perceived and properly understood. Objects that are very similar may be objects of the same class. Objects that have some similarities but notable differences as well may be related somehow in an inheritance hierarchy (parent-child, sibling-sibling). Objects can be constructed with other objects as their components. Once the overall design has been determined, the rest of the development is straightforward. The use of ADTs, inheritance and polymorphism, and frills such as overloaded operators—given a good design to start with—make maintenance much easier than the traditional procedural approach.

Exercises

1. What plagues older I/O routines from `<stdio.h>` (like `printf()`) that the streams classes avoid?

2. Why does `ostream::operator<<()` return an `ostream &` instead of a plain `ostream`?

3. Given a programmer-defined class X, how does defining `operator<<(ostream &, const X &)` also insure that an X object can be saved to a textfile?

Assignments

1. Derive a class called `ExtendedBST<T>` from the `BST<T>` template class introduced in chapter 13. Each `ExtendedBST<T>` node contains a parent pointer that points to the node's parent (in addition to the standard left and right child pointers). (The root node has `NULL` for a parent pointer.) Provide a new member function:

   `ExtendedBST<T>::print_ancestors(const T&element);`

   that finds `element` within the tree and prints out all of the item's ancestors. An appropriate message should be printed instead if `element` is not found in the tree.

2. Derive a class from `String` (as were `SimpleString` and `SortedString`) called `NumericString`. `NumericString` objects should contain only digits ('0'–'9'). All nonnumeric digits should be replaced with the character '0' (notice: not the value 0). Write a cast member operator that converts a `NumericString` object to an integer. Naturally, leading zeroes should be ignored. If the integer will be out of range (too large, since negatives aren't allowed—minus sign is not a digit), `INT_MAX` (defined in `<limits.h>`) should be the value that the object is cast to.

3. Derive a class from `Array<T>` that maintains a separate size member so that the array can grow or shrink as necessary. An array of 100 items could be defined, but it might typically hold less than 100 items. Use this class as the basis for a statistics program as found in the assignments for chapter 7.

4. Add to assignment 1 the ability to print the nodes of the tree in inorder fashion using the streams `<<` operator. (This should allow the printing to be done to disk as well.)

5. Add to assignment 4 the ability to insert an item (or sequence of items) into the tree using the streams `>>` operator. This should allow the input to come from a file as well.

CHAPTER 15

LOWER-LEVEL PROGRAMMING

15.1 INTRODUCTION

C was created in the early 1970s as a tool in developing the Unix operating system. Since C++'s origins lie in C and systems programming, it has a complement of features that assist the kind of lower-level programming that must be done when writing operating systems, device drivers, and other programs that must interact directly with the hardware. Such programs might need to carefully manage the CPU or memory, interact with serial and/or parallel ports, mice, graphics displays, and so forth. Most standard higher-level languages do not provide access to the hardware as C++ does in its language definition. In fairness to other languages, most actual implementations (such as Borland's Turbo Pascal for the PC) make up for the deficiencies by adding extensions to the standard language definitions. These extensions allow the languages to be as useful as C++ for lower-level programming, but since they are *nonstandard* features they are likely to be nonportable to other computing platforms. C and C++ are known for their portability; this makes them the top choice for software being developed for multiple platforms. Most upscale software is available on several platforms. (Consider the WordPerfect wordprocessor which is available for MS-DOS, Microsoft Windows, Unix, OS/2, Macintosh, NeXT, Amiga, and Atari.) Most C++ compilers have a few system specific extensions, such as additional reserved words not defined in the C++ language standard. Fortunately, for the sake of portability, many of these development systems have the option to compile using only standard language rules.

15.2 BITWISE OPERATORS

Normally, a programmer doesn't need to alter the internal structure of a type such as an `int`. The standard arithmetic and relational operators are usually adequate to manipulate `int`s. Consider the situation, however, where a binary data file from one computer system must be read and used by a completely different system. The internal storage of the basic types like `int`s may be different, or the data may be compressed in some way to save disk space. The internal structure of individual bytes of memory can be rearranged by using *bitwise* operators. The bitwise operators are listed in table 15.1.

Table 15.1 The Bitwise Operators

Operator	Name
<<	left shift
>>	right shift
&	bitwise and
|	bitwise or
^	bitwise exclusive or
~	bitwise negation

The ~ (tilda) operator is unary, and the rest are binary. All of the binary operators can be combined with the assignment operator as follows:

```
<<=       >>=       &=       |=       ^=
```

in a manner analogous to +=, −=, *=, etc. For example, x &= y is a shorthand (and potentially more efficient) method of expressing the assignment x = x & y. The shift operators are the same operators that the streams classes redefine for extraction and insertion. The bitwise shift operators came first, however. They have been around since the origin of C; their overloaded use with streams is a recent C++ addition.

In the following examples, unsigned types will be used to illustrate the concepts, since unsigneds don't have a sign bit to complicate matters. The unsigned values will be stored with 16 bits, which is a common size for unsigned types. The actual size of unsigneds are system specific and may be 32 bits or more on some systems.

The *shift* operators slide the bits that make up an object to the left or right a specified number of places:

```
unsigned x = 16, y;    // Internally, x is stored as:  00000000 00010000
                       // (base 2)
y = x << 3;            // y becomes 00000000 1000 0000 (base 2) or 128
                       // (base 10)
cout << x << ', ' << y; // Prints 16, 128
y = x >> 2;            // y becomes 00000000 0000 0100 (base 2) or 4
                       // (base 10)
x <<= 3;               // x becomes 00000000 1000 0000 (base 2) or 128
                       // (base 10)
```

Shifting to the left one bit position doubles the integral value; shifting one bit position to the right halves the value. The following equations describe these relationships:

$$a << b \text{ is equivalent to } a \times 2^b$$

$$a >> b \text{ is equivalent to } \frac{a}{2^b}$$

The bitwise logical comparative operators &, |, and ^ compare the bits in the corresponding positions of their two operands. For example:

```
  00010110 00110111        00010110 00110111         00010110 00110111
& 10111011 11100000      | 10111011 11100000       ^ 10111011 11100000
  00010010 00100000        10111111 11110111         10101101 11010111
```

In base 10 terms, the above `unsigned` expressions translate into

```
5,687 & 48,091 = 4,640     5,687 | 48,091 = 49,143     5,687 ^ 48,091 = 44,503
```

but the decimal representation is not as illuminating as the binary representation. As with the shift operators, the binary forms are easiest to use when calculating the results of applying the bitwise comparison operators. No carries are involved here as in binary addition. With bitwise AND, if both bits in the same position of the two operands are 1 (or on), then the bit in that position in the result will be 1. Otherwise, the bit in the result will be 0. With bitwise OR, if both bits in the same position are 0, the result will have a 0 in that position; otherwise, a 1 will appear in that position. These operators work exactly like logical and (&&) and logical or (| |) except that the logical operators compare the complete value (all the bits simultaneously) and return either 0_{10} (00000000 00000000$_2$) or 1_{10} (00000000 00000001$_2$). The bitwise operators perform the comparisons on a bit-by-bit basis as shown above, thus yielding results that are often different from simply zero and one.

The bitwise EXCLUSIVE-OR operator (XOR) has no direct logical equivalent. XOR yields a 1 if both bits are different (one being 0 and the other 1) or 0 if both bits are the same (both 0 or both 1). To accomplish XOR in logical terms (not bitwise), `x XOR y` would be written

```
(x || y) && (!(x && y))
```

The bitwise NOT inverts each bit within the byte or machine word; zeroes are converted to ones, and ones are converted to zeroes. The `unsigned` value

```
1,090 (00000100 01000010)₂
```

would become

```
64,445 (11111011 10111101)₂
```

when bitwise negated.

To a higher-level programmer, these operators are unnecessary; hence, most other higher-level programming languages do not provide them. Despite their absence in most other higher-level languages, they can be invaluable in certain situations. Consider the need to store as much information into as little space as possible. This is a never ending goal in computer programming. Assume an array of `unsigned` values is going to be stored on disk. The values stored are individual answers to multiple choice questions on a machine readable answer sheet. A typical answer sheet is pictured in figure 15.1. Each question has five options: A, B, C, D, E. For maximum flexibility, all possible responses must be recorded. A test or survey question might allow multiple answers to the same question (A and C, for example). A sample test question might be

76.   Which of the following reserved words is directly involved in building iterative statements?

    A. while   B. do   C. for   D. if   E. Answer not here.

Here, answers A, B, and C would need to be chosen.

If an answer sheet will hold responses to a maximum of 200 questions, what is the minimum amount of storage required to store all the possible responses by one respondent? One approach might store the individual answers to each question in an array of five characters. The array would not be a string, so a null byte would not need to be stored. A typical array might hold only one character, no characters if the question were omitted. It might store 'A', 'B', 'C', 'D', and 'E' if all the options were chosen for a particular question. Five bytes per answer times 200 answers equals 1,000 bytes. If 250 answer sheets are processed, the total storage required would be 250,000 bytes. Can this number be improved?

Use a #2 lead pencil only. Fill oval completely and make mark as dark as possible.

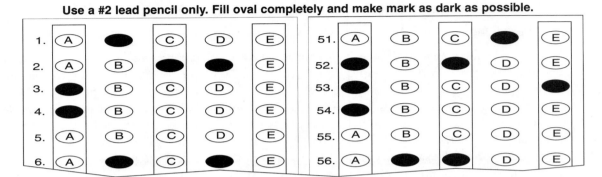

A Machine Readable Answer Form
Figure 15.1

Another approach answers the question: "How many possible combinations of answers per question are there?" Consider the following representation:

$$\frac{1}{E} \quad \frac{0}{D} \quad \frac{0}{C} \quad \frac{1}{B} \quad \frac{0}{A}$$

Here, a one in the first position means that E was chosen, a zero in the first position means that E was not chosen, a one in the second position means that D was chosen, a zero in the second position means that D was not chosen, etc. (The letters are reversed so that the increasing binary powers match the increasing alphabetical order. Any order is fine as long as it is used consistently throughout the program.) With this scheme, only five bits per answer are required. Each answer requires only one-eighth as much storage as the first representation. Five bits per answer times 200 answers equals 1,000 bits. 1,000 bits divided by eight bits per byte equals 125 bytes. Again, if 250 sheets are processed, the total storage required is 31,250 bytes, which is, not surprisingly, one-eighth as large as the first approach.

Each question can be answered by choosing A, B, C, D, or E, or some combination of those letters. A response such as ABE or ABCDE is quite possible. The answer array must be represented as compactly as possible to save space. The answer to each question requires at least five bits of storage, since there are 32 possible combinations of letters that could be chosen for each question. These responses can be indicated by constants defined in the program:

```
const unsigned BLK = 0, A = 1, B = 2, AB = 3, C = 4, AC = 5, BC = 6, ABC = 7,
               D = 8, AD = 9, BD = 10, ABD = 11, CD = 12, ACD = 13, BCD = 14,
               ABCD = 15, E = 16, AE = 17, BE = 18, ABE = 19, CE = 20, ACE = 21,
               BCE = 22, ABCE = 23, DE = 24, ADE = 25, BDE = 26, ABDE = 27,
               CDE = 28, ACDE = 29, BCDE = 30, ALL = 31;
```

BLK = 0, A = 1, B = 2, AB = 3, C = 4, AC = 5, etc. The representation scheme is straightforward. Consider a binary number whose bit positions are labeled

$$\frac{E}{0} \quad \frac{D}{1} \quad \frac{C}{0} \quad \frac{B}{1} \quad \frac{A}{0}$$

The binary number 01010_2 corresponds to the answer BD; the value expressed in decimal form is 10, thus explaining the constant value of BD = 10.

The problem is, if the smallest data type in the system is a char, and a char uses one byte (eight bits) of storage, certainly the smallest amount of practical storage for each answer is eight bits.

While the eight bit solution is still a dramatic improvement over the 40-bit approach above, the five bit solution is attainable. The bitwise operators allow access to the individual bits that make up `chars`. To make the solution realistic, certain limitations are imposed that are common to most computer systems. For the sake of this example, assume a particular computer uses 16 bit machine words (the registers are 16 bits wide). Also, assume it is impractical to spread pieces of data across word boundaries; that is, it is much less efficient, in terms of processing speed, to begin a piece of data at the end of one word and continue it at the front of the next word in memory. In this case, the bitwise operators would not be able to extract and manipulate the data in a reasonable manner. Spreading a single piece of data across a byte boundary is okay, if it is not also a word boundary.

Based on this architecture imposed restriction, the 125-byte response array has to be compromised slightly. The top part of figure 15.2 shows how the individual answers are packed into an array of characters. Since the computer's architecture restricts the way data is arranged in memory in that data cannot be conveniently split over word boundaries, three responses (15 bits total) are stored in two bytes (16 bits) and the remaining one bit is unused (see figure 15.2). Since three responses are packed into two bytes, the total number of bytes required to store all 200 answers would be

$$200 \text{ answers} \times \frac{2 \text{ bytes}}{3 \text{ answers}} = 133.333$$

The `answer` array would therefore need to hold 134 `chars`, or 8 × 134 = 1,072 bits.

Assume that the software that controls the answer sheet scanner stores the information in this form. One task of an analysis program would be to unpack this `answer` array. Instead of storing three answers in two `chars`, one answer would be stored in each `char` of an array of `chars`. This unpacking makes processing the answer more convenient.

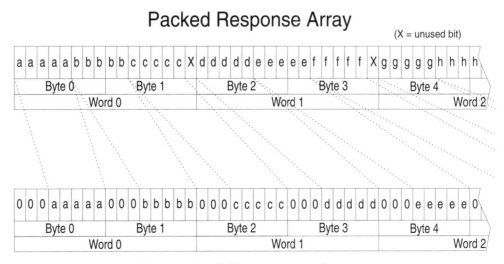

Packed Response Array

(X = unused bit)

Unpacked Response Array

Unpacking the Response Array
Figure 15.2

Copying the first response occupying the first five bits of the zeroth position of the answer array into the first eight bits of the zeroth position of a new unpacked array of answers requires using some bitwise operators. Figure 15.2 illustrates the process. A description of the complete algorithm follows:

The goal is to copy the answers from a packed array of responses to an unpacked array of responses. Let the packed array be called PACK and the unpacked array be called UNPACK. Let there be two indices, pack and unpack, that indicate positions in their respective arrays.

1. Let pack = 0 and unpack = 0.
2. Copy the first five bits from PACK[pack] into the last five bits of UNPACK[unpack].
3. Copy zeroes into the first three bits of UNPACK[unpack].
4. Copy the last three bits of PACK[pack] into the first three bits of UNPACK[unpack + 1].
5. Shift the bits in UNPACK[unpack + 1] to the left two places.
6. Copy the first two bits of PACK[pack + 1] into the last two bits of UNPACK[pack + 1].
7. Copy zeroes into the first three bits of UNPACK[unpack + 1].
8. Copy the third through seventh bits of PACK[pack + 1] into the last five bits of UNPACK[unpack + 2].
9. Copy zeroes into the first three bits of UNPACK[unpack + 2].
10. If all answers in PACK have been converted, stop. Otherwise, set pack = pack + 2 and unpack = unpack + 3, and proceed with step 2.

Steps 2 through 9 can best be written in a function. In this function, ans is a pointer to the unpacked array of chars, and buf is a pointer to the original packed array of chars. All convert() does is look at a portion of each array. A client function increments ans by three and buf by two when the next series of answers are to be unpacked.

```
void convert(char *ans, char *buf) {
    ans[0] = (buf[0] >> 3) & 31;
    ans[1] = ((buf[0] << 2) | ((buf[1] >> 6) & 3)) & 31;
    ans[2] = (buf[1] >> 1) & 31;
}
```

The following function is used to unpack the whole array:

```
void unpack(const char *packed, char *unpacked, int ans_size) {
    int i;
    //  Step through the two arrays copying the unpacked answers
    for ( i = 0;  i < ans_size;  i += 3 ) {
        convert(unpacked, packed);
        packed += 2;  unpacked += 3;
    }
}
```

Once the answer array is unpacked, it can be conveniently treated as any other array of char where each position holds one unit of data.

The & and | operators are often used to mask portions of bytes. It is illustrative to compare the term mask as used here to its use in *painting*. Masking tape prevents paint from getting on surfaces where it shouldn't. It is said that the surface covered by tape or newspapers is being *masked off*. Consider the eight squares in figure 15.3 that are each painted either black or white. To guarantee that the third square from the left is black (no matter what color it is now) and the colors of all the other squares remain unchanged, a mask could be fashioned out of suitable material into the shape shown in figure 15.4.

When the mask is properly aligned over the squares, black paint can be freely applied. The hole in the mask assures that the proper square, and none of the others, is painted black.

If squares two and four are going to be painted white, and the rest of the squares are going to be left unchanged, then the mask in figure 15.5 should be used with white paint.

Painted Squares
Figure 15.3

Masking the Squares
Figure 15.4

Two Bit "Off" Mask
Figure 15.5

If each of the squares represent bits within a byte **B**, and black means *on* (one) and white means *off* (zero), then turning on the bit in the third position is equivalent to bitwise OR-ing **B** with the mask `00100000`. The zeroes mask the "paint," and the one is the hole that allows a one to be "painted" in the third bit. To turn off bits, the mask `10101111` is bitwise **AND**-ed with **B**; thus, the zeroes are the holes through which "white paint" may pass. To summarize:

To selectively turn on (set to one) certain bits:

1. Construct a mask of all zeroes. Place ones in the mask in the same positions that are to be turned on.
2. Use bitwise OR with the mask to turn on the selected bits.

To selectively turn off (set to zero) certain bits:

1. Construct a mask of all ones. Place zeroes in the mask in the same positions that are to be turned off.
2. Use bitwise AND with the mask to turn on the selected bits.

The act of masking assures that certain bit positions are either always on (1) or always off (0). In the code above, the value 31 is used with bitwise AND in several places. Observe the effect:

```
    abcdefgh
 &  00011111

    000defgh
```

The result is guaranteed to have zeroes in its first three bit positions. The final five positions are unchanged; thus, the bitwise & operator can be used as a mask to selectively zero out particular bits of a value. In the example above all the response values were limited to 0 to 31, or five bits. The `convert()` uses a series of shifts and masking operations to produce the value in the form desired.

The bitwise | is often used as a mask to guarantee that particular bits are set (turned on, 1). Consider:

```
    abcdefgh
 |  00011111
    abc11111
```

The final five bits in this example will be set when bitwise OR is used with 31. The first three bits will be unchanged.

The concept of masking is used quite often in systems programming. Sometimes parameters to functions that represent attributes are bitwise OR-ed together. Consider file attributes that can be assigned when opening a disk file:

```
fstream fs("outfile.tmp", ios::out);                                    //  #1
fstream gs("outfile.tmp", ios::out | ios::binary);                      //  #2
fstream hs("outfile.tmp", ios::out | ios::trunc);                       //  #3
fstream is("outfile.tmp", ios::out | ios::binary  | ios::trunc);        //  #4
```

The `ios` class contains a list of enumerated types that can be accessed with the scope resolution operator. They each contain only a single bit (all in different positions, of course). The exact values are implementation dependent, but the following values can be found in one system's class library header file:

```
        class ios {
        //  Other stuff comes before...
public:
        enum {
                in        = 0x01,    // open for reading
                out       = 0x02,    // open for writing
                ate       = 0x04,    // seek to eof upon original open
                app       = 0x08,    // append mode: all additions at eof
                trunc     = 0x10,    // truncate file if already exists
                nocreate  = 0x20,    // open fails if file doesn't exist
                noreplace = 0x40,    // open fails if file already exists
                binary    = 0x80     // binary (not text) file
        };
        //  Other stuff follows...
};
```

The values are listed in hexadecimal form (see below). The equivalent binary form (which unfortunately cannot be represented directly in C++) is:

```
        in        = 00000001,  // open for reading
        out       = 00000010,  // open for writing
        ate       = 00000100,  // seek to eof upon original open
        app       = 00001000,  // append mode: all additions at eof
        trunc     = 00010000,  // truncate file if already exists
        nocreate  = 00100000,  // open fails if file doesn't exist
        noreplace = 01000000,  // open fails if file already exists
        binary    = 10000000   // binary (not text) file
```

When the right-most bit is on, the file can be read from. If the right most two bits are on, the file can be read from and written to. Bitwise OR-ing selected `enum` values turns on just the attributes needed. The notation is easy to read and quite intuitive to use. (Notice that certain attributes are contradictory—one would not combine `ios::nocreate | ios::noreplace`.) The routines that service the file streams behave differently depending upon the values of certain bits in the second argument passed to the `fstream` constructor. All of the examples above that define and initialize an `fstream` object open a file stream for output. The second example opens the file for output in binary mode. The third example opens a file for output erasing any contents it may currently contain. The fourth example combines all three attributes. The process of bitwise OR-ing the attributes together turns on the proper bits to achieve the desired behavior in the file stream.

Exercises

1. What gives standard C++ an advantage over most other standard higher-level programming languages when it comes to lower-level programming tasks?

2. What are the *bitwise* operators?

3. What does the left shift operator do?

4. What does the bitwise negation operator do?

5. What is a *mask*, and how is one used?

For questions 6–25, assume the following type `tiny` is available, which is an unsigned integral type made up of only four bits. All of the possible values of an object of `tiny` type are listed:

Binary Representation	tiny Value
0000	0
0001	1
0010	2
0011	3
0100	4
0101	5
0110	6
0111	7
1000	8
1001	9
1010	10
1011	11
1100	12
1101	13
1110	14
1111	15

Indicate the values of each of the following expressions. Express your answer in both binary and decimal form.

6. 4 << 1　　　　7. 4 >> 1　　　　8. 0 | 5　　　　9. 0 & 5

10. 11 | 5　　　　11. 11 & 5　　　　12. 11 & 3　　　　13. 11 | 3

14. 2 && 3　　　　15. 11 || 2　　　　16. ~5　　　　17. 1 << 3

18. 2 ^ 3　　　　19. 4 ^ 4　　　　20. 1 << 2 >> 2　　　　21. 1 >> 2 << 2

22. 2 & 3 | 5　　　　23. 2 | 3 & 5　　　　24. 2 << 1 & 5　　　　25. 2 & 1 << 2

26.　How can the first four bits of an `int` be turned off with none of the remaining bits affected?

27.　How can the first two and the last two bits of an `int` be turned on with none of the middle bits modified?

15.3　BIT-FIELDS

A bit-field `struct` allows the programmer to specify exactly how many bits constitute a field within a `struct`. A typical declaration is:

```
struct CompactRecord {
      unsigned ID     : 10;
      unsigned age    :  7;
      unsigned status:   4;
};
```

A variable of type `CompactRecord` would require 21 bits for its data fields. Since a byte is the smallest chunk of memory in which an addressable entity can be stored, it would actually require three bytes (24 bits) of storage.

```
CompactRecord r;   //  sizeof(r) = = 3
```

Ten bits are used to store an `unsigned ID` value; thus, its values range from 0 to 1,023. The seven bit `age` field can store the numbers 0 to 127, and the four bit `status` field can represent 0 to 15. A normal `struct`

```
struct NormalRecord {
      unsigned ID;
      unsigned age;
      unsigned status;
};
```

would occupy 6 × `sizeof` unsigned bytes. Few systems use less than two bytes for `unsigned` storage (some use four bytes). This conservative estimate yields six bytes total, or twice as big as the bit-field representation. Bit-fields can be used to pack data within `struct`s so the `struct` uses less memory. The restriction is that the data must be of integral type (`int`, `unsigned`, `long`, `char`, or `enum`). Whether or not individual fields can cross byte or word boundaries is implementation dependent. Depending on how the data is packed and the boundary crossing restrictions, the space savings may be minimal. Some compilers can be set optionally to allow or disallow a field crossing a word boundary. Most systems also limit the size of each bit-field to 16 or 32 bits.

The `convert()` function used above to unpack the array of responses could be rewritten using a `struct` with bit-fields, and all the bitwise operators could be ignored:

```
struct PackedResponseGroup {
      unsigned ans1: 5;    //   First packed answer in group
      unsigned ans2: 5;    //   Second packed answer in group
      unsigned ans3: 5;    //   Third packed answer in group
      unsigned junk: 1;    //   Unused last bit in group
};

void convert(char *unprg, PackedResponseGroup *prg) {
      unprg[0] = prg->ans1;
      unprg[1] = prg->ans2;
      unprg[2] = prg->ans3;
}
```

Observe that this version of convert() looks much less tedious than the original version. The code that calls convert() would be modified slightly. Since the packed array packs three responses into two bytes, it is best to treat a pointer to the array of responses as a pointer to an array of PackedResponseGroups. This can be accomplished through a cast. Each time a pointer to the type-casted response array is incremented by one, it moves three responses (two bytes) along the array. The pointer to the resultant unpacked response array is still incremented by three each time through the loop, since three responses are unpacked with each call to convert().

```
void unpack(const char *packed, char *unpacked, int ans_size) {
      //   Set pointers to the beginning of their respective arrays
      PackedResponseGroup *buf = (PackedResponseGroup *)packed;
      //   Step through the two arrays copying the unpacked answers
      for ( int i = 0;   i < ans_size;   i += 3 ) {
             convert(unpacked, buf);
             unpacked += 3;   buf += 1;   //   Note increment
      }
}
```

This code is actually system dependent since some systems may not allow a bit-field to cross a byte boundary.

15.4 UNIONS

Chapter 8 introduced structs and classes—C++'s means of structuring complex data. From its earliest days, C had two additional related constructs: unions and bit-field structs (or merely bit-fields). Both are used in systems programming; however, unions sometimes find their way into higher-level programs. The syntax for union declaration and manipulation is similar to a struct:

```
union MultiStorage {
      int i;
      float f;
      char c[20];
};

MultiStorage x;

x.i = 3;   x.f = 45.21;   strcpy(x.c, "ABC");
```

Although the syntax may be identical, the semantic differences between unions and structs are great. Recall that a typical struct contains several fields, with each field occupying a distinct storage location. To determine how much storage a struct requires, one needs to add the storage requirements of its various data fields. (Actual storage requirements may be slightly higher because some elements may need to be stored on even machine word boundaries for efficient manipulation.) In a union, all data fields occupy the same memory location; therefore, the size of a union is the same size as its largest field. In the MultiStorage union above, the c field requires 20 bytes of storage; therefore, the whole union occupies 20 bytes in memory. If the reserved word union were changed to `struct`, the storage requirements would jump up to `sizeof int + sizeof float + 20`, certainly more than the 20-byte union.

Since all of its fields occupy the same place in memory, a union cannot be used in place of a `struct` for the purpose of conserving memory. In the sequence of statements above, `x.f = 45.21` destroys the value previously stored in `x.i`. Unions are useful for treating the same data in different ways. Recall the earlier task of unpacking an array of five-bit responses. Data stored in a packed array of five-bit values had to be converted into unpacked eight-bit values for convenient processing. A problem that must be solved quite frequently is data conversion between two different systems. Consider the situation in which a binary file of `long`s stored by a minicomputer must be accessed by a microcomputer. Both systems store `long`s in four bytes, but, unfortunately, the internal arrangement of the individual bytes that make up each `long` differs between the two systems.

Consider the `long` value 369,365,584. In normal binary form it can be expressed as

```
00010110 00000100 00010010 01010000
```

The *least significant byte* (LSB) is `01010000` because it contains the lower valued power of two; the *most significant byte* (MSB) is `00010110`. The microcomputer is an Intel-based PC; therefore, it stores integral types (including `long`s) with the bytes stored in backwards fashion compared to normal binary form. On a PC, beginning with the lowest memory address, it is stored as

```
01010000 00010010 00000100 00010110
```

The LSB is stored at a lower address than the MSB. Reading the four bytes in normal binary form, from left to right, would be equivalent to reading the individual bytes from higher memory address to lower memory address on the PC.

On the minicomputer, beginning with the lowest memory address, the above value is stored as

```
00010110 00000100 00010010 01010000
```

Different computer systems may have different internal arrangements of bits for a particular type, even if the type requires the same amount of memory on both systems. The minicomputer and PC display such a difference in the storage of `long`s. The term *endian* is often used in a discussion of this nature. The PC is a *little-endian* (since its LSB is stored at a lower address) machine, whereas the minicomputer is a *big-endian* machine. If the bytes are labeled `byte0`, `byte1`, `byte2`, and `byte3` proceeding from left to right, a function that converts the minicomputer `long`s to PC `long`s would need to swap `byte0` and `byte3` as well as exchange `byte1` and `byte2`. The individual bits within a byte are not disturbed—only the whole bytes need to be rearranged. A sequence of bitwise operators with appropriate masks could be used to shift whole bytes over and produce the desired result, but the same effect can be achieved at a somewhat higher conceptual level using a union. Consider the following union:

```
union Swapper {
    long long_int;
    char byte[4];
};
```

The data fields `long_int` and `byte` occupy the same memory locations perfectly, since a `long` on both systems uses four bytes and so does an array of four `char`s. The conversion strategy is as follows:

1. Place the minicomputer formatted `long` in a `Swapper` union.
2. Treat the `long` as if it were an array of four `char`s.

3. Rearrange the elements within the `char` array so that the byte arrangement is compatible with the PC format for `long`s.
4. Treat the `char` array as if it were again a `long`.

The function `swaplongbytes()` precisely describes the process:

```
long  swapbyteslong(long mini_value) {
      long  PC_value;
      Swapper  swap;
      char  temp;
      swap.long_int = mini_value;
      /*  Exchange 0th and 3rd byte  */
      temp = swap.byte[0];
      swap.byte[0] = swap.byte[3];
      swap.byte[3] = temp;
      /*  Exchange 1st and 2nd byte  */
      temp = swap.byte[2];
      swap.byte[2] = swap.byte[1];
      swap.byte[1] = temp;
      return swap.long_int;
}
```

If the `swapbyteslong()` function is the only function within the program to perform the conversion, there is no need to define a `Swapper` union. The `swapper` object inside of `swapbyteslong()` can be declared as follows:

```
union {
      long  long_int;
      char  byte[4];
} swapper;
```

Here, the union is defined without providing a type name for it. In this instance, the union's sole usage was in this one function to declare only one variable. This is known as an anonymous union because it has no name. This union is also local to the function and cannot be used outside of the function (unless redeclared). Anonymous unions allow the construction of *free-union variant record* structures. These custom `structs` are occasionally useful in some applications programming situations. The free-union variant record declarations in program 15.1 achieve object-oriented programming without the use of C++'s advanced OOP features:

```
const float PI = 3.14159;

typedef double Real;

enum Shape { rectangle, triangle, circle };

struct Geometric_Object {
      Shape type;
      union {
            struct R {
                  Real length, width;
                  int  sides;
            } rect;
            struct T {
                  Real side1, side2, base, height;
                  int sides;
            } tri;
            struct C {
                  Real radius;
            } circ;
      };
};
```

```
Real area(Geometric_Object *obj) {
        switch ( obj->type ) {
            case rectangle: return obj->rect.length * obj->rect.width;
            case triangle : return 0.5 * obj->tri.base * obj->tri.height;
            case circle   : return PI * obj->circ.radius * obj->circ.radius;
            default       : return -1;   /*  Error value  */
        }
    }

Real perimeter(Geometric_Object *obj) {
        switch ( obj->type ) {
            case rectangle: return 2.0*(obj->rect.length + obj->rect.width);
            case triangle
                        return obj->tri.base + obj->tri.side1 + obj->tri.side2;
            case circle   : return 2.0*PI*obj->circ.radius;
            default       : return -1;   /*  Error value  */
        }
    }

void make_rectangle(Geometric_Object *obj, Real len, Real wid) {
        obj->type =  rectangle;  obj->rect.length = len;  obj->rect.width = wid;
    }

void make_triangle(Geometric_Object *obj, Real s1, Real s2, Real b, Real h) {
        obj->type = triangle;  obj->tri.base = b;  obj->tri.side1 = s1;
        obj->tri.side2 = s2;   obj->tri.height = h;
    }


void make_circle(Geometric_Object *obj, Real r) {
        obj->type = circle;  obj->circ.radius = r;
    }

void main() {
        Geometric_Object figure;
        make_rectangle(&figure, 3.0, 5.0);
        cout << "Area = " << area(&figure)  << " Perimeter = "
            << perimeter(&figure) << n";
        make_triangle(&figure, 2.0, 3.5, 4.5, 1.5);
        cout << "Area = " << area(&figure)  << " Perimeter = "
            << perimeter(&figure) << n";
        make_circle(&figure, 2.5);
        cout << "Area = " << area(&figure)  << " Perimeter = "
            << perimeter(&figure) << n";
    }
```

Program 15.1

A `Geometric_Object` object contains a `Shape` field (`type`), as well as an anonymous `union` that holds three `struct`s: `rect`, `tri`, and `circ`. The programmer can check the `type` to determine which field of the `union` is considered valid and is eligible to be accessed. This form of OOP, which is possible in old C (given minor syntax tweaking), has been made obsolete by C++'s built-in OOP features such as inheritance and virtual functions. Consider the major upheavals that the addition of a new shape would cause to this program. Only functions to calculate `area()` and `perimeter()` are shown, but in practice, many more functions could exist. Each and every `switch` statement would have to be extended to include a provision for the new shape. Modifying old working code is always risky business. It has to be thoroughly tested again to make sure the modification works and that no errors were introduced into the prior working code. In the C++ style of OOP, a new shape would be derived from the base class `Geometric_Object`, and only code pertaining to that new class would be touched. The code referring to the existing shapes would be hidden within the respective classes. Adding new functionality does break old code; this is one precept in software reuse that makes OOP especially valuable.

Exercises

1. How does a union differ from a struct?

2. Consider the following definitions:

```
struct X {              union Y {
    int a;                  int a;
    float b;                float b;
    char c[10];             char c[10];
};                      };
```

What are the minimum sizes of X and Y (assuming one byte characters)?

3. What is a *free-union variant* record?

4. How can anonymous unions be used?

5. What is a *bit-field* struct?

6. Why are bit-field structs used?

7. Given the definition of the following bit-field struct:

```
struct BF {
    unsigned a :   5;
    unsigned b :   4;
    unsigned c :  10;
    unsigned d :   3;
};
```

what are the range of values that the a, b, c, and d fields can assume?

15.5 ALTERNATE NUMBER SYSTEMS

Since the computer manipulates binary numbers, it is only natural that lower-level programming would involve the use of binary numbers. As seen earlier in this chapter, binary masks can be used to assure that certain bits within a value are turned on or off. However, the binary number system has some disadvantages. Expressing relatively small numbers requires many binary digits (e.g., $266_{10} = 100001010_2$). Considering the fact that unsigned longs extend up to $4,294,967,295_{10}$, and that this value would require 32 binary digits, if literal binary values were used frequently in source code, programmers would begin to believe that they spend most of their editing time typing zeroes and ones.

Fortunately, alternate number systems exist that strike a compromise; namely, "binary" numbers can be written in compact form. They are not actually binary numbers, of course, but they can be more easily converted to binary than decimal values can. The base 16 number system, also known as *hexadecimal*, is predominantly used by assembly language programmers today. The other system that is sometimes used is base 8, or *octal*, which is used in many mainframe and minicomputer assembly languages. Notice that both 8 and 16 are powers of 2. This relationship makes the conversion to and from binary painless compared to conversions between binary and decimal.

All hexadecimal numbers are constructed from 16 digits: 0, 1, 2, 3, 4, 5, 6, 7, 8, 9, A, B, C, D, E, and F. Place values are multiples of 16; thus, the number $1A4_{16}$ is represented in decimal as: $1 \times 16^2 + A \times 16^1 + 4 \times 16^0 = 1 \times 256 + 10 \times 16 + 4 \times 1 = 256 + 160 + 4 = 420_{10}$. Since 16 is 2^4, every four binary digits can be represented as one hexadecimal digit. The number $1A4_{16}$ can be quickly converted to binary:

$$1_{16} = 0001_2 \qquad A_{16} = 1010_2 \qquad 4_{16} = 0100_2$$
$$1A4_{16} = 000110100100_2$$

The large `unsigned long` described above that requires 32 bits to write in binary only requires $32 \div 4 = 8$ hexadecimal digits. (Note that the decimal version requires more—ten digits.) The octal number system uses only eight digits: 0, 1, 2, 3, 4, 5, 6, and 7. Values can be expressed in fewer octal digits than binary, but more octal digits are required than hexadecimal digits. In the octal system every three bits in a binary number can be compressed into an octal digit:

$$420_{10} = 1A4_{16} = 0001\ 1010\ 0100_2 = 000\ 110\ 100\ 100_2 = 0644_8 = 644_8$$

In C++, only integral types can be represented in hexadecimal or octal form. This restriction is practical, since systems programming concentrates on moving bytes and machine words among registers, memory, and I/O ports. More complicated types are rarely involved. If a floating point type needs to be manipulated at a lower level, like sending a `float` to the serial port, it would be treated as a series of bytes without regard to how the mantissa, exponent, and sign are going to be interpreted. (In the case of a four-byte `float`, the four bytes occupied by the value would be transferred.) Hexadecimal numbers are prefixed with `0x` or `0X`. Octal numbers are prefixed with `0`.

For example:

Common Representation	C++ Representation
420_{10}	420
$1A4_{16}$	0x1A4
644_8	0644

Programmers should be aware that in everyday decimal notation, `021` is the same as decimal 21, but in C++ `021` means 21_8 which is actually decimal 17.

Integral types may be displayed in alternate bases with streams:

```
cout.setf(ios::showbase);
cout.setf(ios::hex, ios::basefield);
cout << 0x1A4 << ' ' << 420;
```

The above code prints `0x1A4` twice. Substitute `ios::oct` for the `ios::hex` parameter to `cout.setf()` to print integers in octal form (in which case `0644` would be printed twice).

Exercises

1. Convert the following hexadecimal numbers into decimal:

   0x2B   0xAC12   0x7777   0xF02E   0xFFFF   0xCAFE

2. Convert the following decimal numbers into hexadecimal:

   12,023   95   64   48,812   550   1023

3. Convert the following octal numbers into decimal:

   0230   0707   04654   0100

4. Convert the following decimal numbers into octal:

   12,023   95   64   48,812   550   1023

5. Convert the following binary numbers into hexadecimal:

   10101100   01000001   11111111   10101010   01110110

6. Convert the following hexadecimal numbers into binary:

   0x2B   0xAC12   0x7777   0xF02E   0xFFFF   0xCAFE

7. Why is the hexadecimal number system popular among assembly language programmers?

8. How is a hexadecimal numeric constant indicated in C++?

9. What stream functions can be called with `cout` to indicate that a value should be displayed in hexadecimal format?

Assignments

1. Construct a function called `printbyte()` that has the following prototype:

   ```
   typedef unsigned char Byte;
   void printbyte(Byte);
   ```

   The function should print out the contents of its parameter in binary form. All eight bits of the byte should be displayed. For example, the call `printbyte(45);` would display `00101101`.

   You may not use any of the standard arithmetic operators (+, -, *, /, %) to write `printbyte()`; only the bitwise operators may be used.

2. Recall that the left shift operator $x << y$ value shifts all the bits that make up the number x to the left y places. The left-most y bits of x are lost, and the right-most y bits of x become 0. (x itself is not

changed; the value returned may or may not be reassigned to x.) The opposite occurs in a right shift. Write two small functions `leftrot()` and `rightrot()` that act as follows: `leftrot(x, y)` would return a value that is found by shifting the bits of x to the left y places; however, as each left-most bit is "dropped off," it is not lost but becomes the right-most bit (instead of 0). The diagram below illustrates the process:

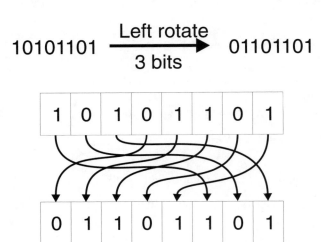

Most processors have left rotate and right rotate op codes in their machine language instruction sets. The following definitions and prototypes should be used:

```
typedef unsigned char Byte;
Byte leftrot(Byte b, int places);
Byte rightrot(Byte b, int places);
```

You should use the `printbyte()` routine in assignment 1 to assist your debugging. (It is possible to write both functions so that each contains only one statement.)

3. Write a program that can be used to translate a binary integer data file from one format to another. The existing format on disk is 1,000 32-bit integers. Each integer is guaranteed to be less than or equal to 10,000. The file is going to be transferred to a machine that processes 16-bit integers. Since none of the values will exceed 32,767, the conversion is possible. The differences between the layout of the 32-bit data file and the 16-bit machine's integer layout is shown:

32-bit Layout

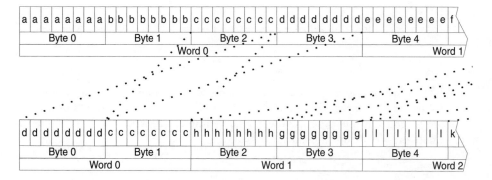

16-bit Layout

The order of the lower bytes must be reversed as shown in the diagram.

4. The data representing a graphics image must be stored on disk. The image is $640 \times 480 \times 16$ colors. If the color information for each pixel on the display is stored as a character, $640 \times 480 = 307,200$ bytes must be stored. Since only the values 0–15 need to be stored, it would be more reasonable to use only four bits for each pixel (two pixels per byte), thereby halving the storage requirement. Write a function called `grafpack()` with the following prototype:

    ```
    void grafpack(int unpacked[], int packed[], int size);
    ```

    It should take `unpacked` (a normal array of characters) and pack them (two values per byte) into the `packed` array.

APPENDICES

APPENDIX A. C++ OPERATOR PRECEDENCE AND ASSOCIATIVITY CHART

Operator	Associativity
`()   []   ->   ::   .`	L to R
`!   ~   -   ++   --   &   *   +   -`	
`sizeof   new   delete`	R to L
`.*   ->*   *   /   %`	L to R
`+   -`	L to R
`<<   >>`	L to R
`<   <=   >   >=`	L to R
`==   !=`	L to R
`&`	L to R
`^`	L to R
`|`	L to R
`&&`	L to R
`||`	L to R
`?  :`	R to L
`=   *=   /=   %=   +=   -=   &=   ^=   |=`	R to L
`,`	L to R

APPENDIX B. STANDARD ASCII CHART

0	NUL	16	DLE	32		48	0	64	@	80	P	96	`	112	p
1	SOH	17	DC1	33	!	49	1	65	A	81	Q	97	a	113	q
2	STX	18	DC2	34	"	50	2	66	B	82	R	98	b	114	r
3	ETX	19	DC3	35	#	51	3	67	C	83	S	99	c	115	s
4	EOT	20	DC4	36	$	52	4	68	D	84	T	100	d	116	t
5	ENQ	21	NAK	37	%	53	5	69	E	85	U	101	e	117	u
6	ACK	22	SYN	38	&	54	6	70	F	86	V	102	f	118	v
7	BEL	23	ETB	39	'	55	7	71	G	87	W	103	g	119	w
8	BS	24	CAN	40	(	56	8	72	H	88	X	104	h	120	x
9	TAB	25	EM	41	)	57	9	73	I	89	Y	105	i	121	y
10	LF	26	SUB	42	*	58	:	74	J	90	Z	106	j	122	z
11	VT	27	ESC	43	+	59	;	75	K	91	[	107	k	123	{
12	FF	28	FS	44	,	60	<	76	L	92	\	108	l	124	|
13	CR	29	GS	45	-	61	=	77	M	93	]	109	m	125	}
14	SO	30	RS	46	.	62	>	78	N	94	^	110	n	126	~
15	SI	31	US	47	/	63	?	79	O	95	_	111	o	127	DEL

APPENDIX C. BIBLIOGRAPHY

Aho, Alfred; John Hopcroft, and Jeffery Ullman. *Data Structures and Algorithms.* Addison-Wesley. 1983.

Barkakati, Nabajyoti. *The Waite Group's Turbo C Bible.* Howard W. Sams and Company. 1989.

Chirlian, Paul. *Programming in C++.* Merrill. 1990.

Dewhurst, Stephen and Kathy Stark. *Programming in C++.* Prentice Hall. 1989.

Ellis, Margaret, and Bjarne Stroustrup. *The Annotated C++ Reference Manual.* Addison-Wesley. 1990.

Turbo C++: Getting Started. Borland International. 1990.

Kelley, Al and Ira Pohl. *Turbo C: The Essentials of C Programming.* Benjamin/Cummings. 1988.

Kernighan, Brian and Dennis Ritchie. *The C Programming Language, 1st Edition.* Prentice Hall. 1978.

Kernighan, Brian and Dennis Ritchie. *The C Programming Language, 2nd Edition.* Prentice Hall. 1988.

McConnell, Steven. *Code Complete: A Practical Handbook of Software Construction.* Microsoft Press. 1993

Kochan, Stephen. *Programming in ANSI C.* Hayden. 1988.

Turbo C++: Programmer's Guide. Borland International. 1990.

Turbo C++: Reference Guide. Borland International. 1990.

Schneider, G. and Steven Bruell. *Advanced Programming and Problem Solving with Pascal.* Wiley. 1987.

Stroustrup, Bjarne. *The Design and Evolution of C++.* Addison-Wesley. 1994.

Stroustrup, Bjarne. *The C++ Programming Language (Second Edition).* Addison-Wesley. 1991.

Tenenbaum, Aaron and Moshe Augenstein. *Data Structures Using Pascal.* Prentice Hall. 1981.

Townsend, Carl. *Understanding C.* Howard W. Sams. 1988.

Turbo C++: User's Guide. Borland International. 1990.

Walker, Harry. *Data Structures: Form and Function.* Harcourt Brace Jovanovich. 1987.

Walker, Henry. *Computer Science 2: Principles of Software Engineering, Data Types, and Algorithms.* Scott, Foresman. 1989.

INDEX